French Pulpit Oratory 1598–1650

A study in themes and styles, with a Descriptive Catalogue of printed texts

PETER BAYLEY

Fellow of Gonville and Caius College and Lecturer in French in the University of Cambridge

Cambridge University Press

Cambridge

London   New York   New Rochelle
Melbourne   Sydney

Published by the Press Syndicate of the University of Cambridge
The Pitt Building, Trumpington Street, Cambridge CB2 1RP
32 East 57th Street, New York, NY 10022, USA
296 Beaconsfield Parade, Middle Park, Melbourne 3206, Australia

© Cambridge University Press 1980

First published 1980

Printed in Great Britain by
Redwood Burn Ltd
Trowbridge and Esher

Library of Congress Cataloguing in Publication Data
Bayley, Peter James, 1944–
French pulpit oratory, 1598–1650
Bibliography: p.
Includes index.

1. Sermons, French – History and criticism. 2. French prose literature – 17th century – History and criticism. 3. Rhetoric – 1500–1800. 4. Preaching – France – History. I. Title.
PQ615.B3   808.5'1   79-50175
ISBN 0 521 22765 8

To the memory of Richard Sayce

Contents

	Page
Preface	ix
Note on the presentation of texts	x

Part I

1	Studying sermons	3
2	Rhetoric in the schools	17
	1. Syllabuses	18
	2. Academic manuals	23
	3. Vernacular commentaries	33
3	Rhetoric in the Church	38
	1. St Augustine	40
	2. Trent and French provincial councils	43
	3. Italian theorists	45
	4. Spanish theorists	53
	5. Jesuit theorists	56
	6. Protestant theorists	61
	7. French theorists	63
4	Prose patterns	72
	1. The early years: 'poetic' and 'plain' preaching	73
	2. Thesaurus sermons	77
	3. Jean-Pierre Camus and catenary prose	85
	4. The rhetorical reaction: Etienne Molinier and conceptist prose	91
	5. Orchestrated prose	97
5	Sermon structure and its stylistic implications	101
	1. The division into points	101
	2. The hierarchy of styles	111
6	Themes and their imagery (i). Illusion and reality	122
	1. Illusion and reality as religious themes	122
	2. Time and eternity	131
	3. Meditation on death	133
	4. Perspectives and reflections	138
	5. Metamorphosis, magic and false gods	142

7	Themes and their imagery (ii). 'Nature, that universal and publick Manuscript'	149
	1. 'Coeli enarrant gloriam Dei'	150
	2. Correspondences	153
	3. The schematic universe and the imagery of disorder	160
	4. Flames	173
Postscript		180
Part II	Descriptive Catalogue of printed texts	185
Explanatory note		187
Abbreviations		190
Catalogue		191
Appendix 1. Some printers' devices		299
Appendix 2. A note on *prônes* and similar material		300
Appendix 3. Some surprising exclusions		301
Select bibliography		305
Index to Part I		317

Preface

It will be obvious to the reader that the second part of this book paradoxically forms the basis of the first part. To have preserved the chronological order of the enquiry would have been tedious and inconvenient, and I discuss in Chapter 1 some of the conclusions which seem to me to flow from my Catalogue. I hope nonetheless that I may be forgiven for repeating here that I have not set out to study the history of French preaching in the period 1598–1650 (with the investigation of areas such as manuscript sources or literary biography which that might imply), but to present a corpus of extant printed texts and to provide some approaches to the interpretation of them.

Most of the research on which this book is based was originally undertaken for a doctoral dissertation at Cambridge, and owes much to the support, both intellectual and material, I received from Emmanuel College as a student and as a Research Fellow there. My greatest debt, however, is one that can now no longer be expressed personally, and my dedication must remain an inadequate token of the gratitude I owe to Richard Sayce for his wise, painstaking guidance and his stimulating encouragement as my supervisor.

My dissertation was examined by Professor Anthony Levi and Professor Odette de Mourgues; and I am grateful to Professor de Mourgues for her subsequent encouragement and advice. I have contracted many debts towards the friends and colleagues to whom I have turned for inspiration and information, and I am glad to acknowledge them here in general terms. In particular, I wish to thank Canon Raymond Hockley, Mr J. H. Prynne and Dr Elizabeth Stopp for their comments on my work in one or other of its earlier forms; Dr Michael Stubbs and Dr Angus Bowie for helping me with various tasks; Mrs Patricia McCullagh for typing my final draft. I am grateful to the Department of Education and Science and the French Ministry of Foreign Affairs for their financial assistance, and to the Ecole Normale Supérieure for its hospitality. Finally, I wish to record my indebtedness towards the staffs of the libraries listed on p. 190 for their constant readiness to answer my questions and for many individual acts of kindness.

This book was already with the publishers when M. Jacques Hennequin's *Henri IV dans ses oraisons funèbres, ou la naissance*

Preface

d'une légende (Paris, Klincksieck) appeared early in 1978. I am pleased to have the opportunity of mentioning here an important new contribution to the study of French pulpit oratory.

Note on the presentation of texts

A subject of this kind naturally involves a good deal of quotation from little-known printed sources. In quoting from sixteenth- and seventeenth-century printed books in French I have endeavoured to transcribe contemporary spelling and punctuation, without needlessly imposing standards which writers and printers did not conform to. Occasionally, I have emended a clear mistake in the text in the light of later editions; such emendations have been placed within square brackets. The marginal references so common in printed sermons I have included in the body of the text between parentheses. For typographical reasons some printers' contractions and suspended letters have been expanded, and the long 's' abandoned. I have, on the other hand, standardized Latin texts, other than short quotations in Latin found in the sermons themselves.

In quoting from sermons and funeral orations in Part I, I refer simply to the short title, date and Catalogue (C.) number of the work. Bibliographical and biographical details are thus almost wholly confined to Part II.

Part I

1
Studying sermons

> There is something in the eloquence of the pulpit, when it is really eloquence, which is entitled to the highest praise and honour. The preacher who can touch and affect such an heterogeneous mass of hearers, on subjects limited, and long worn thread-bare in all common hands; who can say any thing new or striking, any thing that rouses the attention, without offending the taste, or wearing out the feelings of his hearers, is a man whom one could not (in his public capacity) honour enough.
>
> Jane Austen, *Mansfield Park*

In Henry Crawford's uncharacteristically acute observations there is justification enough for the student of preaching. He identifies the genre and its problems in a usefully analytical way: it is an art of persuasion, linked to the European rhetorical tradition; unlike forensic oratory, it takes for its themes great commonplaces which require skilful presentation if they are not to collapse into banality; finally, it is a mirror of taste. The criteria of excellence he establishes are, in other words, literary criteria and the preacher is seen as an artist. If we accept this summary of the aims of preaching, it follows that the genre can demand (potentially at least) a critical consideration of the same order as poetry or drama; and although that notion rings strangely in twentieth-century ears, there is abundant evidence to show that literary craftsmanship in the pulpit was particularly esteemed in the seventeenth century. In England this was summed up by John Donne in a typically pungent remark: 'Religious preaching is a grave exercise, but not a sordid, not a barbarous, not a negligent. There are not so eloquent books in the world, as the Scriptures.'[1]

Donne has himself, of course, been the principal beneficiary of a renewed critical interest in the English sermon. The immense scholarship which Evelyn Simpson and others have devoted to him,

---

1 *Sermons*, ed. Potter and Simpson, Berkeley and Los Angeles, 1953–62, vol. 2, p. 170.

together with T. S. Eliot's famous essay on Lancelot Andrewes,[2] have created an atmosphere where it is as natural for students to read the 'metaphysical sermon' as to read 'metaphysical poetry', and apply much the same critical tests to them. As far as the French literature of the same period is concerned, we have within the last thirty or forty years recovered poetry and drama for critical enjoyment, but we have barely thought to extend the enterprise to sermons. This book is, then, an attempt to enlarge critical horizons by according pulpit oratory the sort of attention which no one thinks misapplied to 'the poetry of meditation' or the religious music of Monteverdi.

This aesthetic priority is particularly appropriate to the first half of the seventeenth century in France, for it is in some ways that of the preachers themselves. The Edict of Nantes in 1598 saw the end of the vigorous partisan preaching which had played such an important role in the Wars of Religion.[3] Henri IV took special measures, based on the most violent of threats, to suppress such activities. On the other hand the mid-century marks both the momentary end of a political truce and the entry of French pulpit oratory into the traditional Pantheon of French literary history with the early sermons of Bossuet. This explains my choice of dates for this study.

If, however, our opening text stresses the need to judge preaching with artistic criteria, it also opens up a parallel avenue of exploration. Preaching is a *littérature engagée*: it aims to convince men of certain ideas and move them to act in accordance with certain principles. The efficient preacher, we are told, has to do this 'without offending the taste, or wearing out the feelings of his hearers'; that is to say, the sermon must appeal to (and therefore reflect) the sensibility of congregations and readers. It is a record of temperament, taste, and convention, and an especially valuable record at a time when church-going is widespread and mass media are unknown. Huizinga showed how it is possible to portray what we might nowadays call the 'structure of feeling' of a whole

---

[2] First published in 1926. See *Selected Essays*, 3rd edn, London, 1966, pp. 341–53.
[3] See Charles Labitte, *De la démocratie chez les prédicateurs de la Ligue*, 2nd edn, Paris, 1865.

civilization with the materials of pulpit oratory.[4] No study of a
single literary genre can of course do this for an age as complex
and as well documented as the early seventeenth century in France;
but even an enquiry as narrowly focussed as this one may provide
a useful portrait of the background of sensibility and convention
against which other creative artists, thinkers, or religious reformers
may be seen at work.

There is a third contribution which an examination of the
sermons of this period can make. The history of French prose
style has not really progressed beyond the schematic, and one of
the major omissions is precisely the early seventeenth century.[5] It
has been agreed by all to be crucial, considered by many to be the
formative period, and yet between the towering figures of
Montaigne and Pascal there is a great gulf fixed. This is partly
because historians have by and large concentrated their attention
only upon major writers, partly because they have tried to see the
development of French prose in isolation, like a river to which
new streams have from time to time added a developed syntax or
a purified vocabulary. Lanson's brief sketch,[6] still one of the most
quoted general surveys, offers only a series of charming museum
pieces, with no serious comparisons or historical remarks. It is true
that St François de Sales[7] and Guez de Balzac[8] have been discussed
from a stylistic point of view; but we have still to be told of the
broad contexts and specific movements of prose style within
which they were working. A great deal of work has, by contrast,
been done in other major European languages to relate the prose
of individual sixteenth- and seventeenth-century writers to broad
movements and traditions. This is especially true of English.
M. W. Croll's fundamental articles,[9] for all their over-simplification

4 *The Waning of the Middle Ages*, English trans., Harmondsworth, 1955. Huizinga draws extensively on the sermons of Jean Gerson and Olivier Maillard.
5 See, for example, W. von Wartburg, *Evolution et structure de la langue française*, 3rd edn, Berne, 1946, chap. 6.
6 *L'Art de la prose*, Paris, n.d. [1908].
7 Antonio Mor, *San Francesco di Sales scrittore*, Rome, 1960. One element in the saint's style has been very fully dealt with; see Henri Lemaire, *Les Images chez Saint François de Sales*, Paris, 1962.
8 G. Guillaumie, *J.-L. Guez de Balzac et la prose française*, Paris, 1927.
9 Collected in *Style, Rhetoric and Rhythm*, ed. J. Max Patrick *et al.*, Princeton, 1966.

of issues and hasty linking of style and ideology, represented a
major step forward in the understanding of Renaissance and
Baroque prose, and in the application of comparative techniques
to further the analysis. George Williamson's *The Senecan Amble*
(London, 1951) throws fresh light on the classical and Renaissance
traditions which were present to the writers of our period, and
incidentally conveys some useful negative lessons by demonstrating
the dangers of entering the maze of over-fine discriminations too
literally applied, as well as by pointing up (unwittingly perhaps)
the discrepancy between the theories and the practice of those writers.
More recently Brian Vickers, in his work on Bacon,[10] has tied up
many of the loose strands in the discussion and emphasized the
need to return to the study of the individual artist. Historians of
French literature cannot yet go as far as this, for the background
of trends, conflicts, fashions and obsessions has still to be painted.
It is possible that the examination of a major prose genre over
fifty years may yield something that will be of value when that
history comes to be written.[11]

Pulpit oratory has then a triple interest: it is a valid autonomous
art form, a guide to understanding some of the conventions of
taste in a period, and a gauge of changing prose styles. Past studies
of the genre have tended, not unnaturally, to view it from only
one of these angles. We can, I think, distinguish four main
approaches in these studies. The most familiar, already mentioned,
is the source-hunting of the historian, who finds in sermons information about daily life, customs and ideas which is not readily
available elsewhere. This technique is of major importance for
medievalists.[12] I shall not be much concerned with this approach,
which is essentially an external one. Previous historians of our
period have stressed this aspect to the detriment of others, so that

---

10 *Francis Bacon and Renaissance Prose*, Cambridge, 1968.
11 There have been stylistic studies of a very high order on preachers in
    other languages, e.g. Raymond Cantel's *Les Sermons de Vieira, étude du
    style*, Paris, 1959, or Joan Webber's *Contrary Music. The Prose Style of
    John Donne*, Madison, 1963. It seems to me more important to gain a
    general view before applying this sort of technique to individual French
    preachers.
12 This 'contribution of sermons to social history' is fully expounded by
    G. R. Owst in his *Preaching and Pulpit in Medieval England*, Cambridge,
    1933, pp. x–xvi.

although accounts of crowds weeping and swooning before a famous preacher may be had in abundance, there has been no attempt to discover and evaluate the reasons (in great part literary and psychological) behind the phenomenon. The second approach is that of the literary historian anxious to paint the continuous tradition of a genre in broad brush strokes which mask rather than throw into relief the character of the individual writer. Rejecting the insights of comparative study or the close reading of texts, this method aims at completeness and often attains only superficiality. The major exponent of it to discuss the oratory which interests us, the Abbé Boucher,[13] accepted unquestioningly the assumptions of previous critics, as this sort of writer is bound to do, and did not hesitate to repeat their judgements verbatim. A later sort of historiography lies behind the third approach, best exemplified by W. Fraser Mitchell's *English Pulpit Oratory from Andrewes to Tillotson* (London, 1932). This is a remarkably complete, sympathetic and scholarly account of English preaching in an important period, but for all its excellence it falls into the trap of contemporary assumptions by taking the notion of 'schools' of preaching as axiomatic. What were, in their time, variations on the central currents of prose are thus made to appear almost like the clashes and manifestoes of modern literary history, and the possibility of a fuller appreciation of past sensibility seems to be diminished in the process. The basic problem here is how to introduce some sort of structure, necessarily prejudged in part, into the study of pulpit oratory; by relying from the beginning on the technique of grouping authors by schools, Mitchell overlooked the prospect of distinctions based more on an analysis of style than on the political or sectarian alignments of preachers. Fourthly, there have been scholarly studies of *la technique du sermon*, what eighteenth- and nineteenth-century critics called a preacher's *méthode*. The best-known exponent of this is Etienne Gilson.[14] Although in this case the laudable aim is to increase our understanding of the way sermons should be read, rather than to classify works for the convenience of textbooks, there is an assumption which should not go unchallenged. Gilson has been

13 *L'Eloquence de la chaire*, Lille, 1894.
14 'Michel Menot et la technique du sermon médiéval', *Revue d'histoire franciscaine*, II (1925), pp. 301-50.

fortunate in finding a preacher who, save in the case of *quaestiones disputatae*, casts his sermons in the precise mould recommended by works of theory; but this should not blind us to the fact that the two are not interchangeable, and that the study of *artes praedicandi* does not dispense us from the study of texts.

That is really the heart of my objection to these approaches: for the reading and appreciation of the sermons themselves, they substitute the study of theory, the life and opinions of preachers, or, worst of all, they impose a historiographical system which crushes its own foundations. An enquiry which is to conform to our initial criteria must remain faithful to the printed texts.

Unfortunately, the information we possess which might help us in such an enquiry is very slight. The standard works for Catholic sermons, Paul Jacquinet's *Des prédicateurs du XVIIe siècle avant Bossuet*,[15] and Adrien Lézat's *De la prédication sous Henri IV*,[16] are, as their dates indicate, unlikely to conform to modern standards of precision and information. I shall discuss their critical standpoints later in this chapter. Of the remaining sources (listed in Section 3 of my bibliography) a number are pure plagiarisms of Jacquinet,[17] the rest studies of individual preachers which, though too outdated to provide much of critical value, occasionally contain matter of biographical or bibliographical importance. The same holds good for the Protestants, where Alexandre Vinet's early-nineteenth-century impressionistic survey[18] remains the standard introduction. There are short theses on selected preachers written by students in the Protestant faculties and a few modern works which touch in passing on preaching in our period. The extent to which research has stood still may be gauged by the fact that in the discussion of Pierre du Moulin's sermons which Lucien Rimbault includes in his recent study of that major figure's pastoral thought and activity, he relies upon Vinet both for an

---

15 Diss. Paris, 1863. Second edn Paris, 1885.
16 Diss. Paris, 1871. Reprinted Paris, 1903.
17 The worst offenders are Boucher, *L'Eloquence de la chaire*, Lille, 1894, and Victor du Bled, in *La Société française, deuxième série*, vol. 2, Paris, 1901.
18 *Histoire de la prédication parmi les réformés en France au XVIIe siècle*, Paris, 1860. This is a posthumous collection of notes taken at Vinet's lectures at Lausanne. He died in 1847.

Studying sermons

account of the works and for a critical appraisal of them.[19] It is clear, therefore, that a completely fresh start has to be made, information collected and collated, and the investigation based upon the results of a general enquiry into the available material rather than upon omissions and prejudices which largely date from over a hundred years ago.[20]

Some of these aims I hope to have fulfilled, if only partially, in my Descriptive Catalogue. The results provide us, I think, with a critique of existing knowledge on the subject, and a basis for a more positive discussion of the lines our further research ought to follow.

The close textual study which has marked the revival of interest in early-seventeenth-century French literature supposes an examination of bibliographical problems which, in the case of pulpit oratory, has not hitherto been undertaken. Such an exercise is in part an attempt to provide evidence on which the choice of printed texts may be based. It is, however, also concerned to answer the broader and even more fundamental questions of who, precisely, the preachers of the period between the Edict of Nantes and the Frondes were, what was published in their name, and to some extent the popularity they enjoyed. These questions have never received even the most inadequate consideration. The Catalogue thus represents a (necessarily incomplete) list based on printed texts. The first thing to strike a student acquainted with present knowledge on perusal of the Catalogue is the discrepancy between the traditional picture and the new outlines which seem to suggest themselves here. From this point of view the most important section is probably Appendix 3, 'Some surprising exclusions', which contains many names prominent in the received canon. To explain this discrepancy it is useful briefly to resume and explain the traditional account.

Students of seventeenth-century French pulpit oratory have been dominated by a scheme of literary history whose legitimacy and usefulness now seem highly questionable. Academic 'good taste' – a central concept in their work – was by definition that of

---

19 *Pierre du Moulin, 1568–1658, un pasteur classique à l'âge classique*, Paris, 1966, esp. pp. 136–42.
20 For instance, Migne's *Collection intégrale et universelle des orateurs sacrés*, 99 vols., Paris, 1844–66, reprints parts of the works of only six of our preachers.

the later seventeenth century as they saw it, and the historian's job consisted in tracing the evolution of the genre from an initial bad taste to the triumphs of reason and clarity in that most elusive of periods, the *siècle de Louis XIV*.[21] The necessity of describing and evaluating a good proportion of the material is thus dispensed with from the beginning, since the *mauvais goût* of the sixteenth century is taken as axiomatic, and the investigation is reduced to the search for an ecclesiastical version of Boileau's Malherbe. There is unfortunately no obvious candidate. To escape from this dilemma a further undiscussed premiss is brought into play: the reform of the pulpit is seen as part of ecclesiastical and moral reform in general. The clearest statement of this principle is offered by Sauvage, although it lies behind every page of Jacquinet: 'Tant il est vrai que dans l'ordre des questions religieuses, sans la pureté des moeurs et la dignité du caractère, les doctrines littéraires et le goût restent impuissants!'[22] The implications of this are immense; it is the first step away from the texts and into religious history. Here the ground is easy, the scheme is ready-made, and the names of men like Bérulle, Vincent de Paul, and even Saint-Cyran make their inevitable appearance. It was not difficult to extract remarks on preaching which might indicate a context of reforming zeal. In Chapter 3 of this study I attempt to show how little we can rely on these often contradictory commonplaces. It is this step from specific texts to vague contexts which lies behind the surprising disparities of my Catalogue, for these luminaries left no published sermons, nothing by which a revolution in taste might actually be judged; but this consideration was by now irrelevant to Jacquinet's enquiry. While the account thus conceived by him and completed by later students gave prominence to a few 'reformers' (whose works we often do not have), it covered the majority of preachers with scorn or else consigned them to oblivion.

21 The impact of evolutionary theory on nineteenth-century critics of sermons is very marked. This methodological assumption is perhaps made most explicit by the Abbé Sauvage, who postulates 'cette loi de continuité qui est aussi indispensable au développement des sociétés qu'à l'harmonie de la nature; nous nous sommes rappelé qu'il y avait eu un moment dans notre histoire littéraire où ce n'était plus l'obscurité, où ce n'était pas la pleine lumière, où nous étions sortis de l'enfance sans être encore à l'âge mûr.' *Saint François de Sales prédicateur*, Paris, 1874, p. 7.
22 *Ibid.*, p. 41.

The subsequent history of this critical canon is not without interest. On the one hand it has been preserved and handed down by a process of repetition and even plagiarism. On the other, however, it was swiftly exposed to destructive criticism based on its own principles. Only eight years after Jacquinet's thesis was published, Lézat opened for the opposition by reinstating, amongst others, François de Sales; a perfectly logical step since how, given the premisses of the argument, can a saint and reformer be an unregenerate author? Criteria of goodness are, of course, elastic, and before long even local piety sufficed to support the claim of some provincial preacher to be a reformer of the pulpit (the only sort of preacher thought to be worth considering); thus in a number of studies the distinction of an author rests on his being a Savoyard, or a Toulousain, or a Limousin.[23] The chief victims of this process have naturally been the texts themselves, and condescending references to 'la poussière des siècles' adorn the road from the library to the world of historical conjecture. Mgr Pioger was obliged to write an entire dissertation on the oratory of St John Eudes without having one sermon by him in a recognizable form.[24] It was possible to write, in 1949, of Molinier:

Les travers que nous venons de constater seraient-ils des motifs de dédain et de délaissement de ses oeuvres? Non; il faut considérer les traits de mauvais goût comme des superfétations de mots fâcheuses et les biffer du texte. Ainsi expurgés, les sermons, les discours, les monographies historiques elles-mêmes seront tout à fait dignes de survie.[25]

This sort of profanation justifies, I think, an insistence on the primacy of the written material.

The confusion of external history and internal evidence has, in fact, its origins in the very scope of the initial enquiry made by Jacquinet. This underlines the second striking fact to emerge from the Catalogue, which is the discrepancy between my list and our modern picture of the religious scene in early-seventeenth-century

---

23 See for example E. Fage, *L'Abbé Pierre de Besse*, Tulle, 1885.
24 A. Pioger, *Un Orateur de l'école française*, Paris, 1940, pp. 3–4.
25 J. Contrasty, 'Le Prêtre toulousain Etienne de Molinier, précurseur des orateurs du siècle de Louis XIV', *Revue historique de Toulouse*, XXXVI (1949), p. 40. Canon Contrasty has honoured Molinier with a *particule nobiliaire* which does not appear on the preacher's title-pages.

France.²⁶ The chief features of this period are administrative reform and the sending out of missionaries into the dechristianized French countryside,²⁷ the reform of the religious orders, the much studied rise of Jansenism, and above all, of course, the development of the 'French School' of spirituality with its far-reaching effects on French and indeed European religious life.²⁸ Yet hardly any of the names connected with these movements appear in the Catalogue and, to look ahead for a moment, very few of these topics are prominent in the extant sermons. It is as if there were two separate worlds, the one occupied with reforms, the other content to repeat the perennial concerns of Christian preaching: elementary doctrine, morality, and religious duties. This divorce between the main currents of contemporary religious thinking and the everyday preoccupations of the pulpit is not without its own intrinsic importance. Here, however, it stands as a warning not to confuse the two, if only because we do not have the evidence on which to base solid conclusions. This is not to deny that reforms took place and that new thinking and new personalities had a considerable impact on pulpit oratory. It is quite certain, for instance, that St Vincent de Paul's manner and instruction were of the greatest importance, but as far as this enquiry is concerned they cannot be judged without the testimony of his written sermons, and this testimony is denied us. Ours must therefore be the position of the agnostic, content to discuss what it lies in our power to know.

If then one cannot, on the basis of the extant texts, write the *history* of the French pulpit in this period, the Catalogue none the less gives ample material upon which to base an enquiry. It reveals the existence of a vast body of published sermons written

26 The most useful recent work of synthesis is Jean Delumeau, *Le Catholicisme entre Luther et Voltaire*, Paris, 1971. Greater detail is to be found in Léopold Willaert, *La Restauration catholique 1563–1648*, Paris, 1960 (vol. 18 of Fliche and Martin, *Histoire de l'Eglise*; part I only has so far appeared).
27 See Paul Broutin, *La Réforme pastorale en France au XVIIᵉ siècle*, 2 vols., Paris, 1956.
28 See Henri Bremond, *Histoire littéraire du sentiment religieux en France*, 11 vols., Paris, 1916–36. Bremond's masterpiece was the first work to study this period for itself and not as a precursor of something else. More recent work has been done by Jean Dagens, *Bérulle et les origines de la restauration catholique*, n.p., 1952.

by between fifty and sixty men. Perhaps the most significant facts about these preachers are as follows. There is an unexpectedly large number of Protestants, most of whose works date from the second half of the period. It will therefore be difficult to trace any sort of evolution in Protestant preaching from the earliest years, which are represented only by the two Durants. Among Catholics, secular preachers predominate over members of the religious orders, with the exception of the Jesuits. There is thus little evidence on which to base comparisons of the style of different ecclesiastical groups; the Dominicans, for example, are notably absent, and there are hardly any Oratorians. A large number of the authors were preachers to the King, or gave Lenten or Advent courses in Paris. This geographical concentration is itself a most important feature.

So much for the external characteristics of the extant material; but what of its internal nature? What is this imaginative and conceptual universe, the background of more original thought and expression, really like? What are its dominant obsessions, and what are the means preachers use to convey them? These are the questions which the central chapters of this book aim to answer. To do this it is obvious that some attention has to be paid to the mode of expression, the vehicle of prose, and so first of all we must try to get as close as possible to the insights and methods of the preachers themselves. Chapters 2 and 3 are partly an attempt to induce this frame of mind, so that when we come to the sermons we can share some of the theoretical perspectives present in their authors' minds. These chapters are also in part an independent investigation into theoretical works and since, I shall argue, these works form a separate tradition, almost a separate genre, it is obvious that they will not exclusively provide the clues to understanding the sermons. There will be variations of tone, and developments in the use of imagery, which rhetoric books leave undiscussed, and to appreciate them we must have flexible responses.

That is also why this does not claim to be a work of scientific linguistic analysis based on the sort of stylistics defined by Bally.[29] Although the number of preachers precludes the close analysis

29 *Traité de stylistique française*, 3rd edn, 2 vols., Geneva and Paris, 1951.

which scholars like Francis Higman[30] or Brian Vickers[31] have devoted to their authors, theirs is nevertheless the literary approach I wish to emulate.

Among aids to the further understanding of these early-seventeenth-century works there is one contribution which has not so far been mentioned: the vast amount of work devoted to elucidating the concepts of Baroque and Mannerist. All students of this period owe an enormous debt to this expansion in our knowledge and sympathy: this enquiry would not have begun without it. Nevertheless, although the insights of the *Baroquistes* are so valuable, it seems to me unprofitable to tie a study to the ball and chain of a terminological debate which, unless based on and leading to free analysis, ends so often in arid controversy.

Before beginning the investigation proper it is perhaps as well to discuss here certain points about the sermons which often intrigue the casual enquirer and which are, I think, helpful for a clearer view of the material. Firstly, the conditions of preaching and their consequences for the published texts. Although ecclesiastical authority required a sermon or homily at Mass on Sundays, these were often brief instructions and were rarely reprinted.[32] The full dress sermon was normally delivered at a separate time, often in the afternoon, on certain major feast days, on Sundays in fashionable town churches, and above all during Lent and Advent. It also formed part of the elaborate ceremonies for the Octave of Corpus Christi. There were also, of course, sermons for special occasions like missions or professions into the religious orders, but few of these survive. The funeral oration, to which distinguished or noble

---

30 *The Style of John Calvin in his French Polemical Treatises*, Oxford, 1967.
31 The first chapter of *Francis Bacon and Renaissance Prose* contains a full discussion of the question of style. I fully agree with Vickers's point that 'the only way to analyse a literary text is to give it a careful and sensitive reading, without preconceptions, and to develop gradually the implications of the significant stylistic factors' (p. 27). That is why I have avoided prejudging the issue by imposing a rigid scheme, pseudo-scientific at the most, on material about which we know so little. Pierre Guiraud, *La Stylistique*, 5th edn, Paris, 1967, comes to similar conclusions; see pp. 117-18.
32 See Part II, Appendix 2. These varieties of pulpit oratory are discussed by Jacques Truchet, 'Prédication classique et séparation des genres', *L'Information littéraire*, VII (1955), pp. 127-33. Professor Truchet's definition of a sermon is that it always 'suit les règles du discours oratoire en traitant des mystères de la religion et des vertus morales' (p. 127).

figures had a right, forms a separate genre and was almost always published separately. The printed collections of Catholic sermons reflect these customs faithfully; Lenten and Advent sermons form the greater part of our material, closely followed by those for Sundays and feasts. There is considerable evidence that such published collections were widely drawn on by other preachers: Camus is said to have once been obliged to listen to a sermon of his own from the lips of a visiting preacher.

None of this applies, naturally, to the Protestants. Preaching was for them a central part of worship, and was closely associated with the reading of the Bible. Thus the practice was for a minister to choose a book of Scripture and expound it verse by verse each time it was his turn to preach; this could be as often as once a week or as rarely as once a month. The resultant collections formed commentaries upon Scripture and were often published as such. The commentary sermon is a tradition, revived by the Reformers, which goes back at least as far as St Augustine. Apart from these series, of which we have a small number, published Protestant sermons were largely delivered at special occasions like feasts, synods, and the frequent fast days. There seems to have been something of a personality cult among Protestants, and collections of the occasional sermons of a famous preacher were not infrequent. Du Moulin's *Dix decades* (C. 139-145) are perhaps the most voluminous example in this period.

The process of transmission or transcription, which determines the relationship between the spoken word and the written text, has been accorded an importance which I think exaggerated. As far as I have been able to discover, most preachers wrote notes for the pulpit which they then developed into a form ready for the printer. Sometimes, of course, they omitted this elaboration, as we shall see in the case of Camus. Occasionally – like Bourdaloue later in the century – they memorized and recited a text written out in full beforehand. A number of texts we have are certainly based on notes taken by the congregation – a very common practice throughout Europe at this time – and have no manuscript relationship with the preacher at all.[33] But comments in notes and

---

[33] Nevertheless, this has led me to be rather cautious when dealing with St François de Sales. Most of his autograph sermons date from before 1598, and the reconstructions from congregational notes of those preached later are often fragmentary. That is why he is not accorded such prominence in this study as might be thought his due.

prefaces all agree that the written sermon was a quite different article from the spoken word, and that extensive elaboration was a most legitimate process.[34] We must therefore be very careful not to confuse the event in church with the published book. It is difficult and hazardous to attempt a reconstruction of the living sermon, and I am not convinced that the effort is worth making.

Questions about the length of sermons lead to the same conclusion. There is considerable scattered evidence that the customary time allotted was an hour.[35] The consequent irrelevance of trying to imagine the reaction of a congregation to one of the extant discourses – an exercise which appears to have held an irresistible fascination for nineteenth-century students of the pulpit – is commented on at some length by one of our preachers, Claude de Voyer d'Argenson:

> Et qu'on ne m'aille pas icy obiecter que i'ay manqué en mes neuf predications à la practique de ce precepte que ie donne aux Predicateurs, proposant au public des sermons qui ne sont pas l'entretien d'vne seule heure, mais de six & sept heures, si les forces de celuy qui parle au public luy pouuoient permettre de prescher aussi long temps: car autre chose est de dresser des predications pour estre proferées dans vne chaire; autre chose de faire imprimer des sermons pour estre leuz de ceux qui n'ont pas le loisir bien souuent d'assister à la predication qui se faict à l'Eglise. Les premiers doiuent estre bornez par vne briefueté qui empesche l'ennuy que causent les trop grandes longueurs. Mais les derniers estant plutost discours predicables, & matieres de predication fort dilatées, il est loisible à celuy qui les couche par escrit, de s'estendre sur son papier tant qu'il voudra, pourueu qu'il se tienne tousiours dans les bornes de sa matiere.[36]

34 See the *Epistre au lecteur* of Pierre Coton's *Sermons sur les principales et plus difficiles matieres de la foy* of 1617 (C. 98) for a full contemporary discussion of the differences between spoken and written language and the consequences of this for published books.

35 E.g. Suarez de Sainte-Marie, *Sermons pour les octaves du S. Sacrement*, 1605 (C. 284), sig. ã4^v: 'ie ne lairray de te donner ces Sermons ... les ayant augmentez de plusieurs choses que la briefueté d'vne heure ne me permettoit de dire'.

36 *L'Enneade sacrée*, 1622, quoted from C. 313, p. 41. This is repeated in the introduction to his ninth sermon, which occupies fewer than 143 folio pages.

2
Rhetoric in the schools

It is now a commonplace to insist on the importance of understanding rhetoric if we are to understand the writers of the seventeenth century. Students of English literature have long been engaged in applying the doctrines of the rhetoric books to Renaissance and post-Renaissance authors and, more recently, the same approach has illuminated not only individual French artists and thinkers but the whole cast of mind of French writing in the period.[1] By the same token, it might seem necessary to apologize for covering such well-known ground, were it not obvious that the training in the art of writing which could mould the profound originality of a Pascal or a Racine[2] must have an even closer bearing on openly oratorical works like sermons.

The schoolboys of the late sixteenth and early seventeenth centuries were subjected in their rhetoric classes to a fairly rigorous training in what amounts to public speaking and literary criticism. In this chapter I wish briefly to survey the several versions of such training available to them and also to attempt a momentary sharing in their experience by examining and quoting from the manuals they used. There are two reasons for this. It has been cogently argued that the rhetorical figures 'had a definite potential for expressing emotional and psychological states',[3] and we must therefore be quite closely familiar with them if we are

1 The list of critical works is extensive and growing, and will doubtless grow even more under the aegis of the recently founded Society for the History of Rhetoric. Among the most stimulating or comprehensive studies, mention should be made of G. Genette, *Figures I*, Paris, 1966; A. Kibédi Varga, *Rhétorique et littérature*, Paris, 1970; P. France, *Rhetoric and Truth in France*, Oxford, 1972. This last study contains a useful bibliographical essay (pp. 265–77).
2 See P. Topliss, *The Rhetoric of Pascal*, Leicester, 1966, and P. France, *Racine's Rhetoric*, Oxford, 1965.
3 Brian Vickers, *Classical Rhetoric in English Poetry*, London, 1970, p. 119. See the whole of his third chapter for a defence of this position.

not to misread the sense of early-seventeenth-century writing. In the second place, however, it can be argued that only by such an exercise can a modern critic free himself from the bondage of too close an adherence to rhetorical sources. When we trace the influence of formal rhetoric in an author's work we are not thereby commenting on its quality nor are we expounding the complete range of organization and expression we discern in the text. There are good rhetoricians and bad ones, and it is in order to distinguish between them that we must acquaint ourselves with the often tedious details of what the manuals of schemes and tropes actually taught. Nor is it possible to assume a uniformity of doctrine; as L. A. Sonnino remarks in her *Handbook to Sixteenth-century Rhetoric*,[4] there is probably 'no consistent organic classification possible for material derived originally from the diverse practices of individuals and of schools'. Before discussing the rhetoric of preaching, we must therefore resume what, in France, these individuals and schools proposed as the subject of their teaching;[5] the more precise application of this teaching to the sermon will then form the subject of Chapter 3.

1. Syllabuses

It is to the educational systems of the late sixteenth century that one must first look for the rhetorical training the majority of our preachers received. This means that none of the more important seventeenth-century movements in education – the Oratorian, the Jansenist – need concern us here, although it is possible to deduce something of this generation's attitude to schooling from the educational views they later held. For one thing, a schoolmaster is apt to choose a familiar manual for his pupils. Furthermore, in France there was no significant seminarian training.[6] The three chief systems were the secular, the Protestant, and the Jesuit.

It is not easy to discover exactly where a given preacher was

---

4 London, 1968, p. 12.
5 Both Kibédi Varga, *Rhétorique et littérature* (esp. chaps. 1 and 2) and France, *Rhetoric and Truth in France* (esp. pp. 5–15) discuss the manuals, but both give a composite account of rhetorical teaching. Moreover, Kibédi Varga limits himself to *inventio* and *dispositio*.
6 See below, p. 38.

Rhetoric in the schools

educated. The best evidence is that given in Haag[7] for the Protestants, of whom a small number were educated in Geneva and the remainder in the various French academies at Poitiers, Saumur, Châtellerault and Sedan (not at that time a part of France). The Jesuits either were educated in their own system or later became teachers in it, and we are justified in looking for their ideas in the *Ratio studiorum*. Paradoxically, it is the education of the majority in schools and arts faculties that is the least clearly documented, but it is not difficult to discover the ancient authors they read or the manuals which collected and ordered the ideas scattered in Cicero, Quintilian and Aristotle.

Despite the monumental changes taking place in education at the time of the Renaissance and the important theoretical contributions of the humanists, instruction in basic rhetoric varied little in secular institutions during the century. The chief innovation seems to be the increasing use made in the latter part of the sixteenth century of the Ramist rhetoric. Two pieces of evidence illustrate the point. L. Massebieau's edition of the *Schola aquitanica*,[8] a programme drawn up for the Collège de Guyenne and reflecting an early-sixteenth-century curriculum, shows that pupils were introduced to rhetoric in the second class (i.e. that next to the highest), though we are left to guess which manual they used,[9] and in the top class, actually called the 'Rhetoric' in later schools, the precepts continued to be taught and demonstrated by the reading of Cicero. The *Programme des écoles d'Aix* for the year 1576 gives us a clearer indication of the manuals prescribed:

Plus que led. M. Arnaud sera tenu de fere les lectures suyvantes: est le matin la Fisico et Dillectique de Cesari [*sc.* Joannes Cesarius, 1460–1550] et apres diner les Particions; – le second, au matin, lira la Retorique de Talley et une horeson de Sicero.[10]

As an editorial note elsewhere confirms,[11] 'les Particions' are Peter

7   E. and E. Haag, *La France protestante*, 10 vols., Paris, 1846; 2nd edn (*Aba–Gas* only), 6 vols., Paris, 1877–88.
8   In *Mémoires et documents scolaires publiés par le Musée Pédagogique*, fasc. 7, Paris, 1886.
9   'In secunda classe mane orationum Ciceronis aliqua praelegitur, et Partitiones, aut aliquid tale rhetoricum.'
10 F. Belin, *Histoire de l'ancienne Université de Provence*, Paris, 1896, vol. 1, p. 623.
11 *Ibid.*, p. 297.

Ramus's *Partitiones dialecticae* of 1543 and 'Talley' is Omer Talon (Audomarus Talaeus), his literary lieutenant who wrote the Ramist rhetoric. Much has been said about the importance of Ramism, and it will be discussed later.

The sixteenth-century university, according to H. C. Barnard,[12] concentrated more on Greek for its set texts, and Demosthenes and Isocrates were prescribed. As far as manuals are concerned, Barnard is clearly wrong in suggesting that Vossius's compendium could have been used in the sixteenth century, since as we shall see it was not yet published. It was, of course, very popular in the seventeenth — when the curriculum had changed but little — as much at the Sorbonne as in contemporary England.[13] The only way to discover what manuals might have been used in class is to consult the *Répertoire des ouvrages pédagogiques du XVIe siècle*,[14] which shows that the only rhetorics to achieve more than ten editions in France were Melanchthon's, dating almost wholly from 1520–30, Soarez's, soon to be discussed, and the one by Talon which we have already met.

While some of the Protestants were, as we have seen, educated at Geneva, where they may in fact have read Melanchthon,[15] the majority learnt their rhetoric in French colleges and academies. However unorthodox their theology may have been, the Protestants' training in the humanities was firmly tied to tradition. At the Académie de Die the top class read Cicero and learnt how to declaim; they had already studied some of the great speeches and poems of antiquity in the class below, and there had read a handbook (irritatingly anonymous) of rhetoric:

En la seconde, les préceptes de l'art poétique ... les oraisons de Cicéron: *Pro Ligario*, *Pro Marcello* et *Dejotaro* et Isocrate; *ad Nicollem* ou l'*Illiade* d'Homère; les *Géorgiques* de Virgile, un abrégé de rhétorique.[16]

---

12 *The French Tradition in Education*, Cambridge, 1922, pp. 9, 190.
13 See H. Lantoine, *Histoire de l'enseignement secondaire en France*, Paris, 1919, p. 33, and C. Richardson, *English Preachers and Preaching 1640–1670*, London, 1928, p. 6.
14 Ed. F. Buisson, Paris, 1886.
15 W. H. Woodward, *Studies in Education during the Age of the Renaissance*, Cambridge, 1906, p. 160.
16 J. Brun-Durand, 'Règlements de l'Académie protestante de Die', *Bulletin historique et philologique* (1891), pp. 315–16.

That this *abrégé* was possibly Talon's is suggested by the rules for the college at Montauban drawn up in 1600:

Sur la fin de l'annee le regent exposera la rhetorique de quelque auctheur bien approuve, comme le quatriesme livre de la rhetorique *ad Herennium*, et la rhetorique de Talena.[17]

'Talena' is another of the numerous forms Omer Talon's name takes in the syllabuses of the period.

As for the Jesuits, there is ample evidence that they read the usual authors: Cicero above all, Aristotle and Quintilian where they reinforce his teaching.[18] F. de Dainville has recently discerned in seventeenth-century Jesuit education three main phases, of which the first – 'fidélité au *Ratio Studiorum*' – lasts until 1660, through the whole of our period.[19] Now, the *Ratio studiorum* expressly commends Cypriano Soarez's manual,[20] and Dainville adduces a great deal of evidence to support his contention that 'son explication deviendra souvent la leçon de préceptes'.[21]

As far as later educational movements go, it is interesting to note Arnauld's approval of the Jesuit's book in his *Mémoire sur le règlement des études dans les lettres humaines*.[22] That there was but a slight tension between what we might now call the two best-sellers of rhetoric is shown by the appearance of 'la rétoricque de Soiare en basane vert' in the inventory of the Oratorian school at Toulon, although according to the editor of this inventory it was only when the school fell into Jesuit hands that the book replaced Talon's in the classes.[23]

The picture is clear: at a college one was introduced to rhetoric

17 M. Nicolas, *Histoire de l'ancienne Académie protestante de Montauban (1598–1659)*, Montauban, 1885, p. 325.
18 F. Charmot, *La Pédagogie des Jésuites*, Paris, 1943, p. 269.
19 'L'Evolution de l'enseignement de la rhétorique au XVIIe siècle', *XVIIe Siècle*, LXXX–LXXXI (1968), pp. 19–43, esp. p. 24.
20 *Ratio atque Institutio studiorum Societatis Iesu*, Rome, 1616, pp. 122–3; 'Praeceptorum Rhetoricae brevis summa ex Cypriano, secundo scilicet semestri, tradetur.' *Cf.* pp. 124, 127.
21 'L'Evolution . . .', p. 21; *cf.* the same author's *Les Jésuites et l'éducation de la société française*, Paris, 1940, vol. 2, p. 97.
22 Quoted by H. C. Barnard, *The Port-Royalists on Education*, Cambridge, 1918, p. 181.
23 E. Poupé, 'Livres de classe en usage au Collège de Toulon en 1624–1625', *Bulletin philologique et historique*, 1932–3, pp. 138–9.

through a manual and the reading of Cicero in the second class, and this was reinforced by a further reading of the classics in the first class. If one attended the arts course at a university one was more likely to read Aristotle and, later, Vossius. Caussin's *De eloquentia sacra et humana libri XVI* was used towards the end of the period. On balance, a Catholic was more likely to read Soarez, a Protestant to read Talon.

To discover whether in these differences we may trace serious literary divergences, one needs to look at the various books more closely. Before doing that, however, two other important elements in the education of the preachers should be emphasized. Since an education in literature still meant the study of works in a foreign language, it is not surprising that teachers were enjoined to discuss linguistic and stylistic questions in detail; nevertheless, the insistence on such points as the derivation of words is not without its importance when one recalls the use that contemporary preachers made of etymology. The method to be used by the Professor of Greek at the Académie de Montauban places the study of language above that of content:

Le professeur en grec ... baillera l'interpretation en monstrant la derivaison des noms et verbes; et pourra s'estendre pour traiter brievement et sommairement la matiere que son aucteur luy fournira, sans obmettre de marquer les figures et ce qui est de la rhetorique et dialectique ...[24]

The rules for the Professor of Rhetoric laid down in the *Ratio studiorum* are almost as insistent on the study of style:

Stylus (quanquam probatissimi etiam historici, et poetae delibantur) ex uno fere Cicerone sumendus est; et omnes quidem eius libri ad stylum aptissimi; Orationes tamen solae praelegendae, ut artis praecepta in orationibus expressa cernantur.[25]

The second element is perhaps better known: not only did the schoolboy study the art of speaking and writing through the medium of texts, but he was expected to be able to compose and declaim an oration of his own, frequently in public. This practice, too, cuts across any boundary of sect or century.[26] When, therefore, one reads that for the Jesuits:

---

24 Nicolas, *Académie de Montauban*, pp. 321–2.
25 Rule 1 (1616 edn, p. 112); *cf.* rule 8 (pp. 116–17).
26 *Cf.* Georges Snyders, *La Pédagogie en France au XVIIe et XVIIIe siècles*, Paris, 1965, p. 122.

L'eloquence n'est pas que la perfection de l'élocution écrite et parlée, l'usage d'un latin pur et élégant, c'est encore un bagage de connaissances positives d'ordre littéraire, historique, géographique...[27]

or that in the sixteenth century as a whole rhetoric was primarily part of the learning of classical culture,[28] it is as well to remember that the practical side of the subject was not neglected. A most interesting recent study of French Jesuit education in the 1620s based on Fr Louis de Cressolles's *Vacationes autumnales* of 1620 demonstrates if anything an increased emphasis upon the practical arts of *actio* and *pronuntiatio*.[29] The sections of the manuals which deal with gesture and pronunciation may be dead for us today, but they had their use when they were written.

Another point stands out clearly from all this: nothing in the educational theory or practice of the time leads us to think that rhetoric was considered as anything other than essential and serious. To regard the application of its rules in the literature of the time as frivolous or insincere is to misunderstand its purpose. This impression will perhaps become stronger as we now examine some rhetorical manuals in greater detail.

2. Academic manuals

We can see from this short survey that although the manuals used by different groups varied, the sources were the same. Cicero is the great source: some of his works were read by every schoolboy; so were Quintilian and (more rarely) Aristotle. Among manuals based on these authorities there are, therefore, more similarities than differences. Soarez's manual is perhaps the most faithful to the full classical tradition, despite its brevity, and gives a good idea of the central substance of rhetorical teaching in our period. It was also the most influential but there are few detailed modern accounts of it.

---

27 Dainville, *Les Jésuites et l'éducation de la société française*, vol. 2, p. 87.
28 W. J. Ong, *Ramus. Method and the Decay of Dialogue*, Cambridge, Mass., 1958, p. 275.
29 Ed. M. Fumaroli, 'Aspects de l'humanisme jésuite au début du XVIIe siècle', *Revue des sciences humaines*, CLVIII (1975), pp. 245-93.

The work[30] is divided into three books, one each for *inventio*, *dispositio* and *elocutio*. Although there is a slight departure here from Cicero – who had stated in the *Partitiones oratoriae* that there were five parts of rhetoric, these three together with *actio* and *memoria*, whereas Soarez deals very summarily with action and memory at the end of his third book – it is clearly not intended to be a significant break with tradition.[31] The opening preface indeed continues with an attack on the 'libidinem temere contradicendi veteribus scriptoribus'. Respect for the ancients is one of the key principles upon which this textbook is based, albeit that Soarez's definition of rhetoric is slightly different from, and indeed an advance upon, Cicero's famous *probare, delectare, flectere*. For the Jesuit the sole aim of the orator is to move, and the means is good expression:

Dicere est ornate, graviter & copiose loqui. Rhetoricae officium est dicere apposite ad persuasionem: finis persuadere dictione. (I, 1; 1ᵛ)

This is repeated throughout the work (*cf.* I, 11; II, 1) and is perhaps most clearly expounded in II, 26:

Locuples enim, & speciosa vult esse eloquentia ... Quo fuerit enim uberior, ac suavior, eo etiam erit credibilior. (30ʳ)

There is a less material reason for studying rhetoric which is also mentioned in the preface, though not repeated elsewhere, that in doing so one becomes pleasing to God.

Speeches are divided into three kinds, epideictic (*exornatio*),

---

30 According to Sommervogel, *Bibliothèque de la Compagnie de Jésus*, vol. 7, pp. 1331–8, the first edition is Coimbra c. 1560. It went through an enormous number of editions, many of them in France, throughout the seventeenth century, and only achieved its last edition in 1735. The edition I have used is one that may well have been read by some of our preachers: *De arte rhetorica libri tres ex Aristotele, Cicerone, & Quintiliano praecipue deprompti*, Paris, 1573. References are to book and chapter, followed by the folio number.

31 *Partitiones oratoriae* [or *De partitione oratoria*], ed. and trans., with *De oratore*, Sutton and Rackham, 2 vols., London, 1959–60 (Loeb Library), i, 3 (vol. 2, p. 312). *Cf. De oratore*, I, xxxi, 142 (vol. 1, p. 98). Perhaps Fr Cressolles's emphasis on *actio* mentioned above springs from a wish to restore this slight imbalance in the rhetorical training given in Jesuit colleges.

Rhetoric in the schools

deliberative (*deliberatio*), and forensic (*iudicium*): an orthodox repetition of Cicero.³²

Soarez then moves on to the subject proper of the first book, *inventio*. This is concerned with the content of the speech and the way the arguments are handled. It is in fact a short guide to the art of arguing, and consists largely of a discussion of the various *loci*, or arguments, that one can use. These are either internal (*loci insiti*) or external (*loci assumpti*). There are sixteen *loci insiti*; to run through them is to discover the methodical way the orator breaks down the problems he faces. They include definition, etymology, contrast, various forms of syllogism, causes and effects, and comparison. The external arguments include the manipulation of witnesses and evidence. Two considerations are constantly mentioned in these chapters: firstly that to use this method of analysis is an easy way to break down an argument (we may expect to see the fruits of this in methodical analyses of Biblical texts), and secondly that the orator is not expected to be a dialectician. This is a re-statement of tradition against the Ramist view that dialectic should supplant the old systems of *inventio* and *dispositio*. Not only are the arguments of the orator less tight:

Est autem argumentatio argumenti explicatio, qua dialecti[ci] pressius: oratores ornatius, & liberius utuntur   (I, 12; 4ᵛ)

but often he may argue in a completely different way from the logician:

Saepe enim definiunt & oratores, & poetae per translationem verbi ex similitudine cum quadam suavitate.   (I, 15; 5ʳ)

Now that he has broken the subject down under several headings the orator must attempt to move his hearers as best he can:

Maxima vis exstitit oratoris in hominum mentibus permovendis, quod amplificatione fit.   (I, 32; 10ʳ)

This *amplificatio* is the expansion of the arguments by showing their consequences or attributes or inherent contradictions, or simply by heaping up the arguments so that they overwhelm the hearer. A further technique is to introduce a debate on the subject with *fictis personis* and *mutis rebus*. Soarez ends with a warning

---

32 *De oratore*, Sutton and Rackham, 2 vols., London, 1959–60 (Loeb Library), *ibid.*; *Part. orat.*, xx, 70(*ed. cit.* vol. 2, p. 362).

against splitting hairs and with advice to refer to those subjects which move men most deeply – charity, love and honour.

These sorts of arguments cannot, of course, be used in epideictic oratory, and so we proceed to a discussion of the ways in which a man (or, for that matter, a city) may be praised or blamed. This is obviously important for panegyrics and funeral orations. The subjects are divided into men of the past and men of the present; the former are to be praised as noble or great, and their promise of future glory emphasized (chap. 43: Soarez gives John the Baptist as an example), while the latters' virtues of justice, fortitude and temperance are to be stressed. If a man has recently died, his posthumous honours and the exploits of his children are also to be included.

Further hints for deliberative oratory are given; the need to bear the hearers in mind and to appear as impressive as possible is insisted upon. Soarez makes an interesting distinction between an audience of *agrestes*, to whom you appeal on the basis of usefulness, and one of *expoliti*, for whom worthy motives are uppermost. The book ends with the very significant idea that an orator should above all be well stocked with examples:

Vis autem ad suadendum exemplorum est maxima, aut recentium, quo notiora sunt, aut veterum, quo plus auctoritas habent. (I, 55; 19^r)

This sort of remark supports the vogue which runs throughout the period of private as well as published commonplace-books, and is thereby linked to the debate on the use of examples we shall meet for instance in Guillaume du Vair's comments on contemporary oratory, and in many comments on preaching.

Book II again follows Cicero in its division of the speech into *exordium*, *narratio*, *confirmatio* and *peroratio*.[33] It is important to note that these divisions are not thought to hold good for every speech: in deliberative oratory the exordium should be either brief or not there at all, and it is only in epideictic oratory that exordia can ramble. The narrative of the facts involved should not be pedestrian – only the exciting speaker wins the hearts of an audience, and hence the value of exaggerated emotions and dramatic forms:

---

33 *De oratore, ibid.*; *Part. orat.*, viii, 27 (*ed. cit.* vol. 2, pp. 330–2).

Rhetoric in the schools

> Ciceroni vehementer placet ut iucunda, & suavis sit narratio, eamque suavem esse narrationem ait, quae habet admirationes, expectationes, exitus inopinatos, quae interpositos motus animorum, colloquia personarum, dolores, iracundias, metus, laetitias, cupiditates. (II, 8; 22^v)

The section on confirmation returns to the technique of handling the essential points (*status*): whether it is a good thing that was done, what exactly it was that was done, and so on; this leads on to chapters on the use of reasoning, examples, *sorites* (the accumulation of arguments) and *dilemma*, where you hold your adversary in a cleft stick. The reader is however warned against making his speech a confused jumble of syllogisms, and the golden rule, already quoted, is once again stated to be that the easier and more pleasing a speech is, the more likely it is to be believed. In the peroration all the stops are out; here you seek to convince not only your audience but also your opponent, if there is one. More important, the use of visual imagery is expressly advocated for this section:

> Miram etiam vim habet in hoc ipsum, imagines rerum absentium ita complecti animo, ut eas cernere oculis, ac praesentes habere videamur: has quisquis bene conceperit, is erit in affectibus potentissimus. (II, 27; 31^r)

Book III opens with a theme that runs throughout, namely that 'copious writing' (a key concept in Renaissance stylistics from Erasmus on) springs from having copious things to say, and that verbal splendour 'ex rei natura existit' (chap. 3, *cf*. chap. 45). This book is naturally the most fragmentary but it is, I think, worth our while to pursue our author through his close analysis of stylistic resources. The single word is dealt with first, and we are warned against *verba sordida* (chap. 5). Chapters 6 and 7 deal with new or unusual words, a matter which was to be at the centre of much seventeenth-century literary debate in France. Soarez not only approves of such words ('si raro ... et in loco adhibeantur'), but gives advice on how they may be invented: by analogy, onomatopeia, derivation, or by making up compounds.

He then begins his discussion of tropes, or ornaments which consist in single words only, and leads us, with copious examples from the classics, through metaphor (with warnings against farfetchedness or disparity), synecdoche, metonymy, antonomasia, catachresis, metalepsis, allegory, irony, periphrasis and hyperbaton (which is permitted only to poets). Here it becomes clear that this part of the book is intended to be as much a companion to the reading of the classics as a practical handbook.

The figures, or ornaments of several words, are divided into two kinds: *figurae verborum* (often called *figurae dictionis*), which depend upon the word order, and *figurae sententiarum*, which depend upon the sense. After noting the considerable variation in ancient writers' classification of these, he divides the *figurae verborum* into three groups: those that function by adding matter, those that leave out matter, and others. At this point our analysis must needs become a bare list, for the book itself is nothing more. Among the first group are *repetitio* (the use of the same word at the beginning of consecutive sentences), *conversio* (the same word at the end), *geminatio* (use of a word twice), synonymy, polysyndeton (the repeated use of conjunctions) and *gradatio* (repeating at each new stage what has already been said). The second group includes *dissolutio* (the avoidance of conjunctions) and *adiunctio* (where several clauses refer to or depend upon one verb). In the third group we find paronomasia (more or less play on words), isocolon (the use of words of the same length), antitheton (the contrasting of words) and *commutatio* (example: 'non ut vivam edo, sed ut edam vivo'). Soarez finishes this list with what we may feel to be a well-timed warning that over-indulgence in such verbal patterns gives rise to suspicions of insincerity (III, 29; 43ᵛ). The list of *figurae sententiarum* is even longer. It is divided into the techniques of forensic oratory, with which we shall not be much concerned – *occupatio*, for instance, where you anticipate the opponent's objections, or *communicatio*, where you actually consult him – and those more general devices, prosopopeia, apostrophe, pretermission, deprecation, execration, exclamation, with which most readers of oratory are familiar.

Soarez then turns to a subject which holds a high place in the rhetorics of the time, the study of Latin prosody and its counterpart in prose, *oratio numerosa* (also known as *numerus oratorius*). It is a subject which exemplifies the ambiguous nature of this and other manuals, since it is both a guide to the study of literature and a recommendation for the student's own writing. The attention given to it certainly had the effect of making vernacular orators more careful with their cadences in those speeches and parts of speeches which were traditionally *numerosae* in antiquity – epideictic oratory and perorations.

The treatment of memory, pronunciation and gesture is extremely cursory. One point, noted earlier and repeated here with some force, is that memory is greatly aided by having in the mind a treasury of anecdotes and proverbs. We shall see in later chapters the results of remarks like the following:

Non immerito igitur thesaurus hic eloquentiae dicitur, cum exemplorum, legem, sapienter dictorum, beneque factorum velut quasdam copias, quibus abundare, quasque in promptu semper habere debet orator, incredibilis eius vis repraesentet.   (III, 53; 58^r)

The book ends with an exhortation to consecrate one's eloquence to God. It may not be fanciful to believe that this is just the step many former readers of Soarez's work thought they were taking when they used these traditional rhetorical methods in their sermons. This analysis shows at least how detailed and complex was the sixteenth-century schoolboy's introduction to literary criticism and practice, and gives an idea of the wealth of stylistic resources likely to appear in the sermons.

To turn from Soarez to Omer Talon[34] is something of a release from bondage. For one thing, the elaborately Ciceronian style of the Jesuit gives way to the racy Latin of the Ramist; the chapters consist of short definitions followed by well-chosen examples. Certainly, one feels, the difference in classroom atmosphere must have been enormous. But this immediate impression does not, of course, tell the whole story: Talon's rhetoric was revolutionary. It simply omits *inventio* and *dispositio* and consists of two books, on *elocutio* and *pronuntiatio*.[35] This was not in itself a great change; other rhetorics had been and were to be concerned with the third part only.[36] The importance lies in Talon's close links with Ramus,

34 The work was begun in 1545, radically revised in 1548, and adapted into French by Antoine Fouquelin in 1555. For Fouquelin's version see Roy Leake, 'The relationship of two Ramist Rhetorics', *Bibliothèque d'humanisme et Renaissance*, XXX (1968), pp. 85-108. Twenty-five editions were published in France before 1600; thereafter the centre of popularity shifted to Germany and England: see W. J. Ong, *Ramus and Talon Inventory*, Cambridge, Mass., 1958, pp. 91-119. As with Soarez, I have consulted a Parisian edition: *Audomari Talaei rhetorica, e Petri Rami professoris regii praelectionibus observata*, Paris, 1577.
35 For a fuller description of what was involved, see F. P. Graves, *Peter Ramus and the Educational Reformation of the Sixteenth Century*, New York, 1912, esp. pp. 134-41, and P. Sharratt, 'Peter Ramus and the reform of the University: The divorce of philosophy and eloquence', *French Renaissance Studies*, ed. P. Sharratt, Edinburgh, 1976.
36 E.g. Sherry's *Treatise of Schemes and Tropes* of 1550. Yet his learned editor specifically denies that Sherry was a Ramist; see the critical edition by H. W. Hildebrandt, Ann Arbor and London, 1958, p. 146.

who had declared that the first two parts of rhetoric should in fact be pure dialectic; and we may suppose (from the *Programme des écoles d'Aix*, for instance) that it was Ramus's own dialectic that was studied.

The work opens with a discussion on tropes, divided into metonymy, irony, metaphor and synecdoche; then Talon, like Soarez, divides the figures into *figurae dictionis* and *figurae sententiae*. In the section on *figurae dictionis* he places his only two chapters on *numerus oratorius*. Considerable stress is laid upon verbal devices, to which he gives slightly different names from Soarez: *epizeuxis* (the energetic repetition of a word), climax, anaphora, various tricks with individual syllables (*epistrophe, complexio, epanalepsis, polyptoton*) and finally paronomasia. The section on *figurae sententiae* is short and clear, dealing with the well-known techniques of the orator in much the same way as Soarez. Book II, on *pronuntiatio*, is not long, but it does give a fuller description of physical devices than most other manuals; an idea of its detail is given by the title of chapter 11: 'De gestu pedis, femoris, pectoris'.

There has been and continues to be considerable debate about the likely effect of a course in Ramist rhetoric. It is certainly to be expected that the replacement of the old system of rhetorical places by the ideas of the professional philosopher would have some influence, as Rosemond Tuve pointed out:

If finding matter and arranging are taught ... as the logician teaches them, we may expect a conceptual strictness in poetry that was not there before ... Any poet who believed what he was taught would look to the strictness of his logic; and no reader who had come to expect the intellectual toughness of good upstanding dialectic in all kinds of discourse could be put off with the old ambling pace.[37]

On the other hand we have Brian Vickers's remark that:

I confess that I cannot detect any ways in which a Ramist's writing differs in style or method from that of a non-Ramist. The case has not been proved on stylistic grounds, and its theoretical foundation is so tenuous it seems unlikely that it ever will be.[38]

There are nevertheless certain emphases in Talon's book that one

---

37 *Elizabethan and Metaphysical Imagery*, Chicago, 1947, pp. 340–1.
38 *Classical Rhetoric in English Poetry*, p. 42. Cf. Ong, *Ramus. Method and the Decay of Dialogue*, p. 283.

might, I think, be justified in seeing as one of the reasons why Protestant sermons in our period tend to strong affective oratory rather than the somewhat automatic and stilted use of figures that we shall often find in Catholic preachers. There is an insouciant, even flamboyant attitude towards the art which indicates a less pedantic concern for the rules than one finds, for example, in Soarez. There is also a much more functional conception of what eloquence is. The introduction plunges the reader into a world of forceful argumentation where *elocutio* is a tool for persuading people by concentrating on their emotions, and is an effective, even dangerous weapon in the hands of a skilled user:

Rhetorica est ars bene dicendi: cuius virtus prudenter adhibita, mirabiles effectus habet. Ideoque Plato sophistis Graeciae et Rhetoribus iratus, hanc ipsam artem . . . quandam obsonandi, fucandi, adulandi, incantandi peritiam appellat. (I, 1; p. 5)

However, attractive though the idea may be of seeking the source of the difference between the Ciceronian elaborateness of Catholic preaching and the affective verve of Protestant (a hypothesis one might rashly extend beyond the borders of France in this period), the theory does have an element of building on sand. There are many other reasons which might also be adduced to explain the dissimilarities of style, and of course Protestant students were not alone in using Ramus and Talon. Certainly later rhetoric books used in France (even those written by Protestants) are formally unaffected by Ramist ideas and continue in the full tradition of Aristotle, Cicero and Quintilian.

It is to two of these later books that we may now turn. We have already seen that the manual of the Dutchman Vossius was widely used in France in the seventeenth century.[39] It is clear at a first glance that only an advanced student of some leisure could read the book through: it consists of two large volumes, both containing over four hundred closely printed pages. The most noticeable feature of the book is the way the traditional tripartite order is expanded and broken up. Book I is a discussion of the nature of

39 Some confusion exists among the authorities as to which of his books was in fact read; investigation shows that it was the *Rhetoricorum oratoriarum institutionum libri VI*, of which the earliest edition I have been able to trace is of 1606. In England his later work, *Rhetorices contractae*, was very popular. The edition of the major work used here is Leiden, 1643.

rhetoric; Book II, ostensibly on *inventio*, is largely a treatise on the passions; and Book III, though concerned with *dispositio*, also contains a lengthy classification of the different kinds of oratory. Although *elocutio* is the subject of the fourth book, it overflows into Book V, which is on schemes (i.e. figures). Book VI is a strange mixture of *pronuntiatio* and further abstract philosophizing on the nature of oratory. This peculiar order is not, of course, entirely new. In Aristotle's *Rhetoric* Book II deals with the passions while *dispositio* is left to the end of the work, and it is probable that Vossius's organization is deliberately close to Aristotle, who was still more widely read in the universities than elsewhere. Certain points of interest may be noted. There is a complete long chapter on the use of neologisms, *mots bas* and poetic vocabulary which reflects the increasing concern felt for these aspects of writing among contemporary critics; and this feeling of contemporaneity is strengthened when we find examples from sixteenth-century writers like Justus Lipsius and J. C. Scaliger. If anything, the exhaustive enumeration of every possible trope and figure, the lengthy discussion of periodic harmony, and the fact that the book was quickly adopted by teachers not of Vossius's nation or religion seem to indicate a more analytical interest in formal rhetoric in seventeenth-century higher education even than in the sixteenth century.

This same inference might justly be drawn from Nicolas Caussin's *De rhetorica sacra et humana libri XVI*, first published in 1619 and quickly adopted by schools outside France as well as by the Jesuits there.[40] Here the three or five books of the traditional manual are expanded into sixteen, with whole books devoted to the separate types of oratory, including for the first time sacred oratory (Books XIV–XVI). The passions are, as in Aristotle and Vossius, allowed a large section of their own (Book VIII), and their crucial role in this subject is picturesquely pointed out.[41]

40 See P. Kehrli, 'Rhétorique et poésie: le *De eloquentia sacra et humana* (1618) du P. Nicolas Caussin', *Travaux de linguistique et de littérature*, XIV, 2 (1976), pp. 21–50. Kehrli's reasons for assigning a new date to the work based on the preliminary documents found in it (p. 22, n. 6) seem to me less than convincing. His interesting discussion naturally focusses mostly on poetic questions. He also discusses Vossius (pp. 32–3).
41 'Ut Deus in ventis, sic orator in affectibus ambulat.' Paris, 1643 edn, p. 459.

Rather more significant is the fact that the work does not waste much time over classical poetry and is clearly intended to be a guide to the study of eloquence pure and simple. This is attested by the author's preface, which forcefully rejects previous types of rhetoric as an 'indigesta rerum farrago', and by the alphabetical order of the ornaments of speech, which are not clearly divided into schemes and tropes as in the other manuals. However, this is not merely a reference book, as its sharp remarks on pulpit oratory will show when we come to study the theory of preaching.

In his schools and universities, then, the Frenchman of the late sixteenth and early seventeenth centuries was put through a detailed and careful course in rhetoric. This course was not only designed to help him identify more clearly the devices and thus enjoy more completely the art of ancient writers, but remained the definite training in practical public speaking that it had been in the time of Quintilian. Here the difficulty arises that whereas school declamations were in Latin, the writer or speaker or preacher had also to use his native tongue. The specific problems of preaching will be dealt with later; I wish now briefly to extend this survey beyond purely academic rhetoric by sampling the work of two eminent French men of letters writing respectively almost at the beginning and end of our period. The layman's attitude to rhetoric in action forms an interesting commentary on the effects of what was being taught in the schools.

3. Vernacular commentaries

Guillaume du Vair, although a bishop, is better known as a figure of importance in public life, and his treatise *De l'éloquence françoise*, first published in 1590,[42] may be taken as indicative of an average late-sixteenth-century practical view of the subject. It is an introduction to his volume of translations from the classics and seeks to justify this work by taking as its theme 'les raisons pourquoy elle [*sc.* French eloquence] est demeurée si basse'. Since preaching is expressly excluded, the chief area of interest is the law and politics.

His opening remarks are organized around a review of contemporary French orators – Pibrac, Margot, Versoris, Despeces, above all Brisson – to whom he distributes praise or blame. It is

---

42 The edition quoted is in the *Oeuvres*, Paris, 1619, pp. 211–32.

this section which reveals some of the criteria used in judging public eloquence. Brisson, who is considered at some length, is praised for his ornateness and order but is taken to task for using precisely that stock of citations and examples we saw recommended by Soarez:

> Mais aussi y auoit-il plusieurs choses qui le reculoient bien loin, à mon aduis, de la perfection. L'vne qu'il aimoit mieux paroistre sçauant qu'Eloquent: & pour ce ne se doit-il pas plaindre s'il a rencontré ce qu'il cherchoit. Ses discours estoient si remplis de passages, d'allegations & d'authoritez, qu'à peine pouuoit-on bien prendre le fil de son oraison. (p. 213)

Du Vair shows how common this was at the time, although his attribution of the fashion solely to Brisson's reputation must be doubted:

> Or ces deffaux-là n'ont pas nuy à luy seul. Car la grande reputation qu'il auoit, a fait aymer à ceux de son temps ce qu'il falloit fuyr en luy, & à son exemple fait passer quasi en tous ceux de nostre temps, cette vicieuse affection de vouloir beaucoup alleguer, & parler long-temps. (*ibid.*)

This interrupted action is contrasted to what Du Vair considers the highest eloquence:

> Mais cette grande et diuine eloquence à laquelle est deu le premier lieu d'honneur, & que Eschines & Demosthenes entre les Grecs, Ciceron et Hortensius entre les Latins, ont trouuee, qui se forme tel stile qu'elle veut: & tel que le subiect requiert, qui est plaine d'ornemens, pleine de mouuemens, qui ne meine pas l'auditeur mais l'entraine; qui regne parmy les peuples, & s'establit vn violent Empire sur l'esprit des hommes, est quelque chose de plus de tout ce que ceux dont nous auons parlé ont peu acquerir. (p. 215)

He then expounds a neo-Platonic theory of eloquence as exemplifying and indeed creating harmony in speech – the highest activity of man. Here there is certainly no anti-oratorical movement, but rather an exaltation of rhetoric, on purely artistic grounds, to a new eminence. The reasons why French oratory has not attained these ideal heights are then given; they are largely based on the difference between a republican system (as in Greece and Rome) and the French system of monarchy.

At this point Du Vair begins the justification of his translations. It is highly significant, since he views translations as an alternative to manuals and condemns these, we may suppose, in much the same way as a number of his contemporaries might have done:

> Apprendre par preceptes est vn chemin bien long, pource que nous auons

peine à les entendre, apres les auoir entendus à les retenir, & apres les auoir retenus à les mettre en vsage: Et difficilement nous imaginons-nous d'en pouuoir tirer le fruict qu'ils nous promettent. (p. 226)

In the place of these *abrégés* he erects an equally respectable and traditional sixteenth-century theory of imitation.

Du Vair's final point is extremely interesting: he opposes borrowed, archaic and newly invented words on the grounds that ambiguity in oratory is always wrong. His stringent criticism of them will become a constant over the next fifty years:

Certainement s'il y a endroit ou ceux de nostre aage ayent besoin de l'exemple des anciens ... c'est en l'vsage des mots empruntez. Car pource qu'ils voyent qu'ils apportent quelque enrichissement à l'oraison, ils en vsent si debordément la plupart, & auec si peu de jugement, qu'il leur semble que c'est vice ou au moins pauureté de langage, d'vser des mots propres à signifier quelque chose; quelques vns mesmes affectent d'en trouuer que l'on n'entende point, & pensent que c'est estre Eloquent, quand ce qu'ils disent a besoin d'estre interpreté. (p. 230)

We find a strong echo of this forty years later in La Mothe Le Vayer's *Considérations sur l'éloquence française de ce temps*:[43]

Car puis que nous ne parlons et n'écriuons que pour estre entendus, d'où vient que la premiere perfection de l'Oraison consiste en ce point d'estre claire et intelligible, il s'ensuit que son principal defaut procedera de l'ambiguité s'il s'y en trouue, comme il ne se peut faire autrement quand nous nous seruirons de termes peu connus. (p. 421)

This insistence upon clarity is indeed the keynote of the entire treatise, and is the strand which connects the three sections: on individual words, periods, and whole speeches. That the violence of the attack is not an overstatement of increasing public outrage at a continuing professional mannerism is confirmed by Ferdinand Brunot, who considers the author a moderate in the movement for the purification of vocabulary, if not an actual opponent of it.[44] A further object of La Mothe's wrath is the form of period which since Croll we have learned to call *style coupé*.[45] His remarks attempt to throw light on the motives of those who use this stylistic device:

---

43 First published in 1638. Quotations are from the *Oeuvres*, 2nd edn, vol. 1, Paris, 1656.
44 *Histoire de la langue française*, vol. 3, Paris, 1909, pp. 198-9.
45 *Style, Rhetoric and Rhythm*, esp. pp. 211-19.

On peut neantmoins reconnoistre par l'inuectiue de cét Empereur [Caligula ranting at Seneca] qu'vn style entre-couppé a tousiours esté tenu pour fort vicieux. Ceux qui s'en seruent encore auiourd'huy le veulent prendre recommandable, parce qu'il semble auoir d'auantage de pointes que celuy qui est plus diffus, & d'autant que beaucoup de figures comme les antitheses, & les allusions y paroissent auec vn éclat nompareil. (p. 435)

To this is opposed the period which excels by being 'nombreuse, bien sonante, ornée de figures, et accompagnée de quantité de conditions, dont les Rheteurs nous ont laissé vn assez grand nombre de préceptes' (p. 436). Despite this re-statement of a classical rhetorical principle, we are warned that ornateness need not be majestic, and conversely that great prose may often scorn to adopt ornaments, 'comme si c'estoit prendre les habits ou le fard d'vne Courtisane qui ne songe qu'à l'exterieur' (p. 438). The discussion of tropes and schemes is limited to the most cursory glance at metaphor, hyperbole and allegory, and we are constantly reminded that they are not to be abused. A similar insistence on clarity and correctness informs the remarks on whole speeches; from a remark like 'ces trois vertus d'estre correcte, claire, et ornée, se doiuent trouuer dans toutes les differentes especes de l'Oraison', we may deduce that the criteria the Frenchman of the period used in judging oratory were not entirely those he had learnt from Soarez. There are loud echoes here of the European debate over 'witty' and 'conceited' writing. However, before we read too much into La Mothe's new accents, we should note that his own manual of rhetoric, composed for Philip of Orléans,[46] follows the standard pattern of Soarez and others extremely closely.

It is interesting to learn that the trend in legal oratory in the first half of the century was indeed away from examples, anecdotes and learned quotations, and towards what has been called 'l'éloquence pathétique'.[47] The evidence seems to show that, although among laymen there was no falling away from the fundamental principle of rhetoric – that verbal persuasion is an art with rules that can be learned – or from the concept of ornamentation, there was perhaps some doubt as to the practical sufficiency of the

---

46 *La Rhétorique du Prince*, in *Oeuvres*, 1656 edn, vol. 1, pp. 817-43.
47 Catherine Holmès, *L'Eloquence judiciaire de 1620 à 1660*, Paris, 1967, p. 32. See also pp. 33, 38.

manuals and certainly a growing transference of interest to questions which had been merely peripheral in the schools: choice of vocabulary and extent of quotation. As with theories of preaching, the vernacular commentaries mirror to some extent that shift in French oratory from the 'thesaurus style' to consecutive, affective, periodic writing which we shall examine in Chapter 4, while the substance of the rhetorical manuals remains largely static. The precepts of Cicero and Quintilian, like those of Aristotle and Horace in poetry, can be called in to justify almost any style of vernacular prose.

3
Rhetoric in the Church

If a thorough grounding in the ancient arts of speaking was the common heritage of educated Frenchmen in the early seventeenth century, there was no less interest in the specialized application of those arts to contemporary circumstances. In a Christian monarchy the pulpit can replace the forum as a focus of rhetorical activity and the preacher naturally assume the role of public orator *par excellence*. But that is not to say that the preacher can simply adopt unquestioned the concerns of classical secular rhetoric. He believes, for instance, that he has received a commission to proclaim the word of God, not to argue a law case, however brilliant; he can trace the origins of his office in Hebrew prophecy and Patristic exegesis. At a more practical level, he knows that the sermon is, at the very least, a special branch of public speaking with its own traditions and rules. And so he has need of other guides, other aids, than those provided by his schooling.

In a later period it is to the seminary that he would naturally go to learn, among other things, how to compose and declaim his sermons. But the diocesan seminary as we know it today did not then exist in France. The Council of Trent's decree on the subject was one of the last to be accepted by the French Church, and the seminarian movement of the 1630s and 1640s aimed at only a very brief training in essentials prior to ordination. During these preparatory courses discussion of preaching was normally confined to a list of obligations and was frequently not mentioned at all. Among Catholics, then (with the exception of the Jesuits), the idea that an advanced secular education and a decent family were sufficient formal qualification for the cleric held good until the second half of the century.[1] On the other hand, there existed a

---

1   *Cf.* Delumeau, *Le Catholicisme entre Luther et Voltaire*, p. 73: 'En fait la France ne se couvrit de séminaires qu'après 1650.' See also Broutin, *La Réforme pastorale en France au XVIIe siècle*, vol. 2, pp. 181ff.

large body of published treatises on preaching, clearly intended to provide the additional information a young priest would need.[2] It was to these that the educated but inexperienced preacher had recourse, and the number of editions most of them went through testifies to their popularity.

The sixteenth century had witnessed a resurrection of interest in sacred rhetoric springing firstly from the revival of more objective classical studies and the new respect accorded to the authority of Cicero and Quintilian. The humanists saw the sermon as the modern equivalent of the ancient oration, and wished to establish the traditions of antiquity in this as in other literary genres. A second and more significant impetus to the study of preaching among Catholics was given by the Council of Trent, with its renewed awareness of pastoral needs and its strong desire to restore the dignity of ancient ecclesiastical practice. The claims of classical authority and pastoral efficiency were not, however, readily reconcilable, and the central ambiguity in contemporary manuals has to a large extent its origin in this uneasy alliance. The conflict between the 'sacred' and the 'secular' remains, under many guises, the dominant theme of preaching theory throughout our period, and may still be found in La Bruyère.

By the turn of the sixteenth and seventeenth centuries, then, there was a vast amount of material available to the enquiring ordinand. Its influence in France has not been seriously studied, and even the one modern attempt made at classifying it is not very useful for our purposes.[3] One may, of course, legitimately wonder whether it is not begging the question to speak of 'schools'

2 For lists of these the four articles by H. Caplan and H. King are indispensable: 'Latin tractates on preaching: a book-list', *Harvard Theological Review*, XLII (1949), pp. 185–206; 'Italian treatises on preaching: a book-list', *Speech Monographs*, XVI (1949), pp. 243–52; 'French tractates on preaching: a book-list', *Quarterly Journal of Speech*, XXXVI (1950), pp. 296–325; 'Spanish tractates on preaching: a book-list', *Speech Monographs*, XVII (1950), pp. 161–70. Since I shall make constant reference to these, only a short title will be given in future.

3 By Father Sagüés, in the introduction to his critical edition of Estella's *Modus concionandi*, Madrid, 1951, vol. 1, p. 237. He proposes a threefold division into intransigent classicists (those for whom the sermon was a mere extension of the classical oration), moderate classicists, and independents. The difficulty with this for us is that all his 'intransigents' turn out to be pre-Tridentine. In other words, what he calls 'extreme classicism' is an early-sixteenth-century phenomenon only.

at all, and I shall return to this point again. Nevertheless, a rudimentary classification has to be imposed. The evidence of the editions, of contemporary references, recommendations and, in some cases, borrowings, points to a fivefold division: Italian works written under the aegis of St Charles Borromeo and inspired by the ideals of Trent, Jesuit ordinances and textbooks, representative Spanish works, standard Protestant treatises, and of course early-seventeenth-century works written in France. Although I think it is valuable to give an individual account of the works thus classified, I shall attempt at the same time to trace the continuous threads of discussion and evaluate the various ways in which the principal themes are treated.

The origins of these themes are not unimportant; I have already mentioned the Council of Trent, and the echoes and developments of its doctrine in French councils will provide us with a starting point for the practical rules of everyday preaching. The concerns of more elaborate theory largely originate with St Augustine, whose *De doctrina christiana* is an indispensable introduction to the whole subject.

1. St Augustine

Augustine's treatise *De doctrina christiana libri IV*[4] is the most frequently quoted authority in works of preaching theory throughout the period, and it is here that we can grasp most firmly some of the central points at issue. It is a pity that many analyses of this work overlook the first three books, since Augustine's statements about the matter of preaching have some important implications for the form which are not always made explicit in the fourth book (on style).

The exposition of Christian doctrine is firmly tied to the interpretation of Scripture; but this is in turn subordinated to what must be the overriding duty of the preacher, to show how all Scripture and theology tend towards the love of God and one's neighbour. The aim therefore is not purely intellectual but moral. The immediate interest of the text, and the possibility of objective discussion, are to be set aside in favour of the unified inspiration which lies behind it. It follows that the moral interpretation is

---

4 References are to the edition by H. J. Vogels, Bonn, 1930 (*Florilegium Patristicum XXIV*).

always right 'etiam si latet quid senserit ille qui scripsit' (III, 27; p. 62). This naturally leads on to the principle that all Biblical texts which do not in their literal meaning encourage virtue or a purer faith are to be read figuratively, and that therefore 'omnia vel paene omnia quae in veteris testamenti libris continentur, non solum proprie, sed etiam figurate accipienda [sunt]' (III, 22; p. 60).

He mentions two chief aids to right exposition. Ambiguities in the literal sense of the text are most easily solved by linguistic science, or philology (II, 11; p. 26). More important is his insistence on the usefulness of pagan learning; for Augustine it is simply foolish to avoid such truths as the pagans possessed:

Neque enim et litteras discere non debuimus, quia earum deum dicunt esse Mercurium. Aut quia Iustitiae Virtutique templa dedicarunt, et quae corde gestanda sunt in lapidibus adorare maluerunt, propterea nobis iustitia virtusque fugienda est. Immo vero quisquis bonus verusque christianus est, Domini sui esse intellegat, ubicumque invenerit veritatem. (II, 18; p. 33)

This is reinforced by a lengthy section on the detailed ways heathen stories and traditions may be of value to the Christian.

This attempt to reconcile the pagan and Christian traditions, a dominant theme in all Augustine's writings, operates on a more detailed level in Book IV, where he discusses the art of preaching properly so called. Although the book opens with a warning that academic rules are not to be sought here, it soon becomes clear that he intends them to be found in and learnt from secular works. His vigorous defence of rhetoric reveals a profound belief in its power:

Nam cum per artem rhetoricam et vera suadeantur et falsa, quis audeat dicere, adversus mendacium in defensoribus suis inermem debere consistere veritatem, ut videlicet illi qui res falsas persuadere conantur, noverint auditorem vel benevolum vel intentum vel docilem prooemio facere, isti autem non noverint?
(IV, 2; p. 72)

The point is brought home by an analysis of rhetorical devices in Scripture in an attempt to show how excellent must be the art which even the Holy Spirit uses in inspired works. Paul's handling of figures and *oratio numerosa* is constantly referred to in the book.

There is, nevertheless, a difference between the pagan faith in the efficacy of rhetorical rules and the Christian belief in divine inspiration. Augustine's handling of this difficult problem is one of the most honest we shall meet. He confronts the books of schemes and tropes with the most directly inspirationist of Christ's remarks (Matthew x, 19–20: 'Take no thought how or what ye shall say . . .') and neatly resolves the conflict by a comparison with prayer: God gives us what we need but expects us to make human efforts to obtain it. Thus rhetoric's place is firmly established, and he wastes no time in explaining its basic principles. Assuming a close knowledge of the rules, he improves on tradition by making teaching and delighting functions of moving. This is in accord with his view of the essentially moral aim of Scriptural preaching:

Oportet igitur eloquentem ecclesiasticum, quando suadet aliquid quod agendum est, non solum docere ut instruat, et delectare ut teneat, verum etiam flectere ut vincat. (IV, 13; p. 84)

To this he links his famous theory of the three styles adapted to Christian ends. The simple style is for instructing, the mediocre (that is, ornate) for delighting, and the sublime for conquering the hearer's will (IV, 17; p. 87). There is here no subordination of the Christian vision to pagan schemes, as his insistence on the significance and power in the Christian story of apparently insignificant things bears witness.[5] Paul continues to be the model, and his functional use of the three styles is examined and praised.

Augustine goes on to give practical advice on stylistic matters (the importance of variety, the avoidance of lengthy excursions into the sublime) and possible causes of embarrassment (tears and how to interpret them). The treatise ends with a brief consideration of the preacher's life and devotion which contains two interesting *prises de position*. Moral qualities in the preacher, according to Augustine, are important but not indispensable for good preaching. The confusion of these two led many later theorists into complicated and often untenable positions. Secondly, intellectual deficiencies can be supplemented by borrowing on a large scale from the work of others, a principle of great significance for later practice.

The central points of the *De doctrina christiana* – the close reference to Scripture interpreted to moral ends by means of

5 IV, 18. The background to these remarks on the hierarchy of styles and values is fully discussed by Erich Auerbach, *Mimesis*, trans. Trask, New York, 1957, esp. pp. 63–6. There is a brilliantly stimulating discussion of *De doctrina* IV in chap. 1 of the same author's *Literary Language and its Public in late Latin Antiquity and in the Middle Ages*, trans. Manheim, London, 1965.

figures, the insistence on the value of secular rhetoric and its necessary adaptation to Christian ends – provided the frame of reference for most of the serious theories of preaching throughout our period.

2. Trent and French provincial councils

The application of Augustine's theories supposes a tradition of cultivated preaching and a highly intelligent trained clergy. The situation faced by the Fathers at Trent could not have been more different. Widespread absenteeism and consequent neglect of basic teaching on the part of the higher clergy, a rural priesthood for the most part ignorant of theology and unaware of their duties, the scandal of wandering preachers: it is against this background that the decrees of Trent and the provincial councils must be seen. Their practical nature and their authoritative status make them the second pillar of contemporary discussion. Nothing, indeed, could be more practical than the Tridentine decree on preaching,[6] which confines itself to setting out the general principle that preaching is the prerogative of the bishop and those approved by him, and that parish priests should instruct their flock on Sundays and feast days in doctrines necessary to faith and morals, 'cum brevitate et facilitate sermonis'. The remainder of the document is devoted to the financial and legal arrangements which will ensure the proper execution of these principles.

On the other hand, the provincial councils held in France after Trent become increasingly detailed in their teaching.[7] While they, too, are concerned to establish the principles of episcopal authority and clerical duty, their decrees contain practical advice which impinges directly on the manner of preaching. Reliance on homilies and the work of others was vigorously commended at Bordeaux in 1583 and at Bourges in 1584, and several simple books of homilies were eventually composed to answer this need.[8] All these decrees

6 Sessio V, decree of 17 June 1546 *super lectionem et praedicationem*, in *Diariorum, Actorum, epistularum, tractatum nova collectio*, vol. 5, Freiburg im Breisgau, 1911.
7 Of the ten councils listed in Mansi, *Sacrorum conciliorum nova et amplissima collectio*, Rome, 1759–1927, vol. 34, those held at Bourges 1584, Cambrai 1586, Toulouse 1590, Narbonne 1609, Bordeaux 1583 and 1624 contain decrees on preaching.
8 See, for example, Part II, Appendix 2, below.

stress the need for a preacher to have received a thorough education; it appears to have escaped the authorities that the learned quotations they go on to condemn were probably an attempt by the clergy to give proof of this education. But the decrees of the Councils consist for the most part of violent attacks on fables, jokes and profane matter generally. It is worth quoting these condemnations, to stress their consistency over forty years and to introduce us to one of the chief topics of contemporary preaching theory:

Caveant summopere praedicatores, ne in suis concionibus fabulas, jocos, dicteria, & scommata, quibus [risus] excitetur, intermisceant: concionatoris enim est, non risum movere, sed lacrymas auditoribus excutere.
(Bordeaux 1583; Mansi col. 770)

Ne historias ex apocryphis scriptoribus populo narrent.
(Cambrai 1586; Mansi col. 1229)

Improbatas historias, fabulas, & alia ad risum invitantia, minime proponant.
(Narbonne 1609; Mansi col. 1483)

Quae autem concionatori sunt fugienda, multa esse norunt omnes, sed haec dumtaxat praescribamus. Ne igitur certum tempus Antichristi, extremi judicii, apocrypha, falsa miracula, fabulas, profana, ambigua, obscura, dubia, difficilia, ac supra plebis captum afferat concionator.
(Bordeaux 1624; Mansi col. 1579)

The mechanical repetition of the same phrases seems indeed to indicate less the correction of abuses than a fixed conception of what this sort of decree should contain. The need to avoid jokes and fables rests on two propositions which are *de rigueur* in preaching theory, but which can be made to lend their support to an almost infinite number of conclusions: they are the phrase about preaching oneself and not Christ, which originates in 2 Corinthians iv, 5, and the insistence that tears and not laughter are the fruit of effective preaching, which is a quotation from Jerome.[9] All these conciliar decrees are, furthermore, based on Borromeo's provincial councils held in Milan from 1565 to 1579, and it would

---

9 *Ad Nepotianum 52*, para. 8. The full quotation is 'Docente te in Ecclesia, non clamor populi, sed gemitus suscitetur. Lacrymae auditorum, laudes tuae sint.' Migne, *P.L.*, XXII, 534.

therefore be unwise to see them as a response to local, or even contemporary conditions.[10]

One aspect of preaching, the funeral oration, is dealt with in some detail by these councils. As well as enjoining great circumspection in this practice, the decrees actually suggest themes the preacher may use. In chronological order these are prayers for the dead (Rheims 1583), human wretchedness and vigilance against sudden death (Aix-en-Provence 1585), the inevitability of death and judgement (Toulouse 1590) and finally, at Narbonne in 1609, the idea that the content should be any of the subjects 'quae audientes ad se parandum ad mortem commovere possint'.[11] Thus there is an evolution from the static exposition of a dogma – prayers for the dead – to a dynamic attempt to shake the spectator into a new vision of life. This may be contrasted with the classical theory as expounded by V.-L. Saulnier in his article on the sixteenth-century funeral oration.[12]

We must, however, be careful not to exaggerate the importance of these conciliar decrees; they are more symptomatic than influential. They are also, like those of Trent, concerned with the village *curé* rather than with the court preacher, and their neglect of detailed method may much more plausibly be ascribed to conciliar tradition than to novel thinking on style or rhetoric.

In Augustine we find the origins of some major concerns in Christian rhetorical theory; in the conciliar tradition we can see administrative injunctions in a pure state. It is the balance of these two elements, I shall argue, that largely determines the emphases of the individual preaching manuals we are now ready to examine.

3. Italian theorists

Italian works on preaching theory were very widely read in early-seventeenth-century France, as libraries and lists of editions

---

10 The link with Borromeo is more clearly established by the 1624 Council of Bordeaux's strong recommendation of his book on preaching. This is the only manual mentioned by any of these councils. See Mansi col. 1579.
11 Mansi cols. 698, 995, 1291, 1503.
12 'L'oraison funèbre au XVIe siècle', *Bibliothèque d'humanisme et Renaissance*, X (1948), pp. 124–57. M. Saulnier draws only on Agostino Valiero.

testify.¹³ This popularity is, of course, part of the wider influence of St Charles Borromeo which marks the whole of the French Church at this time, and which finds one means of expression in the numerous panegyrics devoted to his praise.¹⁴ But too often Borromeo's ideas are seen in isolation from other works which formed part of the same body of teaching, and it is necessary constantly to bear in mind the context in which his theories were elaborated and to complement them with those of his fellow theorists.

Borromeo's *Pastorum concionatorumque instructiones*¹⁵ is a compendium of his previous pastoral decrees on the subject to be found in the instructions of his provincial councils. It is therefore a practical and authoritative document aimed at presenting easily assimilable ideas and correcting the most obvious abuses; a great deal of time is spent in explaining the ordinances of Trent and in giving directions on such matters as the wearing of vestments and the proper times for sermons. The work places almost as much emphasis on the preacher's life and qualifications as on actual sermons. The preacher should be a model of virtue and learned in all theology. Despite this education, and his recommendation of Greek and Hebrew for elucidating the Scriptures, Borromeo insists that similes should be homely and familiar: 'Agricolis porro si concionabitur, plurimum ad rem proderunt similitudines, ab agro, vinea, frumento, vitibus, lino, cannabi, arboribus, stirpibus, aliisque agriculturae partibus ductae' (fol. 14ʳ). The quality of a preacher's spiritual life, and especially the practice of meditation, are vitally important to his ministry. Augustine and Chrysostom are proposed as literary models, and (most important of all) an ecclesiastical rhetoric is enjoined.

His discussion of the sermon itself consists for the most part of condemnations. For *inventio*, once having posed the principle that

---

13   Cf. Dejob, *De l'influence du Concile de Trente*, Paris, 1884, p. 143: 'Leurs livres étaient répandus en France, comme le prouvent encore aujourd'hui les vieux fonds de nos bibliothèques. Plusieurs furent réimprimés ou traduits à Paris, soit dès le premier jour, soit durant le dix-septième siècle, soit même au dix-huitième.'
14   Cf. Broutin, *La Réforme pastorale en France au XVIIᵉ siècle*, vol. 1, pp. 37–95.
15   In *Acta ecclesiae mediolanensis*, Milan, 1583, fols. 212ᵛ–221ʳ. Caplan and King ('Latin tractates', p. 188) give a very long list of editions.

Rhetoric in the Church

Scripture and the Christian life are the proper objects of instruction, he gives a long list of subjects which should be banned: doctrinal subtleties, conjecture as to the date of the Last Day,[16] jokes and new allegories, personal quarrels, and scandals among the public authorities. But he allows the occasional use of pagan quotations:

> Ethnicorum doctrinam, poetarum versus, philosophorum [disciplinas], quae religioni christianae non alienae, sed accomodatae videntur, ad utilitatem, et usum revocari, sancti doctores Augustinus, et Hieronymus, aliique censuerunt. Sed concionator hoc faciat, quam rarissime. (fol. 217^r)

His remarks on style constitute a similar list of condemnations, beginning with a general fulmination against 'exquisite' eloquence and developing into a detailed attack on apparently almost every stylistic device:

> Fucum omnem fugiat ... Verba antiqua, et peregrina fugiat. Fati, fortunae, infortunii nomina, aliaque id generis, ab ecclesiae usu iampridem explosa, omnino cavebit. Epithetorum item nimium usum, et poeticum dicendi genus ne confectetur. Anicularum non adhibeat proverbia ... Exordiatur moderato, et temperato dicendi genere: in quo exordio vitentur similitudines, praesertim poetico more explicatae. Vocabulorum frequentem synonymiam omnino caveat ... Metaphoras, similitudines, et exempla a rebus maxime notis, et insignibus sumat: nam deiicit maiestatem orationis, qui a rebus similibus similitudines frequenter trahit ... Verba ecclesiastica, etsi minus elegantiae habent, ne dicere recuset: at prophana, et nova repudiet omnino. (fol. 220^v)

This may at first sight seem to indicate a total rejection of traditional rhetoric. In fact, there is only one place where Borromeo does this explicitly, and that is in his remarks on pronunciation and gesture (fol. 221^r). On closer examination, this list will be seen to be entirely devoted to excesses – a type of denunciation which has a long rhetorical tradition behind it. Borromeo's work contains, then, the negative side of classical theory. The positive side is to be sought elsewhere.

Borromeo not only recommended the use of an ecclesiastical rhetoric, he actually commissioned his friend Agostino Valiero, Bishop of Verona, to write one for use in the new diocesan seminaries of Milan. *De rhetorica ecclesiastica libri III* appeared in

---

16 Fol. 217^r. This prohibition occurs in many similar documents, and was evidently a burning issue.

Venice in 1574,[17] a year later in Paris, and in France was considered (with Luis de Granada's treatise of the same name) to be the chief representative of this sort of work as late as the eighteenth century.

As we might expect after reading Borromeo's instructions, the problem of inspiration and the legitimacy of rhetoric are discussed at length. Although Valiero admits the possibility of direct inspiration by the Holy Spirit, he insists in chapter 1 that study is the more normal way; thus the implicit accusation of pride can be levelled against those who rebel against the system. The problem is dealt with another way in chapter 3, where he distinguishes between the *causa efficiens* of preaching (the Holy Spirit) and the *proximae causae efficientes* (study and practice). Far from being a pale imitation of classical antiquity, Christian rhetoric is seen as the crowning triumph of the whole tradition, since it elevates a great technique to discourse on the highest truths. Once this problem has been dealt with, he has full freedom to define ecclesiastical rhetoric in terms which leave no doubt as to the importance of 'art':

Ars autem, quae Ecclesiasticam eloquentiam, christiano populo tam utilem, docet, Rhetorica Ecclesiastica appellatur; quae est ars, sive facultas inveniendi, disponendi, & eloquendi ea, quae ad salutem animarum pertinent.   (I, 3; p. 4)

Likewise he can follow the secular tradition very closely in his threefold classification of the oratorical genres into deliberative, demonstrative and forensic; he is in fact much more traditional in this than the majority of his contemporaries. It is in his adaptation of these genres to Christian ends that he introduces a new element. Chapters 5 to 19 of Book I consider the deliberative genre divided into five points, things we must believe, hope, fear, avoid, and practise. The discussion of demonstrative oratory is mostly a (highly secular) method of delivering funeral orations.[18] Forensic oratory is confined to synods, etc. He seems unconcerned by the limited value of these traditional categories and is evidently not interested in giving a descriptive account of normal Christian preaching.

17   Caplan and King, 'Latin tractates', p. 195. References are to the edition of Verona, 1583. A fairly free translation, *La Rhétorique du prédicateur*, is to be found in Migne, *Nouvelle encyclopédie théologique*, vol. 6, cols. 955–1128.
18   An analysis of it is given in V.-L. Saulnier's article 'L'Oraison funèbre au XVIe siècle', pp. 137-40.

The third Book, on *elocutio*, contains the conventional rhetorical attack on disorderliness, verbosity, lengthy periphrasis and puns, together with a vague warning against excessive attention to words: 'Nihil inani verborum strepitu infructuosius, cum de gloria Dei, & de salute animarum agitur' (III, 6; p. 224). This is the only trace of the Borromean diatribe. Otherwise this section is devoted to detailed teaching on how to construct similes, metaphors, figures, allegories and functional imagery. His remark on comparisons clearly demonstrates that these are intended to please as well as convince: 'Similitudines non solum ad probandum, sed etiam ad delectandos animos adhibentur' (III, 23; p. 245). He re-states Augustine's theory of the three styles in Augustine's precise terms. His discussion of decorum is also important, since it lends weight to the idea that the attack on profane and indecorous preaching was in fact directed not against style but against a certain incorrect treatment of themes; thus he reproves self-praise, fictions, lack of respect and heresy.

In the last sixteen chapters of the book he leaves the secular tradition and enters the field of the practical sermon. Thus we are introduced for the first time in chapter 43 to the homily; his remarks show that it is clearly different from the classical oration, but he offers none of the sharp definitions we shall meet elsewhere. It is in this section that he places his discussion of *dispositio*, which wholly conforms to classical rules. The sort of oration (*sermo evangelicus*) which is a commentary on the Epistle or Gospel of the day is accorded a passing reference (III, 51; p. 302), and only two brief chapters (52 and 53) are spent on the fourfold interpretation of Scripture. This is not, however, an indication that he disdains the old style of exegesis; on the contrary he notes that excessive concentration on the literal sense leads to frigidity in the pulpit (III, 53; p. 317). The short final chapter contains the whole of his teaching on memory and gesture, and ends with the characteristic statement that the oration should be written out because the pen is 'optimus artifex dicendi'.

The Milanese triptych is completed by Giovanni Botero, Borromeo's secretary and disciple, whose *De praedicatore verbi Dei libri V*[19] is possibly the most interesting of the three works. It has a structure very similar to that of Borromeo's own

---

19 References are to the Paris edition of 1585.

Instructiones, but certain parts are dealt with much more fully. The first two books give an exalted ideal of the preacher's intellectual and moral qualities, and there is the usual emphasis on the dignity of the office. The claims of pagan learning are accepted on the all-important principle that they can be pressed into God's service, and Botero himself frequently cites classical poets as well as philosophers in the course of the treatise. The purely Christian side of the balance is, however, by no means left unweighted, and after stressing the uniqueness of the Bible as a source of teaching and moving, Botero ends with a splendid exhortation to make every sermon reflect, in its inspiration and in its imagery, the omnipresence of the crucified Christ:

> Ita nihil est, ad animos audientium excitandos, crucis praedicatione accomodatius. Qua de causa, laudare satis non possum sanctissimi, ac sapientissimi Cardinalis Borromaei consilium atque institutum. Is enim nullam habet fere concionem, nullum sermonem ad populum, quem non aspergat Christi sanguine, non distinguat Christi plagis, non exornet Christi corona, non condiat felle, & mirra, non exaggeret Christi mortis & crucis commemoratione.
> (fol. 25)

Book III contains a debate on eloquence which discusses the central points at issue with remarkable vigour and originality. The initial definition departs from the traditional threefold scheme – 'concionatoris duo praecipue officia, docere, & permovere' (fol. 39^v) – and insists on the necessity of the 'vis dicendi'.[20] From this position he attacks all indulgence in verbal artistry for its own sake, 'orationis exquisita quaedam compositio' (fol. 40^r), and indeed all purely human eloquence. This is summed up in the comparison, which will become a commonplace in later debates on rhetoric, with painted women:

> Similes videntur foeminis: quae, quod naturali pulchritudine non multum sibi ornatae esse videantur, accersunt extrinsecus simulati medicamenta candoris, & ruboris: ut quia, naturae beneficio tales non sunt, artifitioso colore, & fucata specie, esse videantur.
> (fol. 40^v)

The pernicious *dulcedo* he dislikes so strongly is identified with the *dicendi genus temperatum* which, he declares, should never be heard in the Christian pulpit. But before we see in this a complete break with the whole classical and Augustinian position, not to say with his own master, it is important to note how, in the next

---

20 F. 39^r. The use of *vis* rather than *ars* is clearly deliberate.

section, 'idem probatur auctoritate Ciceronis' (fol. 41ᵛ). The rather limited object of his attack is finally revealed to be excessive elegance and *oratio numerosa* (fol. 46ᵛ). By contrast, he expounds his new aesthetics, which are based on vigour and, we might almost think, violence:

Non enim muliebrem venustatem, sed virilem quandam dignitatem secantur; nec fuco illitum, sed sanguine diffusum colorem adamant. (fol. 43ʳ)

Realism in oratory is praised through a comparison with painting which we shall meet again in France:

Et ut boni pictores nuda hominum corpora spectatorum oculis, quantum pudor, atque honestas patitur, subiicere student: Ita sapiens verbi Dei praedicator res, ac sententias ipsas, quam maxime nudas, potest, ante mentis oculos constituere conatur. (fol. 56ᵛ)

All this is leading up to the idea that in Scriptural eloquence we have an art in complete conformity with these ideals which has the added advantage of being divinely inspired and therefore binding. This is why he deals at great length with the literary virtues of the Gospels,[21] the Prophets, and of course St Paul. His analyses reveal a constant preoccupation with effective persuasion and the need to castigate the folly of elegance. A parallel to this may be found in the severity and functionalism of the fine arts in the years immediately after the Council of Trent.

It will be obvious by now that this group of works contains a very wide range of theoretical attitudes towards pulpit oratory, and that nothing would be easier than to select and oppose isolated quotations from them. In this way a whole system of schools, attacks and counter-attacks could be constructed. Yet the fact remains that they were written by men who shared exactly the same ideals; indeed, Valiero's and Botero's works were subject to the authority of Borromeo. Without prejudicing the future development of the argument, it does seem that a subtler interpretation is needed to explain the variety of these opinions. The key lies, I suggest, in their functions as revealed by their titles. Borromeo's work quite simply consists of pastoral injunctions, Botero's is a discussion of the ideal preacher, while Valiero is

21 The idea that Christ's *sermo piscatorius* is stylistically praiseworthy represents a considerable advance over the Augustinian position. Augustine refers only to the Prophets and Paul as rhetorical models, and they easily fall into classical categories.

writing in an educational and literary tradition with norms and topics which are not necessarily linked to contemporary realities. The unpractical nature of the *Rhetorica ecclesiastica* seems to support this hypothesis. In other words, these books are trying to do different things, and are even aimed at different audiences. They do not, as we shall soon see, cover the whole range of manuals, but they represent three complementary theoretical activities.

The aspect of preaching theory which is not discussed by these three is the actual mechanical process of composition – the most important from our point of view. It is the subject of the most popular Italian preaching manual, Francesco Panigarola's *Modo di comporre una predica*.²² This was composed for Franciscan novices but was soon recommended for more general use. It evidently met with approval in Milanese circles, since Botero's preface refers to Panigarola as a preacher of 'eximia doctrina' and 'summa eloquentia'. The work corresponds to the *inventio* and *dispositio* sections of rhetoric, but although it opens with the usual division of oratory into three genres, deliberative, demonstrative and forensic, it adds a further, 'que nous appellerons à la maniere Greque, Didascalique' (fol. 1ᵛ), which is to be the subject of discussion. Didactic preaching, according to Panigarola, covers two sorts of sermon, 'de matiere ou d'Euangile' (fol. 2ʳ), thematic or expository. Though a Gospel can if necessary be the basis for a classical oration, it normally requires detailed comment or the development of one of its central ideas. These distinctions are made in other works of theory too, and their absence in the Milanese group underlines the restricted scope of those treatises.

Once the theme has been selected, the preacher's chief task is to find, quite literally, the ideas ('conceptions') which will support it. The account of the way these ideas are to be mined from books,

22 The first edition, at Cremona, Milan and Rome, is 1584 ('Italian treatises', p. 244). A Latin version was published at Cologne in 1605 ('Latin tractates', p. 193). It was translated into French by Gabriel Chappuis as *L'Art de prescher et bien faire un sermon*, Paris, 1604, 1608, 1624; Lyons, 1615 ('French tractates', p. 298). Panigarola was well known in Paris, where he had preached before the Court; see Labitte, *Les Prédicateurs de la Ligue*, pp. 86–9. References are to the French edition of 1604.

and the whole idea that a sermon should be built or woven rather like a nest, is worth quoting at length:

Cecy fait [i.e. having found a proposition], nous commençons à auoir besoin d'autres que de nous-mesmes, c'est à dire de plusieurs liures desquels nous pouuons tirer les conceptions qui prouuent, & qui nous introduisent à la proposition que nous nous sommes esleue: en la maniere, qu'apres qu'aucun a proposé de bastir en la ville, & de faire vne maison de telle forme, il faut qu'il entre en apres, en la fournaise, à fin de se prouuoir de pierres, & au bois pour faire prouision de poutres & soliues, & en somme pour apprester la matiere de son edifice: Ainsi il faut que nous entrions en nostre estude & librairie, & que là de tous les liures que nous auons, nous taschions de tirer & mettre à part comme vn amas de toutes les conceptions, qui nous doiuent seruir en la matiere proposee. (fols. 13^v–14^r)

For this activity a commonplace-book is absolutely essential.[23] This is the first time we have met this recommendation, which recurs in many practical manuals. It is clearly of the highest importance in determining the form of the sermon.

Thus in the group of Italian works whose influence was active in early-seventeenth-century France we have a wide range of preaching theory, ranging from abstract discussion and bald decrees to sensitive, practical aids. It is a microcosm of the whole field and though the emphases may vary in other groups, the basic framework will remain the same.

4. Spanish theorists

The famous *invasion mystique* described by the Abbé Bremond is just one aspect of the general influence of Spanish religious thought on seventeenth-century France. The two most widely read Spanish works on preaching, Luis de Granada's *Rhetorica ecclesiastica* and Diego de Estella's *Modus concionandi*, again exemplify two approaches to preaching theory. One is an elaborate academic treatise, the other a severely practical manual; and there is no evidence that they were ever thought of as other than complementary.

The whole of the first book of Granada's *Rhetorica ecclesiastica*[24]

23 'Amas' in this passage is 'selva' in the original Italian version; it derives from the Latin *silva*, which is the normal word for published compendia of quotations at this time.
24 First published at Lisbon, 1576; Paris editions in 1583 and 1594 ('Latin tractates', p. 190). References are to the French version by Nicolas Binet, *La Réthorique de l'Eglise ou l'éloquence des prédicateurs*, 2 vols., Paris, 1698.

deals with the problem of rhetoric, secular learning and the nature of Christian oratory. Far from seeing a conflict between the sacred and the secular, Granada draws a parallel with the advances in theology brought about by the application of philosophical ideas and, like Valiero, stresses the rarity of direct inspiration:

> C'est pourquoi si nul ne peut réussir avec honneur dans les disputes de Philosophie & de Théologie, sans être bien fondé en l'Art de disputer; il y a non plus personne, à moins qu'il ne soit, ou rempli de l'esprit divin, comme l'ont été les Prophetes & les Apôtres, ou heureusement né pour l'eloquence, ce qui est tres-rare; il n'y a personne, dis-je, qui sans l'un ou l'autre de ces dons extraordinaires, puisse réussir avec avantage dans la Prédication, que par le secours de la Rhétorique. (I, 2; vol. 1, p. 7)

It is this 'secours de la Rhétorique' which the book aims to provide by a complete adaptation of secular doctrine to the special requirements of the pulpit. The result is a strange amalgam. Whole chapters are taken directly from Cicero and Quintilian and he labours hard to fit sermons into the different genres of pagan oratory. Yet he has some practical recommendations, particularly on the use of a personal commonplace-book.[25] The disparity between the concerns of large-scale theory and the practice of contemporary preachers is demonstrated by his omission of any reference to the traditional *avant-propos* and Ave Maria which even preface most of his own sermons translated into French.

Diego de Estella's manual[26] is much more limited in scope; it deals only with the homily or *sermo evangelicus*, the genre which is widely met in practice but rarely discussed in theory. It is this which at first sight gives parts of the book such an unfamiliar look. It will be remembered that Panigarola divides the sort of sermon which does not fall into the deliberative, demonstrative or forensic genres into two categories, *de matière* and *d'Evangile*. Estella does not even consider the thematic sermon and concentrates entirely on the homiletic exposition of Scripture. He does, however, deal briefly with panegyrics and funeral orations.

---

25 Vol. 1, pp. 111–12. Although he does not mention published commonplace-books, he obviously approved of their use since he himself published a *Sylva locorum communium*.

26 *Modus concionandi*, Salamanca, 1576. Twice published in France: Lyons, 1592 and Paris, 1635. The Paris edition and the two Cologne editions of 1594 combine it with Granada's treatise; see P. Sagüés Azcona's critical edition, 2 vols., Madrid, 1951.

The originality of the book lies in its treatment of Scriptural interpretation and in the concept of the 'digression'. Cutting across the whole hermeneutic tradition, he insists that the literal and tropological senses are the only valid ones and rejects the allegorical and anagogical methods:

Nec idipsum assertis nostris obstat. Nam in principio et coadunatione sacrosanctae militantis Ecclesiae, ethnicis et judaeis maxime congruebat sermo allegoricus, ut lex evangelica magis ac magis stabiliri et confirmari posset, et novella fidelium germina crescerent. At vero, cum his nostris temporibus Ecclesiae plantae uberrimos fructus edidere, modo nostra concio non ethnicis, quin potius ad fidelium convertitur animos: qui quidem fideles, quamvis sint piaculis debilitati, et criminibus cooperti, et languoribus delibuti, modo concionator majorem fructum faciet, si moralem doctrinam praedicaverit, qua quidem et crimina taxantur et virtutes docentur.[27]

Furthermore, the moral sense must spring from the literal and develop the straightforward teachings in the text 'absque ipsius litterae contorsione, et chimericae fictionis machinatione' (p. 228). This method is illustrated by a discussion of the miracle of the loaves and fishes in which Estella's comments are almost identical to those of the Protestant Hyperius whom we shall study later. The difficulty of literally interpreting the Old Testament is solved not by the doctrine of prefiguration, but by a system of parallels. Thus David and Goliath are not so much figures of good and evil as an example to which the battle for the soul may be compared.

The structure of the homily owes nothing to classical models, except for the idea of an exordium which should engage the listener's attention rather than divide the points in the medieval manner (p. 296). The principal task thereafter is the selection of three or four topics in the Epistle or Gospel of the day and their development and exposition to a moral end. Estella calls these points *digressiones*[28] and gives a set of clear rules for their content:

Quamlibet autem digressionem debent comitari, et ei connectere, utpote in auctoritate, comparatione, atque exemplo, ex Veteri Testamento desumpto; denique vitiorum fiat taxatio ut doctrinae ratio postulat. (p. 246)

Of these elements, the comparison is clearly the most important, for it is from comparisons that a sermon derives its literary beauty: 'quippe cum lepores quidam sint, et qui concionem maxime

---

27 P. 214. Estella's Spanish version is even more forceful: 'piérdese el tiempo que se gasta en alegorías y anagogías' (p. 18).
28 According to Sagüés (vol. 1, p. 190) this is the only treatise of the period where the word is used in this special sense.

decorant' (p. 259). Most of the remaining chapters deal with ways of embellishing one's work; they are largely drawn from traditional rhetoric, although Estella calls them the 'new style'.

But the finding of Scriptural authorities, examples, and general comparisons naturally demands the use of a commonplace-book and the consultation of digests and thesauri. Here Estella is quite explicit, and (like Panigarola) reserves this information for his most practical section, the chapter 'Uti sermo evangelicus componatur ac fiat':

exceptorium consulito quaternionem, in quo communia loca excepta et notata in laudem alicuius virtutis, aut contra vitii alterius incommodum, vel secundum aliam quamcumque propositam materiam videat, ut huiusmodi evangelii locus amplietur doctrina, Scriptura, et comparationibus, ex alphabetico codice desumptis. Et peractis iam elucubrationibus et antiquis studiis utatur, quae labore et vigiliis consequutus est.[29]

Nor is a personal commonplace-book sufficient: he expressly recommends the published *Summa de exemplis* of Joannes a Sancto Geminiano.[30]

There are innumerable stimulating and important details in this manual which a general review cannot discuss. Nevertheless, even in its broad lines, this handbook provides the only full Catholic account of *sermo evangelicus*, and it is the first treatise we have met precise enough to allow the influence of such practical instructions on actual sermons to be gauged with any accuracy.

5. Jesuit theorists

Unlike the preachers for whom the Italian and Spanish manuals were written, the Jesuit novice received instruction in preaching as part of his general training. Moreover, a young man who showed promise in this direction was picked out and given special reading courses.[31] This training was far from narrow, since preaching was seen as an extension of Christian charity, and therefore all

---

29 P. 240. *Cf.* pp. 214–15: 'Verum, moralibus doctrinis ut abundes, albeolum seu quaternionem habeto, alphabeticis characteribus ordine signatum, et manu tento calamo in evolvendis sacris et ecclesiasticis Doctoribus, ex eis quaecumque notatu digna sunt excipito, serie iam alphabeti dicta, ut quae ad avaritiam spectant, in verbo *avaritia* et quaecumque ad caritatem faciunt, in verbo *caritas*, et sic de aliis.'

30 '... et Joannes de Sancto Geminiano, qui exactum ex his comparationibus librum edidit' (p. 259).

31 *Decreta Societatis Iesu*, Avignon, 1827–8, vol. 7, pp. 233–5.

Rhetoric in the Church

approaches to it were welcomed.[32] Practical experiments were held, and the treatises I shall examine incessantly encourage this custom.[33]

St Francis Borgia's short treatise *De ratione concionandi*[34] is concerned above all with the moral life of the preacher; spiritual preparation and the need for grace are the dominant themes. Nevertheless, this insistence upon inspiration does not lessen the need for the art of rhetoric. For Borgia the *dispositio* and *elocutio* elements are the same as for the classical oration; the secular ornaments of metaphor, example and comparison are expressly commended (pp. 697-8), while the usual attack on stylistic abuse is narrowed down to affected or improper words:

Phrases, dicendique modus, & verba, cavendum ne affectata adhibeantur, & plus aequo conquisita; haec enim & dicentis animum exsiccant, & audientis. Vitanda contra et verba sordida, rustica, & barbara, & obsoleta.   (p. 699)

The treatise is written in a majestic and prayerful manner which suggests that it is intended less as an academic work than as an exhortation; this would explain its emphases.

The same concern for the preacher and his training informs the Jesuit General Claudio Acquaviva's two letters on preaching.[35] The first is a brief instruction to Provincials to encourage preaching, and gives the practice of meditation an important place in the spiritual training of young orators. This is obviously linked to another letter of the same day discussing the use of the *Spiritual Exercises*.

The second letter divides the main points into three categories: aids, hindrances, and means. This text is extremely informative,

32 *Ibid.*, vol. 1, pp. 162-3: 'ut melius et cum maiori fructu animarum id munus obeant, omnibus mediis utantur, quibus commode iuvari possint.'
33 *Cf.* André Schimberg, *L'Education morale dans les collèges de la Compagnie de Jésus en France*, Paris, 1913, p. 24. A note reveals that 'on les appelait les "tons" '.
34 First published Salamanca, 1579 ('Latin tractates', p. 188). It was translated into French and published at Douai in 1603; there were six editions before 1650 ('French tractates', p. 297). References are to the text published in P. Binsfield, *Enchiridion theologiae pastoralis*, Trier, 1609, pp. 686-715.
35 Letters of 14 August 1599 *de formandis, ac bene instituendis nostris concionatoribus*, and of 28 May 1613 *monita complectens formandis concionatoribus accomoda*. In *Epistolae praepositorum Generalium*, Rome, 1615, pp. 297-300 and 373-96.

since his balance sheet of good and bad allows us to grasp much more clearly the implications behind the terms used in debates and attacks elsewhere. Thus Acquaviva recommends the sort of rhetoric found in Scripture, and condemns certain devices in precise enough terms for us to see once again that the real object of attack is extravagance:

> Hic porro innumeris pene modis errari contingit, crebra videlicet epithetorum usurpatione, tum adhibendis phrasibus poeticis, nimiumque exquisitis; audacioribis item, atque frequentioribus metaphoris, longioribus circumscriptionibus earum rerum, quae uno, simpliciue vocabulo essent contentae ... adhaec investigandis vocibus antiquis, obsoletis, recens inventis, compositis aut derivatis, usurpatis interdum (ut de Italicis exemplum afferam) a Boccatio, vel poetis, aliisve, qui linguae gnari, ac bene periti videri voluerunt. (pp. 383–4)

Likewise, although he lists recourse to the 'Sermonarii' as a vice (p. 382), recourse to contemporary preachers' reference books is not:

> Uberrima ad dicendum quasi obvia materia, quae videlicet a plerisque eruditis, gravibusque Doctoribus aucta plurimum est, & hactenus digesta sapienter. Maxime vero cum de Societate non pauci, & Scripturis sacris exponendis, & aliis argumentis pertractandis, eiusmodi conscripserint libros, ut ingentes collectos thesauros nullo prope labore eruere inde cuivis liceat. (pp. 375–6)

His doctrine of right intention shows that affectation and vanity were often thought of less in terms of style than as faults in the spiritual orientation of the preacher:

> [Prima] est intentionis obliquitas. Cuiusmodi esset, praedicare seipsum potius, ac laudem sectari, quam auditorum utilitatibus propter Deum consulere. Haec enim res non modo minuit, aut prorsus tollit meritum: sed etiam, cum circa finem erretur, incredibile est quam detorqueat media, eaque depravet. (p. 380)

His practical advice is rather slight; he obviously does not want to repeat the teaching of Reggio and Mazarini to which he refers the student. The one constantly recurring idea is the necessity of a commonplace-book.

At the opposite end of the spectrum stands Carlo Reggio's *Orator christianus*,[36] a standard ecclesiastical rhetoric and reference book aiming at a comprehensive treatment of the whole subject.

36 Rome, 1612.

It would be tedious to summarize its contents, which are in the main those of the similar works by Valiero and Luis de Granada, but it does display certain features which stress the particular Jesuit perspectives. Reggio's advice about right intention (pp. 85–8) recalls Acquaviva's, and there is the same insistence on the uniqueness of Scripture and the Fathers as the source of examples and rhetorical devices. The secular tradition is similarly adapted in the section on 'Orator vir bonus' (Book III), which discusses the preacher's education almost wholly in terms of Scriptural exegesis. Finally, the increasing attention paid to the condemnation of jokes, lack of respect, and so on, is reflected by a whole book (IX) on 'Prudentia'; this is a coherent treatise on all the vices of preaching. Nevertheless, the greater part of the work by far is given over to the exposition of traditional rhetorical techniques.

Although more limited in range, Mazarini's manual[37] is likely to have had much more impact on the young men it was written for. Here the preacher's intellectual preparation is entirely bound up with the keeping of a commonplace-book, which is in turn the central element in sermon composition. Consequently, he says, one should read only those books which will be useful in the writing of sermons, and he not only proclaims the table of quotations which is the fruit of such reading to be quite indispensable, but gives very detailed advice on how to draw it up. It should, for example, have three heads: for Lent, Sundays, and feast days. To this personal collection should be added the reference lists found in thesauri of all types:

> Le Predicateur ne doit point aussi laisser en arriere les autheurs, tant anciens que modernes, qui ont fait des notes, des commentaires, des annotations, des questions, des concordances, des remarques morales, des paraphrases, des tables, & des pandectes; ny moins mespriser ceux qui font vn grand meslange de choses diuerses: parcequ'ils peuuent aider grandement à l'inuention des plus retifs, fournir de matiere aux plus steriles, & n'estre point du tout inutiles aux mieux entendus. (p. 34)

Despite his apparent downgrading of pagan authorities, he recommends here not only contemporary Christian compilers like Felipe Diez and Tomás de Trujillo, but Petrarch and Aulus Gellius as well.

---

37 Giulio Mazarini, *Pratica breve del predicare*, Venice, 1615. References are to the French version by J. Baudoin, *Practique pour bien prescher*, Paris, 1618.

The way in which such material is to be transformed into a sermon is illustrated by a panegyric of St Agatha which he builds up before our eyes as the book progresses. The subject of the sermon is divided up into three or four main points which are then filled out with 'remarques'. This is his version of *inventio* and *dispositio*; the function of *elocutio* is compared, as in Panigarola, to the artist's use of his materials:

Tout cét appareil des poincts particuliers & requis pour faire vn Sermon est au Predicateur ce que sont les os d'vn corps à la vertu formatiue; Au masson ses materiaux entassez peslemesle; Au peintre ses couleurs broyées, & son crayon; & Au Sculpteur le marbre ou la pierre qui n'est point encore polie. D'où il s'ensuit qu'il est necessaire de ranger derechef les poincts de chasque membre, si bien qu'ils soient encheinez & liez ensemble, afin de les pollir par apres, vsant de l'instrument de l'Elocution comme d'vn burin. (pp. 136-7)

Beauty in a sermon consists in the use of figures, and *copia* (p. 140). The text of his panegyric of St Agatha, similar (as we shall see in the next chapter) to very many contemporary French sermons, bears out the suspicion that an oration composed along these lines tends to be a tissue of short comparisons and maxims, with very little continuous discourse.

Mazarini is so bound to the internal dynamic of the preaching manual, however, that although the method outlined above seems sufficient in itself, he also states the secular rhetorical theories in the traditional way. There are two insights to be gained from his account. Firstly, the threefold function of teaching, delighting and persuading is transformed into three facets of the same activity, in conformity with the post-Tridentine emphasis on the need for persuasion and the idea that beauty is the gilding on the pill of conversion. Secondly, there is an open tension between his classical exposition of the seven parts of the oration (exordium, proposition, etc.) and his use of a division into three parts both in the general discussion and in the text he offers as an example. This is the more surprising since, of all genres of pulpit oratory, the panegyric was normally considered to be the closest to classical practice. We can draw from Mazarini, then, not only a deeper insight into the processes of composition than we found even in Panigarola and Estella, but also an idea of the increasing difficulty of combining the theories which originate in rhetorical tradition and those which spring from rhetorical practice.

Rhetoric in the Church

6. Protestant theorists

French Protestant preachers drew their inspiration largely from the expositions of Scripture which form the greater part of the Reformers' writings, but I shall nevertheless examine two manuals which, apart from the direct influence they may have exercised, show the drift of Protestant thought on this subject in the second half of the sixteenth century.

Andreas Hyperius of Marburg's *De formandis concionibus sacris, seu de interpretatione Scripturarum populari*[38] had an influence not only through its French translation[39] but by virtue of Villavicencio's adaptation of it in his popular *De recte formando studio theologico ac de formandis sacris concionibus.*[40] Thus his ideas were known to the whole range of Christian theorists in this period. These ideas are strikingly different from most secular theory, despite Hyperius's fondness for the rhetorical tradition. The central concept of the work is the list of five major categories – 'doctrinale', 'redargutivum' (refutation of error), 'institutivum' (morals), 'correctorium' and 'consolatorium' – which form the basis of his discussion of aims, method and genre. Although, as the title would suggest, the sermon is seen as essentially a commentary on the literal sense of Scripture, Hyperius rejects any approach which does not openly aim at edifying the people in these five ways. Thus the only sorts of sermon he will discuss are those based on a text or a whole Biblical story, and Book II substitutes these new genres for the unhelpful classifications of other theorists.[41] Hyperius deals with the structural problems posed by this method in a remarkably original way by reinterpreting the traditional parts of the oration (narration, confirmation, etc.) as techniques of argument to be used within the framework of the point. Thus

---

38 Marburg, 1553 ('Latin tractates', p. 191). References are to the Basle edition of 1573.
39 *Enseignement à bien former les sainctes predications et sermons*, Geneva, 1563. It was also translated into English by John Ludham, 1577.
40 P. Sagüés Azcona's introduction to his edition of Estella, vol. 1, p. 263, contains an account of Villavicencio's work which tallies exactly with Hyperius.
41 'Frustra mihi videntur se torquere, atque iniuriam non levem inferre Theologiae ... qui conantur tria illa genera causarum, Demonstrativum, inquam, Deliberativum, Iudiciale, e prophano foro in ... Ecclesiam inducere' (p. 115).

there are to be as many confirmations as there are points, and confutation should, when necessary, be used throughout (I, 13; p. 81).

Apart from these novel adaptations, however, Hyperius is a thoroughgoing classicist:

> Breviter, quicquid in dispositione, elocutione, & memoria est concionatori necessarium, accurate rhetores id omne in suis officinis tradiderunt: quocirca (meo quidem iudicio) multo commodissime concionatores easdem partes ex illis discent. Certe qui aliquo modo exercitatus in rhetorum scholis prius fuerit, quam in concionatorum recipiatur ordinem, is multis aliis instructior & magis idoneus adveniet. (I, 4; p. 22)

With the proviso that they are best drawn from Scripture, all the traditional rhetorical techniques are allowed. He assumes a wide knowledge of classical values in the preacher and expects him to put them into practice.

The second Protestant work, Bartholomaeus Keckermann's *Rhetoricae ecclesiasticae*,[42] shows more freedom from traditional teaching, and bears the marks of the developments in preaching theory which took place in the last decades of the sixteenth century. Keckermann was familiar with these developments: he mentions not only Augustine and Erasmus, but Estella, Luis de Granada and Valiero among his predecessors (pp. 19-20). Unlike all but Estella, however, he limits his discussion to the Biblical commentary favoured by the Reformed Churches and the consequent methods of what he calls 'textualis inventio' (p. 21). He distinguishes texts which contain a general moral point from those which require a close historical explanation, and gives detailed advice on the latter which includes etymology. Where he principally differs from traditional theory is in his rejection of the divisions; for him the structure of the sermon is a simple exordium, a 'tractatio intermedia', and a peroration (p. 105).

The most significant feature of the treatise is the constant emphasis placed on strong persuasion. Beginning with his very definition of ecclesiastical rhetoric as 'ars persuadendi Ecclesiae Christi res ad salutem necessarias' (p. 29), it leads him to proclaim the virtues of novelty and shock, to condemn profane elements as distracting and, most important of all, to urge the use of exaggeration and dramatic, immediate imagery:

42 First edition Hanau, 1600 ('Latin tractates', p. 191). References are to the Hanau edition of 1606.

Rhetoric in the Church

Moventur affectus duplici ratione; magnitudine & praesentia; seu, ut magis perspicue dicam, amplificatione sive exaggeratione & deinde hypotyposi, id est, repraesentatione, si videlicet ita res & personae suis descriptionibus & imaginibus ante oculos ponantur, ut non tam dici, quam geri in praesentia videantur. (p. 57)

His treatment of elocution proper, though it contains the age-old praises of harmony and clarity, is heavily weighted towards those figures like exclamation, interrogation and obsecration which have the greatest impact on the listener. It is this emphasis on the relationship between preacher and congregation that leads him to spend the whole of Book II on the delivery of the sermon.

7. French theorists

Very little preaching theory of any substance was produced in France in the first half of the seventeenth century, but the few texts we have are important for the light they shed on developments peculiar to France, and they need to be examined in a European context because they have been used in the past to support certain conclusions about preaching in general in this period which I believe to be erroneous.

The text which has been most widely discussed is St François de Sales's famous letter to André Frémiot.[43] This was written in answer to a request for advice from the newly appointed Archbishop of Bourges, and thus the saint is given an opportunity to expound the teaching of Trent and of his hero Borromeo on the necessity of pastoral instruction. One of the distinctive elements of the work is thus explained by its origin. But it is much more than a Borromean instruction: it is a whole manual of sermon composition, and should therefore be read in the same way as similar works.

François begins by defining the aim of preaching as to make people have life and have it more abundantly, and links this to a twofold definition of the office of preaching, 'enseigner et esmouvoir' (p. 304). Much has been said of his exclusion of the third function of rhetoric, to delight. He in fact includes it, but

---

43 Dated 5 October 1604. It was translated into Latin and many other languages, and went through an enormous number of editions the world over ('Latin tractates', p. 194). References are to vol. 12 of the *Oeuvres complètes*, Annecy, 1902, pp. 299–325.

uses this as an opportunity to distinguish functional from futile ornamentation. It is worth quoting the whole passage:

Je sçai que plusieurs disent que, pour le troisiesme, le predicateur doit delecter; mays quant à moy, je distingue, et dis qu'il y a une delectation qui suit la doctrine et le mouvement. Car qui est cette ame tant insensible qui ne reçoive un extreme playsir d'apprendre bien et saintement le chemin du Ciel, qui ne ressente une consolation extreme de l'amour de Dieu? Et pour cette delectation, elle doit estre procuree; mais elle n'est pas distincte de l'enseigner et esmouvoir, mays qui fait son cas a part et bien souvent empesche l'enseigner et l'esmouvoir. C'est un certain chatouillement d'oreilles, qui provient d'une certaine elegance seculiere, mondaine et prophane, de certaines curiosités, ageancemens de traitz, de parolles, de motz, bref, qui depend entierement de l'artifice: et quant a celle cy, je nie fort et ferme qu'un predicateur y doive penser; il la faut laisser aux orateurs du monde, au charlatans et courtisans qui s'y amusent. Ilz ne preschent pas *Jesus Christ crucifié*, mais ilz se preschent eux mesmes. (pp. 304-5)

It will be seen that François is here doing much the same as most other theorists, namely recommending functional ornament; normally, however, only the negative side of this passage is quoted.[44] In any case, the terms he uses ('elegance seculiere, mondaine et prophane'; 'de traitz, de parolles, de motz') are not precise enough for us to base any firm conclusions on them.

Fortunately he goes on to give a list of things which may or may not be used in sermons, and we get a much clearer picture of the exact nature of his prohibitions. This section is, incidentally, a first-rate example of the way a deceptively simple principle – 'Il y a suffisamment dequoy en l'Escriture Saincte pour tout cela, il n'en faut pas davantage' (p. 305) – can be expanded into a whole system of references and examples. The same expansion is implicit no doubt in many similarly austere remarks. First the Fathers: 'Mais qu'est-ce autre chose la doctrine des Peres de l'Eglise que l'Evangile expliqué?' (p. 305). Then the lives of the saints, beautifully presented: 'Il n'y a non plus de difference entre l'Evangile escrit et la vie des Saintz qu'entre une musique notee et une musique chantee' (p. 306). Not even beautiful comparisons can provide a link between the other points and the initial principle, but he goes on nevertheless to advocate the temperate use of 'histoires profanes', once adapted to Christian truth: 'Elles sont bonnes, mais

44 For a typical misreading see Sauvage, *Saint François de Sales prédicateur*, p. 241: 'C'était dire en d'autres termes: le prédicateur doit s'attacher à instruire et à toucher, mais à plaire, jamais. Et c'est en cela que, par excès de prudence, François de Sales irait peut-être trop loin.'

il faut s'en servir comme l'on fait des champignons, fort peu, pour seulement resveiller l'appetit' (*ibid.*). He makes an original and interesting distinction between the verses of pagan poets ('Leurs vers sont utiles ... Saint Paul fut le premier a citer Aratus et Menander') and their fables, that is, their fictions and mythologies. This lends weight to the suspicion that it was the dangerous content of some classical poetry more than a general dislike of quotation which inspired the attacks against profane citations in the treatises of the time. Indeed, even fables are not totally excluded from François's system: 'O de celles la point du tout, si ce n'est si peu et si a propos ... que chacun voye qu'on n'en veut pas faire profession' (*ibid.*). It is, in fact, only 'faux miracles' and 'histoires ridicules' which are completely banned (p. 307). 'Histoires naturelles' are openly welcomed, on the principle of 'Coeli enarrant gloriam Dei'. This vision of almost unlimited reference appears again in his discussion of examples: 'Les exemples ont une force merveilleuse, et donnent un grand goust au sermon; il faut seulement qu'ilz soyent propres, bien proposés et mieux appliqués. Il faut choisir des histoires belles et esclattantes' (p. 312)

François's treatment of Scriptural interpretation is equally broad and traditional; he recommends the use of the four senses, and gives an example of interpretation in action that would have shocked an earlier and more rational exegete like Diego de Estella.

His section on sermon structure owes little to classical rhetoric. This is all the more surprising because he is not limiting himself to *sermo evangelicus*, but includes even panegyrics and funeral orations. Although he is nowhere explicit, it seems that he expects a sermon to have three points, which the preacher then amplifies with material gathered from the sources above. This is also where, like Panigarola, Estella and Mazarini, he recommends the use of a commonplace-book, recourse to the 'table des auteurs'[45] and to printed thesauri. His particularly warm praise of Diez's sermons and *Summa praedicantium* gives an important insight into his criteria of excellence:

Il va a la bonne foy, il a l'esprit de la predication, il inculque bien, explique bien les passages, fait de belles allegories et similitudes, des hypotyposes nerveuses, prend l'occasion de dire admirablement, et est fort devot et clair.
(p. 320)

45 He is obviously thinking of the great lists of 'belles matières' which are printed at the end of contemporary collections of sermons.

It is at this point of amplification, then, that you construct your comparisons, and the close attention he gives to the construction of artifices is finally much more important than the oft-quoted phrase 'le souverain artifice c'est de n'avoir point d'artifice' (p. 321), which in any case forms part of a section dealing with *actio*, not style. There is nothing in this text to support the idea that François de Sales was aiming at anything more revolutionary than a broad account and synthesis of contemporary theories, weighted if anything towards the practical type of manual as exemplified by Panigarola, Mazarini and Estella. Its real importance lies in the light it throws on the methods of composition used by the saint and his disciples.

Nicolas Caussin is another theorist for whom considerable claims have been made by those who saw the history of pulpit oratory in this period only in terms of a slow march towards classical perfection.[46] When we met his treatise *De eloquentia sacra et humana libri XVI*[47] in our discussion of secular rhetoric, it was pointed out that the inclusion of three books on sacred oratory was a novelty in this sort of treatise. Therein lies the explanation of the first book on preaching, 'Theorhetor, sive de sacrae eloquentiae maiestate' (XIV), which is a massive attempt to raise Christian preaching to the status of pagan oratory. This is done by pointing out, at length, the importance of its subject matter and by exalting its exponents, for whom very great claims are made. The final book (XVI) is devoted to 'Chrysostomus sive Idea'. Book XV, 'De forma et charactere sacrae eloquentiae' contains therefore the essential matter, and it is presented in a striking way. The first half of the book consists of a debate between Logodaedalus, representing the worldly school of preachers, and Theophrastus, who takes a stand for majesty against profanity. The central characteristic of Logodaedalus's speech is less the use of ornament than constant reference to pagan antiquity:

Allii reconditam vim sapientiae mirabantur, quod tam subtiliter Andromedam, cum natura humana, Perseum, cum Christo, Danaen, cum Beata Virgine, & nescio quem Pandorae calceum, cum aeterna beatitudine comparasset.

(p. 929)

---

46 E.g. Jacquinet, *Des prédicateurs du XVIIe siècle*, pp. 204–16.
47 La Flèche, 1619. References are to the edition of Paris, 1643.

Although this has escaped some of Caussin's commentators, it does not escape Theophrastus, who states his central objection to Logodaedalus in precisely those terms.

Mihi vero idem, in re haud multum dissimili contingit exclamare, quo mihi fabulae cum veritate? quo mihi phalerae verborum cum sanctimonia? quo cum igne vigili, & tremenda Christi ora Silenorum, & Satyricorum lusus? (p. 930)

So this is very much in the line of traditional condemnations of fables; it is therefore not surprising to find him making similarly conventional distinctions between a rhetoric which is 'elaborata, & circumtonsa, & manu facta' (p. 941) and Christian eloquence which is 'non putida, & nitida fluens, & colorata, sed vis quaedam ineluctabilis, victrix, triumphatrixque animorum' (p. 944). It is, however, worth noting that in Book XIV Caussin had praised Christian orators by comparing them to the best pagans (p. 913), and that Theophrastus himself is not above allusions to Rhodopeian snows.

Theophrastus is then urged to outline the ideal preacher's training. At this point the work turns into a standard ecclesiastical rhetoric with few new elements except a particularly vigorous attack (p. 949) on the sort of commonplace-book which contains pagan rather than Christian quotations. This is rather important because, although Caussin makes it clear that his remarks are intended to be general and timeless,[48] it is obvious that commonplace-books are essential to the methods of composition which lead to what in the next chapter I shall call 'Thesaurus sermons'. Caussin's reaction against the 'thesaurus style' is thus mirrored in this theoretical work of his, although it has nothing to do with 'moral reform'.

This antagonism between the sacred and the secular was not universally felt, however, as Claude de Voyer d'Argenson's short treatise[49] testifies. Although many of Voyer d'Argenson's remarks are clearly inspired by the ideals of Trent and the French councils – for example, his remarks on legitimate authority, times and places of sermons – he insists that the preacher should be learned in all branches of letters, and seems to distinguish good pagan

---

48 'Haec dico, non ut insultem aut nostri saeculi penuriam accusem...' (p. 949).
49 The *avant-propos* to his *Enneade sacrée*, Paris, 1622. References are to the edition of Paris, 1628 (C. 313), pp. 1–47.

mythology from wicked pagan fictions in his recommendation of 'la Mythologie que les Sages de la Gentilité ont tiré de toutes les mensongeres inuentions que leurs Poëtes auoient proposées' (p. 30). This support of antiquity's place in the pulpit is evident in the sermons which follow, each one of which is placed under the protection of a Muse.

Antoine de Balinghem's *Praeparatio in locos communes*[50] results, on the other hand, from the increased use of the Bible in the search for examples and *sentences*. But even he refers to the advice preachers may find in the works of 'authores profani' like Cicero, Plutarch, Quintilian and Aulus Gellius.

As far as secular influences on the structure and composition of the sermon are concerned, there appears to have been no appreciable decline as the century progressed. Simplicien Gody's *Ad eloquentiam christianam via*[51] is, if anything, closer to the secular tradition than any of the earlier treatises we have been studying. His respect for the authority of Cicero and Quintilian is absolute: 'sine qua non staret satis oratoria disciplina' (p. 7). His only departure from the classical path is into recommendations of themes for funeral orations, which lay a definitely unclassical accent on 'fluxarum rerum instabilitas & levitas' (p. 308), mirroring the change of emphasis in this genre we saw in the decrees of provincial councils. This identification of secular and ecclesiastical rhetoric is also to be found in Antoine Sirmond's remark that 's'il a le bien dire en main, [l'orateur] s'en sert, parcequ'il l'a, et en donne dans le viscère de l'ennemi'.[52] It recurs in Arnauld's declaration that 'le prédicateur évangélique peut et doit se servir utilement de l'éloquence qui s'enseigne dans les écoles'.[53]

Side by side with this tradition there was growing up a critical movement which concentrated all its attention on attacking the more obvious manifestations of a training in rhetoric. There is a parallel here with the increasing concern about choice of vocabulary

50 The preface to his huge concordance, *Scriptura sacra in locos communes ... ad concionum usum digesta*, Douai, 1621. A very untrustworthy paraphrase of this was published by the Abbé Morel as *Le Prédicateur*, Paris, 1837.
51 Paris, 1648.
52 *Le Prédicateur*, 1638, quoted by J. Truchet, *La Prédication de Bossuet*, Paris, 1960, vol. 1, p. 58.
53 *Réflexions sur l'éloquence des prédicateurs*, quoted *ibid*.

Rhetoric in the Church

and extent of allusion among the critics of secular oratory. The only representative in our period is Antoine de Laval, whose short treatise 'Des prédicateurs qui affectent de bien dire'[54] sums up all that is supposedly wrong with preaching:

> Le Vice de la saison le porte si auant à la recherche de mots nouueaux, de Metaphores, de Paroles non communes, de Periodes mesurées en cadence nombreuse, d'infinis Epiphonemes, Erotemes & autres figures de Rhetorique tellement sensibles à l'oreille, que ce sermon ... m'a esté vne pure Declamation de College (p. 175)

and selects as a specific abuse obscure vocabulary: 'ces mauvaises paroles peintes, fardées, figurées, & tirées à vive force du sein des Antres plus profonds de l'obscurité mesme, pour s'esloigner du parler commun & moins entendu' (p. 185). As well as being thoroughly inspired itself by a long tradition, this attack is also, to a large extent, vitiated by a violent attack on foreigners, who turn out to be anyone from south of the Loire. Another point also needs to be emphasized: this sort of bad rhetoric is for him 'le Vice de la saison', and he hankers for the purity sermons had in his youth.

It is to this tradition that the famous attacks of Rapin and La Bruyère much later in the century belong, and it is worth stepping out of our period to note how, there too, certain elements have become *topoi*, repeated more in deference to a tradition than in response to realities. Thus Rapin attacks foreigners,[55] and, as late as 1694, La Bruyère insists on the novelty of the vices.[56]

To return to the general problem of how to classify treatises on pulpit oratory, it seems to me that a fairly clear distinction emerges from this study between elaborate theoretical works and practical manuals of composition. The close similarity between the various *rhetoricae ecclesiasticae* suggests that they form a distinct genre

---

54 In his translation of the *Homélies de S. Jean Chrysostome*, Paris, 1621.
55 'Elle [*sc.* l'éloquence de la chaire] n'ayme dans le discours que ce qui est droit, simple, naturel. Le commerce avec les Sermonaires Italiens et Espagnols, pour y trouver de l'esprit, luy est fort contraire.' *Réflexions sur l'éloquence*, in *Oeuvres diverses*, Amsterdam, 1693–5, vol. 2, p. 98.
56 'Depuis trente années on prête l'oreille aux rhéteurs, aux déclamateurs, aux énumérateurs.' 'De la chaire', 5, in *Les Caractères*, ed. Garapon, Paris, 1962, p. 447.

with rules and *topoi* of its own, and are by no means descriptive. In many of them, remarks which appear at first sight to concern style have in fact to do with the preacher's interior life, and certainly cannot be used to support arguments about an antirhetorical movement. Nevertheless, their insistence on matters like meditation and literary imitation have stylistic implications which we shall meet in succeeding chapters.

It is the practical manuals – those of Panigarola, Estella, Mazarini, François de Sales – which offer us the key to the complexities of the sermons themselves, not least in their common insistence on a personal commonplace-book and on the published digests where similar material can be found. These digests or thesauri were very numerous in this period, and their importance cannot be exaggerated. At the turn of the sixteenth and seventeenth centuries a number of much earlier encyclopedias were reprinted especially for preachers,[57] though their range continued to be encyclopedic. At the same time there was a spate of digests and concordances of a specifically ecclesiastical nature, ranging from Felipe Diez's *Summa praedicantium* and Tomás de Trujillo's *Thesaurus concionatorum*, which give full sermon plans and detailed advice on similes and metaphors, to a Biblical concordance like Balinghem's. Many of the 'profane' quotations so frequently attacked in this period could be traced back to works like Luis de Granada's *Sylva locorum communium* or Jean Dadré's *Loci communes*, both of which proclaim on their title-page that they contain sayings from sources of every kind. For the comparisons from nature so highly recommended by a theorist like François de Sales, there was Pliny's *Natural History* and Binet's modern counterpart.[58]

With the exception of some works published very early in the period, the development of prose styles in our French sermons can be studied very largely in terms of the influence of these commonplace-books and the various ways in which preachers

57 E.g. Joannes a Sancto Geminiano's *Summa de exemplis*, first published c. 1480, reprinted at Venice in 1576 and at Antwerp in 1615, or Marko Marulić's *Dictorum factorumque memorabilium libri VI*, dating from the very early sixteenth century and reprinted at Paris in 1586.

58 Etienne Binet, *Essay des merveilles de la nature et des plus nobles artifices. Piece tresnecessaire à tous ceux qui font profession d'éloquence*, Rouen, 1621.

strove to adapt, improve upon, or reject them. That is the subject of the next chapter. Meanwhile, readers of Swift will recall his comments on the sort of text such a training can easily lead to:

Whoever only reads, in order to transcribe wise and shining Remarks, without entering into the Genius and Spirit of the Author; as it is probable he will make no very judicious Extract, so he will be apt to trust to that Collection in all his Compositions; and be misled out of the regular Way of Thinking, in order to introduce those Materials which he hath been at the Pains to gather: And the Product of all this, will be found a manifest incoherent Piece of Patchwork.[59]

59 *A letter to a Young Gentleman lately entered into Holy Orders*, in *Irish Tracts and Sermons*, ed. Davis and Landa, Oxford, 1963, p. 76.

4
Prose patterns

Many of the real implications of the *artes praedicandi* emerge clearly only as one looks at the actual styles and shapes of the sermons. I want therefore in this chapter to survey some stylistic trends in early seventeenth-century pulpit oratory, using categories which have deliberately been made somewhat general so as to reflect the flavour of a work and the broad principles underlying its use of the means of expression, rather than any close technical classification. The profusion of stylistic devices obviously cannot be classified in detail. By the end it will, I hope, be clear that this is intended as an impressionistic picture of the developments in preaching taste during the period, and that – like any account of changing taste at such a time – it can only be historical or chronological in a loose sense. There is as complex an interaction between the style of an individual and the style of a period, as there is between the specific artistic achievements of a talented writer and the tradition in which he works. A sermon of 1600 and one of 1650 are palpably different things, but the influences which go to make that difference are manifold. Many of them are evidently not religious or rhetorical; of those that are, only a few fall within the scope of this enquiry. But undeniably influential debates on the nature of preaching do occur in our printed books, and the voice and practice of a Camus or a Molinier may be seen as symptomatic of those debates, if not actually formative.

Very little help is given us in all this by contemporary commentators; preachers in France were not labelled 'witty', 'plain' or 'golden' in the manner of their English counterparts (although some of these definitions might well have been applied to them). It is nevertheless possible to propose labels for the stylistic patterns to which the bulk of our sermons conform – the 'thesaurus' style, the 'catenary' style, the 'conceptist' style, and finally 'orchestrated' prose. First of all, though, some account must be given of the curious mixture of styles in vogue at the very opening of the period.

1. The early years: 'poetic' and 'plain' preaching

It is not my purpose here to survey the development of French prose styles in the closing years of the sixteenth century; the task would be a mammoth one, complicated by the towering figure of Montaigne and the cross-currents of what is known as the 'Senecan' movement. The most noticeable feature of the sermons written at the turn of the sixteenth and seventeenth centuries, however, is a distinctive blurring of the frontiers between prose and poetry. Not for nothing were two of the more renowned preachers of the time – Cardinal du Perron and Jean Bertaut – also renowned as poets.

Bertaut's *Sermons sur les principales festes de l'année* (C. 26) was published posthumously by his brother Pierre in 1613. The way in which the quondam court poet of Henri III bridged the gap between sixteenth- and seventeenth-century modes of preaching as Bishop of Sées under Henri IV is evident from the first in the sources of emotion that he exploits – the horrors of civil and religious strife, the veneration of the heroes of the medieval past, aristocratic, chivalrous and crusading ideals. That these chords should have been struck in his funeral oration of Henri IV[1] is of course perfectly natural, but they also occur in his volume of sermons. His discussion of the great controversy over transubstantiation in sermon 9 begins, in much the same way as a hundred others, with close theological argument about the relevant Scriptural texts interspersed with side-swipes at the weaker of the Calvinist positions. Its ending, however, is strikingly different, for Bertaut introduces a moving lament over France strife-torn and divided by precisely this kind of controversy, and enriches it with references to the heroes of old:

> Que diroient, mais plustost que ne disent point au Ciel, vn Roy Clouis, vn Charlemagne, vn Godefroy de Bouillon, vn Roy S. Loüys, & tant d'autres valeureux & religieux courages dont ils estoient accompagnez és saintes expeditions & conquestes qu'ils entreprenoient pour la seule gloire du nom de nostre Seigneur, reuoyans l'Empire tant spirituel que temporel, qu'ils auoient rendu si fleurissant par leur vaillance & pieté, reduit aux plaintes & regrets de sa felicité passée? (p. 322)

Thus contemporary arguments are prejudged by appealing to the ancient reverence for these royal (and orthodox) saints or demi-saints, internal warring is contrasted with the glorious religious

---

1 *Discours funebre sur la mort du feu Roy*, 1610 (C. 25).

and military exploits of the Crusades, and Catholic belief is subtly associated with prosperity and peace. The preacher's last words are, in addition, a clear reminder of the poet's famous (and much quoted) quatrain from one of his *chansons*:

> Félicité passée
> Qui ne peux revenir,
> Tourment de ma pensée,
> Que n'ay-je, en te perdant, perdu le souvenir![2]

The traditionalist note is struck here not only by the loyalist conservative appeal but by the use of epic technique – in this case the conjuring up of the ancient heroes.[3] Similar devices are common in these sermons, where Bertaut uses a poetic type of structure rather than a careful, logical and exhaustive detailing of the points under consideration. Another discussion of a controversial doctrine, the Immaculate Conception (sermon 2), moves, in much the same way as sermon 9, from complex theological debate to a remarkable epic procession of Old Testament women – Eve, Sarah, Judith, Esther and others – who detail their titles to glory and then lay them at the feet of the Virgin. Our Lady, Bertaut concludes, is the *summa* of all their graces. The preoccupation with the problems of smooth transitions which is a perennial concern of the poet is likewise evident; the preacher moves as unobtrusively as possible from exposition to amplification, carefully underlining in his treatment of the text those elements of drama, personification and allegory which he will eventually draw together to form his final poetic coda.

Stylistically, Bertaut's work contains passages where the poetic element is purely decorative. The obvious and traditional place for such a *captatio benevolentiae* is the *avant-propos* – that of sermon 4, for example:

Messieurs, Ie ne sçay si ie vous oserois dire, comme en riant, que voicy le plus hardy iour de l'annee, car tout petit qu'il est, [&] combattu le plus souuent des iniures de l'air, comme sont les neiges, les glaces, les frimats, il ne laisse pas de marcher le premier en bataille, à la teste de toute l'armee, des autres iours ses freres, sous la conduitte de leur pere: le Soleil, qui desormais retournant à nous du voyage qu'il a fait vers le pole Antartique, recommence à nous faire esperer le Printemps, & les autres douces saisons de l'an, pour nous

---

2 J. Bertaut, *Oeuvres poétiques*, ed. A. Chenevière, Paris, 1891, p. 357.
3 *Cf.* N. Edelman, *Attitudes of Seventeenth-century France toward the Middle Ages*, New York, 1946, esp. pp. 215–45.

montrer que toutes les choses du monde se remuent & conduisent par les
inuisibles rouës du changement & de la vicissitude. (pp. 108-9)

In other words, it is New Year's Day. This piece again exemplifies
Bertaut's love of personification and periphrasis, and he is careful
to end it on a moral note much favoured by his contemporaries.
There is, however, no connexion between this and the sermon that
follows it: it is a purely inconsequential episode designed to please
the audience and show off the preacher's imaginative talents.

All this is not simply the result of a coincidence – a preacher
who also happens to be a poet writing early in our period. Similar
openings are by no means uncommon in sermons published
around this time, and even Camus's earliest work – the *Panégyrique
de la Mere de Dieu* of 1608 (C. 65) – begins with an unusually
elaborate and ingenious set piece clearly inspired by a poetic aim.
In the following passage Archbishop Du Bec, another very early
preacher in our period, combines secular as well as Scriptural
pastoral in his imagery:

Comme quand le pasteur a laissé les pleines & conduit des troupeaux aux
montagnes, les voyant las au retour, les faict rafraischir & reposer sur le
bord des fontaines: Ainsi l'Eglise au milieu de ce caresme, voyant la
bergerie Chrestienne presque lasse de monter & courir si souuent en la
montagne où se depart le pain de l'Euangile, où Dieu donne le pain de
sa parolle, le pain spirituel aux spirituels & celestes, l'amene à l'humilité
des vallées sur le bord des fontaines & fertiles herbages, dont le Prophete
dit: *Dominus pascit me, in loco pascuae collocauit me, super aquam
refectionis educauit me.*[4]

The attempt is rather heavy-handed. The word-pairs ('rafraischir
& reposer', 'monter & courir', 'spirituels & celestes') are of course
characteristic of much prose in this period, and before,[5] and here
give the impression of a somewhat depleted imagination straining
for effects rather than the impression of *copia* they were doubtless
intended to convey. As in the earlier example from Bertaut,
there is no connexion between this and what follows.

On the other hand, Bertaut is the only preacher among his
contemporaries whose genuine poetic vein is not exhausted at the
end of the *avant-propos*. In the emblems he chooses in order to

4 *Sermon de la Samaritaine*, 1600 (C. 133), pp. 1-2.
5 For a discussion of the stylistic phenomenon of word-pairs which goes well
   beyond the individual case of Montaigne, see R. A. Sayce, *The Essays of
   Montaigne, a Critical Exploration*, London, 1972, pp. 301-8.

illustrate or clinch an argument he takes care to unite religious and secular sensibilities. Listing the Virgin's graces he explicitly uses emblems which, though sanctioned by Scripture and long devotional usage in the Litany of the Virgin, for example, do not ring harshly to the reader of Renaissance poetry. There is something of the poet in his very remarks on the inadequacy of plain language, for these, he says, are graces which

> veritablement ne se peuuent representer à l'egal de leur verité, & que l'Eglise a plustost d'escrites en termes qui sentent l'hieroglyfic, & l'Embleme, qu'en paroles expresses & nuës, soit l'apellant vn iardin clos de tous costez, afin que les bestes sauuages du vice & du peché n'y peussent auoir leur entree pour gourmander les belles fleurs de ses vertus, soit vn Paradis terrestre, pource que veritablement elle a porté, l'arbre & le fruict de vie, dont quiconque mange dignement il a la vie Eternelle, soit vne fontaine cachetee de l'image propre de Dieu, soit vne Aurore qui se leue & qui tire apres elle sur la face du monde le Soleil de Iustice, soit vne rose des champs pour la bonne odeur de ses vertus, & pource que comme l'escargot se meurt entre les roses, ainsi l'autheur du peché meurt aupres d'elle, soit vn lys des vallées ... (p. 67)

This sense of decorum forms a strong contrast to the love of bizarre and surprising conceits typical of later preachers' use of emblems. It is the same sensibility which leads Bertaut in the same sermon to use a dense metaphor in a place where his successors (as we shall see) would delight in a rambling explanatory simile. The Old Testament women confess before Mary 'n'estre que de petites bourbeuses fontaines au prix de ceste calme & douce mer de vertus & de benedictions, Marie mere de nostre Sauueur' (p. 52). The antithesis ('fontaine'/'mer') and pun ('mer'/'mere') are introduced with a speed and a sharpness which do not recur until much later in the period, and then in a different stylistic context.

The other characteristic mode of sermons published very early in the century stands at the opposite end of the stylistic spectrum. 'Plain prose' as the flat and relatively unemotive language of exposition is found of course in sermons all through the period; what is remarkable in the work of preachers like Burlat[6] and Benoist is its unvarying use throughout the action. Just as Bertaut does not confine poetic elements to the *avant-propos*, so these preachers have no sense of stylistic differentiation and make only a few concessions to ornamentation. As in Bertaut, this springs in

---

6 *Deux sermons de la resurrection du Lazare*, 1603 (C. 64).

Prose patterns 77

part from a desire to maintain the cohesion of the argument by avoiding awkward transitions. These sermons are all of a piece; sometimes, it seems from this example from Benoist, of a single, massive, sprawling sentence:

> Pourquoy faisons ie vous prie vne vraye & Chrestienne penitence, detestant par vne parfaicte contrition, confessant & delaissant nos pechez, afin que ayant la grace de nostre Dieu, executant les causes & articles du present Iubilé (figuré au Leuitic. 25. c.) nous soyons tellement deschargez de tous nos pechez, que nous facions ceste feste de Pasques auec toute exultation & ioye, y estans tellement confirmez en grace, que nous ne retournions à nos pechez, à la maniere des hypocrites mondains, & charnels mocqueurs, lesquels prennent (en abusant) occasion du Iubilé de pecher plus librement, & de ne faire des bonnes oeuures, tant de penitence que de iustice, auec vne presomption de payer tousiours de la bourse d'autrui, lesquels il ne faut suiure: mais les euitant & fuyant comme souilleures & scandales en l'Eglise, lauons par humilité & charité (laissant les actions brutales, & suiuant les humaines & Chrestiennes) les pieds les vns des autres, nous aduertissant & corrigeant fraternellement, suiuant l'example de Iesus Christ, lequel nous esleue du lauement corporel, au spirituel.[7]

A single example suffices for us to see the essential elements of this style, with its looseness of syntax, repetition, use of word-pairs and elaborately irrelevant parentheses.[8] This sort of peroration (for it is one) is not met with again in this period.

2. Thesaurus sermons

Side by side with the kind of preaching which sees the sermon in much the same terms as the long poem or the expository tract, and gradually displacing it, there exists a type of pulpit oratory in which the preacher's main function is the presentation and connexion of a wide range of anecdotes, illustrations and analogies. The bulk of sermons printed in the first half of our period fall into this group. Behind what appears to the modern reader as a totally foreign method of prose composition, there lies of course a long and respectable tradition. The use of parables and analogies to illustrate a point is one of the major features of the Gospels, and the importance of the *exemplum* in the medieval sermon is well

---

7 *Sermon de la disposition requise pour le lavement des pieds*, 1601 (C. 23), pp. 23–4.
8 There is a discussion of this sort of style in the mid-sixteenth century in F. M. Higman, *The Style of John Calvin in his French Polemical Treatises*, Oxford, 1967, esp. chap. 3.

known.[9] But in our period the traditional *exemplum* – or a modified version of it – ceases to play a merely illustrative role and becomes the central element in the presentation of a doctrine or the exposition of a text. To give the flavour of this sort of prose is not easy without very extensive quotation; perhaps the nearest examples familiar to most readers are the early *Essais* of Montaigne. The parallel is not without significance, for just as Montaigne's essays developed from a commentary on a selection of favourite anecdotes and passages from the classical writers, so the chief sources of this type of preaching are the thesauri, encyclopedias and collections of *exempla* which, as we saw in Chapter 3, were constantly recommended by the manuals. Very often a sermon is built up by the indiscriminate heaping together of undigested material culled from these reference works and the preacher's own commonplace-book;[10] and it is appropriate to define the group as 'thesaurus sermons'.

A further factor in the encouragement of this sort of composition was the need to appear learned; breadth of reference was taken as evidence for breadth of culture on the part of the preacher. It satisfied a considerable demand: richness of learned quotation is deliberately advertised in several prefaces,[11] and the title-pages describe authors as 'docte & celebre' (Seguiran) or 'l'vne des grandes memoires de nostre temps'.[12] A quatrain in praise of

---

9 See, for example, J. T. Welter, *L'Exemplum dans la littérature religieuse et didactique du moyen âge*, Paris and Toulouse, 1927. Welter defines an *exemplum* as 'un récit ou une historiette, une fable ou une parabole, une moralité ou une description pouvant servir de preuve à l'appui d'un exposé doctrinal, religieux ou moral' (p. 1).
10 This emerges very clearly when a preacher gives his sources; see, for example, sermon 6 of Lor's *Sermons salutaires sur tous les jours de l'Advent*, 1623 (C. 208), where all of Lor's chief authorities turn out to be those recommended in manuals of sermon composition.
11 E.g. the printer's note to Seguiran, *Sermons doctes et admirables sur les Evangilles des Dimanches & Festes de l'annéé*, 1612 (C. 268): 'Tu trouueras chez luy & aux riches coffres de ceste espargne dequoy satisfaire aux plus sçauans, contenter les deuotieux, soulager les ignorans, & dequoy battre en ruyne les heresies' (sig. ã2ᵛ).
12 Thus the title-page of Humblot's *Sacrifice d'Isaac*, 1617 edn (C. 181), *Conceptions admirables sur toutes les festes de l'année*, 1619 edn (C. 183), and *Conceptions admirables sur les lamentations de Ieremie*, 1618 (C. 186).

Pierre de Besse illustrates the sort of tastes for which these sermons were composed:

> Ainsi que dans Paris preschant tu rauissois
> Aux deuots auditeurs le coeur par les oreilles:
> Ainsi tu rauiras aux plus doctes François
> Par la veuë les coeurs en lisant tes merueilles.[13]

The point seems to be that learned surprises ('merueilles') were what the reader of these sermons wanted to find. Hence no doubt the fact that Besse's sermon series all go under the title of *Conceptions theologiques*. The word *conception* in this period can, as we shall see, be placed almost anywhere on a semantic scale running from 'theological idea' to 'metaphysical conceit'.

The function of these autonomous anecdotes varies considerably in the work of different preachers. The typically medieval *exemplum*, or story drawn from daily life to illustrate a moral point, is found in only a few cases. It is most common in a preacher like Antonin de Paris who deliberately eschews elaborate similes and classical maxims in favour of more homespun sources.[14] Boucher uses a contemporary story of a Spanish lady afflicted with leprosy who informs her bishop of the joy she has in seeing her carnal prison rotting away,[15] Lor draws an object lesson from contemporary ophthalmic practice,[16] and Valladier's *Saincte Philosophie de l'ame* is packed with current anecdotes, often of the most scurrilous kind.[17] Valladier is the only one of our preachers to make a point of emphasizing his personal knowledge of the characters in his *exempla*; after discussing the role of the devil in the night-flying activities of Philiberte Maurin, who came from his native town, he insists that 'ie l'ay veuë depuis sa guerison fort particulierement, ay conferé auec tous ceux qui l'auoient traittee, assistee, exorcisee, me suis enquis des singularitez de ce grand

---

13 *Premieres conceptions theologiques sur le Caresme*, 1604 (C. 27), vol. 1, sig. *4ᵛ.
14 *Tresor admirable tiré de l'Escripture saincte*, 1613 (C. 17): p. 439, ploughing; p. 507, archery; p. 526, shipbuilding; p. 823, sewing.
15 *Les Magnificences divines*, 1620 (C. 53), pp. 93–4.
16 Quoted in Chapter 6 below, p. 140.
17 1614 (C. 304): pp. 197–241, werewolves; pp. 463–70, gossip about the death of Henri IV; pp. 668–70, gang rape.

desastre: ay prins d'elle-mesme tout ce narré qu'elle m'a donné, escrit & signé de sa propre main'.[18] This testimony of personal experience in Valladier's work is at odds with the general reliance elsewhere on irrefutable authorities and widely known stories.

It is the analogy (*parallèle* or *comparaison*) which holds pride of place in the thesaurus sermons. The great majority of analogies are drawn from nature, and the theories underlying their use will be discussed in Chapter 7. But the idea of the analogy as nothing less than the central substance of preaching has important implications for composition and style. In one of the most perceptive comments made by any critic about the pulpit oratory of this period, Antoine Albert remarked of the various disparate *sentences*, *remarques* and *citations* that the application of them 'fait toute la preuve et tout l'ornement du discours'.[19] Now, the whole classical technique of composition depends on posing an argument logically, giving examples, and then developing it affectively; the style is naturally modelled on the function language is fulfilling in the given section of the discourse. But when the subject matter (and not the mode of presentation) is itself both proof and ornament, there is no question of a movement in three stages − argument, illustration, exhortation − and therefore no question of stylistic variation.[20] Nor, of course, is there any necessary link between a given analogy/demonstration and those that follow it: the reader is just bombarded with one self-contained proof after another, and it is by the accumulation of these, not by the development of a theme, that the writer hopes to convince him. This accounts to some extent for the monotony created for the modern reader by a list of *belles comparaisons*, for these preachers were concerned to squeeze as much as possible out of the parallels they had lighted upon. In addition, many of the writers who use this method were still bound to the stylistic tradition which I have labelled 'plain prose', and the combination produces considerable flatness and repetition. Here is Boucher on humility:

18   *Ibid.*, p. 625.
19   *Dictionnaire portatif des prédicateurs françois*, Lyons, 1757, p. xiii. The whole passage is quoted by Truchet, *La Prédication de Bossuet*, vol. 1, p. 19.
20   Joan Webber makes a somewhat similar distinction between Ciceronian and Senecan style in Donne's prose, and links the latter with the analogy, in her *Contrary Music. The Prose Style of John Donne*, esp. pp. 21-2.

Prose patterns

> Or ceste vertu est si belle & si agreable à Dieu, aux Anges & aux hommes, que la gloire & l'arrogance mesme, se veut couurir & orner de son lustre: car la gloire ressemble à vne Courtisanne & femme mondaine laide & deffigurée, laquelle s'efforce de tout son pouuoir à couurir la laideur & deformité de son teinct basané & plombé par l'artifice d'vn fard mensonger & trompeur: ainsi l'arrogance qui est laide & affreuse sur tous les pechés, met peine tant qu'elle peut de cacher sa deformité par vne humilité apparente, en quoy paroist la grandeur & excellence de ceste vertu, puis que la gloire sa capitalle ennemie est contraincte d'emprunter sa faueur & secours pour cacher sa laideur affreuse: de sorte que si on me demandoit que c'est qu'vne arrogance desguisée; ie respondrois que ce n'est autre chose qu'vne humilité apparente: tout ainsi que l'humilité feinte de plusieurs qui veulent paroistre vertueux afin d'estre estimez, n'est autre chose que le fard de leur orgueil caché: car l'humilité feincte faict à l'endroit d'vne personne glorieuse ce que faict le fard sur le visage d'vne femme laide & difforme, dautant qu'en tous deux la beauté paroist à l'exterieur seulement, mais la difformité demeure tousiours au dedans.[21]

This is an absolutely typical passage not only because of the persistent squeezing of the parallel but because it avoids all affective rhetorical techniques. It is dreadful writing. In the hands of an infinitely more talented preacher with a greater sensitivity to traditional rhetoric, some of these inherent drawbacks are overcome. François de Sales, discussing the Assumption, links together a number of disparate *conceptions* which constitute the substance of his sermon; he moves from texts of Paul through a discussion about arrows to Aristotle on wild goats, then back to a Scriptural text, and then on to the phoenix. But within a single point he manages considerably more than a flat analogy:

> Le phoenix meurt par le feu, et ceste sainte Dame mourut d'amour. Le phoenix assemble des busches de bois aromatiques, et les posant sur la cime d'un mont, fait sur ce buscher un si grand mouvement de ses aisles, que le feu s'en allume aux rayons du soleil (Plin. *Hist. Nat.* 1. X. c. II). Ceste Vierge assemblant en son coeur la croix, la couronne, la lance de nostre Seigneur, les posa au plus haut de ses pensees, et faisant sur ce buscher un grand mouvement de continuelle meditation, le feu en sortit aux rayons des lumieres de son Filz. Le phoenix meurt en ce feu la; la Vierge mourut en celuy ci, et ne faut pas douter qu'elle n'eust en son coeur gravees les armes de la Passion. Ah, si tant de vierges, comme sainte Catherine de Sienne, sainte Claire de Montefalco, ont bien eu ceste grace, pourquoy non Nostre Dame, laquelle ayma son Filz et sa mort et sa croix incomparablement plus que ne firent onques tous les Saintz et les Saintes? Aussi n'estoit elle plus qu'amour, et en nostre langage, l'anagramme de Marie n'est autre chose que aimer: aimer c'est Marie, Marie

---

21   *Les Magnificences divines*, 1620 (C. 53), pp. 320–1.

c'est aimer. Alles, alles heureux, o beau phoenix, ardent et mourant d'amour, dormes en paix sur le lict de la charité![22]

Here the basic parallel between Mary and the phoenix is elaborated with interrogation, exclamation (a favourite Salesian figure), varied periods, and the final anagram, which is clearly intended to persuade by delighting with ingenuity.

The developed analogy is also a technique for expounding a Scriptural metaphor at some length. This is a favourite with Protestant preachers: Du Moulin devotes a whole sermon to the exposition of the metaphor in Luke xxiv, 32 – 'Did not our hearts burn within us . . .?'[23] It is not exclusive to them, however: the Jesuit Seguiran works from the other end, gathering together various texts and ideas about Christ and then introducing at the climax the now fully comprehensible metaphor of the Sun of Righteousness.[24]

So far we have been looking at analogies of a type which a classical critic, although probably offended by their form, might nevertheless call appropriate parallels. There is between the objects compared a certain evident or traditional connexion which makes the comparison plausible as well as expected. But this sort of analogy is hardly a *docte merveille*; if the element of surprise is going to be effective, much more unusual associations have to be sought. This is done by jettisoning the normal connotations of one part of the comparison (the 'vehicle' in I. A. Richards's well-known definition of metaphor) and retaining only certain relevant factors which are perceived by the intellect, or 'wit'. There is some evidence that a sensibility conducive to this was widespread even among highly 'unwitty' preachers. Boucher, for instance, can use St Peter asleep in prison to represent the unrepentant sinner undisturbed in his *cachot* of spiritual darkness, despite the disparity between the sanctity and sinfulness of the two halves of the comparison.[25] But more often this cultivation of implausible comparisons is quite intentional, and constitutes the essential element

22 C. 168, vol. 7, p. 451.
23 *Cinquième decade de sermons*, 1642 (C. 142), sermon 6.
24 *Sermons doctes et admirables sur les Evangilles des Dimanches & Festes de l'annéé*, 1612 (C. 268), p. 245.
25 *Les Magnificences divines*, 1620 (C. 53), p. 344. Boucher does not go on to develop the only plausible connexion by introducing the story of St Peter's deliverance.

Prose patterns   83

in what is often called the seventeenth-century conceit. J. A. Mazzeo has defined the conceit as 'the harmonic correlation between two or three knowable extremes, the act whereby the understanding discerns the correspondences between things' and, in addition, as 'the *elaboration* of "witty" correspondences'.[26] This is a definition which perfectly fits many of our analogies. It is this harshly intellectual perception of relationships which aroused admiration among the readers and critics of thesaurus sermons.

The conceit can often emerge as an extension of a traditional analogy. Pierre de Besse conventionally compares the Church to a ship – 'navis instituris de longe portans panem' – and continues:

> Le Pere eternel est ce riche marchand, Iesus Christ ce sacré pain, l'Eglise le nauire qui le porte, pain qui est porté de loin, parce qu'il vient du ciel, *à summo coelo egressio eius*: ô le voilà bien venu de loin, pain attendu si longtemps, pain qui a rauitaillé tout le monde. Vne docte conception sur ce subiect, le pain qu'on porte sur les nauires doit estre biscuit, & Iesus Christ est vn biscuit, *Bis coctus, bis genitus*: Cuit & engendré eternellement dans le sein eternel du pere: Cuit & engendré vne autrefois au sacré ventre de la Vierge.[27]

It is precisely the fact that our intellects do not normally relate Christ to biscuits which makes of Besse's ingenuity a 'docte conception'. Playing with theological ideas in this way is a very fruitful source of conceits. Seguiran explains at great length[28] why Our Lady is a 'ciel animé' – a recurrent conceit found not only in the Jesuits, but in Molinier and (outside preaching) even in the work of the solemn Bérulle.[29] We are here very close to the 'violons ailés' and 'miracles volans' of early-seventeenth-century poetry.[30] What characterizes the use of the conceit in these

26 *Renaissance and Seventeenth-century Studies*, New York and London, 1964, pp. 32, 33. His italics.
27 *Premieres conceptions theologiques sur le Caresme*, 1604 (C. 27), vol. 1, fol. 50.
28 *Sermons doctes et admirables sur les Evangilles des Dimanches & Festes de l'anneé*, 1612 (C. 268), p. 479.
29 *Vie de Jésus*, chap. 19: The Virgin 'est un ciel en la terre et un ciel animé, un ciel que Dieu a fait pour porter un soleil plus luisant que celui qui nous éclaire'. Quoted in Flachaire, *La Dévotion à la Vierge dans la littérature catholique au commencement du XVIIe siècle*, ed. A. Rebelliau, Paris, 1916, p. 51.
30 See Jean Rousset, *La Littérature de l'âge baroque en France*, Paris, 1954, pp. 184–9.

thesaurus sermons is its wholly dominant position in the argument and the space devoted to the explanation of it, whereas later preachers use it as one element in the orchestration of their ideas in continuous prose.

It is a short step from the conceit to the emblem, the visual depiction of a relationship or analogy which, in emblem books, is usually explained in the accompanying verse. Well-known emblems are accordingly used as the starting point for lengthy analogies. These are often introduced in rather a gauche way, exemplifying the nonchalant approach to transitions typical of thesaurus preachers. Suffren, discussing the reasons why Christ died on a cross, merely adds that there is another reason 'qui est que le Seigneur estant mort sur ceste croix, s'est comporté ny plus ny moins que le Pellican'.[31] This is then expounded at very great length – rather like François de Sales's comparison between the Virgin and the phoenix – in a passage where one can see how the traditional medieval symbol is being used, developed and visualized in the attempt to squeeze more meaning out of a conventional analogy. References to emblems seem in fact in this period particularly common among Jesuits: Seguiran on more than one occasion refers to Alciati's *Emblemata*,[32] and clearly expects some familiarity with that book when, for example, he uses the candle emblem as an analogy to good works:

Les bonnes oeuures faites en particulier & à l'escart de la veuë des hommes sont meritoires de la vie eternelle, & causent la mort au peché: mais si vne fois il arriue qu'vn homme face des actions vertueuses publiquement ... au lieu que ces oeuures, quoy que bonnes d'elles-mesmes, luy deuroient donner la vie, [elles] luy causent la mort: mais mort eternelle s'il meurt en telle maniere de faire. A cela se peut rapporter cest ancien embleme de deux flambeaux, l'vn tourné vers le Ciel, l'autre vers la terre auec ceste inscription, *quod me alit, me extinguit*, c'est icy où se retrouue ceste merueille, il est vray que les bonnes oeuures sont comme des flambeaux pour ardre & brusler: mais il faut que ce soit vers le Ciel seulement. Elles ne doiuent estre faictes que pour le respect de Dieu: car si vous tournez ces flambeaux vers la terre, si vous faictes des oeuures seulement pour estre veus des hommes, *quod vos alit, vos extinguit*, icelles qui deuroient cooper[er] à vostre iustification, cooperent à vostre damnation eternelle.[33]

31 *Le Victorieux et triomphant combat de Gedeon*, 1616 (C. 290), p. 78.
32 *Sermons doctes et admirables sur les Evangilles des Dimanches & Festes de l'annéé*, 1612 (C. 268), pp. 42, 122.
33 *Ibid.*, p. 37.

In the work of preachers of this kind, therefore, we can see how the medieval type of *exemplum* and the classical anecdote, sometimes transformed by an extension of the method of analogy into the conceit, the emblem, or the explicated metaphor, gained a dominant place in sermon composition. This had two effects. Firstly, it led to considerable monotony and flabbiness of language: each relationship is painstakingly (and often repetitively) pointed out and analysed. Secondly, it tended to transform the books of sermons back into the thesauri from which they had themselves drawn their material. It was his reaction to this situation that led Jean-Pierre Camus to develop the most highly individual technique of sermon composition in our period.

3. Jean-Pierre Camus and catenary prose[34]

As a welcome change from the shocked comments of most critics on Camus's sermon style, a modern scholar has analysed in some detail the rhetorical figures found in the three homilies Camus preached before the States-General in 1614.[35] M. Descrains gives an excellent account of Camus's prose; his long examples bring out clearly the 'enchaînement des images' (p. 74), the nonchalant linking together of strings of analogies, allusions, anecdotes, Scriptural figures and quotations which combine, he says, to form a sort of 'prose poétique' (p. 73). To describe this profusion of disparate elements and entire lack of continuous argument I shall use the term 'catenary prose'.[36] What has not, however, been sufficiently pointed out is that this unusual style is not a mere accidental idiosyncrasy, but the result of a carefully thought out theory of the printed sermon.

This theory is expounded in the unusually long prefaces to the

---

34   Several of the points made in this section are reproduced from my article, 'Les Sermons de Jean-Pierre Camus et l'esthétique borroméenne', in *Critique et création littéraires en France au XVIIe siècle*, ed. M. Fumaroli, Paris, 1977, pp. 93–8.

35   Jean Descrains, 'La Rhétorique dans les homélies de Jean-Pierre Camus aux Etats Généraux de 1614', *XVIIe Siècle*, LXXX–LXXXI (1968), pp. 61–78.

36   See the primary meaning of 'catena' in *O.E.D*. The same image seems to underlie Descrains's use of words like 'enchaînement' (in the remark quoted above) and 'concaténation' (p. 72).

Premieres homelies quadragesimales of 1615 and the *Premieres homelies dominicales* of two years later.[37] In addition, the preface to the *Premieres homelies festives* of 1617 (C. 74) refers the reader to the latter discussion. Written in the breathless, inchoate style they serve to defend, these critical prefaces demand careful elucidation. The primary idea is a frank acceptance of the sermon/ thesaurus ambiguity. This ambiguity is, it is true, sometimes made explicit by other preachers: Voyer d'Argenson refers to his published sermons as 'discours predicables, & matieres de predication fort dilatées',[38] and Antonin de Paris advises his reader that 'si tu es Predicateur, & que tu veuilles seruir des Sermons qui y sont, tu les trouueras si bien disposés, que si tu ne veux traittér que d'vn poinct, il est assés ample en chacun'.[39] But this consideration had no effect on their method of composition, and the intending preacher would find it difficult to sift through their elaborate prose in search of central and adaptable points. Camus, on the other hand, bears in mind right from the beginning 'celuy qui se voudra seruir de ce trauail' (*Dominicales*, sig. ã4ᵛ). He has deliberately shaped his work so that it can serve not only as a model for direct imitation, but as a conceptual framework for the sermons of others:

il te preste, Lecteur, vn large champ à la transformation, de tout mien il t'est tres-aisé de la rendre tout tien. Quand tu n'y apporterois autre industrie que l'extension, & apportes des paroles, marchandise si vulgaire, & si vile, que l'ose presque dire, qui plus en a, n'en vouloir à l'auanture que moins. Il est en toy auec ce seul outil, de metamorphoser tous ces discours que ie te presente en masse, & les rendre absolument tiens, y adioustant autant de façon que ie leur en ay osté, pour espargner mon loisir & ta patience.
(*Dominicales*, sig. ẽlʳ)

These remarks already contain some clues as to how this concept of *disponibilité* has been translated into the reality of the text: the borrower has only to add 'l'extension' or 'façon'. The idea is clarified elsewhere by means of a series of metaphors:

---

37 The *Premieres homelies quadragesimales* are C. 71; quotations from the *Premieres homelies dominicales* are taken from the 1619 edition (C. 73). For brevity I shall simply give a short title and page or signature reference after quotations.
38 *L'Enneade sacrée*, 1622; quoted from C. 313, p. 41.
39 *Tresor admirable tiré de l'Escripture saincte*, 1613 (C. 17), sig. ẽ3ʳ.

Ie suggere aux apprentifs, la matiere & l'Art tout à nud; ce sont diamans de roche, que ie baille aux plus aduancez à tailler & polir. Ie trace le crayon que d'autres y mettent les couleurs, le fonds de l'image, d'autres fournissent les enlumineures; le corps du tableau, d'autres y adioustent les crotesques & corniches des entrées, sorties, Apostrophes, Prosopopées, saillies, figures oratoires, cadences, fleurs, digressions, extensions, descriptions, persuasions, & des grands helas & exclamations, qui souuent ont plus de force sur l'auditoire que les raisons. (*Quadragesimales*, sig. ẽ3ʳ)

Interpreted in terms of traditional rhetoric, this means that he has simply left out the stage of *elocutio*; and indeed he uses these terms himself to describe his sermons as 'des matieres inuentées & disposées, mais indigestes' (*Dominicales*, sig. ã4ᵛ). There is, therefore, more here than a convenient method of compiling a thesaurus; after all, these works are published as sermons. It is clear that his sacrifice of *elocutio* is a very willing one, and it enables him to develop a critique of precisely that verbosity which characterizes thesaurus preaching. He echoes the contemporary criticisms which have led him to this method of composition:

Ceux-cy se plaindront que quelques prescheurs ont trop de parolles & peu de suc, des autres qu'ils sont trop entassez, de ceux la, qu'ils sont trop grossiers aux discours, appelleront ceux cy confus, les autres trop contemplatifs & subtils, diront que ceux la font des commentaires non des harangues, que ces autres sont des beaux diseurs qui quittent les choses pour les parolles, que ceux la ne font que repeter & sont ennuyeux à lire . . .
(*Quadragesimales*, sig. ã8ʳ)

This lamentable state of affairs will be corrected, he suggests, in his own work: 'aussi n'y [a] il icy aucune dragme de Rhetorisme' (*ibid.*, sig. ã8ᵛ). The word is significant; it suggests his agreement with what at first sight seem the anti-rhetorical comments of the theorists, comments which we have seen to be confined to *elocutio* and its misbegotten child verbosity. In its place he proposes an aesthetic of brevity:

C'est vn consommé, vn precis, vn suc, vne quinte essence alambicquée, qui en peu de mots [a] beaucoup de sens, j'y a tant visé à la briefueté que j'y redoute l'obscurite. (*Quadragesimales*, sig. ẽlʳ)

C'est icy du biscuit sec, mais succulent, serré, mais substancieux, peu de chair de discours, mais prou de nerfs, de cartileges, & de mouëlles de Concepts.
(*Dominicales*, sig. ã4ᵛ)

These images recall those used by the Italian theorists of preaching. At almost exactly the same time Mazarini was writing that

'Tout cét appareil des poincts particuliers & requis pour faire vn Sermon est au Predicateur ce que sont les os d'vn corps à la vertu formatiue ... Au peintre ses couleurs broyées, & son crayon ...', and Botero had already compared the bold realistic style of his ideal preacher to the painter of nudes.[40] If one recalls, too, the reservations on *elocutio* expressed by Borromeo, it becomes clear that Camus was attempting to put into practice the realistic, energetic aesthetic of surprise and shock emanating from Italian reformist centres and carried, together with other Counter-Reformation ideas, into devout humanist circles in Savoy. There is further evidence of this strong Italian influence in the *Homelies panegyriques de sainct Charles Borromée*.[41]

The moment was remarkably propitious; it would have been difficult to find a style more adaptable to this kind of energetic pruning of verbosity and consequent heaping-up of conceits than that of the thesaurus sermons. The pruning process may be seen in Camus's own work; in his earliest printed sermon, dated 1608, he elaborates an analogy between Our Lady and the Ark of the Covenant:

Le Cofin du propitiatoire de l'arche d'alliance deuoit estre d'or pur, dans lequel on reserroit les tables de la loy, la manne celeste, & la verge d'Aaron: le bastiment du sainct des saincts deuoit estre du boys de Sethin, lequel estoit incorruptible, leger, noüeux, espineux, & outre cela ne se pouuoit brusler. Et nostre Emperiere n'a elle pas esté incorruptible quant à sa chair, incombustible à tous les feux des concupiscences, legere par ces celestes contemplations entierement denuées, & espurées de terrestreité: espineuse outre cela par l'austerité de sa vie? En fin elle a esté ce coffret d'or tres-pur, *de auro purissimo*. Ce sont ses sacrées entrailles, dans lesquelles a esté formée la vraye manne de l'humanité du fils de Dieu, representée aussi par la verge ...[42]

In the catenary *Homelies festives* published eight years later this becomes:

Voulez-vous des figures de ceste pompe? ... Voicy l'Arche d'Alliance, qui a porté en soy la manne de l'humanité, & la verge de la diuinité de IESVS, qui est rapportee des terres des Philistins en la terre promise.[43]

40   Both quoted above, pp. 60 and 51.
41   1623 (C. 86). See especially homily 4 where, incidentally, Panigarola is called 'le Chrysostome de l'Italie' (p. 117).
42   *Panegyrique de la Mere de Dieu* (C. 65), fols. 7^v–8^r.
43   Quoted from C. 75, p. 471.

Prose patterns 89

The compressed, allusive nature of catenary prose lends itself particularly well to the use of emblems. A Maundy Thursday sermon opens with a direct reference to one:

La Mort & l'Amour, tous deux aueugles dict l'Embleme, inopinément changerent vn iour de trousse, & voyla que voulans faire leurs ordinaires exercices
    Tunc pereunt iuuenes, depereuntque senes.[44]

The emblem is Alciati no. 154 in the 1618 Paris edition; the allusions compressed into the remark are brought out by Mignault's commentary, which traces the story in Guicciardini, Jean Lemaire de Belges and Joachim du Bellay – an illustration of the way the sensibility of devout humanism links spiritual and secular traditions. Occasionally one is bombarded by an emblematic, or at least an extremely concrete image, based on an analogy and seen from several different angles:

Comme en vn miroir nous voyons les taches de nos visages, quoy que le miroir soit de soy net & poly, ainsi N. S. est *vn miroir sans tache*: mais ce sang, ces crachats, ces mains troüees, ces pieds percez, ce chef herissé d'espines, ce sont les figures hydeuses de nos crimes, sur le cristal de son innocente personne.

On dit qu'en certaine ville d'Afrique les femmes immondes impriment par leur veuë certaines taches sur les miroirs plus terses, ô que nos impuretez soüillent d'horribles playes le beau corps de nostre Espoux.

Du moins regrettons d'estre cause par nos coulpes de sinistres effets: & comme la belle Helene: *Fleuit vbi in speculo rugas conspexit aniles*, ainsi lamentons sur la laideur exterieure nostre interieure deformité: *& emendemus in melius quae ignoranter peccauimus.*[45]

This is often the nearest catenary prose approaches to a consecutive passage; elsewhere, as Camus says, there is 'nul fil d'agencement oratoire, pas vne digression ny dilatation, mots expressifs & energicques le plus que i'ay peu' (*Quadragesimales*, sig. êl^r). Does not this correspond precisely with Croll's classic summing-up of 'baroque prose': 'periods advance wholly in the direction of a more imaginative realization: a metaphor revolves, as it were, displaying its different facets; a series of metaphors flash their lights; or a chain of "points" or paradoxes reveals the energy of a single apprehension in the writer's mind'?[46] In Camus's work, then, a

---

44 *Quadragesimales*, p. 244.
45 *Homelies sur la Passion*, 1617, quoted from C. 77, pp. 319–20.
46 *Style, Rhetoric and Rhythm*, pp. 218–19.

serious aesthetic of energy, a missionary attitude to the use of his sermons by others, and the development of the proof/ornament unit as the substance of *inventio* combine to push such a stylistic tendency to its furthest imaginable extremes.

At this point some modification may be made to this general picture. The catenary style is not exclusively limited to Camus, nor is he enslaved to its use. Some of the earlier preachers were also moving in the direction of greater punch and brevity in the listing of analogies. Pierre de Besse has a passage on 'the world' where the sentences are still fully formed, but the references flash past much more quickly than elsewhere in Besse's work.[47] Here are the beginnings of a process to which Camus was to bring the support of a coherent theory. Again, not all of Camus's sermons are written in catenary prose; as well as the early thesaurus style of the *Panegyrique de la Mere de Dieu*, we find poetic exordia remarkably similar in tone to those of Bertaut or Du Bec.[48] Is the catenary style, then, restricted to collections intended exclusively for use as source-books for other preachers, and called 'homélies'? The catenary States-General sermons, also called homelies, contradict that hypothesis; so too does the fact that all his sermons are published under that title, whatever their length

47 *Premieres conceptions theologiques sur le Caresme*, 1604 (C. 27), vol. 2, fol. 73: 'Le Basilic vn serpent fort venimeux, en veut seulement à l'homme, lequel il empeste de sa seule veuë, & au reste des animaux ne porte point de domage, son venin n'est que pour l'homme. Le monde plus dangereux mille fois, que n'est point ce Crocodile, ne nuyt point aux bestes, mail il est si contagieux pour l'homme qu'il tue par sa frequentation, & l'infecte de sa seule veuë. Le tyran Pharaon (*Exod.*) rompoit tout le corps du iour, les Hebrieux de trauaux & de fatigues, & sur le soir à la retraicte leur faisoit donner les estreuieres. Le monde regne auec ceste tyrannie, & rompant l'homme de trauaux tout le iour de sa vie, sur le soir de la mort qui est sa derniere retraicte (*Genes.* 39.), il le precipite bien souuent aux enfers. Vne autre Allegorie, Ioseph ne fut pas si tost abordé à la maison de cet AEgyptien Putifar que voyla sa Dame qui le sollicite au peché, & son Maistre qui le iette dans les prisons. Helas nous n'auons pas si tost receu l'estre que voyla la nature qui nous porte au vice, & le monde cet AEgyptien Putifar qui nous iette dans les cachots de peché, & de la mort, d'où nous ne sortons iamais que pour aller à l[a] damnation. ô malheureux monde.' And so on for several pages.

48 E.g. the opening passages of the *Premieres homelies eucharistiques*, 1618 (C. 78), or the *Homelies panegyriques de S. Ignace de Loyola*, 1623 (C. 85).

Prose patterns 91

and style.⁴⁹ Nor were the *Dominicales, Quadragesimales*, and so on, written exclusively for the use of others; Camus did compile such collections, and he called them 'prônes'.⁵⁰ The key seems to lie less in the function of the given sermon than in the nature of its subject matter. Clearly, an early-seventeenth-century panegyric on Borromeo or Ignatius Loyola would incorporate a good deal of material that was new to the reader or listener, whereas the themes of Lenten or festival (or even routine political) sermons would be familiar to everyone. Catenary prose, as we have seen, works by sparking off the memory of a fully developed analogy, and it can therefore be applied, in the words from Jane Austen which open this study, only to 'subjects limited, and long worn thread-bare in all common hands'.

4. The rhetorical reaction: Etienne Molinier and conceptist prose

So eccentric a method of prose composition was bound to call forth criticism. The most violent and sustained attack is to be found in a preface by the only preacher in this period to rival Camus in the number and variety of his sermons, Etienne Molinier.⁵¹ Molinier's case rests on his opposition to the proof/ornament *conception*. For him, something has to be added if preaching is to fulfil its aim, which he sees as 'porter les ames à la fuite du peché, & à l'amour de Dieu' (sig. ẽ2ʳ); there has to be that affective development which he finds pre-eminently in St Paul (sig. ẽ5ʳ). This fullness of development is incompatible with any practical possibility of making the sermon series into a commonplace-book, and he rejects this central idea of Camus and his forerunners:

Or ie produits au iour ces Sermons auec les mesmes auant-propos, entrées, amplifications, exaggerations, exclamations, perorations qu'ils furent prononcez: car ie ne suis pas de l'aduis de quelques vns qui n'ont voulu donner en la publication de leurs Sermons que la diuision, l'ordre, & le gros de la matiere, qui neantmoins sans la forme n'a pas la moitié de son estre, tant s'en faut de sa beauté: & apres tout, il n'y a pas manque de repertoires, Calepins, thresors, lieux communs, où les esprits steriles en inuentions, ou foibles en sçauoir,

---

49 Descrains also comes to the conclusion that the word 'homélie' has no particular significance for Camus ('La Rhétorique', p. 61).
50 See Appendix 2 to Part II, below.
51 The preface to *Le Mystere de la Croix, et de la Redemption du monde*, 1628 (C. 241). References are to the 1635 edn (C. 242).

peuuent supleer à leur indigence, sans qu'il semble estre besoin de produire tous les iours de nouueaux inuentaires des Tables des Liures, ou transcrire en autre papier le Bercorius, ou le Polyanthea, qui peuuent rendre autant de seruice en leur original qu'en leur copie. (sig. ē1^v-ē2^r)

There is no doubt whom he is attacking; the opening words are almost Camus's own. Even the title-pages of the thesaurus preachers are ridiculed:

comme si ces coquilles s'adressoient à des enfans qui prinssent le grauois pour perles, les Imprimeurs nous les debitent sous le titre de conceptions, rares, admirables, & diuines, craignans peut-estre que ce soit trop peu pour des hommes de n'escrire qu'humainement. (sig. ē3^r)

He even takes one of Camus's key analogies – painting – and turns it against him: this art has so much 'rudesse' that 'on n'eust peu recognoistre les lineamens & les traicts de la chose qu'ils auoient voulu pourtraire, s'ils n'eussent adiousté son nom dans l'inscription' (sig. ē3^r). It is precisely the search for bizarre new forms, the indiscriminate heaping of them together, and the lack of a continuous thread that he objects to. The following passage is probably as good a description of catenary prose as one could find:

Car qu'est-ce, ie vous prie, qu'on y voit pour l'ordinaire, que conception, comme ils parlent, apres conception, pensée apres pensée, adaptation apres adaptation, curiosité apres curiosité, sans liaison ie ne diray pas des periodes, mais mesmes des matieres, sans nerfs de raisonnemens, sans vigueur de sentences, sans dessein d'instruction & de persuasion; fables, humanitez, histoires profanes, ou bien passages de l'Escriture ambigus, obscurs, tirez à contrepoil, interpretations monstrueuses, & qui choquent le sens commun par des subtilitez & dez arguties pareilles à ces noix dorées qui n'enserrent que du vent, specieuses à l'oeil qui n'en void que l'escorce, creuses & vuides à la main qui en espluche le noyau? (sig. ē3^v)

It is important to note that Molinier's central objection – that this sort of prose is 'sans dessein d'instruction & de persuasion' – comes not from some new theoretical development, but from fidelity to the ancient doctrines of rhetoric. It is Camus who is the innovator, not Molinier. This point is extended when he defends traditional *elocutio* against the sweeping condemnations of the Italian school: they merely show their ignorance when they scorn ancient techniques as 'figures, & fleurs de Rhetorique'

ne sçachant pas discerner, ou ne voulant pas aduoüer la difference qui se troue entre les viues raisons, & les ornemens affetez; entre les couleurs naturelles, & le fard emprunté; entre le bon teinct d'vn visage animé de ses propres graces, & le vermillon qui accuse ses defauts en les plastrant: bref, entre les colonnes qui soustiennent & affermissent l'edifice d'vn discours en le decorant, & les grotesques ou peintures qui ne font que cacher ses fentes, & couurir non guerir ses ruines.[52] (sig. ã7ʳ)

Antoine Albert's final criticism of the thesaurus prose style he summed up so well was that 'il y a très-peu de morale solide, moins encore de raisonnemens', and he complained elsewhere of the lack of 'la morale et le pathétique'.[53] This criticism naturally springs from a sensibility for which affective development of a logically posed argument is essential to persuasion. Since this may be taken to be the essence of 'Ciceronianism', it is not surprising that Molinier found allies in his resistance to catenary prose on this account; the same attitude emerges (if anything more clearly) from Caussin's preface to *Le Buisson ardent*:[54]

I'ay attrempé la science de l'Escriture, & des saints Peres, par la moralité, & i'ay pris souuent vne façon affectueuse & mouuante . . . (ã5ᵛ)

Ie n'ay pas voulu faire vne chaisne continuelle de conceptions, de remarques & d'allegations, dautant que cela tient plus de l'annotation que du discours. I'ay fait regner le raisonnement, & l'ay orné conuenablement de passages, plustost pour embellir que pour estouffer la raison. (ã7ʳ)

However, we must not be misled by this deliberate return to older rhetorical theories. The coming together of the thesaurus tradition and a revived sense of rhetorical values results not in some identifiably 'classical' prose style, but in the thoroughly

---

52 It is interesting to speculate how much this conservative, rhetorical reaction owes to Molinier's early admiration for Du Vair, and to his sense of an author's style as something worth imitating. See the *Discours funebre sur la mort de Mgr du Vair*, [1621] (C. 240), esp. p. 43, where Du Vair is praised as 'le vray modelle de la naïfue eloquence' in a passage devoted to the classical theory of imitation. The dedication to that work makes it quite clear that it is a purely literary exercise on Molinier's part. There is a good deal of the *littérateur* in Molinier, e.g. his remark in the preface we are examining (sig. ã8ʳ) that the early works collected in the *Mystere* were written when 'ie voulus commencer de sonder et tenter le gué du costé de la prose'.
53 *Dictionnaire portatif des prédicateurs françois*, pp. xiii, 4.
54 1647 (C. 89). *Cf.* Caussin's theoretical *prises de position*, discussed above, p. 66–7.

European style known as 'conceptist'.[55] Preachers of the stamp of Molinier and Caussin remain profoundly marked by the style against which they are reacting; they retain the analogy, the maxim, the classical anecdote and the emblem, but they embed them in passages of consecutive writing. Abra de Raconis provides a useful illustration of this:

Il [sc. the experienced soldier] bondit d'aise au son de la trompette qui l'appelle au combat: il se mire dans les blessures comme le Paon dans son plumage, il les caresse, comme les tesmoings plus certains de sa valeur, les bresches de l'honneur, & les escarboucles de sa gloire ... En vn mot, il tient pour maxime, que comme la musique ne s'apprend qu'en frappant & battant la mesure, de mesme le courage ne s'acquiert que parmi les coups, & l'honneur ne se recueille que parmi les plus rudes & perilleuses escarmouches. Que comme les orgues ne joüent point si elles ne sont pressées, la valeur ne se descouure qu'en la presse des ennemis. Que tout ainsi que l'escarlatte doit estre battuë pour estre haute en couleur: ainsi le courage ne se releue qu'à la mesure qu'il est aux coups, & qu'il soustient sans s'esbranler la gresle & la tempeste des fleches ennemies.[56]

Since the *conception* no longer has to play the double role of both proof and ornament, the element of decorative wittiness can be exaggerated; word-play and ingenious analogies unite to form conceits of extreme brevity. Thus Caussin on Mme de Beauvillier:

Elle esclaroit iusqu'à l'ombre de la mort par les rayons de sa constance, & son ame dressoit autant de trophees, que ses yeux iettoient de regards, & que sa langue prononçoit de paroles.[57]

---

55   An immense amount of critical work has of course been done on the subject of conceptist or 'pointed' prose in most major European languages other than French. There are useful references, and a welcome attempt to view a French prose writer in this European context, in Jeanne Goldin, 'Jeux de l'esprit et de la parole', in *Critique et création littéraires en France au XVIIe siècle*, ed. M. Fumaroli. It is sometimes claimed that France produced no theorists of this style; clearly Molinier and Caussin are not of the standing of a Gracián or a Tesauro – in particular because they are so tied to traditional rhetoric in their theories – but they are not negligible.
56   *Oraison funebre sur le trespas de feu Mgr le Mareschal de Schomberg*, 1633 (C. 2), pp. 36–8.
57   *Les Devoirs funebres rendus à l'heureuse memoire de Mme ... de Beauvillier*, 1634 (C. 88), p. 34. Cf. *ibid.*, p. 1: 'ie forceray l'estat de mort, qui est vn silence, pour parler d'vne vie qui ne peut estre muette à la posterité'.

Prose patterns 95

This sort of fleeting, ingenious *pointe* even finds its way into such a sober preacher as Daillé, who speaks of St Paul's epistles as 'arôsant avec la plume, ce qu'il avoit planté avec sa langue'.[58] Emblems are still found – Caussin, especially, continues this tradition – and again they are used to reinforce a logically made point with a vivid image. The listeners' familiarity with them now permits great brevity in allusion.

The way in which the tradition of the thesaurus preachers is modified but nevertheless in some way continued in conceptist prose may perhaps be seen most clearly in the striking *avant-propos* with which Molinier begins a sermon preached at the consecration of a *Pietà* painting:

Les Autheurs Romains Remarquent (*Pline* 1. 37. cap. 2.), qu'en la pompe de cet auguste & magnifique triomphe que Pompée dressa pour les victoires, & conquestes des prouinces de l'Asie, il fit porter deuant le char triomphant vne sienne image en relief, & en bosse, toute bastie de perles & de marguerites, qui en estoient & l'ornement, & la matiere, laissant en doute les spectateurs qu'est-ce qu'ils deuoient y admirer dauantage, ou, le prix, ou la nouueauté. Voicy, Chrestiens Auditeurs, vne Image de la Vierge, Image toute de perles, qu'on a ce jourd'huy solemnellement beniste, & consacrée par les ceremonies de l'Eglise; ie dis de perles, puisqu'elle represente les larmes que la Vierge respandit le iour de la Passion sur le corps pasle & defiguré de son cher Fils descendu de la Croix. Larmes qui furent autant de perles que les Anges ramasserent, & que nous deuons recueillir pour en faire vn carquant à nostre col, vne plaque à nostre poitrine, vne couronne à nostre deuotion. Les perles s'engendrent de la rosée du Ciel, la Vierge est vn ciel animé, & ses larmes vne diuine rosée, d'où naissent en nos coeurs les perles de mille sainctes pensées. C'est de la rosée de ces larmes sacrées que le peintre a formé les riches perles ie veux dire les beaux traits, & les viues, ou plustost mourantes couleurs, qui enrichissent ce tableau, où l'amour & la mort sont pourtraits. C'est de ces mesmes larmes que nous deuons dresser dans nostre coeur à nostre Mere pleurante, & desolée auprès de la Croix, vne image de perles, Nom que ie donne aux sainctes Meditations que nous deuons former sur la representation de la Vie morte, & de l'Amour pleurant, du Sauueur percé de cloux, & de la Vierge naurée du glaiue de douleur, laquelle nous saluërons, *Aue Maria*, etc.[59]

The classical anecdote with which it opens is there primarily as ornament; this sort of opening is very widespread among preachers and almost universal in Molinier. It is a favourable comparison

58 *Exposition de la divine Epître de S. Paul aux Filippiens en XXIX sermons*, vol. 1, 1644 (C. 120), p. 3.
59 *Le Mystere de la Croix et de la Redemption du monde*, 1628, quoted from C. 242, pp. 667–8.

for the painting being discussed; it sets an appropriate tone of magnificence; above all it allows the preacher to introduce the idea of pearls. He begins his exploitation of the visual similarity between pearls and tears with an image which refers to a whole tradition in *Pietà* painting: 'Larmes qui furent autant de perles que les Anges ramasserent'. This sort of play on visual similarity is of course a commonplace of conceptist poetry: one thinks of Góngora's constant use of the crystal/skin/water conceit, couched in this very construction, in the *Soledades*. The construction recurs later in this same sermon (p. 674) with 'sa saincte Mere naurée ... d'autant de playes, qu'elle voit de cicatrices'. Beneath the mention of the pearl there lie not only reminiscences of the 'pearl of great price' (Matthew xiii, 45) but theories about the way pearls are formed in oysters by dew, and about the pearl/tear ambiguity in the interpretation of dreams. In thesaurus and catenary sermons these theories are normally very fully explained before play is made on them,[60] whereas here our knowledge is assumed and the preacher goes on to complicate the play with the Virgin/'ciel animé' conceit we met in section 2 above (p. 83). Brevity in allusion is, indeed, a major characteristic of this passage. 'Vn carquant à nostre col' recalls the opening picture of the Roman triumph and unites it to the Biblical 'my yoke is easy' (Matthew xi, 30); 'vne plaque à nostre poitrine' weaves in the Text of this sermon – *Pone me ut signaculum super cor tuum* (Song of Songs viii, 6) – which will be expounded later. The emblem tradition is here too, in the fleeting mention of 'l'amour & la mort', and so is the technique of embellishment with witty word-play and the contrast of opposites ('les viues, ou plustost mourantes couleurs'; 'la Vie morte, & ... l'Amour pleurant'). Yet for all the brilliance and concision of the tapestry of conceits, the note of devotional pathos is not entirely absent. Here too the emphasis is on the concrete and visual images of pain: Christ's body is 'pasle, & defiguré', he is the 'Sauueur percé

Cf. Seguiran, *Sermons doctes et admirables sur les Evangilles des Dimanches & Festes de l'anneé,* 1612 (C. 268), p. 173; Camus, *Premieres homelies eucharistiques,* 1618 (C. 78), p. 193, and *Premieres homelies dominicales,* 1617, hom. 29, 'Des larmes de nostre Seigneur' (see C. 73, esp. pp. 305–16). Molinier, *Sermons pour toutes les feries, et dimanches du Caresme,* 1641 (C. 253), vol. 2, p. 608, gives one of the sources as Artemidorus of Daldis's *Oneirocritica*. An edition of this had been published in Paris in 1603 and may partly explain the extreme popularity of the theme.

de cloux'; Mary, 'pleurante, & desolée auprès de la Croix' is 'naurée du glaiue de douleur'. By inserting here an echo of Simeon's prophecy (Luke ii, 35), Molinier taps the stream of devotional feelings associated for centuries with the traditions of the *Mater Dolorosa* and the *Pietà*.

The debt that Molinier owes in this passage to the preachers of the thesaurus tradition and to Camus is, then, much greater than his theoretical attacks on them would lead one to expect. The chief difference between him and Camus lies in the strength of the unifying scheme into which previously disparate conceits are now grafted, and in a certain variety and flexibility of sentence structure. Even so, the matter continues to dominate as the chief ornament of style, and few rhetorical figures are exploited other than those particularly adaptable to the still paratactic structure of conceptist prose.

5. Orchestrated prose

The rhetorical values that Molinier and Caussin were expounding in their prefaces other preachers were putting into effect. Central to the nature of what I shall call 'orchestrated' prose is that an argument has to be developed affectively in order to persuade readers or listeners fully to accept it; and so writers turn again to the treasure-house of persuasive techniques found in the rhetoric books. The concept of *le naturel* also makes its appearance; when Macé praises 'vne Eloquence d'autant plus ou moins artificielle, qu'elle se monstre naturelle',[61] he speaks (for all his word-play) from an aesthetic standpoint which is wholly different from, say, Camus's. The development of the ambiguity in the meaning of *artificiel* is enough to reveal the extent of the change.

It is amongst Protestant preachers that this approach to prose composition is earliest found. The reasons for this are of course extremely complex, but it may be remembered that the separation of argument (logic) from development (rhetoric) was the central point of Ramist teaching, and that Protestants were, on balance, more familiar than Catholics with the work of Ramus and Omer Talon. Close study and conscious imitation of the Bible is a

---

61 *La Couronne des saints*, 1637, quoted from C. 210, sig. ã4^r.

further crucial factor, and Protestant preachers often discuss their texts in terms of the rhetorical techniques used.[62]

The most striking contrast between this style and those discussed above lies in the sentence structure. In the sermons of the thesaurus and catenary tradition, even in the work of Molinier or Caussin or Abra de Raconis, one would be surprised to find a sentence like the following from Jean de Croï:

> Ignorans, & aveugles Mortels, qui ne considerez les Cieux, & les Elemens, que comme des corps d'eternelle durée, qui ne vivez sur la Terre, que de la mesme façon que s'il n'y avoit point, ny de mort, qui deust arrester le cours de vostre vie, ny de sepulcre, où vos corps deussent estre iettez, pour y estre reduits en poudre, ny de lieu de supplice, ou de recompence; & qui n'eslevez iamais vos Esprits à la contemplation de la iustice de Dieu, & des choses qui doivent arriver à la fin des siecles, vostre aveuglement vous dérobe la connoissance de l'un des plus grands & des plus importants mysteres de la Religion Chrestienne, & vos passions, qui se sont renduës maistresses de vostre volonté, arrachent de vos coeurs, autant qu'elles le peuvent, l'apprehension du iour du dernier Iugement, de mesme qu'elles destournent vos pensées de la consideration & de la crainte de la mort.[63]

The profusion of subordinate and especially relative clauses allows a progressive elaboration of the ideas already contained in the opening 'aveugles Mortels'; and this elaboration is affective rather than intellectual.

There is a strong contrast, too, in the way similes, metaphors and allusions are handled; where a Camus would delight in the variety and continual shock of his images, a Daillé is normally careful to preface them with a 'comme' or a 'si je puis dire' (itself a significant imitation of Cicero). Word-play and assonance are the only devices common to both traditions.

The particular quality of this sort of prose is often due to a combination of delicate but firm allusion and the use of classical rhetorical figures. Take for example the remarkable peroration of one of Amyraut's university sermons, on the Lord's Supper:

> C'est ce Christ que nous vous presentons icy mort pour vos offenses & ressuscité pour vostre iustification [.] Il a souffert que son corps ait esté rompu en la croix pour vous. Il a voulu que son sang ait esté respandu pour le lauement de vos ames. Il vous donne maintenant sa chair à manger, il vous donne son sang à boire: c'est à dire, les gages de l'vn & de l'autre, pour vous

---

62 For a particularly exhaustive example of this, see Amyraut's discussion of Ezekiel xviii, 32, in *Six sermons*, 1636 (C. 5), pp. 6–12.

63 *Le Dernier Jugement*, 1645 (C. 107), p. 5.

asseurer que si vous croyez, vous auez en luy la vie. Mais ie dis si vous croyez. Que ceux qui ne croyent pas que c'est leur Redempteur, que ceux qui pensent se pouuoir passer de ce Redempteur, ne s'approchent pas de sa Table; ne pensent pas auoir aucune part en ses graces. C'est la source dont vous auez à puiser vostre salut; & le moyen de la puiser c'est la foy. C'est l'arbre de vie dont vous auez à manger; & le moyen de le manger, c'est croire. C'est le serpent esleué dans le desert de ce monde, par lequel vous deuez estre gueris, & le moyen d'estre gueri, c'est de le contempler. C'est le Sacrificateur & la victime par laquelle vous auez à estre sanctifié; & le moyen d'en estre veritablement sanctifié est d'estre couuert de son sang, & le receuoir auidement, quand par la predication de l'Euangile & l'administration des Sacremens on vous en arrouse. C'est le rocher frappé dont vous auez à estre rafraischis & desalterez; & le moyen de se rafraischir, c'est de boire, c'est de croire.[64]

The urgent, strongly persuasive rhythm of this passage is based firmly on the so-called Gorgianic figures of parison and anaphora. Amyraut has adopted short sentences and has given them all a closely corresponding structure. This is reinforced by the repetition of initial words (anaphora: 'Il a souffert'; 'Il a voulu'; 'Il vous donne'; 'Il vous donne'; 'Que ceux qui'; 'Que ceux qui'; 'C'est ... & le moyen, ... c'est' – five times). This basic structure is varied by the occasional addition of subordinate clauses ('par lequel vous deuez estre gueris'; 'quand par la predication ... on vous en arrouse'), and by the sudden shock of the final paronomasia ('c'est de boire, c'est de croire'). But this sequence of rhetorical figures is also a sequence of Scriptural figures. The tree of life, the brazen serpent and the smitten rock are all types of Christ's redemptive power and, by extension, of the power of the sacramental act of faith. Classical rhetoric and Scriptural exegesis combine to move the hearer to an act (communion) and a state of mind (the Protestant notion of faith as a 'clinging to Christ').

The use of a fluid, flexible, and yet tightly controlled style enables the preacher to orchestrate more subtle moods. The crude chunks of abuse hurled at their opponents by the thesaurus preachers are replaced by the repeated insinuations rising to a crescendo of anger which may be found in the work of almost any of the later Protestants who preach against Rome. Civilized irony, too, finds a place in the pulpit; Retz introduces a typical note into a sermon on St Louis preached before the king:

64 *Six sermons*, 1636 (C. 5), pp. 45–6.

> Sire: J'apporte aujourd'hui aux pieds du crucifix ce qui n'a presque jamais servi que de trophée à la vanité des hommes. Je lui présente des couronnes, qui n'est pas le sacrifice le plus ordinaire que l'on lui fasse. Je lui offre des armes, qui ne sont pas les instruments les plus communs de la piété[65]

– an example of courtly charm, slightly précieux in tone, which reminds us of the important developments in secular prose taking place at this time.

It is important to avoid thinking of these categories of prose style in terms too rigid, whether chronologically or personally. A preacher may choose, as we have seen in the case of Camus, to adopt an uncharacteristic style in certain circumstances. Direct imitation, too, is an important factor. When Valladier bases part of his funeral orations over Henri IV and Anne d'Escars on St Bernard's lament for his dead brother, the style changes radically.[66] Caussin borrows an entire sermon from Gerson, and reverts to a wholly medieval mode of presentation.[67] Perhaps the most striking example occurs when Bertaut's flowing poetic style suddenly becomes pointed and antithetical in a sermon on the Nativity. A marginal reference provides the clue: the whole passage is modelled on St Leo.[68] Similarly, the persistence of personal styles would ruin any attempt to base a classification on too precise a division into, say, decades. Twenty-five years, for instance, separate Besse's 1604 Lenten sermons from his Lenten series of 1629, and yet there is absolutely no stylistic change. On the other hand, it is possible to see how some styles definitely develop out of others, or by reaction to them. In given circumstances therefore – geographical as well as chronological – one of the stylistic traditions tends to be dominant; and yet their variety and flexibility are such that a preacher's choice of his individual means of expression is never totally determined.

---

65 *Sermon de S. Louis*, 1649, quoted from C. 263, p. 112.
66 *Harangue funebre de Henry le Grand*, 1610 (C. 297), p. 17; *Epitaphe panegyrique, ou le Pontife chrestien*, 1612 (C. 301), pp. 149–54.
67 *Le Buisson ardent*, 1647 (C. 89), discours 23.
68 *Sermons sur les principales festes de l'année*, 1613 (C. 26), sermon 3.

5
Sermon structure and its stylistic implications

1. The division into points

In attempting to give an account of the formal structure of sermons at this period, one necessarily encounters the same difficulties as described in the last chapter. It is a delicate task to reduce the welter of variety to classifications of manageable proportions without at the same time imposing a wholly false picture of sharply drawn distinctions and conflicting groups. As far as formal structures are concerned, however, we have at least a rough guide-line in the existence of two well-known systems which respectively precede our period and emerge at the end of it, together with the fact that these systems – the medieval and the late-seventeenth-century – were the subject of some contemporary theoretical discussions and have been closely described by modern scholars. The medieval *méthode*, with its *prothema*, *thema* and elaborate division and subdivision of the matter into innumerable separate points, has been analysed by Etienne Gilson.[1] The classical system whereby (after an *avant-propos* and an exordium) the subject was regularly divided and discussed under three heads has been rescued from the gibes of La Bruyère by Jacques Truchet.[2] Truchet shows how the classical technique expresses a sense of order and offers a means of grasping spiritual verities while avoiding the hair-splitting complexities of rigorous subdivisions. There is also a suggestion of an almost Hegelian resolution of paradoxes in the third point. These two long-lived and firmly established techniques form the poles between which the sermons of the early seventeenth century constantly oscillate.

---

1 'Michel Menot et la technique du sermon médiéval'.
2 'La Division en points dans les sermons de Bossuet', *Revue d'histoire littéraire de la France*, LII (1952), pp. 316–29. For La Bruyère's criticisms see *Les Caractères*, ed. Garapon, p. 447.

By calling these techniques of division formal structures I do not wish to imply that they merely represent the convenient but purely artificial and arbitrary *cloisonnement* of a subject; they do not, however, always follow that 'deep structure' of a work which is now one of the most closely investigated aspects of literature. In the hands of a master like Bossuet they can express this controlled internal movement of ideas and emotions, but more often they merely form the backbone, the general outline of the discussion.

Division was the essential first step the preacher had to take; the argument flows directly from it, the seeds of the conclusion are contained in it. This is especially true of Protestants analysing the words of their Biblical texts: to divide is to 'open the Scriptures'. In the 1604 Canons of the Church of England an incumbent is directed to 'preach one sermon every Sunday of the year wherein he shall soberly and sincerely divide the word of truth to the glory of God and to the best edification of the people'.[3] Techniques of division were not, on the other hand, restricted to preaching; the decisive first step of *partitio* was regarded as essential to any analytical discourse, and recommendations as to the breaking-down of a topic in terms of the various *loci* abound (as we saw) in the rhetoric books.[4] But there is a distinction to be made between the methods of logical analysis prescribed for each and every author and the clear and simple divisions needed more particularly in works intended for oral delivery. It is remarkable that most of the post-Renaissance works on sermon theory tend to ignore the latter while concentrating on the former; as Truchet says, 'ils n'étaient pas arrivés à se dégager des cadres fixés par la rhétorique latine'.[5] As we saw in Chapter 3, however, some of the more practical theorists did discuss methods of division and occasionally even made recommendations. Panigarola, it will be remembered, made the crucial distinction between preaching *d'Evangile* and *de matière,* Estella recommended only the former kind, while Keckermann dealt exclusively with what he called *textualis inventio.* Thematic division (*de matière*) is much more widespread in Catholic sermons, where the text is often merely a starting point or even a purely decorative element, stripped of any

3 *The Stuart Constitution*, ed. J. P. Kenyon, Cambridge, 1966, p. 140.
4 See Brian Vickers, *Francis Bacon and Renaissance Prose*, chap. 2, for a very thorough discussion of *partitio*.
5 'La Division en points', p. 317.

analytical function; this is particularly true of Camus's works. Protestant preachers not unexpectedly favour close analysis of the text, and in this period we see amongst them the emergence of two quite different approaches: the Scriptural commentary sermon, where there is often no thematic unity at all, and the selection of a particular subject found in the text and expounded by reference to it.

Very little of this applies to the poetic or formless sermons described at the beginning of Chapter 4; their structure, if any, follows an internal and highly flexible movement of ideas and emotions. There is, however, a curious example of the vestigial survival of an earlier technique in Benoist's *Abrégé d'un sermon* of 1600 (C. 22). The abridger has been naturally led to use section headings, thus: 'Theme' (three distinct texts), 'Preface selon la coustume au commencement des Predications' (disparate comments on the circumstances of the sermon, the small numbers attending, etc.), and 'Proposition des choses pour lesquelles nous deuons principalement prier en la presente procession'. Under this heading comes a discussion of the texts chosen for the 'Theme', and a completely unrelated division into seven points of the aims of the procession; these points are then briefly gone over, with an exhortation added at the end of each, and the whole ends with two prayers. An elaborate technique for the analysis of texts has been rather clumsily imposed on a simple politico-religious speech for which it is clearly unsuited.

This tension between a rigorous adherence to traditional forms and a rambling freedom of treatment is apparent in large numbers of sermons – both Catholic and Protestant – written early in our period. Some preachers manage quite successfully to maintain their discussion on the lines of the numerous points given in the formal division: among Protestants this is most particularly true of the Englishman Primrose. Boucher dispenses with a full proposition section but replaces it (after a long *avant-propos*) with a numbered list of the points to follow. The continuing influence of the medieval subdivisions and the obsession with numbered points is very clear in the following break-down of the text *Magnificat anima mea Dominum* (Luke i, 46):

1. Dauid a receu dix faueurs speciales de Dieu.
2. La Vierge a receu dix graces speciales.
3. Elle chante en son Cantique dix perfections diuines.

4. Son Cantique diuin couronné de dix epithetes.
5. Magnifier, signifie cinq choses.
6. La Vierge pour trois raisons chante Magnificat.
7. Cinq moyens pour magnifier Dieu.
8. Trois sortes de personnes chantent vn triste Magnificat, bien esloigné de celuy de la Vierge Saincte.[6]

The most elaborate of all numerical divisions comes (surprisingly late) in Caussin's sermon based on Gerson.[7] The 'douze grandeurs de la Principauté de Iesus' form the subject of the first point, and are broken up into three main subdivisions, each with four sections. The mathematical precision of the *partitio* and the exact balance in the use of abstract terms gives this first point medieval qualities which are not only lacking in the second but which, to my knowledge, are not found in any other sermon of this period.

At the other extremity of this pendulum swing between rigour and licence there stands, characteristically enough, the figure of Camus. In the first sermon of his *Homelies spirituelles sur le Cantique des Cantiques* he exclaims impatiently that it is impossible to impose an order on a subject as exuberant as love:

Mais quel ordre obseruerons-nous en ce sujet d'Amour; le mesme ordre de l'Amour: & quel est l'ordre de l'Amour, c'est de n'auoir point d'ordre, *Amor ordinem nescit:* l'ordre gesne la franchise & liberté naturelle ... vous auriez aussitost reduit en forme vne masse d'argent vif, qui s'esparpille plus on le serre & ammoncelle, que ramené à vn ordre reiglé tous les excez d'Amour.[8]

Clearly it is difficult to reconcile traditional *dispositio* with catenary prose; and yet there are basic principles to which most of Camus's homilies conform. Almost all, for instance, are of the *de matière* type (although he uses *divisio textualis* in the *Homelies festives*), and there is a rough and ready typographical distinction between points, of which there are frequently two or four, rarely three.[9] Within the points a statement is normally supported by quotations from authorities, then by examples from Nature, and followed by a very brief exhortation. The peroration is replaced by an *application* in which the moral lessons are rapidly

---

6 *Les Magnificences divines*, 1620 (C. 53), sermon 1.
7 *Le Buisson ardent*, 1647 (C. 89), *discours* 23.
8 1620 (C. 82), pp. 12–13.
9 Camus calls them 'traittes' throughout.

Sermon structure and its stylistic implications

enumerated. In some ways this reflects the advice laid down in St François de Sales's letter to Frémiot.

Under the heading of free division come, too, the great majority of funeral orations. There was never a fixed pattern laid down for these; even Bossuet was to retain considerable flexibility in the *Oraisons funèbres*, despite his largely antithetical mode of thought. Sometimes the points follow different episodes in the life of the hero,[10] sometimes they are based on key ideas, or on a theological appraisal of his or her actions.[11]

A large number of sermons, however, conform to neither of the two tendencies discussed above. One is often able to discern a number of different schemes of organization imposed on a single work, and the division proposed in the opening pages frequently gives way to a separate order which, though nowhere made explicit, is nevertheless clearly based on a properly conceived principle of organization. A point which goes a long way towards clearing up some of the potential confusion inherent in this situation is made by Truchet in the opening words of his article, where he distinguishes the two meanings of the word 'division' as 'tantôt le partage d'un discours en ses divers points (ce que nous nommons aujourd'hui le plan), tantôt ... la partie de l'exorde qui sert à indiquer ce partage, et qu'on pourrait appeler l'annonce du plan'.[12] Now, the medieval tradition of according supreme importance to the announcement of the division resulted in an obsession on the part of many preachers with highly elaborate schemes of organization which, unlike their medieval predecessors, they were not inclined to obey too rigidly in the body of their sermons. Behind a title-page like that of Molinier's *Douze fondemens de la Cité de Dieu, ou les douze articles du symbole des Apostres, expliqués par les douze pierres precieuses de l'Apocalypse*, 1635

---

10 E.g. Boucher, *Oraison funebre de ... Emery de Barbezieres*, 1609 (C. 52); Macé, *La Tres-eloquente Harangue funebre du Pere Joseph*, ?1639 (C. 213).

11 E.g. Caussin, *Les Devoirs funebres rendus à l'heureuse memoire de Mme ... de Beauvillier*, 1634 (C. 88); Hersent, *Le Sacré Monument dedié à la memoire de ... Louis le Juste*, 1643 (C. 175), part I.

12 'La Division en points', p. 316. In many theoretical works the second sense of 'division' was conveyed by the word *propositio*; this was in fact always thought of as following the exordium and quite separate from it.

(C. 251), there lies not only the attraction of number mysticism,[13] but also the whole tradition of memory systems so thoroughly traced by Frances Yates in *The Art of Memory* (London, 1966). Theologians, and indeed their congregations, were in any case steeped in mnemonic lists like the seven deadly sins or the nine angelic orders, and it is quite natural that an oral and partly catechetical art like preaching should make use of the same methods. Nevertheless an excessive love on the part of preachers of classification and ornamentation for their own sakes must have led to diminishing returns as far as the retention of major doctrinal or moral points by the congregation was concerned, and so simpler structures emerged. Number systems were not of course restricted to theological concepts; the world of classical learning abounded in them, and preachers seem to have carried over the memories of their schoolboy exercises into their sermon organization. Voyer d'Argenson's *Enneade sacrée*, 1622 (C. 312) connects the nine Muses to nine Christian feasts, and the engraved frontispiece to his book (described in the Catalogue) is perhaps the best example of this interrelation of secular and religious found in any preacher's work of the period. His sermons themselves reveal the further point, since there is in fact no mention of the Muses in any of them once the initial connexion between Muse and feast has been briefly established, that this complex system is simply an elaborate exercise in ingenuity. Once the *propositio* has been brilliantly composed, the structure of the sermon follows a perfectly straightforward exposition of the meaning of the feast.

A further factor leading to this highly complex interrelation of structures is the celebrated fourfold interpretation of Scripture.[14] This method of extracting the full implications of a text is only rarely used in its complete form, except among the more old-fashioned of the Protestant preachers. Du Moulin, for instance,

13 See V. F. Hopper, *Medieval Number Symbolism*, New York, 1938. It seems quite possible that the classical three-point division has its origins in Trinitarian symbolism.

14 For a very full examination of this in an English context, see J. W. Blench, *Preaching in England in the Late Fifteenth and Sixteenth Centuries*, Oxford, 1964, chap. 1. There is a more general discussion in Helen Gardner, *The Business of Criticism*, Oxford, 1959, esp. pp. 79–100. It will be remembered that Estella, the proponent of greatly simplified structures, was also strongly opposed to any interpretation of Scripture which was not literal or tropological.

interprets Psalm 16, 9, 'Ma gloire s'est esgayée, aussi ma chair habitera en asseurance', anagogically as referring to the general resurrection, allegorically ('Dauid comme estant figure de Iesus Christ'), and tropologically ('car nous deuons tous . . . nous fortifier contre la crainte de la mort, par l'asseurance de la resurrection'). He is however careful to defend this use by the authority of St Peter's example in Acts ii.[15] More often the particular interpretation is chosen with the aim of making a connexion between the text and the single theme of the sermon. One can almost detect a note of scorn on the part of Seguiran for his text (the account of the healing of the widow's son in Luke vii) as he quickly moves on to the more general subject he wishes to discuss:

Ce n'est pas maintenant mon intention de parler de la Resurrection de ce petit adolescent: mais tout ainsi que nous voyons que du petit grain de moutarde croist vn arbrisseau, & comme de ceste petite pierre, en Daniel creut vne montagne: aussi soubs la Resurrection de ce ieune adolescent, nous parlerons de la Resurrection generale, pource qu'elle en est la figure & le pourtraict.[16]

It is easy to see how the automatic application of a method of non-literal interpretation could be imposed on a discourse where the author's real intention is to say something else, and how this could lead to a conflict of structures. This is the case with Suarez de Sainte-Marie's funeral oration of Henri IV (1610, C. 287) where the text is Zechariah xii, 11–14. The aim of the oration is to make the nation weep for the king's death, but so much time is taken up in explaining the minute parallels not simply between Henri and David, but between Marie de Médicis and Rebecca (for he does not stick closely to his brief), as well as the innumerable Old Testament figures who are revealed as types of seventeenth-century ones, that the reasons for our grief are only intermittently touched upon. To add to the confusion, the *avant-propos* had already drawn a detailed parallel between Henri and Brutus. A more successful attempt at providing this sort of figurative framework in a funeral oration is made by Valladier in his *Epitaphe panegyrique* of 1612 (C. 301). Taking the text 'Moyses, & Aaron in sacerdotibus eius, & Samuel inter eos qui inuocant nomen eius' (Psalm 98, 6;

15 *De la mort du fidele, et de sa resurrection*, 1649 (C. 149), p. 11.
16 *Sermons doctes et admirables sur les Evangilles des Dimanches & Festes de l'anneé*, 1612 (C. 268), p. 863.

Psalm 99 in A.V.), he divides the life of Anne d'Escars into his period as a monk (Samuel), a bishop (Aaron) and a cardinal (Moses). The need to establish these parallels, however, still works against the narrative flow since he makes a detailed and learned exposition of Jewish vestments and the way they symbolized virtues. He also finds great difficulty in incorporating obligatory material like genealogy into this scheme. In the peroration, by contrast, freed from these structural shackles, Valladier succeeds – with the help of imitation from St Bernard – in providing emotional relief by means of a personal and yet objective lament written in remarkably moving language.

The emergence of clearer standard forms springs in great part from a rejection of these exegetical methods. Amyraut begs to be excused 'si nous ne taschons pas à anatomiser ce texte en toutes ses parties. Ni le temps ne le permettroit pas quand nous le voudrions: ni nostre dessein de maintenant ne permet pas que nous ayons ceste pensee.'[17] Elsewhere he comments drily that to think we are saved by allegories is 'vne opinion merueilleusement bigearre',[18] and demonstrates how the literal sense of a text is much more interesting than any anagogical meaning.[19] This reaction is common to both Protestants and Catholics. In other ways, however, the slow crystallization of fixed divisions takes different forms in the two separate traditions, and they are better traced separately.

The earliest example of a Catholic rigid three-point division in our period comes, interestingly enough, from Richelieu's sermon of 1608 (C. 264). The figure three is played with in the exordium to this Christmas sermon (Christ's three births: eternal, temporal, and spiritual in our hearts, reflected by the three Christmas masses), and the text (selected verses from John i) is neatly divided thus: 1. 'In principio erat Verbum'; 2. 'et Verbum caro factum est'; 3. 'et habitavit in nobis'. Thereafter the order breaks down, but Richelieu is careful to apologize for this:

---

17 *Six sermons*, 1636 (C. 5), p. 50.
18 *Ibid.*, p. 169.
19 *Sermons sur quelques sentences de l'Ecriture*, 1647 (C. 15), sermon 4. In 1636 he had already used the significant phrase 'claire et distincte' of proper Scriptural exposition; see *Six sermons*, 1636 (C. 5), p. 4.

C'est de ces trois naissances desquelles je parlerais aussi, si le jour ne me conviait particulièrement à me restreindre aux deux dernières. (p. 7)

The distribution of matter also sets a pattern which others later will repeat: the first point contains elaborate theological arguments, reinforced by Scriptural and Patristic quotations in Latin, while the second (and longer) is 'à la portée des simples' (p. 10). The feeling for order which underlies the organization of the sermon is made explicit here in a long exhortation to civil harmony and unity. This ordered pattern is still more apparent in the next sermon collection[20] to use three-point divisions, nearly twenty years later: Abra de Raconis's *Riches et excellens paralleles* of 1625 (C. 1). These sermons have an *avant-propos* and three points; there is no real exordium and no *propositio*. Unusually, the *avant-propos* serves as a real introduction, not just as an ornamental preface. The author rejects a *propositio* or formal division:

ie ne m'arreste point à vous marquer l'vn apres l'autre les points de ce discours, par ce que ie suiuray ma methode & distribution ordinaire en trois points: pour les doctes, contre les errans, & en faueur des deuotieux. (p. 40)

The third point combines an *application* with a peroration; it is noticeably longer than the others and makes much more use of rhetorical figures. This method seems to be the ideal model on which other three-point divisions later in the period were based even though they rarely conform wholly to it. Whence this model emerged and by whom it was propagated remains a problem.

Among Protestants the development of a model is much clearer. We find preachers struggling towards a three-point division, though unable to abandon earlier methods. Charles de Beauvais, for example,[21] divides his sermon into thirty-three sections but places them under three main headings, which he calls 'parties'. The sermons in Du Moulin's *Décades* move chronologically from very variable divisions[22] to a point where the basic structure is at least attempting to conform to a standard. Even then he finds it difficult

---

20 If one excepts Suffren, *Le Victorieux et triomphant Combat de Gedeon*, 1616 (C. 289), where the three-point division is inevitably lost sight of in the course of no fewer than 290 pages.
21 *De la protection et sauvegarde divine*, 1636 (C. 20).
22 E.g. *Decade de sermons*, 1637 (C. 139), sermon 2, which is divided into six sections, each of which discusses a single word of the text – a good example of *divisio textualis*.

to carry through the plan outlined in the *propositio*. Sermon 1 of
the third *décade* of 1639 (C. 141) has a classic three-point division
but the third point contains continuations of arguments supposedly
dealt with in the previous two, and is far too bulky and general to
allow the sermon any balance. Once he is deeply interested in his
subject, Du Moulin is unable to remember the limitations inherent
in the structure he feels obliged to choose. Amyraut, too, is conscious that his audience is accustomed to a norm and apologizes
more than once for departing from it:

Nous entreprendrons donc de la vous exposer; & cela d'vne methode vn peu
differente de ce que nous auons accoustumé. Mais toutes choses ne
conuiennent pas à tous temps & à toutes occurrences.[23]

What was then this Protestant structural norm? It is to be seen most
clearly in the work of Mestrezat, who indeed adheres to it with a
rigidity that is not always appropriate. After the reading of the
text, he begins with a general exordium which sometimes discusses
the sacred author, sometimes the circumstances in which the
sermon is being preached, and sometimes more abstract topics.
This is followed by a close examination of the text, its historical
background, its context in the book from which it is taken, and
the difficulties raised by its language. This is often the place for
a display of etymological scholarship. Then comes the *propositio*
or division, almost always into three points. The body of the
sermon is followed by a sort of extended peroration often entitled
'Applications' or 'Enseignements et consolations'. Somewhere in
the sermon there is a controversial point aimed at Rome; normally
it comes in the third point or in the final section. Mestrezat
occasionally deviates over the number of points,[24] and the typographical conventions vary considerably. But it is to this model
that the majority of the Protestant preachers in the second half of
our period approximate, even when, like Aubertin,[25] they dispense
with an exordium or, like Le Faucheur, discuss the context after
the division.[26] It was, as the sermons of Jean Claude show, to
remain the model for many decades, although the inclusion of a

23 *Six sermons*, 1636 (C. 5), p. 5; cf. *ibid.*, p. 50.
24 *La Pentecoste chrestienne*, 1633 (C. 223), and the second sermon of the
    Trois sermons sur la venue et naissance de Jesus-Christ, 1649 (C. 238),
    have two points rather than three.
25 *Sermon sur les versets 3 et 4 du Psalme 130*, 1637 (C. 19).
26 *Trois sermons*, 1632 (C. 197), sermon 1.

controversial point came to be less and less automatic. In the work of Daillé the *méthode* is no longer a rigidly imposed structure; it has become the natural convention within which the preacher thinks as well as writes, and he adapts it with the flexible imaginativeness which comes from a secure knowledge that both preacher and congregation are thoroughly familiar with a clear and fruitful convention.

It will have been noticed that this Protestant *méthode* has considerable affinity with the traditional technique of meditation, with its movement through composition of place and effort to comprehend to a formation of resolutions, often ending in an affective colloquy with God.[27] Terence Cave has pointed out the use of sermon tones in formal meditations;[28] the same is true in reverse. In fact, Amyraut occasionally calls a sermon 'ma meditation'.[29] This interrelation of religious exercises, although it is not exclusive to Protestants, nevertheless had a considerable influence on their use of varying styles within the sermon. It is to such stylistic implications of formal structures that we may now turn.

2. The hierarchy of styles

The rhetorical theorists of antiquity distinguished three main styles a writer or orator might use, the *genus sublime*, *genus mediocre* and *genus humile*. They were linked to specific functions, the persuading, delighting and teaching which were the aims of rhetoric. In St Augustine's words, 'is erit igitur eloquens, qui ut doceat, poterit parva submisse, ut delectet, modica temperate, ut flectat, magna granditer dicere'.[30] Although this definition lays stress on the appropriateness of style to subject matter, it was also possible to define the three styles in terms of the rhetorical devices used. The sublime style relied on techniques like apostrophe, exclamation, interrogation; the middle style was characterized by ornamental figures – chiasmus, isocolon, paronomasia – and the plain style concentrated on expounding its subject in clear, short

27 See Louis Martz, *The Poetry of Meditation*, revd edn, New Haven and London, 1962, esp. pp. 25–39.
28 *Devotional Poetry in France c. 1570–1613*, Cambridge, 1969, esp. pp. 36–7.
29 *Deux sermons sur 1 Jean, v, 7–8*, 1646 (C. 13), pp. 11 and 61.
30 *De doctrina christiana*, IV, 17.

sentences. These were early connected with the various parts of an oration, narration, refutation, amplification, etc., terms which initially describe possible techniques (much in the way grammarians use the expression 'parts of speech'), but which soon came to be identified with distinct sections. Thus the middle style was for the exordium, the plain style for the exposition, and the sublime for the peroration.

Obviously a preacher in the thesaurus tradition, or an exponent of the catenary and even conceptist prose styles, would not be able to fit his sermons into a scheme which required the use of the full register of rhetorical techniques. And yet, with the development of the feeling that a sermon ought to be more like a classical oration, some stylistic differentiation was needed. In order to achieve this, preachers developed a remarkable convention in which, although the sentence structure and the use of schemes remained unvaried, the subject matter in the traditionally ornate passages was itself of an exotic or decorative nature. This need for ornate matter to replace an ornate manner was often supplied by Pliny or Binet, with their treasure-houses of rare and rich jewels, animals, plants, to all of which some symbolical meaning might be attached.

'Jewelled prose' in fact fills a vast number of early-seventeenth-century *avant-propos*; a characteristic example from Molinier was analysed at some length in Chapter 4.[31] Exordia, too, were frequently written in this way: after another *avant-propos* all of pearls and tears, Molinier turns in the exordium to flowers:

Iam hiems transijt, imber abijt, & recessit, flores apparuerunt in terra nostra: l'Hyuer est passé, les pluyes ont cessé, les fleurs commencent de poindre, & de paroistre. L'hyuer du peché est passé en Magdeleine, les pluyes de ses larmes sont arrivées, les fleurs de sa Conuersion ont commencé de s'éclorre. Voicy paroistre vne belle rose, premierement sortie d'emmy les espines du vice; & de là transplantée parmy les espines de la mortification, arrosee des larmes de la contrition, espanouye aux rayons du S. Esprit, rouges des flammes du diuin amour, & respirant par toute l'Eglise les soüefues odeurs de la penitence dont son exemple nous parfume. Que si l'odeur de la rose tuë l'Escarbot, & attire l'Abeille pour y succer le miel, la senteur respanduë de ceste fleur mystique n'a pas moins de vigueur, pour faire mourir le peché, & venir à soy les ames, afin d'y recueillir le miel d'vne saincte imitation. C'est Iesus-Christ, qui s'appelle la fleur des champs, & le lys des valées, qui a premierement alleché par ses odeurs celestes ceste Penitente; laquelle

---

31 See above, pp. 95–7.

d'espine est deuenuë fleur, de pecheresse saincte, aussi-tost qu'elle l'a touché comme Iosephe raporte que le sable touchant les eaux d'vne fontaine de Iudée, se transforme en crystal; ou comme la torche esteinte que l'attouchement de la source de Dodone change en torche brûlante.[32]

Similarly, without any of the *oratio numerosa* classically associated with ornate sections, using only his characteristic asyndeton, Valladier creates a tapestry of lights as the introduction to his philosophical reflections on the soul:

Domine probasti me & cognouisti me, tu cognouisti sessionem meam, & resurrectionem meam: c'est de vostre soleil que m'est venu ce rayon, de vostre rayon ceste lumiere, de vostre lumiere ceste aurore, de vostre aurore ce beau iour, de vostre iour ce beau midy, de vostre midy ce beau lustre de mon ame: de vostre or ceste lueur, de vos carquans ce brillant, de vostre astre cét esclat, de vostre miroir ceste espece, de vostre oracle ceste verité, de vostre foudre cét esclair, de vostre vision ceste oeillade, de vostre brasier ceste estincelle, de vostre diafane ceste clarté, de vos pierreries ceste splendeur, de vos reuelations ceste foy, de vostre escole ceste saincte, diuine, admirable, & tres-necessaire PHILOSOPHIE.[33]

Preachers utterly bound to the thesaurus tradition use the same technique in perorations. Thus Seguiran departs not at all from the nature parallels and the quotations which make up the substance of his prose, but chooses his examples from the field almost automatically associated with ornamentation:

Pline dit, que la perle ne peut viure hors de son escaille, ny plus ny moins que l'ouytre: Ainsi l'ame qui est ceste perle precieuse, ne peut viure sinon en son escaille, c'est à dire, en la gloire, qui est le lieu d'où elle est sortie. *Fecisti nos, Domine, ad te, & inquietum est cor nostrum donec quiescat in te, in ipso viuimus, mouemur, & sumus*, dit sainct Augustin, ô perle plus riche & plus precieuse que celle que Cleopatra fit fondre en du vin-aigre: Aussi c'est auiourd'huy que nostre Seigneur fait fondre ceste pretieuse perle de son ame dans le vin-aigre, & excez de sa mort & passion: C'est de ceste perle d'estime que ce mesme Seigneur parloit, *Simile est regnum caelorum, homini quaerenti bonas Marguaritas, inuenta autem una, &c.* Ou bien en fin ie pourrois dire que par ces perles, que sainct Iean dit estre à la porte du Paradis (*Apoc.* 21.) sont representees les larmes & trauerses de ceste vie, par lesquelles il faut passer pour entrer au Ciel, la perle se nourrit par la rosee du Ciel, aussi ceste gloire celeste ne s'acquiert & ne se peut obtenir que par les larmes, c'est là ceste rosee.[34]

32 *Sermons pour toutes les feries, et dimanches du Caresme*, 1641 (C. 253), vol. 2, pp. 609–10.
33 *La Saincte Philosophie de l'ame*, 1614 (C. 304), p. 35.
34 *Sermons doctes et admirables sur les Evangilles des Dimanches & Festes de l'annéé*, 1612 (C. 268), p. 173.

Much the same effect is to be seen in those passages of thesaurus sermons where, doubtless remembering some classical doctrine learnt long ago, the preacher suddenly switches to a 'sublime mood' which in no way springs from the general theme of the sermon, and does not amplify a point already argued. Such is Valladier's extraordinary burst of vituperation used to ornament an *avant-propos*:

> Et quoy, les Astres peuuent ils toucher à l'ame qui est vne substance spirituelle? a elle quelque dependance, ou correspondance auec les Planetes? ou auec les constellations & signes du firmament? bourdes, impostures, piperies des mocqueurs Astrologues, colporteurs d'Almanacs, pantalons de theatre, qui embaboüinent le monde de leurs farces, crochetent les bourses, amusent les idiots, renuersent les esprits, perdent & ruinent les ames, les conduisans petit à petit à l'atheisme.[35]

It is in this tradition, perhaps, that we can place Retz's use of irony, stylistically so different from these thesaurus preachers, with which he decorates the exordia of sermons.[36] A rather different technique, but one which is obviously intended to give an impression of ornamentation – to delight, in fact – is the widespread use of word-play in these sections. Not unexpectedly this is very common in Camus. Some preachers combine word-play with flowers, like Macé preaching on St Louis:

> Le Lys est la fleur des Roys, & la Reine des fleurs . . . France, ma chere patrie, tu es sans doute ce delicieux jardin. Le Lys qui te couronne, apres que tu l'as heureusement couronné, n'est autre que l'incomparable S. Louys.[37]

The technique of jewelled prose is also occasionally used to give a sermon the tone appropriate to a great festival. Thus Voyer d'Argenson, in a sermon on the Assumption which has no great

---

35 *La Saincte Philosophie de l'ame*, 1614 (C. 304), pp. 419–20. *Cf.* the sudden attack on the Protestants, *ibid.*, p. 756: 'Ils desadouënt les morts: ils secondent les demons: ils meprisent les Anges; ils denient le sens, dementent la raison: controuersent la foy: vilipendent les Docteurs: meprisent les traditions, corrompent l'Escriture: se mocquent des hommes: ne se soucient de Dieu: doutent du Paradis: nient le Purgatoire: se iouent de l'Enfer: incredules, vagabonds, reprouuez, profanes, sacrileges, blasphemateurs, que Dieu reserue patientant auec eux, iusques au iour de son ire.'
36 C. 263, p. 112 (quoted above, p. 100); *cf. ibid.*, p. 135.
37 *Panegyrique de S. Louis*, 1648 (C. 212), pp. 1–2 (*avant-propos*).

Sermon structure and its stylistic implications 115

stylistic differentiation between the parts, deliberately selects precious stones as the source of his comparisons in order to convey a greater richness than in his other sermons.[38]

Nevertheless, whereas almost all thesaurus or conceptist preachers use jewelled prose as their version of the *genus mediocre*, only Seguiran and Valladier use it to replace the *genus sublime* proper to perorations. Among the others it is revealing to discover that, however committed they may be to the thesaurus method with its unvaried prose, they still depart from it in order to produce affective conclusions.[39] Often this is done less by strikingly forceful rhetorical techniques than by a quiet meditative colloquy, common among both Catholics and Protestants. The following example from Besse contrasts strongly with the examples of his style in other parts of the sermon quoted in Chapter 4:

O Seigneur, nous vous en faisons auiourd'huy les protestations, *Zelus domus tuae comedat nos*: Nous n'affectionnerons iamais rien tant, comme l'honneur de vostre saincte Eglise, le respect de vos sacrez Temples, la gloire de vostre magnifique nom, & la fidele continuation de vostre diuin seruice: ce sera nostre seule ambition, & qui nous durera autant que la vie. Seigneur nous serons si reformez, & si sinceres aux charges esquelles vous nous auez esleuez, que vous n'aurez iamais plus d'occasion de vous en mettre en cholere, & nous chasser de vos Temples.

Seigneur que la mort nous arriue plustost que de prophaner ces sacrés lieux, que d'y rien vendre ou acheter. Mais mille morts plustost que d'y commettre des simonies, [ou] y nourrir des hypocrisies: Seigneur nous sommes resolus de vous y seruir si fidelement que nous meriterons, sortans comme bons seruiteurs de l'Eglise militante, de vous aller voir en la triomphante.[40]

In contrast, too, to the jewelled exordia of Molinier is this peroration to a Corpus Christi sermon:

38 *L'Enneade sacrée*, 1622 (C. 313), pp. 75–6. *Cf.* the sumptuous comparisons introduced to honour the feast of Easter in Seguiran, *Sermons doctes et admirables sur les Evangilles des Dimanches & Festes de l'anneé*, 1612 (C. 268), sermon 15.
39 With the exception of Camus, whose conclusions for the most part consist of numbered résumés or resolutions.
40 *Premieres conceptions theologiques sur le Caresme*, 1604 (C. 27), vol. 2, fols. 284^v–285^r. *Cf.* meditative colloquies in Suffren, *Le Victorieux et triomphant Combat de Gedeon*, 1616 (C. 289), and Voyer d'Argenson, *L'Enneade sacrée*, 1622 (C. 312), sermon 4.

Ouurez, ouurez les yeux, & si vous auez quelque sentiment, si quelque connaissance, si quelque raison, aymez Dieu qui vous ayme, honorez vostre Dieu qui vous honore. Si ses commandemens n'ont assez de force sur vous, que ses dons surmontent vostre obstination. Si ses menaces ne vous peuuent toucher, que ses bien-faits vous esmeuuent. Si vous ne cedez à la crainte de sa justice, laissez vous vaincre aux attraicts de son amour. Puis que Iesus-Christ s'est donné à vous, donnez-vous à luy; puis qu'il s'est sacrifié pour vous, sacrifiez-vous à luy; puis qu'il a baillé pour vostre salut la chair qu'il a pris [sic] de vous en sacrifice sanglant sur la Croix, & la baille tous les iours en sacrifice non sanglant sur l'autel; ne refusez pas de luy offrir vos esprits en sacrifice d'attention à ses sacrez mysteres, vos corps en sacrifice de mortification, vos volontez en sacrifice d'obeyssance, vos affections en sacrifice d'amour, vos langues en sacrifice de loüange, vos mains en sacrifice de bonnes oeuures, vos actions en sacrifice de iustice, vos biens en sacrifice d'aumosne.[41]

With its use of parison, anaphora and *communicatio*, or direct address, this passage falls very much into the category of orchestrated prose. Running, therefore, beneath the thesaurus and conceptist traditions all through the first thirty years of the century there is this vestige of classical practice, and this ability to manipulate rhetorical techniques when thought appropriate. This probably explains why the first orchestrated Catholic sermons are written in an exceptionally elevated tone: when the conventional ('thesaurus') forms used for the middle and plain styles were first rejected, the only familiar consecutive prose style was the sublime.

As fixed sermon structures crystallized, so the feeling for a clear hierarchy of styles grew. Abra de Raconis often fulfils his intention of combining an *application* and a peroration in his third point 'pour les deuotieux' by means of a torrent of 'sublime prose'.[42] The end of his second sermon is advertised in the margin as a 'paraphrase emphatique de la sentence des meschans':

Ite maledicti, Allez maudits, *Ite* o quel depart; *Maledicti*, o quel malheur, *In ignem*, o quelle demeure, *aeternum*, o quelle longueur, *Qui paratus est*, quelles preparations; *Diabolo*, o quelle compagnie, *Et Angelis suis*, o quels Anges, *Ite*, irreuocablement, *Maledicti*, Malheureusement, *In ignem*,

---

41 *Le Banquet sacré de l'Eucharistie*, 1635, quoted from C. 249, p. 119. It must however be said in fairness to Molinier that, on one occasion at least, he produced an absolutely classical exordium in the style of the law courts; see *Sermon sur les festes des saincts*, 1648 (C. 257), vol. 1, pp. 154-5.

42 Though he, too, occasionally ends with a meditative colloquy in the first person, e.g. sermons 11 and 16.

Sermon structure and its stylistic implications 117

Cruellement, *Aeternum*, Desesperément, *Qui paratus est*, Dignement, *Diabolo*, Premierement, *Et Angelis suis*, Consecutiuement. *Ite*, Depart trop ennuyeux, *Maledicti*, Malediction furieuse, *In ignem*, Demeure trop douleureuse, *Aeternum*, Longueur pleine de desespoir, *Qui paratus est*, Preparatifs espouuantables, *Diabolo*, Compagnie trop effroyable, *Et Angelis suis*, Ministres impitoyables.

Ite, Tout beau est-ce vne menace de vostre misericorde qui nous fasse craindre pour nous corriger de nos vices? ou vne sentence de vostre Iustice qui nous condamne, & nous enuoye au supplice? Ah Seigneur! si c'est vne ordonnance de vostre Iustice, nous appellons au Tribunal de vostre Misericorde, surintendante de vos vertus, & qui preside souuerainement sur toutes les oeuures de vos mains – *Vbi sunt antiquae Misericordiae tuae Domine*, Que sont deuenuës vos anciennes Misericordes, o Seigneur![43]

There are still elements here of the close commentary on the text, but textual elements are amplified by paraphrase (of a rather vacuous sort) rather than transformed wholly into the continuous prose which was more normal later. Amyraut actually announces the change of style which marks the beginning of the *application-peroration*:

Nous ne laisserons pas d'vser de quelques exhortations pour la fin de cette action, & de vous coniurer par le soin que vous aués de vostre salut, d'embrasser de plus en plus étroitement ce Redempteur.[44]

'Exhortations', 'coniurer': these aims are reflected in the energetic use of the highly affective techniques of which we earlier saw Amyraut to be a master.

Protestant preachers in the second half of our period standardized this hierarchy of style just as they standardized sermon structures. Their sermons are models which might serve as examples in the classical textbooks. Perhaps the most effective of them all was Jean Daillé, one of whose sermons[45] is worth analysing in detail as an illustration. It opens a series of Scriptural commentaries, and is therefore at the same time an example of that tradition in Protestant preaching rather than of the often more sumptuous occasional sermon.

That Daillé was familiar with rhetorical techniques, as well as sensitive to them, emerges clearly from his work. Elsewhere in this collection he speaks not (as an earlier preacher would have done)

43 *Riches et excellens paralleles*, 1625 (C. 1), pp. 61–2.
44 *Deux sermons sur 1 Jean, v, 7-8*, 1646 (C. 13), p. 108.
45 *Exposition de la divine Epître de S. Paul aux Filippiens en XXIX sermons*, vol. 1, 1644 (C. 120), sermon 1.

of Paul's fascination and complexity, but of the reasons why he is so 'patétique & affectueux'.⁴⁶ In the Dedication he is concerned to defend Paul against criticisms of his style:

> S'ils [sc. ses écrits] n'ont pas les graces de la terre, ils ont celles du ciel; & encore que l'industrie de l'art humain n'y paroisse nulle part, une naïve, & vigoureuse beauté y reluit par tout, née de la hautesse des choses mesmes, & de la hautesse des pensées de ce divin écrivain. (p. 7)

When analysing Paul's technique in the opening words of the Epistle (the text is Philippians i, 1-6) he gives a faithful classical account of the function of the exordium:

> Les maistres de l'art de bien dire nous apprenent, que la tasche de l'exorde, c'est à dire du commencement de nos discours, est de gagner la bonne grace de ceux, à qui nous parlons. En effect puis que la haine, l'aversion, & l'indifference ferment l'entrée des coeurs des hommes, il est necessaire, quand nous avons dessein de les persuader, qu'avant toutes chose nous preparions leurs ames, & les remplissions de bons prejugés en nôtre faveur, afin que nos raisons puissent estre receuës dans leurs espris. C'est à quoi travaille l'Apôtre en ce verset, & dans les suivans iusques au douzieme. (p. 17)

And indeed his own exordium is a model of its kind:

> Entre les avantages, que Dieu a donnés à l'homme au dessus des animaux, à peine y en a-il aucun plus marveilleux, ni qui tesmoigne plus clairement l'excellence de nôtre nature que l'invention & l'usage des lettres. Aussi lisons nous que les peuples de ce nouveau monde, qui fut découvert du temps de nos peres, ne treuvoient rien de plus étrange, que cet artifice; ne pouvans comprendre, comment une petite feuille de papier marquée de quelques lignes & de quelques traits, étoit capable de reveler à un homme le secret d'un autre absent de plusieurs lieuës de là; & avant que d'en avoir appris la raison s'imaginoient, qu'il y devoit avoir quelque ame, ou quelque vertu divine renfermée dans les caracteres des lettres pour produire un si admirable effet. Qu'eussent ils dit, s'ils eussent sçeu, que cette invention nous communique les discours, & les pensées non des absens seulement, mais des morts mesmes? & malgré les distances des lieux & des temps nous rend presans, ceux, que non seulement plusieurs climats, mais mesmes plusieurs siecles ont éloigné de nous d'un espace presque infini? (p. 2)

It captures the interest of the audience by referring them to a fascinating and relatively recent event, the discovery and opening up of America; the level of discussion is general, and intended to revive in the hearers' minds the excitement of Bible reading as well as to make the presence of the Apostle more nearly felt. There is, admittedly, no great use of rhetorical figures – discretion and

---

46   Sermon 8, p. 293.

sobriety were doubtless calculated to appeal to the faithful of Charenton – but the sentences are flowing and complex, and he ends the exordium with the striking *pointe* (already quoted) about St Paul 'arôsant avec la plume, ce qu'il avoit planté avec sa langue'.

This is followed by the context section, in which the circumstances of the Philippians and the reasons why Paul wrote to them are fully discussed. The three-point division proposes a consideration of the opening greeting of the Epistle, the thanks and prayers, and the Apostle's assurance of his disciples' perseverance. The body of the sermon is a very thorough exposition of these, written in the plainest of styles. The contrast with other preachers, even with other Protestants, is seen in the sparing use of examples and comparisons, of which there are only three or four in all the three parts. The following passage, from the first point, is typical for its quiet and unemotional explanation, and for the interesting way in which the obligatory controversial point is muted to a simple reconstruction of circumstances in Apostolic times, backed up with Patristic authority:

Quant à ceux, qui gouvernoient l'Eglise des Filippiens l'Apôtre les nomme *les Evesques, & les Diacres*; comprenant sous le mot d'*Evesques* tous les Pasteurs, & docteurs, qui travailloient à la parole, soit pour enseigner, soit pour exhorter, soit pour catechizer, soit pour consoler; sous le nom de *Diacres* ceux, qui avoient soin des tables, & des povres, & administroient les deniers sacrés, selon la distinction des ministeres de l'Eglise, qu'établirent les Apôtres des le commencement, comme nous le lisons dans les Actes (Act. 6.). Il est vrai qu'aujourd'huy, & depuis plusieurs siecles, le mot d'*Evesque* se prend autrement en la Chretienté pour celui, qui preside sur une Eglise & sur tout son clergé, y exerceant une autorité particuliere. Mais ici Saint Paul prend evidemment le mot d'*Evesque* autrement. Car il met plusieurs Evesques dans une seule Eglise, au lieu que comme on l'entend communement il n'y en peut avoir qu'un. En effet il est clair & par ce passage, & par plusieurs autres, qu'au temps des Apôtres les mots *d'Evesque & de Prestre*, c'est à dire ancien, signifioit une mesme charge, celle que nous appellons le saint ministere; & ne paroist par aucun lieu du nouveau Testament qu'il y ait eu en ce premier siecle quelque autre dignité dans le ministere ordinaire de l'Eglise au dessus de celle-là. Et il y a longtemps, que Saint-Jerôme a fait cette judicieuse remarque en divers endroits de ses livres, concluant que le Prestre & l'Evesque sont égaux de droit, & selon la premiere institution Apostolique, la difference, qui y est maintenant, ayant été établie depuis pour conserver l'ordre, & l'unité, n'étant par consequent que de droit positif & humain, & non divin.
(pp. 12–14)

Daillé's persistence in keeping to his preordained structure and his awareness of the need for the congregation to follow it clearly is underlined by the opening words of the peroration:

> Ainsi avons nous expliqué, mes Freres, les trois points que nous nous étions proposés au commencement.[47]

Much of the peroration is characterized by the traditional figures of the *genus sublime* – anaphora, parison, *interruptio*, even hyperbaton. Its conclusion reverts to a more soberly hortatory tone:

> Ce n'est pas en vain qu'il vous a recous de tant d'embrasemens, sauvés de tant de naufrages, r'assemblés de tant de dispersions, & conservés par miracle au milieu de tant de confusions. Freres bien aimés, comme ses benefices sont illustres sur vous, y ayant tres peu de troupeaux au monde, où sa protection & ses faveurs reluisent si magnifiquement, que dans le vôtre; que vos reconnaissances soient aussi remarquables entre tous les Chrestiens; Que vôtre gratitude ne paroisse pas moins, que sa grace. Ce n'est pas assés, Fideles, de le remercier en paroles, & dire amen aux loüanges, & benedictions, que nous lui rendons ici solennellement en nos saintes assemblées. Le remerciment, qu'il vous demande, & que vous lui devés en effet, c'est que pour la grace, qu'il vous a communiquée vous ayez soin de sa gloire; que vous cheminiez en la lumiere, dont il vous éclaire; que vous suiviez la guide, qu'il vous a donnée; que vous ayes une ardente charité pour vos freres ses serviteurs, comme il a eu une amour infinie pour vous; que vos meurs soient conformes à sa doctrine & que vôtre vie ne soit pas moins Evangelique que votre foi.

The most obviously new figure is *communicatio*; direct address is almost wholly absent from the other sections. The short, sharp phrases of preachers like Amyraut have been replaced by greater *copia dictionis*, and a real attempt to render *oratio numerosa* more natural, but there remains ample use of anaphora and antithesis.

Not all later preachers conform slavishly to this model; nor did Daillé himself, who is not beyond using the older practice of including a short peroration within each point when he thinks it necessary[48] or of using ornate style in normally plain sections, as when, for instance, he apostrophizes Paul and invents the Apostle's

---

47 P. 41. *Cf.* sermon 12, p. 491: 'C'est où je finiray, Chers Freres, apres vous avoir brievement touché les principales leçons, que nous avons à tirer de la doctrine de l'Apôtre pour nôtre edification.'

48 E.g. *Le Sacrifice des chrestiens*, 1633 (C. 110), or *Sermon pour le jeusne celebré à Charenton le Jeudy 21 Aoust 1636*, 1636 (C. 115).

replies in the *propositio* section of a sermon.[49] But a sermon of this type demonstrates clearly how firmly the notions of fixed structure and stylistic differentiation were held by the closing years of our period.

49 *Exposition de la divine Epître de S. Paul aux Filippiens en XXIX sermons*, vol. 1, 1644 (C. 120), p. 131.

6
Themes and their imagery (i)
Illusion and reality

'Un thème', a student of our period observed not long ago, 'n'est rien d'autre qu'un certain domaine privilégié dans lequel un auteur choisira ses images.'[1] The remark makes even more sense if the terms are reversed: the author's choice of imagery reveals, at the level of the text, the principles which underlie his writing. By examining what Ortali calls the 'réserves d'images' characteristic of our preachers, we can arrive at an idea of the thematic structure on which their writing rests. I do not mean by this the obvious doctrinal and moral teachings which recur explicitly in their every sermon, but the cast of mind which moulds and colours their presentation of those teachings. What emerges most strikingly on analysis is the unity of this thematic structure; however disparate the images may appear, they are rooted in a single apprehension of the meaning of life.

1. Illusion and reality as religious themes

This view of existence is fundamentally antithetical: the insubstantiality of the physical world is set in opposition to the solidity of the spiritual. Worldly pleasure, says Daillé, is 'une figure qui passe ... une figure parce qu'il n'a qu'une fausse apparence, & une vaine couleur pour recréer les yeux, mais non aucune vraie & solide substance pour contenter l'ame'.[2] *Vrai et solide*: whenever both parts of the antithesis are fully expressed, this is the vocabulary associated with the realm of spiritual reality. Daillé uses these same words more than once;[3] Camus speaks of our being heirs of Christ 'solidement & solidairement, reellement & substantiellement,

---

1. Raymond Ortali, *Un Poète de la mort: Jean-Baptiste Chassignet*, Geneva, 1968, p. 67.
2. *Exposition de la divine Epître de S. Paul aux Filippiens en XXIX sermons*, 1644 (C. 120), vol. 1, p. 285.
3. E.g. *ibid.*, p. 221.

non imaginairement & fantastiquement'.[4] Molinier illustrates the folly of neglecting the spiritual message of a feast in appropriately culinary terms:

> Ce sera cueillir les fueilles, & laisser tomber les fruicts, embrasser l'ombre, & laisser eschaper le corps, humer la vaine odeur de la fumée, & ne toucher pas à la substance des viandes.[5]

Apart from the witty way in which they explore the connotations of the word 'feast', Molinier's metaphors deserve attention for the manner in which they make explicit the true sense of the 'baroque' obsession with illusion. We shall meet again and again the shadows and smoke which represent the unreality of this world, but shall more rarely be told of their opposites. The very intensity with which early-seventeenth-century authors point up the first half of the antithesis has often led commentators to neglect the second; and yet for those authors it was the more important, because it endows the elaboration of metaphors of transience with a clear moral purpose and an element of hope. What would otherwise remain a tragic lament over man's estate is transformed by the revelation of an alternative reality and the prospect of an ultimate triumph. We must, from the beginning, always bear in mind the implicit religious vision which accompanies the contemporary insistence on the vanity of life.[6]

It is nevertheless true that more attention is devoted by our preachers to creating a sense of insecurity than to discoursing upon the 'solid joys and lasting treasure' that await the faithful. The reasons for this are obvious. Firstly, the theme is associated with a wealth of Biblical and classical imagery which is not only at the preachers' immediate disposal but has the advantage of increasing the authority and strengthening the emotional impact of their remarks by allusion to memorable passages familiar to most hearers. Secondly, the need to denounce the wiles of the world must have a clear priority, if only because their attraction is

---

4 *Premieres homelies eucharistiques*, 1618 (C. 78), p. 87. Since it may be objected that this is merely the technical vocabulary of Eucharistic controversy, it is worth noting that the contrast is with 'images... tableaux... ombres... figures'.
5 *Sermon sur les festes des saincts*, 1648 (C. 257), vol. 1, p. 154.
6 *Cf.* Terence Cave's remark that 'the *vanitas* tradition and moral generalisation are virtually inseparable' (*Devotional Poetry in France c. 1570-1613*, p. 155).

so strong and so constant. One might add that a realm of spiritual realities, based as it is largely on metaphysical speculation, is unlikely to prove a rich source of literary invention.

Drelincourt's sermon *La vanité du monde* of 1639[7] exemplifies this natural tendency. The basic antithesis is enshrined in the two points: 'nous n'auons point icy de cité permanente', but 'nous recherchons celle qui est à venir' (Hebrews xiii, 14). The way Drelincourt deals with the problem of expressing the nature of the continuing city to come is simply to reverse the images of transience he has used in the first point; the mountain torrent becomes an ever-flowing river, the consumed candle an ever-burning flame. The second point is thus merely a negative copy of the first, with its series of powerful images:

> Qu'est-ce de cette vie-là même que nous respirons icy bas? Ce n'est qu'vn soufle en nos narines & vne vapeur qui aparoit pour vn tems & puis s'éuanoüit: c'est la vanité même. Elle s'écoule comme vne rauine d'eaus. Elle court plus vite qu'vn cheual de l'oüage, ou vne barque de poste. Elle passe comme vne ombre & s'éuanoüit comme vn songe. Elle s'enuole comme la parole en l'air & se consume comme vne pensée. Le plus beau de nos iours n'est rien que fâcherie & tourment: il s'en va soudain & nous nous enuolons (Ps. 90). Comme la chandelle se consume en éclairant, ce qui entretient nôtre vie c'est cela même qui la détruit. La lumiere qui l'éclaire est vn feu qui la deuore. (pp. 349-50)

The power of this passage derives partly from the uses of anaphora ('Elle s'écoule'; 'Elle court'; 'Elle s'enuole'). Much more significant is the use of Biblical allusions and of the marginal note which refers us back to a psalm famous for its expression of just these sentiments.[8] The final image comes from another source – that emblem of the candle which we have already met.[9] But Seguiran and the other thesaurus preachers would never have attempted to sum up the moral of the emblem in a beautifully balanced sentence

---

7   Quoted from the Geneva reprint (C. 129).

8   See esp. vv. 4–7 of Psalm 90: 'For a thousand years in thy sight are but as yesterday: seeing that is past as a watch in the night./ As soon as thou scatterest them they are even as a sleep: and fade away suddenly like grass./ In the morning it is green, and groweth up: but in the evening it is cut down, dried up, and withered./ For we consume away in thy displeasure: and are afraid at thy wrathful indignation' (Prayer Book version). All this may flash through the reader's memory as well as the verse (10) which Drelincourt actually alludes to.

9   See above, Chapter 4, p. 84.

Illusion and reality

which rests, without ponderous explanations, on an awareness of the twin properties of flame: 'La lumiere qui l'éclaire est vn feu qui la deuore.' With its evident affective intent, its use of functional rhetoric, its Biblical inspiration and its preference for allusion over explanation, this passage clearly belongs to the tradition of 'orchestrated prose'. It is in fact generally the case that preachers in this tradition, as its Scriptural and classical origins would lead one to expect, are much more effective in their handling of this sort of imagery. The point emerges clearly if, in the light of the example from Drelincourt, we look at the way an earlier preacher deals with the same theme:

Les quatre elements qui se rencontrent les premiers, ne nous representent autre chose, que les quatre passions desreiglées qu'il faut dompter. La ioye desordonnée fondée sur des changeantes prosperitez representée par l'eau, soit parce qu'elle resioüit la veuë, soit parce qu'il n'y a rien de plus mobile & plus facile à s'escouler; & au lieu de celle-là ne nous resioüir qu'en Dieu. La tristesse mal fondée, c'est à dire, sur des motifs bas & terrestres d'afflictions & d'aduersitez, marquée par la terre, pource que ceste tristesse ne nous arriue que par des considerations terrestres ... La troisiesme est l'esperance mal appuyée, sur des considerations mondaines, sur des souhaits des grandeurs du siecle, & autres motifs de vanité (helas! nous n'en auons que trop) & celle là symbolisée par l'air, qui ne se dissoult pas si facilement en vapeurs & fumées, que toutes [c]es esperances se reduisent en peu de temps à neant, & au lieu de celle là n'auoir esperance qu'en Dieu. La quatriesme c'est la crainte, passion qui nous faict balancer en nos actions, & par vne folle apprehension que nous auons de la difficulté du chemin du Ciel, nous le fait le plus souuent abandonner entierement, representée par le feu qui chancelle continuellement, & ne s'esleue iamais droit, & au lieu de celle là auoir la crainte de Dieu, qui sera lors veritablement vn feu lequel embrasera nos coeurs des viues flammes de la charité, plus ardantes que ne sont les brasiers qui allument & font chanceler nos feux ordinaires.[10]

It is the very precision with which Voyer d'Argenson establishes his parallels that gives this sort of writing its flatness. Metaphors are replaced by carefully underlined symbols ('representée par l'eau'; 'marquée par la terre'; 'symbolisée par l'air'); emotional factors are reduced to an interjection ('helas! nous n'en auons que trop') and the occasional adjective ('ioye desordonnée'; 'folle apprehension'). The whole passage leaves the impression of a mechanical construction, with none of the customary remarks

---

10 Voyer d'Argenson, *L'Enneade sacrée*, 1622; quoted from C. 313, p. 97.

omitted,[11] and not a spark of novelty or vehemence to shock the reader into accepting the religious commitment he proposes.

Beneath these differences of treatment, however, the vocabulary of illusion and reality and transience consists fundamentally of a small number of images. The difficulty that many of our preachers faced was how to amplify these. Several of them, as we shall see, preferred to concentrate on one symbol of vanity which they then thoroughly explored. But a few were able to orchestrate the basic material so as to render it more immediate. We have already seen how Molinier elaborated the illusion/reality antithesis in its pure state by the use of physical imagery. The same emphasis on physicality appears in his sermon for St Lucy's day, where he is discussing the reasons for the saint's rejection of marriage and, by extension, the world:

Elle considera meurement, & par vne prudence esclairée de la lumiere du Ciel, que la beauté n'est qu'vne fleur qui se fane, la ieunesse qu'vn Printemps qui fait bien tost place à l'Hyuer, la vie qu'vne vapeur qui se dissout en vn moment, le monde qu'vne figure qui passe, & s'éuanoüit, les choses presentes qu'vne peinture en l'air, qui n'ayant que la couleur apparente, sans fondement qui la soustienne, se laisse voir, mais non prendre, ny retenir, trompant la main qui se laisse tromper aux yeux. Que le mariage promet de douceurs, & donne des amertumes, montre de fleurs, & cache des espines, apaste de miel, & saoule de fiel, & tel qui pensoit ne s'y repaistre que de laict, n'y boit que de l'absynthe.[12]

Many of the customary metaphors are there. They are, however, supplemented with images which relate directly to the body, and which are in fact graded in terms of the senses. The transition from the conventional to the novel occurs at the same point as the break-down in the sentence pattern, that is, when he begins to qualify the 'peinture en l'air' comparison. The sight is deceived by the 'couleur apparente' and in turn deceives the sense of touch. Then he switches to the sense of smell, which deceives the sense of taste. And yet, despite this firm sequence, there is no purely mechanical progression. To form his contrasts he draws on a simple antonym ('douceur . . . amertume'), a highly conventional and quasi-emblematic image ('fleurs . . . espines'), paronomasia ('miel . . . fiel'), and leaves his most violently physical image to the

11 Though he does appear to be rather bored with listing them, and takes refuge in the blanket phrase '& autres motifs de vanité'.
12 *Sermons sur les festes des saincts*, 1648 (C. 257), vol. 1, pp. 196–7.

Illusion and reality

end. A talented writer can, then, by a skilful use of balance and gradation, amplify the traditional metaphors and give them a remarkable vividness and beauty.

This sort of talent is, however, rare. More often a preacher has to supplement this basic material by introducing allied themes. For most ages one of the almost inevitable corollaries of the *vanitas* theme has been the ultimate meaninglessness of worldly honours; it was, indeed, a central motif in the medieval *danse macabre*. It is, by contrast, remarkably infrequent in the first half of the seventeenth century, when implied criticism of authority might perhaps be taken for a manifestation of a definite political attitude. Even when the cry of *sic transit gloria mundi* does make itself heard, it is singularly muted:

Ma langue N[osseigneurs] n'a garde de flestrir les dignités, dont la reuerence est imprimée dans mon coeur. I'honore trop religieusement les Saintetés, & les Eminences, les Maiestés & les Excellences, pour t[r]euuer à redire, dans ces illustres tiltres. Seulement, cette verité m'eschappe quasi malgré moy, la liberté de l'Euangile luy ouurant la porte. Si ces tiltres n'ont la foi pour fondement, la pieté pour base, la Religion pour leur premiere substance; apres tout, ce sont des couleurs trompeuses, des accidens superficiels, des grandeurs imaginaires, souuent criminelles: au moins vaines, & fantastiques; *Sepulchris similes, nil nisi nomen retinent.*[13]

This was published in 1648 and, although it was preached in Rome, it was clearly not the time for a court preacher to fulminate against royal or religious titles in a sermon on St Louis. The extraordinarily circumspect tone of the passage shows that this, at least late in our period, was not a theme on which preachers could safely draw to orchestrate their denunciations of this world.

They turned instead to subjects of a more general nature, and preferred to illustrate their teaching with images designed to instil the lesson rather by delighting than by terrifying their audiences. Most of the symbols of vanity and transience they chose are familiar to readers of contemporary literature. But here again one may repeat a point made in an earlier chapter and underline the way in which the metaphors of seventeenth-century poetry are unravelled and commented upon in seventeenth-century sermons. Take for instance the classical *exempla* Boucher uses to develop his contrast between the Virgin's exultation and the vanity of earthly joys:

13 Macé, *Panegyrique de S. Louis*, 1648 (C. 212), p. 8.

Les sages Antiens auoient raison de figurer la vanité du monde par la representation de Iunon, accompagnée de l'Iris, ou Arc-en-ciel & du Paon: Car la gloire, pompe & beauté du Paon, qui ne consiste qu'en ses plumes, diuersement esmaillées par la faueur passagere des rayons du Soleil, s'éuanoüit & se pert incontinent, si tost qu'il contemple la deformité de ses pieds, & la gloire & vanité du mondain est promptement effacée par la consideration de la triste & miserable fin à laquelle aboutissent toutes les choses sur lesquelles il fonde ses contentemens & plaisirs.

Quant à l'Iris, qu'est-ce sinon vne nuée enflée de vapeurs, & regardée du Soleil pour quelque temps, laquelle se dissipe incontinent par le vent? Et la vanité, qu'est-ce encore sinon vn amas de desirs & pensées grossieres & terrestres, lesquelles estans pour vn temps suyuies de bon-heur, nous semblent estre quelque chose d'illustre & de beau: mais qu'à la fin le vent d'vne disgrace, d'vn changement de fortune & d'estat, ou de la mort mesme, reduit tout à neant?[14]

For all the dull repetitiveness of Boucher's prose, this is a significant passage. It has become so much of a commonplace to cite this sort of symbol as characteristic of 'baroque man's' 'passion de la métamorphose jointe au déguisement, son goût de l'éphémère, de la "volubilité" et de l'inachevé'[15] that we are in danger of missing its message, namely that ephemeral magnificence is only one side of the coin. The constant and widespread reproduction of these symbols in the century after Trent depends essentially on the fresh impetus given to the classical *utile dulci* teaching at that Council. Thus even the sober Daillé can quote the 'Monstre des Poëtes changeant à tous momens de forme, & de couleur', but only to show how it teaches us 'qu'il n'y a point de dignitez au monde capables d'asseurer le repos, & le bonheur aux hommes'.[16] As with the peacock and the rainbow, so with the other key images of contemporary literature and art.

Among Protestants the vocabulary of illusion and reality has a further application: with almost no adjustments it can serve to contrast true evangelical religion with the pomp of catholicism. Eustache, in a long controversial passage, applies the traditional images:

Les honneurs du monde sont des pieges, où vous prenez plaisir de vous enlasser. Mais ils ne sont que fumée au prix de ceux que Dieu vous reserue, si vous vous adjoignez à son Eglise. Vous prisez cette pompe de ceremonies

---

14 *Les Magnificences divines*, 1620 (C. 53), pp. 96–7.
15 Jean Rousset, *Anthologie de la poésie baroque française*, 2nd edn, Paris, 1968, vol. 1, p. 6.
16 *Sermon pour le jeusne celebré à Charenton le Jeudy 21 Aoust 1636*, 1636 (C. 115), p. 49.

Illusion and reality

qui rehausse quant à l'apparence vostre Religion, mais vous trouuerez parmy nous la verité dont vous n'auez que les ombres. Vous auez des chapelles pour vos Saincts, & nous des ames pour Dieu: vous auez des images dont vous parez vos Temples materiels, & nous les vertus Chrestiennes dont nous ornons nos Temples spirituels.[17]

In the hands of Du Moulin this technique, far from generating a monotonous series of antitheses, becomes a vivid attack on the religious chameleons of the period:

Il y a vne autre sorte de feintise & tromperie en la religion, par laquelle vn homme instruit en la vraye religion, est honteux d'en faire profession, & va à la Messe contre sa conscience. De tels la religion est masquée, & leur vie est vne espece de Comedie qu'ils iouënt deuant Dieu & deuant les hommes. Ils contrefont leur langage de peur d'estre recogneus Galileens.[18]

Here we have once again a striking example of the power of a fleeting Biblical allusion: the last sentence crowns the argument that has gone before by associating those who conform outwardly to the state Church with St Peter's denial of Christ.

The other images Du Moulin uses in this rather specialized context – the mask and the stage – are of course commonplace in the wider discussions of illusion and reality. Yet these, too, are capable of misinterpretation. The theatre is an obvious symbol of worldly pomp and brilliance, but perhaps a slightly less obvious symbol of unreality and disillusion. If, however, it is viewed in the light of another concept which frequently accompanies it, its meaning becomes clearer:

Il arriue tous les iours au monde tant de changemens si inopinez, si promts & si remplis de merueilles, que quand nous y pensons il nous semble que c'est vn songe ou vne comedie qui vient d'estre representée sur le theatre.[19]

The whole point behind the insistence that 'life's a dream' is that you wake up; the play on the stage ceases to be real when you leave the theatre. There is perhaps no need to stress the importance of what is, after all, one of the great themes of European literature in this period, but it is worth while paying some attention to images which can arguably only be understood in the context of

17 *Sermon sur Matthieu xxvi, 26: 'Ceci est mon corps'*, 1648 (C. 161), p. 77.
18 *Premiere-cinquiesme decades de sermons*, 1642-3 (C. 143), part IV, p. 38.
19 Drelincourt, *La Vanité du monde, sermon sur Hebreux xiii, 14*, quoted from C. 129, p. 357.

this interpretation of the stage/dream idea. Artificial lighting is one of the most powerful agents in the creation of theatrical illusion, and it is a short step from this to the false lights of the world:

> Il se faict des flambeaux artificeusement composez de certains ingrediens, qui font paroistre à nos yeux des ombres monstrueuses; Les fausses lumieres du monde composees des graisses de ses delices & vanitez, representent mille chimeres à ceux qui les veulent quitter, pour se refugier à la Penitence.[20]

These images have a great power of suggestiveness which recalls the bewitching effect on Néron of 'Les ombres, les flambeaux, les cris et le silence' when he first sees Junie at night.[21] But in the sermons there is always the other side; the house-lights, as we might now say, are turned on and reveal the instruments of sorcery for what they are. For Daillé it is the light from the tomb of the risen Christ which shows the glitter of the world's stage to be mere tinsel.[22] For Caussin it is 'le iour de Dieu':

> Tout passe icy bas, tout s'escoule, & le meilleur mestier que l'on sçauroit faire en ce monde, c'est de bien passer & de bien couler. Il y en a qui viuent vne vie de limaçon, qui font force tirades d'argent dans la nuit du siecle: mais le soleil à son leuer faict paroistre que ce n'est que de la baue d'vn chetif animal. Tant de parures du monde, tant de fortunes d'or & d'argent, tant de pompes, tant de bruit autour des grands & des riches; mais le iour de Dieu faict voir que tout cela n'est que pourriture.[23]

This remarkable passage with its striking and unusual comparison and its carefully constructed climaxes and anticlimaxes sums up much of the substance of the imagery associated with the theme of illusion: the flux, the magnificence, the wealth, pomp and titles of the world. But it is not a self-indulgent exercise; this was preached at the funeral of a nobly born nun who had, in the neat

---

20 Camus, *Premieres homelies dominicales*, 1617, quoted from C. 73, p. 38.
21 Racine, *Britannicus*, act II, scene 1.
22 *Deux sermons ... prononcéz à Charenton, les deux Dimanches, 5. & 12. de Septembre 1647*, 1647 (C. 124), p. 73: 'Cette belle lumiere, que vous voiez sortir de son tombeau, dissipera en un instant les charmes, & les illusions du monde. Dites tout ce qu'il vous plaira, mondains, de la commodité de vos richesses, de la douceur de vos plaisirs, & de la gloire de vos grandeurs. Ce n'est apres tout, qu'une noire fumée, & une ombre legere, au prix des biens, que nôtre divin ressuscité nous presente.'
23 *Les Devoirs funebres rendus à l'heureuse memoire de Mme ... de Beauvillier*, 1634 (C. 88), p. 52.

Illusion and reality

phrase Molinier uses in a similar context, preferred 'la solidité de l'estre à la vanité du paroistre'.[24]

2. Time and eternity

If we now examine more closely one of the subordinate themes which flow from the antithetical view of existence, the same point emerges. The contrast between time and eternity possessed the added advantage of having, from the earliest antiquity, been expressed in terms of an image: the river flowing into the sea. The traditional nature of this comparison is made explicit in this passage from Du Moulin, with its clear reference to Heraclitus:

> Ceste difference est telle qu'est la difference entre la mer qui ne change iamais de place, & entre vn ruisseau qui coule, tellement que c'est tousiours vne autre eau; & comme tous les ruisseaux se perdent finalement en la mer, ainsi tout le temps est englouti par l'eternité.[25]

The remarkable thing is that our preachers for once accept the comparison as established, and spend their energies in constructing variations on it and in drawing out its moral implications. The first sermon of Du Moulin's *Troisiesme decade* illustrates this very clearly; the preacher begins to discuss time and eternity in an abstract meditation on Psalm 90, 10, but deliberately turns away from philosophizing to teaching:

> Car l'eternité ressemble à vne mer calme; mais le temps ressemble à vn ruisseau coulant: c'est tousiours vne autre eau, & celle qui est passée ne reuient plus. Ainsi c'est tousiours vn autre temps, & le present se perd dans l'abysme du passé. Mais ceste meditation n'est pas de ce lieu, & vaut mieux nous arrester aux doctrines qui naissent de la brieueté & de la misere de la vie, & du flux des annees qui nous eschappent.[26]

His subsequent exposition of these doctrines is interesting inasmuch as he does not, like most Catholic preachers, merely direct our attention to spiritual realms. There is, for the Protestant especially, a definite lesson to be practised within time itself, in our worldly conduct:

> Item la nature des iours & des annees, lesquelles estant passées, ne se r'appellent plus, & dont la perte est irrecouurable, nous aduertit de bien employer le temps, & d'en estre chiches, & ne le dissiper pas en choses inutiles.

24 *Sermons sur les festes des saincts*, 1648 (C. 257), vol. 1, p. 127.
25 *Decade de sermons*, 1637, quoted from C. 143, part I, p. 52.
26 *Troisiesme decade de sermons*, 1639 (C. 141), p. 9.

> Car l'argent perdu se peut recouurer, mais la perte du temps est irreparable. En quoy nous monstrons que nous cognoissons fort mal le prix & la valeur des choses. Car si on nous derobbe nostre argent, la colere nous transporte, & sommes outrés de douleur iusqu'au bout. Mais si quelqu'vn nous derobbe nostre temps en nous diuertissant de bonnes & sainctes actions, nous le remercions de sa compagnie agreable: cependant nous auons à rendre conte à Dieu du temps & des heures, & de l'auancement que nous y faisons en la pieté[27]

a comparison which seems to reflect the mid-century society of the Protestant merchants, with their busy lives and their meticulous accounts.

This is not what Catholic preachers took as the chief lessons to be learnt from considering the passage of time. They concentrated instead on developing the fundamental image, and often their amplifications are too obvious and too vague to inculcate a real lesson, or even to surprise the reader with an unusual insight: the mechanical drawing-out of parallels is a trap for even the best preachers of the period. But a piece from Antoine de Lor shows that the river/sea image *was* capable of imaginative development:

> Mais helas! plus nous viuons, & plus nous accumulons de vices & de mauuaises habitudes: nous faisons comme les riuieres, qui serpentent beaucoup de païs, auant que se rendre dans la mer, lesquelles quoy que belles, claires, & nettes en leur source, par ceste longue trainee de leurs eaux ne font qu'assembler vn grand tas d'immondicitez & d'ordures, qu'elles vont finalement descharger dans l'Ocean: ainsi nous sortans purs & nets du lauoir du Baptesme, plus nous viuons en ce monde, plus nous nous salissons parmy ceste grande diuersité d'affaires, de personnes, de conuersations [,] de commerces, & de negociations: si bien qu'apres auoir longuement roullé durant tout le cours de ceste vie, nous nous trouuons à l'heure de la mort bien esloignez de ceste premiere pureté, auec vne conscience trouble & chargée de la lie des affaires du monde.[28]

This is in the best tradition of the elaborated conceit: it takes a single property of the original comparison and then introduces it into another even more traditional one, grace symbolized by the waters of baptism. The resulting play is intended to delight, but the final tone is one of disillusion; the ground is prepared for the

---

27   *Ibid.*, p. 17.
28   *Sermons salutaires sur tous les jours de l'Advent*, 1623 (C. 208), pp. 224-5.

Illusion and reality

proposition of an alternative goal, the scaling of the heights of spiritual perfection.[29]

3. Meditation on death

In many of the metaphors of illusion and reality there is a point of transition between the two worlds: the stage-lights, as it were, are replaced by the full glare of the day, the river of time meets the sea of eternity. In terms of an individual's experience, this moment of revelation is death. The fact of death has two functions in the eyes of those who preach this antithetical vision of existence; it underlines the truth of the message that the visible world is merely transitory, and it provides a useful stimulus to living in conformity with the moral code. Although these two points are obviously intimately connected, it is easy to stress the first rather more than the second, and this is in fact the case with the preachers of this period, especially Catholics. Amendment of life is urged on the hearers only when the whole context of illusion and reality has been thoroughly described. Thus a number of funeral laments or sermons on death draw on the full range of the themes discussed above before coming to the moral teaching; many of them are cast in the form of meditations, in which considerations deduced from a broad spectrum of experiences lead to a series of firm resolutions. This in itself is noticeably different from the Renaissance funeral oration, which is a catalogue of the deceased hero's virtues and deeds; and it will be remembered that precisely such a shift from the subject's life to the hearer's was prescribed in the decrees of the post-Tridentine provincial councils in France.[30]

This technique, whereby the usual message that the visible world is an illusion is presented with a heightened vividness and given the stamp of evident truth by reason of the presence of death, receives its fullest expression in this period in Molinier's

---

29 Although these examples are characteristic of meditations on the subject of time in the sermons of this period, there is an interesting exception. Sermon 18 of Nicolas Caussin's *Buisson ardent*, 1647 (C. 89), contains a long passage on the similarities between time and God, cast in the language of metaphysical speculation. There is mention of a river – the Nile – but Caussin concentrates his attention on its hidden source rather than on its flow.

30 See above, Chapter 3, p. 45.

Oraison funèbre de M. Pons de Bardion.[31] Molinier begins by rejecting the static view of the funeral oration as a literary monument to the dead, and insists on the lesson to be learnt by the mourners. In the old orations, he says, 'nous pleurions la mort des autres, & ne meditions pas la nostre pour nous y preparer. Tous ces objects s'estoient arrestez à nos yeux sans penetrer & passer iusque dans nos coeurs' (p. 459). The meditative nature of what follows is expressed in his use of first person verbs: at first *nous* and then *je* become the subject of an increasingly personal and urgent enquiry into the frailty of human nature. Similarly, as the meditation becomes more personal, its scope is enlarged. The first stage consists largely of thoughts connected with death. Transience is expressed in rather conventional terms, but he quickly moves to a series of sharply pointed antitheses on the subject of the dissolution of magnificence into nothingness:

Aujourd'hui sain, demain mort; aujourd'huy couuert de musc, demain puant de corruption; aujourd'huy vestu de soye, demain d'vn suaire; aujourd'huy dans vn carrosse, demain dans vne biere: aujourd'huy triomphes, demain funerailles; aujourd'huy sur vn tribunal ou sur vn throne, demain dessous la terre, n'est-ce pas la fable que ioüent les hommes, voire les Princes, & les Roys, sur le theatre de ce bas Vniuers? Toutes choses passent, grandeurs & dignitez, pompes & richnessess, estats & benefices. Rien n'est ça bas de stable, que l'instabilité; rien ne s'y trouue de permanent, que l'inconstance, rien n'y demeure d'immortel, que la mort qui faict mourir tout, & ne meurt iamais elle-mesme. (p. 462)

This is clearly the place for the great commonplaces, the equality of all conditions in death,[32] and the comparison with the stage.[33]

31 First printed in the *Mystere de la Croix, et de la Redemption du monde*, 1628 (C. 241), pp. 376–400. Page references are to the 1635 edition (C. 242). Many of the points Molinier makes are touched on individually in the context of death by the other preachers referred to in my next few footnotes.

32 *Cf.* Drelincourt, *La Vanité du monde, sermon sur Hebreux xiii*, 14, 1639 (C. 129), p. 351. Valladier, *Harangue funebre de Henry le Grand*, 1610 (C. 297), pp. 89–90, builds up a very similar series of antitheses.

33 Cf. Hersent, *Le Sacré Monument dedié à la memoire de . . . Louis le Juste*, 1643 (C. 175), oration 3, p. 4: 'D'ailleurs la vertu, qui dans la plupart des hommes est masquée par les apparances trompeuses du bien, est ordinairement sans masque & sans dissimulation à l'heure de la mort. C'est lors, que la scene de nos actions, déguisée par tant de personnages faux & affectez, rend au theatre de nostre vie, sa face veritable & naturelle.' A very clear statement of the idea expounded above that death is the moment which confirms the truth of a preacher's metaphors.

In the second section Molinier casts his net wider and produces a variation on the *coeli enarrant* theme:

portant mes yeux sur toute la face de ce monde corruptible, ie contemple en toutes chose l'image de la mort, & descouure par tout, les embusches qu'elle me dresse. (*ibid.*)

Like all meditations on this theme, the analysis follows a highly schematized view of the natural world and man's place in it. The element of water is an obvious source of comparisons, the sky can only furnish a rather strained parallel with its counterpart, the earth, and he quickly introduces the macrocosm/microcosm parallel:

Ie voy tout l'Vniuers en branle continuel, & toy ô homme, petit monde, n'es-tu pas emporté par vn cours, qui n'a pas d'arrest? (*ibid.*)

The schematic break-down continues with the seasons, the ages of man and the wonders of the ancient world. The tone of meditative soliloquy is intensified in the conclusion to this enquiry:

Qu'attends-ie doncques? Que fay-ie? Quelle est ma folie? Tout ce qui est au monde, toute la Nature, le Ciel, la terre, l'eau, les fleurs, toutes les creatures me representent l'image de ma fragilité; la raison me l'inculque, l'example me la fait toucher au doigt; l'experience journaliere ne permet pas que i'en doute: & cependent ie n'escoute pas, ce que toutes choses me preschent! (p. 466)

It is only at this point that Molinier introduces the other side of the antithesis, lays emphasis on the solidity and eternity of Heaven, denounces worldliness, and provides an alternative: good works are the key to this real world, they alone matter at death:

La vraye vie gist en l'obseruation des commandemens de Dieu, vie qui n'a pas de fin, vie qui ne craint pas la mort, vie qui accompagne l'ame saincte, quand elle sort de ce monde, & passe auec elle du temps à l'eternité. (p. 469)

Now, although this full-dress recital of the meditation on mortality may seem straightforward, it is rarely stated in as complete a form when the subject of death is discussed. And yet it is, I would argue, the context in which we must set the more familiar manifestations of this theme in this period. What is often spoken of as the obsession with death at this time[34] is in fact an obsession with conversion and amendment of life. Georges de La Tour's

[34] See, for example, Madeleine Maurel, 'Fastes mortuaires et déploration. Essai sur la signification du baroque funèbre dans la poésie française', *XVIIe Siècle*, LXXXII (1969), pp. 37–54.

Madeleine au miroir is not indulging a morbid taste for the macabre as she fingers the skull on her table; she is attempting to experience that sense of the immediacy of death which precedes, in the meditative scheme, the resolution to amend one's life. The religious artists of the early seventeenth century are interested in the ghoulish chiefly as a potent moral stimulus.

As it happens, vivid descriptions of corruption are relatively rare in our pulpit oratory. (The older sort of funeral oration prefers to show the hero on his deathbed calmly preparing to meet his Maker,[35] while morally orientated works tend to generalize in the manner described above.) Of the few examples there are, the most striking again comes from the pen of Molinier, who is incomparably the best preacher on death in our period. Significantly, it occurs not in a funeral oration, but in a sermon for Ash Wednesday:

Proposons nous maintenant de descendre à la lumiere d'vn grand nombre de flambeaux dans la profonde, & épouuantable obscurité d'vn grand, & vaste Charnier, où soient assemblez tous les hommes, & femmes qui sont morts depuis Adam iusqu'au dernier qui meurt en ce moment que ie vous parle. Helas que voyons-nous Messieurs? Que voyons-nous? ie fremis à cet objet, & le poil me dresse en teste; ici ie voy de grands amas de terre relante, & pourrie; là des tas grouïllans de vers, & de corruption; là des squelettes arides, qu'il ne faut que toucher du doigt, ou souffler de la bouche pour les faire voler en cendres: ici se presentent des faces aualees, à qui ne reste plus que l'ombre, & la trace sechee de la figure humaine [,] les traits en estant perdus; là sont plantees des carcasses hideuses, où ne paroissent que les trous des yeux, les bouches qui rechignent, les os secs, les costes nuës, & les troncs decharnez, qui se soustiennent, pour nous faire & compassion, & horreur, sur l'épine du dos. Voilà ce qui est demeuré des Philosophes, des Poëtes, des Orateurs, des Dames, des Princesses, des Euesques, des Cardinaux, des Roys, des Monarques, des Pontifes, de toutes les grandeurs que tous les âges ont produit; voilà ce qui nous reste de la pompe de tous les siecles iusques à ce moment. Où sommes-nous, Messieurs? dormons-nous, ou veillons-nous? sont-ce des illusions qui se presentent deuant nous, ou bien des choses reelles? Ce Monde est-il quelque chose d'existant, & de veritable, & non plustost vn songe qui nous abuse, vn phantosme qui nous deçoit, vne ombre qui trompe nos yeux, & s'enfuit de nos mains? *In imagine pertransit homo; Praeterit figura huius Mundi; Transierunt omnia illa sicut umbra.*[36]

35 E.g. Bosquier, *Harangue funebre sur la mort de Messire Charles de Croy*, 1612 (C. 50); Boucher, *Oraison funebre de . . . Emery de Barbezieres*, 1609 (C. 52), *Oraison funebre sur le trespas de . . . Charlotte du Gué*, 1622 (C. 55); Coton, *Oraison funebre sur le trespas de feu M. de Villeroy*, 1618 (C. 105); Humblot, *Discours funebres . . . de feu . . . le Duc de Montpensier, et de . . . Pere Ange de Joyeuse*, 1608 (C. 179).

36 *Sermons pour toutes les feries, et dimanches du Caresme*, 1641 (C. 253), vol. 1, pp. 65-6.

This, in the meditative scheme into which the theme of death is so often fitted, is the 'composition of place'. The hearer's sense of immediacy is heightened, here as in the oration for Pons de Bardion, by the use of first-person verbs which create an almost conspiratorial bond between the guide and the 'Messieurs' he leads – 'à la lumiere d'vn grand nombre de flambeaux' – in the almost sacrilegious descent to the charnel-house. The conventional major themes ('Voilà ce qui est demeuré des Philosophes . . .') are interspersed with his personal, physical reactions ('le poil me dresse en teste'). An addition like 'iusqu'au dernier qui meurt en ce moment que ie vous parle', coming unexpectedly into the normal evocation of the historically dead, shocks the hearer into realizing the closeness of the subject to himself and his contemporaries. But for all the qualities of this description, Molinier does not linger over it; the underlying message emerges clearly, heightened by the dreamlike situation he has induced in the imaginations of his audience: 'Messieurs, dormons-nous, ou veillons-nous?' Meditation on death is not an isolated theme, but an integral part of the whole message of our preachers.

This is also true of Protestants, but, as with the theme of time and eternity, the emphases are rather different. Death is regarded mainly as the entry into a better life, and the lament over our mortality is correspondingly subdued. For Du Moulin, in fact, a consideration of death is merely an added goad to the practice of piety, a sort of audit in the spiritual life:

La brieueté de ses iours & la contrarieté des temps, & l'inimitié du monde, l'aduertira de racheter le temps, & empoigner les occasions, & se seruir des moyens que Dieu lui presente pour s'auancer au chemin du salut . . . & pour se haster il se demandera souuent conte de son auancement, quel profit il a fait en la pieté depuis tant de temps que Dieu l'instruit par sa parole: quel amas il a fait de bonnes oeuures: & quel thresor d'aumosnes: s'il est plus patient en iniures qu'il n'estoit l'annee passee: si ses prieres sont plus ardentes qu'auparauant, & moins diuerties de pensees vaines & estrangeres.[37]

The absence of exhortations to inner conversion gives the clue: Protestant preaching in France is mostly restricted to the already converted, who may be lukewarm but still think of themselves as orientated in the right way. There is a greater need to confirm the elect than to remind the worldly of the error of their ways: that is the duty of an established Church. Nevertheless, in some ways the

37 *Premiere-cinquiesme decades de sermons*, 1642–3 (C. 143), part IV, p. 87.

later Protestants seem to prefigure the more general reaction against the physical depictions of decay which characterizes the pulpit in the second half of the seventeenth century. When Daillé preaches on death,[38] it is entirely to reassure his people that they need not fear it and that it should be an object of joyful expectation. This is one of many places in Daillé's work where, by modification of or even reaction against the received ideas of the early seventeenth century, he points to later modes of thought.

4. Perspectives and reflections

The themes and imagery associated with a basically religious antithetical view of existence overflow into more general fields. A deliberately cultivated and constantly stimulated awareness of the illusory nature of appearances colours one's appreciation of the physical world, even where there is no explicit urge to conversion or amendment to be drawn from the perception. The natural world is introduced into sermons largely through comparisons, and in many of these it is the importance of scale and perspective that is stressed. Bertaut underlines the commonplace character of these perceptions when, wanting to bring out the point that it is man's sin which makes the devout life seem so hard to attain, he remarks that 'nous mesmes le disons à toute heure sans y penser'. For, he goes on,

> quand nous iettons les yeux en-haut, & principalement quand nous considerons que la moindre estoile du Ciel est plus grande que toute le terre: & que ce qu'elle nous semble si petite, c'est la merueilleuse distance qu'il y a d'icy iusques au Firmament, où elles sont attachees.[39]

Astronomy also provides a comparison for Camus when he wants, oddly enough, to show how the signs of the Last Days will be seen, not objectively in Nature, but by the eye of faith:

> Comment! les estoiles peuuent-elles tomber des Cieux? nullement, mais elles sembleront cheoir, fallace de la veuë; car, en soustrayant visiblement leurs clartés, elles seront estimees tomber, comme ces fausses constellations que le grand Poëte nomme, *Cadentia sydera caelo*.
>
> > Ainsi le baston droit paroist courbé dans l'eau.
> > Ainsi en nauigeant nous semblent cheminer les riuages.[40]

38 *Exposition de la divine Epître de S. Paul aux Filippiens en XXIX sermons*, 1644 (C. 120), vol. 1, sermon 5.
39 *Sermons sur les principales festes de l'année*, 1613 (C. 26), p. 241.
40 *Premieres homelies dominicales*, 1617, quoted from C. 73, p. 5.

Illusion and reality 139

Typically, he reinforces his explanation with two other frequently recurrent observations. There is even some evidence that this interest in the influence of scale on our perception of the external world was written into sermons for its own sake. Seguiran uses a navigational parallel to expound at length how God appears distant to sinners but close to the righteous:

> ainsi que ceux qui cinglent en haute mer, de loin les hautes montagnes leur semblent petites pour estre grandement esloignees, & si le mont Olympe estoit sur la mer, de loin il ne monstreroit rien: mais faisant voile sur la mer & approchant auprés, il esleuera ses cornes & se fera voir & apparoistre grand comme il est: de mesme est-il de Dieu qui consideré par les pecheurs & par ceux qui s'arrestent sur ceste terre leur semble tres-petit: mais laissant le monde & ce qui est du peché pour s'esleuer à la cognoissance de Dieu, alors Dieu qui leur sembloit petit, paroist fort grand & admirable.[41]

However, he immediately reverses this argument by insisting that 'tant plus l'homme s'approche de Dieu, tant plus il se recule de luy', and weakly attempts to overcome this contradiction with the words 'laissant à part ceste explication'. The 'explication' appears to have been inserted merely for the sort of pleasure an illustration of perspective and its tricks might afford the audience.[42]

This interest in perspective naturally leads preachers to the problems of painting; here there is the added curiosity of the relationship between the artistic depiction and the natural reality – which is the more real? – and the difficulties inherent in the painter's own limitations. From this web of complexities Bertaut constructs a convincing comparison with the preacher's inability to describe the perfections of the Virgin:

> Il y a des beautez accomplies qu'on ne sçauroit exprimer par le peinture, mais qu'on trahit & diminuë en les voulant pourtraire. Vn Nain qui s'efforceroit de representer le Geant Polipheme, auroit beau se dresser sur ses orteils, & comme se voulant mal de sa petitesse, tascher à se monstrer plus grand que soy mesme, il amoindriroit tousiours la grandeur du Cyclope en la cuidant exprimer.[43]

---

41 *Sermons doctes et admirables sur les Evangilles des Dimanches & Festes de l'anéé*, 1612 (C. 268), p. 418.
42 A somewhat similar example occurs in Le Faucheur's *Trois sermons*, 1632 (C. 197), pp. 158–60, where the preacher expounds a fairly simple point about God's prescience by means of an elaborate analogy with the limited perspective of a soldier marching in a long column.
43 *Sermons sur les principales festes de l'année*, 1613 (C. 26), pp. 65–6.

Even the sober Amyraut crowns a discussion of the entangled problems of moral theology with a reference to trick paintings:

> Car il en est de certaines affaires à peu près comme de ces portraits à deux visages, qui nous monstrent vne face hideuse & épouuantable d'vn costé, & si nous venons à changer vn peu la situation dans laquelle nous les contemplions, ils nous en presentent vne autre pléne d'agrément & de bonne grace.[44]

Painting, then, in this period of *trompe l'oeil*, seems almost to become a symbol of complexity. But the problems which concern these ingenious minds do not only involve the image or its creator; the eye of the beholder is a third factor in these intricate webs of illusion. In one of Lor's parallels this point is introduced first in the prosaic terms of ophthalmic illness, but then, as he draws the two parts of the comparison together, with the more unusual and more arresting image of distorting spectacles, 'les fausses lunettes'.[45]

This fascination with depiction and the distortions of depiction extends to the observation of mirrors and the reflected image. Very often a lengthy discussion on this subject follows a reference to Genesis i, 27: 'So God created man in his own image.' In his exposition of this text Du Moulin draws again the distinction between art and nature and emphasizes the reflection of movement:

> Mais il y a deux sortes d'images. Il y a des images immobiles, comme sont les statuës & les portraits des visages en tableaux. Et des images mouuantes, comme sont les images qui se voyent és eaux coyes & es miroirs, qui representent les mouuemens & les actions des personnes. Telle est l'image de Dieu à laquelle il a creé la creature raisonnable, afin qu'elle imite les actions de Dieu & se forme à son exemple.[46]

---

44 *Sermons sur quelques sentences de l'Ecriture*, 1647, quoted from C. 16, p. 84.

45 *Sermons salutaires sur tous les jours de l'Advent*, 1623 (C. 208), pp. 362-3: 'Tout ainsi que les yeux offensés de ce genre de maladies, que les Medecins nomment Ophthalmies, ont les operations de la veuë tellement troublées, qu'ils ne pouuent iuger naifuement des couleurs, tous objects leurs [sic] paroissant iaunes & rouges: de mesme l'homme transporté de passion, & de cholere ne se peut rien representer qu'a trauers les fausses lunettes de ceste violente & impetueuse passion, qui luy faict voir tousiours les choses plus grandes qu'elles ne sont en effect: *Et sicut per nebulam corpora, sic per iram res maiores videntur*, comme dict Plutarque.'

46 *Deuxiesme decade de sermons*, 1638, quoted from C. 143, part II, p. 103.

Illusion and reality

It is, however, one of the differences between the sermons and the poetry of this period that the reflective qualities of water with its connotations of flux and disruption are mentioned less often than are looking-glasses; attention is thereby diverted to a static relationship between object and image which can then be explored. It is a favourite device for illustrating the operations of God through the saints.[47] Boucher develops a (somewhat unscientific) conceit whereby the Virgin, as a concave mirror, 'magnifies' the Lord, at the same time focussing the divine light on her devotees, who are consumed by the flame of God's love.[48] Seguiran explains the feast of the Purification in similar terms:

Ceste Vierge imaculee (qui est appellee par son Espoux, *Speculum sine macula*) auoit receu en sa conception vne diuine lumiere, ie dis le fils de Dieu, (que le vieillard Simeon appelle lumiere, *Lumen ad reuelationem gentium*) qu'elle auoit conceu en son ventre, & voicy qu'auiourd'huy, au moyen de l'opacité de l'humilité, elle renuoye à Dieu ceste lumiere de grace qu'elle auoit receu de luy, *Tulerunt illum in Hierusalem vt sisterent eum Domino.*[49]

Seguiran cleverly extends this conceit in a sermon on the Feast of SS. Peter and Paul.[50] The traditional text for this day's sermon was Genesis i, 16: 'Fecitque Deus duo luminaria magna.' Seguiran shows that this applies to the Apostles since they were 'des miroüers tournez vers ce Soleil de Iustice, vers celuy de qui toute la lumiere procede', but is able too to bring out their humanity by seeing their weaknesses as precisely the opacity which made them able to reflect the glory of God. The comparison, which clearly owes a great deal to the preacher's delight in the complexities of

---

47 It is in Europe generally at this time also a common motif in the visual depiction of saints, particularly the ceiling frescoes of saints in glory. The best-known example is probably Padre Pozzo's *Glory of St Ignatius* in the Gesù, where one of the rays emanating from Christ through Ignatius is reflected downwards by means of a mirror held by an angel. Continuing the theme right into the German Rococo, F. J. Spiegler's remarkable *Inspiration of St Benedict* of 1751 in the church of Zwiefalten (Baden-Württemberg) shows a ray of light from the Virgin reflected off a painting of the Virgin and Child on to the heart of the saint, whence it splits up into tongues of fire which cascade over the other saints of the Order below.
48 *Les Magnificences divines*, 1620 (C. 53), pp. 35–40.
49 *Sermons doctes et admirables sur les Evangilles des Dimanches & Festes de l'anneé*, 1612 (C. 268), p. 77.
50 *Ibid.*, pp. 585–6.

reflection, is given a final twist to extract a moral lesson for the congregation:

> nous sommes tous miroüers, si nous tournons vers Dieu nous sommes Dieux, si vers le Diable nous sommes diable.[51]

The quasi-scientific observations of natural distortions and reflections were in fact taken as the basis of metaphysical speculations, especially in the debate about substance and accidents so central to eucharistic controversy. In one of his controversial sermons Valladier draws together, to show the superiority of the eye of faith over the physical eye, a wide range of images which recur again and again in this period – the rainbow, the dove's neck, the 'broken' stick in water, the mirror:

> Il n'y a rien de plus trompeur, & de plus variable que le sens, que la phantasie, mesme que la raison de l'homme. Il me semble à voir le bel Arc en ciel, qu'il y ait de belles couleurs, & il n'y en a pour tout point, ce ne sont que refractions, ou reflechissements des rayons solaires reuerberez en la nuée opacque, & diaphane, comme vn miroüer: tout ainsi que nous le voyons par experience au col terse, & ploy de la Colombe bigarée, & rio-piollée de mille couleurs apparentes. Ce baston dedans l'eau me semble rompu, & le tirant, ie le trouue tout droict: c'estoit l'espece du bout, qui estoit dans l'eau receuë par le diaphane terminé de l'eau, & renuoyée à mon oeil de l'endroict de l'eau, où elle estoit receuë: tout de mesme que le miroüer me renuoye l'image de ce qui luy est opposé à droite ligne pyramidale: nos sens sont esgarez, nostre veuë emoussée, l'imagination volage, la raison fallacieuse, & sophistique: il ne faut qu'vn Lutin pour nous tourner, & amuser le cerueau de mille, & mille phantosmes, qui n'auront autre existence qu'en nostre imagination.[52]

There is, however, here a most important addition: the mention of a 'Lutin' introduces the new idea of positive interference with our perceptions.

5. Metamorphosis, magic and false gods

Metamorphosis, understood as the deliberate provocation of visual changes, is used widely in the sermons as a literary technique closely allied to the conceit. Thus we have already seen passages where tears are not only like pearls, but actually become them.[53] When similes

---

51 The comparison is used similarly by Protestants, e.g. Du Moulin on the beatific vision in *Cinquième decade de sermons*, 1642, quoted from C. 143, part V, p. 95: 'L'effect de ceste veuë est que par icelle les ames bienheureuses sont transformees en la ressemblance de Dieu, en mesme fa[ç]on qu'vn miroir exposé au Soleil s'embrase & deuient en quelque façon vn petit Soleil.'
52 *Les Divines Paralleles de la saincte Eucharistie*, 1613 (C. 302), pp. 112–13.
53 Molinier's *Nostre Dame de Pitié*, above p. 95.

are thus translated into reality – or the reality of the text, at least – and emphasis is placed upon the change effected, it is normally in order to express the miraculous power of God: these changes are miracles. For this reason the most striking occurrences of this technique are found in sermons on the saints. Often the miraculous nature of the event, precisely because it may appear merely metaphorical, is supported by Biblical references. Thus the conversion of Mary Magdalene:

Si iamais vous n'auez peu apprendre cest admirable metamorphose, de laquelle parle le Prophete Royal Dauid, disant; *Qui conuertit petram in stagna aquarum, & rupem in fontes aquarum*: maintenant vous la pourrez apprendre, puisqu'en ce iour ce changement & ceste metamorphose se voit & se recognoist clairement en la personne de la Magdaleine. Veritablement ce changement est estrange, de dire qu'vne pierre soit conuertie en plusieurs fontaines d'eauë, & de faict il n'y a personne de vous qui ne s'en estonne: mais bien plus admirable est le changement & la metamorphose d'vne ame pecheresse conuertie en saincteté, en graces & en merites, & d'vn coeur plus dur que les marbres, que les rochers, ny que les pierres changé & metamorphosé en torrens de larmes.[54]

The mythical metamorphoses of antiquity, too, are used as this kind of support. In Molinier's account of St Stephen's martyrdom, mention of physical changes enables him to make more concrete the workings of grace, thereby producing that kind of jewelled painting which is the hallmark of his style:

on leue les pierres, il éleue son coeur; on le lapide, il prie; on luy iette de caillous, il reçoit des couronnes; & au contraire qu'vn certain fleuue nommé Sylarus, qui change en rochers les rameaux, & les branches des arbres qui tombent dans ses eaux:
    quo gurgite tradunt
 Duritiem lapidum mersis inolescere ramis.

Il change par sa constance les pierres qui touchent son sacré sang en palmes, & en lauriers.[55]

The life of Christ naturally abounds with material for this sort

---

54 Seguiran, *Sermons doctes et admirables sur les Evangilles des Dimanches & Festes de l'annéé,* 1612 (C. 268), p. 673.
55 *Sermons sur les festes des saincts,* 1648 (C. 257), vol. 1, p. 278.

of elaboration. The Transfiguration is an obvious example,[56] and the Resurrection provides Bertaut with an opportunity for using this technique to contrast the crucified and the risen body:

sortant du sepulchre ... il semble que ce fust le Soleil, qui contre sa nature, se leuast à minuict, sans estre deuancé d'aucune aurore, non qu'il ne portast tousiours les euidentes ouuertures des cinq plus grandes playes qu'il auoit receuës en la Croix: mais elles-mesmes, à l'heure luy seruoient d'ornement, comme elles sont encore, & surmontant en clarté le feu lumineux des plus excelens pyropes & rubis de la terre, versoient alors plus de rayons & de lumieres, que n'agueres elles n'auoient épandu de sang.[57]

Contrast, as one might expect, is expressly cultivated in those sermons which allude to famous metamorphoses; as with the conversion of Mary Magdalene, it heightens the reader's awareness of the power of God. The story, from 2 Macchabees i, of how the sacred fire was found in the muddy well is repeated again and again, often to show the transforming power of God's grace.[58]

Metamorphosis – both the idea and the word – is then closely associated with power. It need not be God's; Bertaut includes among Henri IV's virtues his ability to 'changer par vne Royalle Metamorphose, auec le charme de ses bienfaits, ses propres ennemis en fideles seruiteurs'.[59] But a distinction is generally made between divine and other agents, whether human or supernatural. Only God's metamorphoses can be called miracles. The point at which this distinction touches the general theme of illusion and reality is in the doctrine of transubstantiation, according to which it is the substance of the bread which becomes the body of Christ, not the accidents – a miracle which is perceived by the eye of faith while deceiving the senses. It is in this context that most mentions of miracles proper occur:

---

56 E.g. in Voyer d'Argenson's *Enneade sacrée*, 1622 (quoted from C. 313, p. 111), it is called 'ceste belle metamorphose que vous faictes auiourd'huy en vous mesmes, rendant transparente vostre saincte humanité'.
57 *Sermons sur les principales festes de l'année*, 1613 (C. 26), p. 6.
58 To take only one preacher, this story occurs in the work of Camus at least six times. See *Premieres homelies dominicales*, 1617 (1619 edn, C. 73), p. 10; *Homelies spirituelles sur le Cantique des Cantiques*, 1620 (C. 82), pp. 90, 142, 243, 387; *Homelies panegyriques de Sainct Charles Borromée*, 1623 (C. 86), p. 9.
59 *Discours funebre sur la mort du feu Roy*, 1610 (C. 25), p. 6.

Illusion and reality

Confessez vne fois convaincus de la verité que celuy qui a basty le monde de rien, Adam de boue, Eve d'vne coste, que celuy qui a changé les eaux en sang, les verges en serpens, les rochers en fontaines, & les femmes en rochers comme celle de Loth, que le mesme peut bien aussi changer, conuertir, & transubstancier la substance de pain & de vin en la substance de son corps & de son sang.[60]

This general confusion of the senses can be expressed in terms of metamorphosis, as in this extraordinary exclamatory passage in one of Camus's *Homelies eucharistiques* of 1618:

ô laict vous estes du sang blanchi! ô sang vous estes du laict rougy! ô qui pourroit en faire vn meslange pareil à ce chaudeau du S. Espoux qui nous inuite à boire son vin auec son laict (*Cant.* 5), & à receuoir le miel de sa diuinité, auec la cire de son humanité, mon ame, te pasmes tu pas emmy ces sacrez transports?[61]

In Valladier's *Divines Paralleles de la saincte Eucharistie* there is constant mention of miracles, many of them exceptionally ingenious. All this is justified by seeing the Eucharist as the 'chef d'oeuure de toutes les Sainctetez, & de tous les miracles que iamais ce grand Dieu a faict de sa main'.[62]

The distinction becomes more interesting when applied negatively: those metamorphoses which are not miracles must be the work of other powers. Besse gives a fairly comprehensive list:

Nature vous pouuez bien faire faire sortir des Ecclipses dans les Cieux, des tonnerres, des feux, des foudres en l'air, des Euripes dans la mer, des monstres sur la terre, & autres sortes de merueilles: mais non pas iamais de miracles. Demons vous pouuez bien mettre en armes les Elements, eschauffer les tempestes, donner la poste aux vents, faire boulionner l'Ocean, & remuer les montagnes: Mais au partir de là ce ne sont que merueilles, & non pas des miracles.[63]

More often, however, the frame of reference is narrowed down to the more spectacular manifestations of the supernatural, especially

---

60 Besse, *Premieres conceptions theologiques sur le Caresme*, 1604 (C. 27), vol. 2, fol. 101^r.
61 C. 78, p. 91.
62 1613 (C. 302), p. 3.
63 *Premieres conceptions theologiques sur le Caresme*, 1604 (C. 27), vol. 1, fol. 68^r.

witchcraft and lycanthropy.[64] Many of the sermons in Valladier's *Saincte Philosophie de l'ame* attack the notion that astrology and magic have any real effect on the soul, but abound with fascinating descriptions of their other effects. Werewolves, again, do not suffer from any 'estranges metamorphoses de l'ame', but from a 'remuëment & alteration de fantaisie' (p. 210); they are not really seen by others, who are suffering from 'apparitions fantasques, estant troublée l'imagination ou naturellement, ou par art diabolique' (p. 208). Lor also inclines to the latter theory,[65] whereas Camus, on the other hand, favours a more human origin, for he speaks of 'la lycanthropie de ces abominables Magiciens'.[66] Nevertheless, all the authorities are making the same point, namely that this sort of phenomenon, however dangerous and hair-raising, is part of the world of physical illusions.

From this it is a short step back to the moral exhortation which lies always beneath these themes, even in their most fantastic manifestations. To know that it is the devil who sends distractions in prayer is, for Du Moulin, a powerful aid to concentration.[67] Molinier strikes a note calculated to bring the nature of temptation more closely home to a superstitious audience when he speaks of the sinner's eyes – again the visual illusion – as 'aueuglez, ou charmez, par la tentation'.[68] Camus, using the same technique in

---

64 A great deal of attention has recently been paid to the vogue of witchcraft in this period, and there is a useful discussion and review in K. Thomas, *Religion and the Decline of Magic*, London, 1971. Robert Mandrou, in his *Magistrats et sorciers en France au XVIIe siècle*, Paris, 1968, pp. 88–91, devotes a section to 'l'autorité de l'église'. Although contemporary preachers are by no means as obsessed with the subject as he claims, the connexion which he makes between witchcraft and the panoply of the law emerges clearly. Valladier, *La Saincte Philosophie de l'ame*, 1614 (C. 304), p. 204, is most explicit on this point: 'Nos Parlements depuis quelques annees en ça n'en ont eu que trop d'exemples: i'en ay veu iuger vn à Bordeaux, confez & conuaincu par arrest donné l'an 1602. arrest solennel & presidental, prononcé en robbe rouge par Monsieur d'Asys premier President, d'vn ieune garçon Perigourdin, qui auoit desja deuoré deux filles, & descouuert sur la troisiesme, qu'il auoit entamée.'
65 *Sermons salutaires sur tous les jours de l'Advent*, 1623 (C. 208), p. 130.
66 *Premieres homelies festives*, 1617, quoted from C. 75, p. 352.
67 *Sermon de la priere en temps d'affliction*, 1624 (C. 136), p. 146.
68 *Sermons pour toutes les feries et dimanches du Caresme*, 1641 (C. 253), vol. 1, p. 886.

Illusion and reality 147

reverse and giving new life to an old cliché, castigates impurity as 'ce vice miserable qui change l'homme en beste: ce que les Anciens nous ont appris sous la fable des breuuages de Circé'.[69]

This reference to Circe indicates a further way in which our preachers use the more diabolical extensions of the illusion and reality theme. It enables them to condemn the gods of antiquity as being 'unreal', while at the same time giving some place in their sermons to the pagan mythology in which they were so thoroughly steeped. There is a wide range of attitudes to this subject. At one extreme the Protestants quite simply dismiss the pagan gods as devilish idols, and do not indulge in recounting their exploits. Du Moulin, for example, straightforwardly opposes the truth of Christianity

aux faux Dieux forgez ou deifiez par les hommes, & aux Idoles desquelles sainct Paul, en la premiere aux Corinthiens chapitre dixiéme dit, que l'idole n'est rien, pource que leur diuinité & leur valeur ne consiste qu'en l'imagination des hommes.[70]

Eudemare, though not a Protestant, includes the Magi among the worshippers of Satan.[71] But more often such references take the form of detailed stories. Valladier notes how the devil can affect the imagination:

par changement de l'obiect, ce qui se peut ... le cachant soudainement, & en supposant à l'instant vn autre, comme au lieu d'Iphigenie, que son pere sacrifioit à Diane, Satan suppose vne biche, faisant ainsi accroire qu'elle auoit esté changee en biche.[72]

To a great extent this manner of introducing the pagan myths solves the problem posed by the works on preaching theory of how to remain faithful to the Christian message while supplying the classical allusions expected by the audience and intended as proof of the preacher's culture. The theorists and reformers had thundered against the *feintise des poètes*; for a preacher like Molinier, this merely provides a convenient verb to introduce a story:

69 *Homelies spirituelles sur le Cantique des Cantiques*, 1620 (C. 82), p. 227.
70 *Cinquième decade de sermons*, 1642, quoted from C. 143, part V, p. 11.
71 *Tapisseries sacrées*, 1617 (C. 159), pp. 125ff.
72 *La Saincte Philosophie de l'ame*, 1614 (C. 304), p. 631. Cf. *ibid.*, p. 216, where he applies the same ideas to Circe and the companions of Ulysses.

les Poëtes voulant exprimer la force de la douleur en tels sujets, ont *feint* vne Niobe, qui pleurant la mort de ses fils fut changée en pierre; mais, *disent-ils*, perdant sa forme elle ne perdit pas pourtant son dueil, & ne se contentant pas d'auoir pleuré mere, pleuroit encore rocher.[73]

In its most subtly developed variations, then, the theme of illusion and reality proves to be a fertile method of 'finding matter'. The antithesis between the things of God and the things of this world is discerned in the whole spectrum of human and literary experience.

---

73 *Le Mystere de la Croix, et de la Redemption du monde*, 1628, quoted from C. 242, p. 475. My italics.

7
Themes and their imagery (ii)
'Nature, that universal and publick Manuscript'[1]

It is not easy for post-Romantic readers to appreciate the role of Nature in early-seventeenth-century literature. It was difficult enough even a generation or so later, as we discover from Eachard's satirical portrait of the metaphysical preacher:

> It seems also not very easie, for a Man in his Sermon to learn his parishioners how to dissolve Gold; of what, and how the stuff is made. Now, to ring the Bells, and call the People on purpose together, would be but a blunt business; but to do it neatly, and when no Body look'd for it, that's the rarity and art of it. Suppose then, that he takes for his text that of *St. Matthew, Repent ye, for the Kingdom of God is at hand.* Now tell me, Sir, do you not perceive the Gold to be in a dismal fear, to curl and quiver at the first reading of these words? It must come in thus: *The blots and blurrs of our sins must be taken out by the* Aqua-fortis *of our Tears; to which* Aqua-fortis *if you put a fifth part of* Sal-Amoniack, *and set them in a gentle heat, it makes* Aqua-Regia, *which dissolves Gold.* And now 'tis out. Wonderfull are the things that are to be done by the help of metaphors and similitudes![2]

Amusing though this may be, it is not much of a distortion or gross parody of the sort of thing one reads in sermons; it even points out the key function of metaphors and similitudes, which are indeed almost always the vehicles of this sort of information. What enables Eachard to turn alchemical preaching into an object of ridicule, however, is his isolation of the parallel from its context. This chapter will attempt in part to describe that context – of ideas as well as of literary decorum – and show how within it such an apparently strange approach to Nature becomes perfectly normal. If, in fact, we are to speak of impoverishment and abnormality, the fault lies rather more with that very development of the natural sciences in the mid- and later seventeenth century (the

---

1 Sir Thomas Browne, *Religio Medici*, I, 16.
2 John Eachard, *The Grounds and Occasions of the Contempt of the Clergy and Religion*, 1670. Quoted in the *Pelican Book of English Prose (2)*, ed. P. Ure, Harmondsworth, 1956, p. 248.

generation of Eachard in England) which rendered the detailed description of natural phenomena inaccessible to literature.[3]

1. 'Coeli enarrant gloriam Dei'

The view of Nature which is shared by all the preachers of our period has, of course, its roots in Scripture. Everywhere one finds references to Psalm 19: 'The heavens declare the glory of God: and the firmament showeth his handiwork.' The second sermon of Abra de Raconis's *Riches et excellens paralleles*, 1625 (C. 1), consists entirely of a gloss on this text, and contains the extremely important remark that a study of Nature not only tells us that God exists, but provides a whole approach to theology:

> Dieu donc pour soulager nostre infirmité, & subuenir à nostre foiblesse a parlé vn langage plus familier par la bouche de toutes les creatures, qui nous disent & qu'il est, & aucunement ce qu'il est. Qu'il est, comme trompettes; Ce qu'il est, comme tableaux. (p. 43)

There are then in this theme two main points: firstly that by a general consideration of the universe we can arrive at the idea of God; secondly that each part of the universe, if examined closely, will be seen to represent in some way one of God's attributes or an element of his plan for the world.

These two points are emphasized rather differently by different groups. The first occurs much more frequently in Protestant sermons, probably because of St Paul's gloss on the theme in Romans i, and Calvin's almost exclusive reliance on it in those parts of the *Institution* where he wants to demonstrate man's culpability in ignoring God's existence.[4] It is indeed in this same context that one of the most effective large-scale Protestant expositions of the theme is to be found. In the third of his *Six sermons*, 1636 (C. 5), Amyraut repeats Calvin's words in the course of a lengthy consideration of the whole of creation. The consideration

---

3 *Cf.* Antoine Adam's remark that 'les progrès des sciences de la nature ont rendu impossible certaines formes traditionnelles du sentiment de la nature et de la poésie descriptive'. 'Le Sentiment de la nature au XVIIe siècle en France dans la littérature et dans les arts', *Cahiers de l'Association Internationale des Etudes Françaises*, VI (1954), p. 13.

4 See esp. I, 5, i: 'non seulement il a engravé ceste semence de religion que nous avons dite en l'esprit des hommes, mais aussi il s'est tellement manifesté à eux en ce bastiment tant beau et exquis du ciel et de la terre ...' Ed. J.-D. Benoît, Paris, 1957–63, vol. 1, p. 68.

is highly schematic (as we shall later see all descriptions of Nature to have been) but it is nonetheless built up from examples which have an emotive as well as a philosophical force. Amyraut stresses this from the beginning:

Ie ne diray que les choses qui sont exposees aux yeux de tout le monde, & dont non les Philosophes & les sçauans seulement, mais les femmes & les enfans peuuent estre capables (p. 114)

and a further emotive note is struck by the quotation of Psalm 19 itself. It is important, too, to see how closely Amyraut is tied to a view of the universe as ordered in a definite chain-like hierarchy – a view we normally associate with the previous century and its neo-Platonist thinkers. In the context of Amyraut's sermon it may well be that the humanism of Calvin himself is largely responsible, but we find it in other preachers as well. The portraits of a disordered world associated with our period are in fact deviations from this norm, employed when it is the sinfulness of man rather than the existence or nature of God that is in focus.

Amyraut begins with the revolution of the stars and planets, which in turn determine the measurement of time and the succession of the seasons; this is the immediate gloss on the text of the psalm. Then we are asked to lower our sights to the air, with its birds and water, storms and angels: the natural or supernatural agents of God's favour and wrath. Here, as at the end of each section, an affective commentary follows the observations. Water and earth, fish, plants and animals are fully and interestingly dealt with. His picture of bountiful creation includes, by a use of preterition, the decorative as well as the useful; of the sea, for example:

Ie ne parleray pas de l'vtilité de ses poissons pour la nourriture des hommes. Ie ne diray rien des choses medicinales qu'elle produit: de l'ambre qu'elle iette à ses bords; des perles & des precieux coquillages qui se trouuent à ses riuages. (p. 116)

Man, too, is not merely considered as the microcosm of Nature, though this idea inevitably occurs; the preacher includes even governments in his celebration of God's world:

Et force nous est ... de passer soubs silence la sapience qui paroist en l'establissment des polices du monde, accomodees à chacune nation selon son naturel, & qui bigarrent la face de l'vniuers à la verité, mais d'vne bigarrure qui la rend extremement belle, par la iuste symetrie de tous ses membres, & le bel ordre auqel tout le genre humain est composé en ses parties. (p. 118)

It is perhaps as much the neo-Platonist background of this sort of meditation as the principle of inclusiveness and universal goodness that leads this austere Calvinist to borrow for his peroration a (somewhat amended) version of Plato's cave simile:

> De façon qu'il faut reuenir à la belle meditation de ce Payen, qui disoit autresfois que s'il y auoit quelques gens, nourris dés leur naissance en des cauernes soubs la terre, qui tout d'vn coup, la terre venant à s'entrebailler, sortissent de ces lieux esquels nous habitons, pour considerer d'vn costé la terre & de l'autre costé la mer, & puis en leuant les yeux vers les cieux apperceuoir la grandeur des nuées, la force des vents, le Soleil & sa beauté, & la faculté qu'il a de creer le iour par la lumiere qu'il espand dessus la terre. Puis qui vinssent apres, quand la nuict enueloppe l'habitation des hommes, à contempler le ciel si orné & si embelli d'astres, la varieté des mouuemens de la Lune, son croissant, son plein, & son declin, le coucher & leuer des estoiles, & leurs courses si constantes, ils s'escrieroyent pour le certain, qu'il y a vne Diuinité, & que c'est là son ouurage. (pp. 119–20)

Amyraut's persuasive skill in this passage is very considerable. By shifting our attention from broad generalizations about the physical world to the personal reactions of the liberated cave-dwellers, he forces us to identify ourselves with them in this moment of discovery and wonder. The contemporary listener would doubtless seize on the unspoken analogy between the cave and the darkness of the sinful life, and associate himself with the fresh perception of God's existence and power. For this is the moment to which the entire exposition has been tending: a revelation of God and a submission to him.

This idea of an ascent through creation to a personal encounter with the Creator is largely absent from Catholic sermons on this theme. Instead, emphasis is shifted to the symbolic qualities of natural objects. Creation sings its Author in order to praise him and reveal his nature:

> Vous diriez que toutes les creatures ne soient qu'vn carquois, d'où se tire vne trousse de fleches, qui ne sçauent tirer à autre but qu'à l'Amour, & à la gloire de leur facteur; ny entonner autre chose que ce motet, *Sçachez que le Seigneur est Dieu, & qu'il nous a faictes, & que nous ne sommes pas de nous-mesmes* (Ps. 99).[5]

There are of course few preachers whose treatment displays this brevity and charm; that would be to miss a fruitful source of

---

5 Camus, *Homelies spirituelles sur le Cantique des Cantiques*, 1620 (C. 82), p. 386.

invention of matter. Some of the vast catalogues of God's attributes which originate in complete expositions of Psalm 19 are minutely detailed and often extremely tedious. Even Molinier at one point runs the risk of monotony, but his summing-up of the theory which lies behind his lists is rather more succinct, and provides the starting point for further developments:

> Bref ce monde en toutes ses parties, n'est autre chose qu'vn liure qui propose, vn tableau qui exprime, vne voix qui presche, vne trompette qui annonce, vn heraut qui publie la Majesté, la grandeur, & les perfections de la Diuinité.[6]

2. Correspondences

The last quotation contains the highly significant phrase, 'ce monde en toutes ses parties'. It is not only by considering the whole vast scheme of creation that one achieves the knowledge of God, but through an examination of any created object. Molinier states this elsewhere in more explicit terms:

> C'est la maxime de la Theologie que les choses sensibles & corporelles portent l'image & la ressemblance des intelligibles & spirituelles, *Corporalia spiritualium similitudinem gerunt*: si bien que comme de la veüe du pourtrait on s'eleue à la consideration de la chose representée, ainsi la presence des objets materiels faict monter l'esprit à la contemplation des objets intellectuels. Et au lieu qu'Origene, & quelques autres Anciens resueurs ont dit que tout ce qui arriue sur la terre est écrit és corps celestes, & que le Ciel est vn liure, les Astres la charte, & leurs rayons les characteres où l'on peut lire tout ce qui se faict en ce bas Vniuers; au contraire nous pouuons dire veritablement que les choses celestes sont écrites és terrestres, les spirituelles és corporelles, les intelligibles és sensibles, les eternelles és temporelles, les surnaturelles és naturelles, & qu'il ne faut qu'ouurir les yeux de l'esprit pour lire en la terre comme en vn liure les plus beaux secrets du Ciel, en la nature les merueilles de la grace, & de la gloire, és creatures visibles la grandeur, & la majesté du Createur inuisible.[7]

This is very much a method of theological discovery: by including 'les merueilles de la grace' Molinier allows discussion of the Redemption and the Christian life as well as the divine attributes.

---

6 *Le Mystere de la Croix et de la Redemption du monde*, 1628, quoted from C. 242, p. 63. The previous four pages contain a monotonous catalogue.

7 *Les Douze Fondemens de la Cité de Dieu*, 1635 (C. 251), p. 5. This comes from a defence of his use of twelve precious stones as a basis for expounding the Apostles' Creed.

One of the early Protestant preachers even puts the investigation of Nature on a par with Scripture.[8]

This theory of correspondences was not, however, considered by all preachers to have the same value. Camus, as one might expect from the emphasis on utility which informs almost all of his work, tends to restrict it to devotional purposes. The following example is strikingly different from Molinier's idea; single natural objects are referred to precise devotional sentiments:

Quelqu'vne [sc. des ames vrayement esprises de Charité] regardant la courtine des Cieux parsemee d'Astres estincellans, Ce qui sert de lambris à ce monde, n'est, disoit-elle, que le paué & le march-pied du Paradis. Quelqu'autre voyant ces estoilles briller dans le cristal d'vne fontaine, Que mon coeur, disoit-elle, n'est-il ainsi remply de celestes imaginations. A la venuë du Printemps, Quand sera, disoit-elle, que le Zephir de la grace fera esclorre autant de fleurs en mon ame. En l'Automne, Mon coeur plus insensible que la terre ne fera-t'il iamais de fruict. En voyant des roses que des espines enuironnaient, Tels sont les plaisirs & les honneurs du monde. En considerant vn soucy, Que n'ayme-je autant mon Soleil. En escoutant le murmure d'vn ruisseau, La grace de mon Dieu coule ainsi doucement.[9]

This is evidently the beginning of that movement away from an intellectual to an emotional perception of Nature which was commented on at the beginning of this chapter. Thus Du Moulin expressly warns against what we might call scientism:

Le but de ce propos n'est pas de vous rendre sçauans en la Nature, mais de vous mener par le chemin aux suiets particuliers de glorifier Dieu, que Dieu donne à son Eglise . . .[10]

The warning at least reveals the persistent attraction of the quasi-scientific approach. It is obvious that for many preachers, and indeed for their congregations, such explorations of Nature were extremely interesting in themselves. They had the twin effect of adorning the sermon and of revealing the wide reading of the preacher. This intellectual factor is given prominence in another

8 Samuel Durant, *Six sermons sur quelques textes*, 1623 (C. 154), p. 83: 'Et nous esperons trouuer aisément excuse [sc. for the relatively simple allegory he is about to embark upon], puisque nostre excés en ce point n'a autre but que de reformer vos moeurs, & vous rendre plus gens de bien, & que pour cuëillir vn tel fruict il est loisible de tirer des enseignemens de toutes les paroles & actions, & en general, de tout ce que nous voyons, & en la nature, & en l'Escriture.'
9 *Homelies spirituelles sur le Cantique des Cantiques*, 1620 (C. 82), p. 393.
10 *Deuxiesme decade de sermons*, ? 1638, quoted from C. 143, part II, p. 216.

'Nature, that universal and publick Manuscript'

way, too, inasmuch as the precise analogies which flow from and in turn prove the general theory of correspondences are almost always expressed in terms of a comparison or a conceit.[11] Now, as we saw in our discussion of thesaurus preachers, it was ingenuity in the establishment of analogies, the *doctes merveilles*, which was esteemed the highest quality of the witty preacher. The treatment of Nature as a system of correspondences provides a vast field for this sort of intellectual effort, as well as proving the hypothesis of *coeli enarrant*.

Inevitably, therefore, sermons in the thesaurus and catenary traditions are where the widest ranging and the most unusual analogies from Nature can be found. And indeed, although many adhere in a somewhat pedestrian manner to Pliny and Etienne Binet, the variety of some is exhilarating. Obviously the first example of a detailed and exhaustive use of Nature that comes to mind is St François de Sales's bees. Henri Lemaire cites forty-one instances of references to this general area from the sermons, authentic or reconstructed, alone.[12] Others, in order to stimulate closer interest, draw on the flora and fauna of exotic lands. Thus Seguiran on the bird of paradise:

Cet oyseau de Paradis naist en Arabie, & est vulgairement appellé *auicula Dei*, il a la teste iaune comme l'or, le col d'vn plumage vert gay, les aisles de plumes tanees & pourprees, & le reste du corps d'or paillé, & a ceste belle proprieté, que tousiours il est en l'air, & iamais ne touche la terre; car lors qu'il est las de voller, il s'accroche aux branches & rameaux des arbres, auec

11 K. K. Ruthven, in his book *The Conceit*, London, 1969, pp. 9–11, takes to task the theory of J. A. Mazzeo (see above, p. 83) because of the lack in English Elizabethan and Metaphysical poetry of 'hints at any theoretical basis for literary conceits'. This combination of literary theory and practice is precisely supplied by our preachers, whose justifications for their use of Nature imagery seem in the main to support Mazzeo's interpretation. Ruthven also hints that this interpretation sees the post-Renaissance theory of universal analogy as 'an occult term like Baudelaire's *correspondances*' (p. 11). This is a crude linking of two quite separate ideas; metaphysical poets and witty preachers relied on ingenious intellectual perceptions of relationships, not on a poetic intuition founded on the senses, and they would certainly not have described Nature as uttering 'confuses paroles'.
12 *Les Images chez Saint François de Sales*, Paris, 1962, pp. 73–6, 193. As Lemaire remarks in his introduction (p. 5), 'De l'avis général Saint François de Sales est de tous les écrivains français celui qui a employé le plus de comparaisons.'

deux petits filets d'or qui luy seruent de pieds: ainsi est-il de l'ame iuste, qui
iustement peut estre appellee *auicula Dei*, oyseau de Dieu, oyseau de Paradis,
de laquelle la teste iaune est la charité, le col de vert gay, l'esperance, les aisles
tanees & pourprees, la patience, l'or paillé, son humilité: mais sur tout elle n'a
point de pieds pour toucher ceste terre, & pour mettre son coeur à la terre, &
aux richesses & grandeurs de la terre, mais au contraire le tourne incessamment
vers le ciel.[13]

This sense of the exotic and of the new is sometimes indulged in
quite gratuitously; but a remark like the following from Le Faucheur
does show how a serious scientific interest was beginning to
impinge on literature before a shift of sensibility led to its rejection.
He is building up to the traditional analogy between the Apostles
and suns, and finds that new knowledge helps his argument, for

Ces grands Soleils si esclattans en toute sorte de vertus ont eu leurs taches
aussi bien que ce beau Soleil, qui nous esclaire icy, a les siennes selon les
obseruations des Astrologues modernes.[14]

Modernity even becomes a central point in Molinier's elaborate
parallel between the passion flower and St Francis Xavier:

On dit, Messieurs, qu'il s'est trouué en ce dernier siecle vne nouuelle fleur
és Indes dont nous auons veu le pourtraict en Europe, qui represente en la
beauté de ses feuilles épanoüyes les cinq playes, la couronne d'espines, les
cloux, les verges, la Croix, toutes les marques empraintes du Fils de Dieu
crucifié, tirées au vif sur ce papier animé, par le pinceau de la Nature. Voicy
vne nouuelle fleur apparüe en nostre siecle, née dans la Nauarre, cultiuée en
France, mais transplanté és Indes, S. François Xavier, où la grace plus
ingenieuse encore que la Nature, a exprimé naifuement tous les traits de
l'image de Jesus-Christ, non seulement mourant, mais aussi naissant, &
conuersant au monde, sa pauureté, son humilité, son zele, sa charité, ses
trauaux: sa Croix, ses tourmens, sa mort, si bien qu'il a pû dire veritablement,
ce que disoit l'Apostre, *Ego stigmata Domini Iesu in corpore meo porto*.[15]

It is in this kind of description of a natural object and discernment
of its analogy to a 'merueille de la grace' that Molinier is closest to
the thesaurus tradition. Every element is detailed, and finds a
point of comparison in the story of the saint. There is an added

---

13 *Sermons doctes et admirables sur les Evangilles des Dimanches & Festes de l'anneé*, 1612 (C. 268), p. 1029.
14 *Trois sermons*, 1632 (C. 197), p. 94. The discovery of sun-spots, made almost simultaneously by Fabricius in 1611 and by Scheiner and Galileo in 1612, had raised important questions debated by Galileo and Gassendi amongst others.
15 *Sermons sur les festes des saincts*, 1648 (C. 257), vol. 1, pp. 42-3.

analogy in the first half of the parallel itself, since the flower too is a living representation of the instruments of the Passion, and this analogy on two levels is pointed up by the characteristic use of the conceit 'tirées au vif sur ce papier animé, par le pinceau de la Nature'. The creation of such balances displays a powerful and ingenious intellect; every possible meaning is squeezed out of the natural object. Needless to say, thesaurus preachers are not often able to achieve this, and often concentrate more on the object itself than on its spiritual relevance:

Les Naturalistes nous enseignent que la Grece porte vne Arbre nommée Ostys, laquelle est accompagnée d'vne proprieté admirable mais dommageable: car quand vne branche de ceste plante se trouue dans quelque maison, elle sterilize tellement la femme qu'elle ne peut conceuoir, & si elle est grosse, elle tuë le fruict de son ventre & la faict auorter.
    Telle est l'auarice, plante malheureuse & ennemie mortelle de la generation spirituelle.[16]

Boucher's scientific teaching, though informative, is largely irrelevant, and he himself appears to realize this when he breaks off his parallel almost entirely undeveloped. It was this sort of gratuitous self-advertisement which attracted the criticism of later generations; but generalized criticism may overlook the fact that criteria of excellence can be established within the tradition of the Nature analogy.[17]

In its normal state, then, the Nature analogy places as much emphasis on the object as on the spiritual truth it is intended to represent, and occasionally it betrays a greater interest in the object. This is what one would expect of a sensibility fascinated with Nature and with perceiving relationships and messages on the basis of ingenuity. Clearly, the advent of a more affective prose style spells the end of this device. But there is an interesting intermediate stage where a quasi-scientific approach has not yet been completely

---

16 Boucher, *Les Magnificences divines*, 1620 (C. 53), p. 357.
17 To be fair one ought to point out that analogies are frequently abused. Molinier himself can devote almost a page to the sterilizing properties of the laurel, or the slow but unquenchable wrath of the rhinoceros, and then feebly round off the story with a brief reference to St Lucy's virginity or Christ expelling the buyers and sellers from the Temple. See *Sermons sur les festes des saincts*, 1648 (C. 257), vol. 1, p. 187; *Sermons pour tous les dimanches de l'année*, 1631 (1639 edn, C. 247, vol. 2, p. 269).

replaced by conventional and 'literary' references to Nature. Among our preachers, Camus above all exemplifies this stage:

Est-il rien de plus mol que l'eau? est-il rien de plus dur que la pierre? D'où vient donc que la dureté de celle-cy est cauee par la mollesse de celle-là? grande force de la douceur, qui tient vn empire si puissant sur les coeurs les plus endurcis. Qui diroit que le diamant qui ne cede ny aux limes ny aux marteaux, s'amollist & se rendist taillable & flexible au sang du cheureau, si l'experience ne le rendoit manifeste? Que ne doit faire le sang tout boüillant d'Amour de l'Agneau sans tache sur les coeurs plus diamantins? O diuine Loy du sainct Amour, que tu es puissamment suaue, que tu es doucement forte. O Amour sacré, rien n'esgale ta puissance.[18]

Camus's treatment of natural phenomena here is very similar to the way he reacts to the thesaurus style of preaching. The basic structure of ideas is the same as in a full-dress analogy, but the painstaking construction of parallels has been whittled down to brief references to facts the reader is assumed to know. The comparison is not established in all its points; there is no symmetry. Instead it is the paradoxical element which is stressed, and which forms the bridge to the spiritual truth. And this truth itself is not of an abstractly theological kind; it takes the form of a devotionally potent idea which is directly relevant to the task of persuading the hard-hearted listener. That is why it is so quickly followed by the affective exclamations of the submissive soul. This change of emphasis from the descriptive to the emotive leads to a lessening of the shock element in Camus's conceits and comparisons. In order to charge them with maximum persuasiveness, he needs more than an ingenious and learned connexion between the two parts; there must be an element of appropriateness too. So we find him abusing Protestants by means of a comparison which not only explains their errors 'scientifically', but directly and unfavourably compares them to the ugliest of beasts:

Seroit-ce point que comme les singes haïssent les miroirs, où ils apperçoiuent leur laideur, & les chameaux l'eau claire où ils voyent leur deformité, ceux-cy troublans les sources, ceux-là cassans les glaces cristallines, pour s'oster le deplaisir de se recognoistre ridicules: Ainsi les Errans brisassent & troublassent la Verité de la reelle presence du corps du Sauueur en l'Eucharistie, par ce que *c'est vn miroir sans tache*, par ce que *c'est vne source d'eau viue*, parce que là

[18] *Homelies spirituelles sur le Cantique des Cantiques*, 1620 (C. 82), p. 39.

est celuy qui est appellé, *le plus beau de tous les enfans des hommes* (Psal. 44), aupres duquel leur hydeuse deformité a honte de comparoistre.[19]

In all these instances of correspondences a single natural object is used to represent a single spiritual truth. But there were limits to the inventiveness of preachers, and some natural phenomena could be made to mean a very wide variety of things. A small number of natural objects occur with an astonishing frequency in the sermons, and have a very wide field of reference. We have seen in previous chapters some of the meanings attached to one of these *topoi*, the pearl. It may represent tears in dreams, or the hidden treasure of the spiritual life, or virginity by its supposed origin in the oyster's reception of dew. Similarly, the *topos* of the rose amid the thorns is treated with remarkably few 'romantic' connotations. It is assumed that we know the rose to be the queen of flowers, with a superlative scent and visual beauty, and this assumption depends more on a hierarchical classification of flora than on any personal response to the blossom itself. The range of possibilities it offers are such that Camus was able to compose an entire homily on the theme of *Les Espines preferables aux roses*.[20] Molinier offers a fairly comprehensive range:

rose qui dans nos iardins enuironnée de pointes aiguës, qui la font autant craindre que sa grace desirer, semble nous dire en son silence: O hommes! tous vos plaisirs en cette vie, sont meslez d'amertumes & de mescontentemens, comme moy d'aiguillons, & de picquerons; la tristesse y suit la ioye, la viduité le mariage, le soucy les richesses, l'inconstance les faueurs, la charge les dignitez, l'infortune les succez, la satieté les voluptez, les maladies la santé, la mort la vie, l'espine la fleur. Voyez les effets de vostre peché qui a semé les espines ez roses, les trauaux en tous vos estats, les douleurs en toutes vos ioyes. Ne vous attachez pas à cet exil, où la terre vous produit les espines auec les roses, les afflictions auec les consolations: aspirez à vostre patrie dont le peché vous a bannis, où les roses sont sans espines, les plaisirs sans repentance, le bien sans meslange de mal.[21]

This representation of heaven as a garden where the roses have no thorns is quite common. Although the comparison between thorns and sin is certainly the most frequent interpretation, Protestants often view the thorns of the world as the necessary but transitory

---

19   *Premieres homelies eucharistiques*, 1618 (C. 78), p. 64.
20   *Premieres homelies quadragesimales*, 1615 (C. 71), Hom. 4.
21   *Le Banquet sacré de l'Eucharistie*, 1635, quoted from C. 249, p. 290.

condition for obtaining the rose of eternal life.[22] Daillé is even able to synthesize the two elements:

Les tribulations sont sa ioye, & les supplices sa gloire. Il n'y a point d'épines si maudites, où il ne cueille les roses des consolations de son Christ.[23]

This brief allusion to the *topos* only becomes possible when its range of implications is firmly embedded in the sensibility of those for whom the sermon is intended.[24] We may now consider more closely this process whereby the explicit connotations of the *coeli enarrant* theme become implicit and allusive in Nature imagery; firstly in the broad sphere of universal order, then by examining a single image.

3. The schematic universe and the imagery of disorder

Despite their lengthy affective amplifications and detailed descriptions, the major expositions of the *coeli enarrant* theme are based on a very simple structure. The complexity of the natural world is discussed within certain fixed compartments: the heavens, the air, the earth with its flora and fauna, and so on. When stripped down to its essentials, this becomes an enumeration of the elements, with the heavens remaining as a vestigial reminder of the scriptural origin of the theme. This schematization allows a preacher to treat the theme and its message with extreme brevity:

Nous voyons que les choses naturelles retiennent le naturel & l'ordre qui leur est donné de Dieu. Le Ciel recognoist Dieu son createur en retenant le

22   E.g. Le Faucheur, *Trois sermons*, 1632 (C. 197), p. 65.
23   *Sermon pour le jeusne celebré à Charenton le Jeudy 21 Aoust 1636*, 1636 (C. 115), p. 45.
24   A similar *topos* is the story of hinds calving through fear of thunder. It occurs in the Psalms (29, 8: 'The voice of the Lord maketh the hinds to bring forth young, and discovereth thick bushes'), and in our sermons is often the image which accompanies the text 'Initium sapientiae timor Domini' (Proverbs ix, 10). The following by no means exhaustive list of references gives an idea of its popularity: Besse, *Premieres conceptions theologiques sur le Caresme*, 1604 (C. 27), vol. 1, fol. 323^v, vol. 2, fol. 34^v, *Conceptions theologiques sur les quatre fins de l'homme*, 1606 (C. 35), vol. 2, p. 8; Molinier, *Sermons pour toutes les feries, et dimanches du Caresme*, 1641 (C. 253), vol. 1, p. 246, *Sermons sur les festes des saincts*, 1648 (C. 257), vol. 1, pp. 66-7; Seguiran, *Sermons doctes et admirables sur les Evangilles des Dimanches & Festes de l'anneé*, 1612 (C. 268), p. 258.

mouuement qui luy est ordonné de Dieu. Le feu, en rendant aux creatures inferieures la lumiere & chaleur, pour laquelle donner il est crée de Dieu. L'air, donne la respiration. L'eauë arrouse & humecte les corps. La terre produit son fruict pour l'vsage des hommes & des autres animaux. L'homme de bien louë & glorifie son Dieu.[25]

There are two distinct points in this schematic résumé of the ordered world. The part accorded to Nature is based on a quasi-scientific description, whereas man's place is couched in terms which are normative and exclusive; not every man fits rightly into the scheme, only 'l'homme de bien'. This union of two quite different considerations, with dissimilar functions, proves a useful source of didactic material.

The first part of the enumeration on its own has its use as a pure description of Nature. Since Nature can be reduced to the elements, a bare list of them is a shorthand way of encompassing the whole world in the space of a brief remark. It is particularly serviceable for those vast hyperbolic compliments in funeral orations where a preacher suggests that the mourners' loss is humanity's loss too, and that the whole of creation is expressing its grief. A long digression on the world's involvement would be tedious, a bald statement would be ineffectual; the pageant of the elements offers a neat solution which is both ingenious and picturesque. Still, there are occasions when it comes dangerously near to empty bombast, for example in Boucher's exhortation to the mourners in his oration on a provincial nobleman:

C'est maintenant ô noble assistance! que tous ensemble, & particulierement les enfans de ceste Prouince Poicteuine, pouuons à bon tiltre donner à nos l'armes liberté de couler sur la terre, à nos souspirs congé de voller par les Cieux, à nos plaintes licence de voguer par les mers, & à nos sanglots permission de vaguer par les airs, affin que les Airs, que les Mers, que les Cieux & la terre soyent desormais les tesmoins oculaires de nos pleurs; comme ils ont esté iadis spectateurs des vertus de celuy, pour l'amour & la mort duquel nous faisons vn tel duëil.[26]

Perhaps it would have been better not to have specified the 'Prouince Poicteuine'. It is in any case a technique more safely reserved for royal funeral orations or sermons on subjects of sufficient grandeur. Caussin uses it to great effect in a sermon on Mary

25   Burlat, *Deux sermons de la resurrection du Lazare*, 1603 (C. 64), fol. 4.
26   *Oraison funebre de . . . Emery de Barbezieres*, 1609 (C. 52), sig. A4^v.

as the *abrégé* of Nature's wonders (an extension of the traditional microcosm idea):

Son amour estoit ce feu honorable qui brusloit & luisoit tousiours chez elle, plus purement que ne font mesme les flammes immortelles, dont les Astres sont allumez. Sa douceur tenoit lieu de l'air serein, paisible & delicieux, que tant de mortels ont respiré dans la revolution de tous les siecles, & que nous respirons encore dans l'ardeur de nos miseres. Sa misericorde sembloit l'eau viue & crystalline, qui portoit l'esprit vital dans les veines de l'Vniuers. Enfin sa constance estoit la terre ferme, qui n'estoit iamais esbranlée dans les esbranlemens de la nature vniuerselle. O quel monde, chers auditeurs! quel monde que le monde de Iesus!²⁷

Caussin is playing a little with his audience here; it is only slowly that one realizes that he is building up a list of elements, and the key to this schematic enumeration is left to the end: the sum of air, fire, earth and water is the world.

This poses a problem for the more literally minded, for after all these elements are mutually exclusive, and it is difficult to see how someone can be represented as both fire and water. That it was not a question which exercised our preachers to any great extent only demonstrates the more clearly how conventional a device it was. If such objections are to be found anywhere, one would expect them in those slow, detailed expositions of Scripture which form the substance of most Protestant sermons; and indeed Mestrezat, perhaps the most thorough, and certainly the dullest of the Scriptural commentators, does spend some time on the question of how the Holy Ghost can cleanse like water and purge like fire.²⁸

Man, however, is missing from these tableaux, and without him this convenient way of representing the world remains a static literary device. The didactic element which Burlat contrives to slip into his summary of ordered creation is missing from the other examples. When preachers want to stress man's part in the whole and develop moral teaching from it, they return to the idea, closely allied to a schematic view of the universe, of the great chain of being:

Apres cela considerez la liaison & accord de toutes ces creatures entre elles. Les Astres temperent les elemens, les elemens nourrissent les plantes. Les

---

27 *Le Buisson ardent*, 1647 (C. 89), p. 516.
28 *La Pentecoste chrestienne*, 1633 (C. 223), pp. 40–1.

'Nature, that universal and publick Manuscript' 163

plantes nourrissent les animaux. Les animaux nourrissent l'homme & lui seruent afin que l'homme serue à Dieu.[29]

Such concise prefaces to some lengthier discussion of the duties of man are not infrequent in the sermons. Nor did preachers forget the origins of the theories: Macé is quite explicit about 'cette chaisne d'or tracée dans les tableaux du diuin Platon'.[30]

This theory can be put to a number of uses. It is possible to show that any man who does not participate in this universal system of cooperation is acting unnaturally; vice takes on cosmological proportions. This is the most common point to be made. But this system whereby every creature is subordinated to another can also be applied to social relationships. Loyalty and responsibility to one's superiors are signs that one is acting in accordance with God's will expressed in the structure of creation. This explains, for example, the imagery Raconis uses when he wants to portray the Maréchal de Schomberg as an obedient soldier:

C'estoit vne Heliotrope qui tournoit tousjours vers son Soleil, c'est à dire son Roy, Soleil vnique qui esclaire la France, & qui en la ronde du Zodiaque de son Estat, nous fait voir vn doux Printemps en la serenité de son visage, vn chaud esté en l'ardeur de son courage animé, vne Automne abondante aux fruicts de sa bonté Royale, & vn Hiuer glacé aux chastimens de sa Iustice.[31]

Thus not only is the soldier acting naturally, but the king by his ordered actions shows himself to be worthy of this obedience. If comparisons of this sort are frequent in funeral orations, it is because preachers conceive the greatest men to be those who find their right place in the scheme of things.[32]

29   Du Moulin, *Deuxiesme decade de sermons*, ? 1638, quoted from C. 143, part II, p. 215.
30   *Panegyrique de S. Louis*, 1648 (C. 212), p. 3.
31   *Oraison funebre sur le trespas de feu Mgr le Mareschal de Schomberg*, 1633 (C. 2), pp. 61–2.
32   Cf. Macé's comparison of Père Joseph's life with the daily round of the sun, *La Tres-eloquente Harangue funebre du Pere Joseph*, 1639 (C. 213), pp. 10–11: 'Ce sont des formes generalles, des ames vniuerselles, des soleils qui portent cette deuise, *Idem per diuersa*. Le soleil qui se leve au matin esclaire sur le midy, se couure sur le soir, qui fait sa ronde dans l'Asie, L'Affrique, l'Europe & l'Amerique, colorant les vallées & les montagnes, semblable à soy-mesme dans la diuersité de ses mouuemens, *Idem per diuersa*. Les Religieux de ce sainct Ordre [*sc.* the Capuchins] vous asseurent, je l'aduouë, & vous le confessez, que leur deffunct Pere estoit de cette trempe-là.'

In the sermons the idea has a broader application to social and political structures. Du Moulin applies it to marriage, and then extends it to the whole of society, relying heavily on imagery drawn from Nature.[33] Authors of royal funeral orations were not slow to point out to their hearers how easily monarchy can be demonstrated to be in harmony with the universe.[34] But monarchy does not have the exclusive rights of access to this theme; an ingenious and thoughtful preacher like Amyraut can draw almost infinite conclusions from it:

Il [sc. God] fait produire à la terre ses fruicts par le moyen des pluyes & de la chaleur; & fait sentir la chaleur à la terre, & en esleue la matiere des pluyes & des rosées par le moyen du soleil, [&] donne en fin au Soleil son mouuement

33   *Decade de sermons*, 1637, quoted from C. 143, part I, sig. H8^v–I1^r [mispaginated 118–19] : 'En ceste societé du mariage Dieu n'a pas voulu que les parties fussent égales, mais il a donné la superiorité au mari, laquelle inegalité sert à nourrir la concorde: car comme de plusieurs voix toutes de mesme ton vous ne ferez iamais vn accord de musique, & le main seroit vn outil mal propre si tous les doigts estoyent de mesme longueur, ainsi mal-aisément y aura-il vne ferme concorde entre personnes entierement égales: Vn corps de peuple composé de personnes d'égale condition ne se meut qu'auec grande incommodité: c'est ceste inegalité qui entretient la societé des Republiques, entant que les grands ont besoin de seruice des petits, & les petits ont besoin du support des grands, & d'estre conduits par la prudence des superieurs. Partout où Dieu a mis de l'ordre, il y a mis quelque superiorité, il a establi des Archanges sur les Anges, & des Princes sur les peuples: il a voulu que les enfans obeyssent à leurs peres & meres, les seruiteurs à leurs maistres, & les femmes à leurs maris: l'ame commande au corps, & l'entendement gouuerne les appetits. Mesme entre les diables il y a vn Prince, & vne troupe de voleurs se dissipe incontinent si elle n'a vn maistre, & vn conducteur: Dont Dieu a mais des exemples en quelques animaux irraisonnables, commes és mouches à miel qui ont vn Roy, & és gruës qui ont vn conducteur.'

34   E.g. Hersent, *Le Sacré Monument dedié à la memoire de . . . Louis le Juste*, 1643 (C. 175), oration I, p. 10: 'Il [God] se sert tous les iours des regards & des mouuemens des Cieux & des Astres, pour donner au monde la diuersité des temps & des saisons, l'estre aux pierres & aux metaux, la vie aux plantes, & le sentiment aux animaux. Mais comme le plus noble ouurage de sa puissance, & le plus digne objet de sa prouidence est le genre humain, il n'a point trouué vn principe plus legitime, & vn fondement plus asseuré de sa gloire dans le monde, & dans la nature, que l'ordre du gouuernement politique, qu'il a institué parmy les hommes, pour les vnir ensemble comme freres dans vne mesme famille, & membres d'vn mesme corps.'

afin qu'il puisse distribuer sa chaleur & sa vertu viuifiante en tous les endroits du monde. En la police de mesmes. Il conserue chacun particulier par le moyen des vtilités qu'il retire de la societé commune. Il maintient la societé par l'ordre des recompenses & des punitions. Il conserue l'ordre par l'autorité des Magistrats. Il establit les [Magistrats] par les loix & les droits qui sont receus en chacun peuple . . . Et n'establit pas les Magistrats à contresens, pour constituer vn gouuernement populaire parmi les peuples à qui la monarchique conuient mieux, ou vn gouuernement monarchique entre les peuples à qui le populaire est plus sortable. Il donne ordinairement à chacune nation la police selon son genie.[35]

For later readers this has almost the ring of Montesquieu: it is obviously based on a closely considered political theory, with great care taken not to brush aside complexities and difficulties. But it is still firmly orientated towards God and the order and balance which are the marks of his presence in creation.

Descriptions of the ideal state of human affairs, moral, social and political are, then, frequently accompanied by references to a schematic picture of the external world. Since the majority of sermons are aimed at persuading men to act in conformity with this order and reproving their deviations from it, it is natural that the same fund of imagery will be drawn on in passages dealing with disorder. There are a number of ways in which this can be done, of which the simplest is direct contrast. The idea was already implicit in Burlat's reference to 'l'homme de bien'. Camus reproves man's rejection of worship for meaner and lower loves by constructing a long account of the great chain of being and then, at the end, contrasting man's behaviour with that of the other creatures:

Or est à remarquer que toutes ces choses aiment ordinairement les obiets qui leur sont prescrits par l'autheur de leur nature, & sera-il dit que l'homme aduantagé par dessus toutes les creatures de la raison, & creé pour ce seul effet d'aymer parfaitement son facteur, se reuolte de son obeissance, & s'adonne à vn autre Amour? O ingratitude! ô desloyauté! ô peruersion de tout ordre![36]

This simple contrast is not, however, so commonly found as one might expect. More often preachers use the much more devious device of confusing elemental imagery to imply human disorder. This confusion had, of course, always been associated with the Last Days, and it is significant to see how much the brief references to cosmic chaos in the New Testament are amplified in seventeenth-

35 *Sermon sur ces mots . . . 'C'est Dieu . . .'*, 1640 (C. 7), pp. 69–70.
36 *Premieres homelies dominicales*, 1617, quoted from C. 73, p. 398.

century accounts of the Second Coming. Let one example, from Jean de Croï's *Le Dernier Jugement*, suffice:

La Mer elle mesme, quoy qu'elle soit la Mere, & l'assemblée de toutes les Eaux, ne pourra pas conserver son humidité, ny sa froideur naturelle. Ce sera en vain qu'elle voudra opposer ses Eaux aux feux du dernier iour du Monde. Ses Eaux n'auront plus la qualité desteindre [sic] le feu, de mesme qu'auparavant. Elles ne seront que bitume, que Naphthé, & que Soulfre. Les fontaines ne jetteront que du feu; & les vagues elles mesmes se changeront en flammes. Les Fleuues, qui vont maintenant apporter les Eaux dans la Mer, comme un tribut necessaire, qu'ils luy doivent, n'y apporteront alors que des charbons ardens. Les flammes des Airs, qui tomberont dans la Mer, n'y trouveront que leur matiere, & que leur nourriture; & les flots n'y rencontreront que leur embrasement. Ces vastes abysmes de l'Ocean, qui recueillent maintenant toutes les Eaux, qui coulent sur la Terre, sembleront alors estre une fournaise ardente, pour fondre, & pour dissoudre les Airs & la Mer mesme.[37]

The capitalization of certain words is particularly interesting, for it is on these words that an obsessive emphasis, not present in traditional apocalyptic, is placed. Croï uses the confusion among the elements to represent universal chaos; their unnatural mingling becomes symbolic of the end of the old order. Now, developed from these apocalyptic tableaux and intended perhaps to convey a faint reminder of them, one also finds representations of vice in terms of elemental confusion. If the heavens declare the glory of God, they can also speak out the sinfulness of man. A quotation from Camus's denunciation of lust makes this very plain, and will serve to illustrate what is a very widely used technique:

C'est vne fontaine ardente, c'est vne ardeur boüillonnante, c'est vn feu Gregeois qui flambe dedans les eaux.

Mirez le symbole de ce vice en la chaux qui arrosee aboutit en vne ardeur petillante, en vne fumee puante, en vne visqueuse dissolution.

Chose estrange que l'eau & le feu deux elements si contraires, concourent neantmoins en ceste impureté...

Les yeux, sources de ce desreiglement, sont composez d'eau en soy, & neantmoins si nous en croyons Platon, leurs rais visuels sont Ignees.

Si nous consultons la poësie, boutique des anciennes moralitez, elle nous fera voir vne mere nee de la mer, qui engendre vn fils de Vulcan tout entouré de flammes, ce qui nous confirmera à croire que *luxuria est fluxus urens*, ou *lux urens*.

37 1645 (C. 107), pp. 37-8. This is by no means restricted to Protestants; there is an almost identical passage in Lor's *Sermons salutaires sur tous les jours de l'Advent*, 1623 (C. 208), p. 38. Many Advent series begin with a similar passage.

L'escoulement de Narcisse changé apres en vne fleur chaude en quelque degré, nous represente la mesme chose.

Si nous feuilletons le liure de la nature, nous rencontrerons la Salemandre, symbole de l'amour, qui prenant sa naissance de l'eau, tire sa nourriture des flammes, c'est donc l'incontinence vne ardeur humide, vne ardente humidité...[38]

This is a use of imagery which has been noticed by numerous commentators on the literature of this period. Perhaps more interesting is the fact that from this general fund our preachers selected an image which occurs with almost obsessive regularity in their work: the sea-storm and the resultant shipwreck.

Storms offer an ideal example of partial elemental confusion; it is the effect of the wind (air) on the waves (water) which is their immediate cause, and the result is often the invasion of the land by the sea. When a ship is involved one has the added situation of land-dwellers dying by being submerged in an element in which they cannot naturally live. And all this is caused by mysterious forces over which man has no control, forces behind which the hand of God may be discerned. This is often the meaning attached to storms, especially to the Flood, in the Old Testament;[39] and references to such phenomena were doubtless partly intended to convey these Biblical overtones. It is also a theme which lends itself to picturesque and vivid treatment based partly on imitations of the descriptions of storms which abound in ancient and Renaissance poetry, partly on the experience of contemporary voyagers.

Even in the most vivid accounts this literary and Scriptural tradition is dominant:

Monseigneur, Les matelots gaillardement assaillis de la tormente, affranchis en fin de la trouble marine, cinglans à vogue-rancade au haure desiré, font retentir la coste à l'echo d'vn ioyeux Thalassion: saluent le port au cry de leurs acclamations marinieres, font ioüer le canon, accollent le sol natal, baisent la terre ferme, & redimez de la tyrannie flottante du superbe element, salutairement animez à la gratitude, portent leurs premieres pensees [à] rendre leurs voeux au Sainct Tutelaire, de leur heureux abord. Tous les vents des sinistres inuentions, les brisans & escueils des horribles trahisons: les vagues & les flots des passions desreglees, les Pirates mesme & escumeurs des cupidités auidement cruelles, iusques aux Tritons, petits Dieux de ces confusions marinieres,

---

38 *Premieres homelies dominicales*, 1617, quoted from C. 73, p. 465.
39 See Philippe Raymond, *L'Eau, sa vie, et sa signification dans l'Ancien Testament*, Leiden, 1958, esp. pp. 35-53, 77, 196-8.

monstres marins redoutables, pieça complotez, & mutinez, ont assiegé & tenté de toutes parts, du Nord, & du Su, la petite fregate de ma mediocre fortune: pour luy faire perdre la Tramontane si leur pouuoir eust secondé leur vouloir: l'ont poussee plus de deux ans entiers en haute mer à la mercy du Ciel, & des ondes agitee de toutes parts, hormis d'elle mesme, & portee à deux doigts du naufrage imaginaire, phantasié sous l'espaix de leur menee songe-creuse.[40]

By embellishing the account of his personal woes in this way, Valladier is able to do two things. He associates the crimes of his enemies with universal forces of disorder, and he manages to draw on to himself the sympathies normally and traditionally felt for the victims of storms. Not all sea-storm passages are as exclusively indebted to tradition as this, of course. Voyer d'Argenson actually suggests practical remedies should any of his readers find themselves so placed.[41] But it is certainly this indebtedness which explains why preachers so immediately and naturally selected this means of amplifying their remarks on disorder. Nor was it by any means necessary each time to introduce a highly elaborate picture; it was evidently assumed that audiences were so well acquainted with fuller accounts that the briefest reference would produce the desired effect.

Most descriptions of storms and shipwrecks are therefore fairly schematic and can be used in most contexts. They occur most frequently in discussions of civil and religious strife, although the imagery is not always used with much care or consistency in the latter case.[42] In the context of social or political disorder this imagery is often more effectively handled. Here, for instance, is Langle arguing against Huguenot complacency amid the political troubles of the 1630s:

---

40   Valladier, *Les Divines Paralleles de la saincte Eucharistie*, 1613 (C. 302), sigs. ã1–ã2. This is from the preface.
41   *L'Enneade sacrée*, 1622 (1628 edn, C. 313), p. 142: oil in the mouth saves you from drowning.
42   A couple of very flat examples from two of our best preachers. Daillé, *Sermons sur l'Epître aux Colossiens*, 1648 (C. 122), vol. 2, pp. 25–6, discussing the discord of heresy: 'C'est donc encore pour empescher ce desordre, & pour retenir au milieu d'eax l'union en charité, que l'Apôtre avoit un si grand combat. Car comme la mer demeure paisible, & unie durant le calme, mais s'eleve toute en flots se choquans violemment les uns les autres, dés que le vent vient à y souffler; ainsi les faux Docteurs, qui sont comme les vents, & les tourbillons de l'enfer, n'ont pas plustost donné dans une Eglise, qu'ils en troublent la paix, & en remuënt toutes

'Nature, that universal and publick Manuscript'

Il n'est pas raisonnable que nous, qui sommes en vn mesme vaisseau auec nos Concitoiens, & qui voyons tous les matelots crians vn chacun à son Dieu, comme durant la tempeste qui battoit le nauire de Ionas, que nous cependant tous mornes & tous descouragez comme luy, demeurions endormis au fond de la nasselle. Plutost crions au Dieu de nostre Salut dés lieux profonds, & reclamons auec chaleur & auec zele ses compassions en nos detresses.[43]

It is only a brief illustration to crown a long and detailed explanation of the issues involved, yet Langle manages to pack into a few dense lines a good deal of Biblical allusion. There is Jonah, of course, but there is also Psalm 130 and perhaps a fleeting reminiscence of Christ stilling the waves. By comparing the state to a boat in the first place, the preacher emphasizes the impossibility of escape and the need for disciplined cooperation. In that sense it remains a common but perhaps rather faded metaphor in modern English.

The shock and confusion implied in the shipwreck image are particularly appropriate when the political disorder is itself brought on by a sudden and inexplicable intervention of fate. It is hardly surprising therefore to find Valladier making great play with it in his funeral oration for the assassinated Henri IV.[44] Indeed, the metaphor was so closely associated with that assassination that Camus, preaching a few years later on the duty of princes to be accessible to their people, has no need to go further than an allusion:

les parties, les détachant, les soûlevant, & les faisant miserablement entrechoquer les unes les autres, à leur commune ruine, & à la joye de l'ennemi.' Molinier, *Sermons sur les festes des saincts*, 1648 (C. 257), vol. 1, p. 119, describing the scene of St Ambrose's election at Milan: 'il trouue le peuple assemblé dans l'Eglise, il l'exhorte à l'vnion & à la paix, & à deposer les partialitez pour conspirer tous ensemble à la nomination d'vn digne Pasteur, & assaisonna son discours de tant de prudence, l'anima d'vne si viue eloquence, que tous estans rauis de l'oüir, & fleschis par ses persuasions, on vit cette multitude semblable auparauant à vne mer irritée, s'appaiser soudain & reprendre le calme, & la tranquillité, comme la mer quand vn doux Zephyr a dissipé les vents orageux, qui sousleuoient ses vagues & causoi[en]t sa tourmente'.

43 *Sermon sur S. Luc, xiii, 1–3*, 1636, quoted from C. 191, p. 202.
44 *Harangue funebre de Henry le Grand*, 1610 (C. 297), p. 85. Valladier characteristically provides a Patristic reference, to Tertullian's *De anima*, 52.

Les nostres, tres-bons Princes, ne se prodiguent que trop, nous sommes encore tous moüettes des naufrages que nous venons d'en faire.[45]

Similarly, a neat reversal of the normal comparison allows Bertaut, apostrophizing Marie de Médicis in his funeral oration for the same occasion, to compliment the Regent on the way she has restored 'ce merueilleux calme qui regne par vostre conduitte sur les vagues d'vne si grande mer d'affaires publiques'.[46]

Such is the obsessive frequency with which the image occurs, and so definite are its connexions with disorder of one sort or another, that the dangers of the sea are often the first to enter the mind of someone compiling a list of disasters.[47] It is the chief among those afflictions to which Du Moulin devotes a whole sermon.[48]

Closely allied to this conception of the shipwreck as the image *par excellence* of disorder is another obsessively recurrent subordinate theme, the world as a sea. This again is an idea common to most literature at most periods, but it is accorded particular attention in our sermons. Many of the religious and literary connotations that support and explain the shipwreck image naturally support this extension of it. Thus it occurs primarily in the context of the ship of the Church and the story of Christ calming the sea. It is precisely during a homily on this text (Matthew viii, 23ff.) that Bourgoing elaborates the comparison:

Et puis que le monde est vne mer pleine d'orages & d'écueils, ainsi que la mer est vn monde de trauaux & de dangers, que nostre vie est vne perilleuse nauigation: ie vois deux sortes de vie; l'vne des meschans pecheurs, figurée par la Nauire, en laquelle Ionas estoit, & dormoit profondement... l'autre vie est celle des gens de bien, & des seruiteurs de Dieu, qui est signifiée par la nasselle, en laquelle Iesus estoit dormant auec ses disciples; l'vne & l'autre est agitée de la tempeste & des vents contraires; cela veut dire, que les bons & les meschans sont sujets à mille souffrances & afflictions en cette vie: mais auec cette difference, que les bons en vsent bien, & pour leur salut; les meschans en font vn mauuais vsage, & en tirent des motifs de nouueaux pechez.[49]

45 *Premieres homelies dominicales*, 1617, quoted from C. 73, p. 465.
46 *Discours funebre sur la mort du feu Roy*, 1610 (C. 25), p. 30.
47 E.g. Charles de Beauvais, *De la protection et sauvegarde divine*, 1636 (C. 20), p. 4.
48 *Sermon de la priere en temps d'affliction*, 1624 (C. 136), p. 143.
49 *Homelies chrestiennes sur les Evangiles des dimanches et principales festes de l'année*, 1642, quoted from C. 63, pp. 101-2.

Le Faucheur establishes a similar parallel in a rather less heavy-handed way, and adds the idea of the compass to give it a more concrete, more convincing value:

Mais comme l'esguille marine, encore qu'elle tremble tousiours, pource qu'elle n'est appuyee que sur vn poinct, demeurant suspenduë de tout le reste de son corps, est neantmoins si ferme & si constante que quelque orage qui agite le vaisseau où elle est, elle ne change iamais d'assiette, ains regarde tousiours fixement son North: ainsi encores que l'Eglise toutes les fois qu'elle est ou affligee ou menassee de l'estre, venant à regarder combien ses ennemis sont puissants, ses dangers eminents, ses tentations vehementes, & son infirmité extreme, en tremble & s'en effraye; neantmoins parmy toutes ses agitations & tous ses mal-heurs elle s'affermit tousiours en la foy en regardant constamment à son Dieu, & destituee de tout appuy quant au monde, demeure fixe sur ce poinct qu'elle a vn garent & vn Redempteur qui ne la laissera point perir.[50]

Now these examples of explicit association between a Biblical story and the idea of the *mer du monde* come from sermons published in the second half of our period. Preachers in the first half did not feel themselves bound in this way to provide the background to their use of the image. They tend to use it as a metaphor rather than a simile, despite the fact that the cult of the elaborate comparison was at its height in these earlier years. There is an important point to be made here about the way these fundamental thematic complexes work. Although in this reconstruction of them I have spoken of developments and extensions of a basic comparison, this does not necessarily coincide with a historical progression. The automatic association of certain images with certain themes had occurred before our period began, often in antiquity, although all the elements which brought about that association are still present as vestigial traces of the process, and may be included at will. If anything, the explanation and setting in context of these familiar metaphors occur later, when the sensibility that appreciated them is already changing.

The earliest example of the *mer du monde* in this period occurs as a metaphor in a sermon of 1600, where Du Bec speaks of the story of the woman of Samaria as one which 'attire à soy tant de peuples errans par la mer impetüeuse de ce trompeur Monde',[51] and runs right through the period to Bourgoing. Another early example,

---

50 *Trois sermons*, 1632 (C. 197), pp. 63–4.
51 *Sermon de la Samaritaine*, 1600 (C. 133), p. 5.

again metaphor rather than simile, comes from Richelieu. He is telling his audience the story of a sea-captain fearing shipwreck who suddenly sees a young child on board:

> Il prend courage, il court à lui sans dire mot, il le charge sur ses épaules, croyant que Dieu aurait pitié de cette âme innocente et que par ce moyen il pourrait se sauver. Imitons, Messieurs, je vous prie ce brave capitaine. Nous sommes en la mer de ce monde, agités de mille tempêtes, battus de mille orages qui menacent nos âmes de leur perte, ayons recours à un enfant, ayons recours à Jésus-Christ qui prend naissance aujourd'hui. Mettons-le, non sur nos épaules, mais dans nos coeurs et sans doute son innocence nous garantira du naufrage et nous conduira au port de salut.[52]

Retz, on the other hand, feels a need to defend his comparison:

> considérant Saint Charles dans ce trouble et dans cette agitation des affaires et des occupations du grand monde, que l'on peut appeler un Océan d'iniquités, et pour les écueils qui s'y rencontrent, et pour ces monstres d'avarice qui se nourrissent d'ordinaire dans les cours . . .[53]

The various guises of the *mer du monde* idea provide us, in fact, with a convenient recapitulation of a number of points we have already discovered about imagery and themes in this period. First of all, because it is part of a wider view of Nature as a source of analogies of human problems, it is capable of great flexibility. It can take the form of a brief image inserted to suggest this wider context, to spark off memories of a fuller consideration.[54] At the other end of the scale it can be used as the subject of a whole sermon.[55] Although in the majority of cases it is introduced, like almost all Nature imagery in this period, without any affective reference to the reader's own experience and without any purely

---

52 *Un Sermon inédit de Richelieu (Noël 1608)* (C. 264), p. 14.
53 *Sermon ou Panégyrique pour la fête de S. Charles Borromée*, 1646, quoted from C. 263, p. 90.
54 E.g. the two references Lor makes to it in the fifteenth sermon of his *Sermons salutaires sur tous les jours de l'Advent*, 1623 (C. 208): 'nostre ame tandis qu'elle est dans le corps, comme dans vn bateau, se treuue agitée de mille furieuses tempestes de la chair . . . les flots & les boüillons de la sensualité l'environnent, & les ondes de la concupisence le battent de tous costez' (p. 310); 'Apres que l'homme est embarqué sur l'Ocean de ce monde . . . il se treuue encores attaqué de trois grands Pirates & escumeurs de mer, qui sont le monde, le diable, la chair' (p. 311).
55 Camus, *Premieres homelies dominicales*, 1617 (C. 72), Hom. 6, *De la mer du monde*, on the text 'Motus factus est in mari' (Matthew viii, 24).

picturesque elaboration, there is one example of a highly sensitive preacher, Amyraut, selecting it as an especially effective image for the people of La Rochelle.[56] It makes its appearance, then, both as a commonplace the frequency of which can tell us much about the structure of a sensibility universal in the period, and as a touchstone whereby sensitivity and effectiveness in the handling of imagery may be judged.[57]

4. Flames

Although in the last two chapters I have aimed at the non-historical reconstruction of a thematic structure and its attendant imagery – a method imposed by the complexities of the two great themes of

---

56 *Sermon sur... l'Epistre aux Hebrieux x, 26*, 1646 (C. 14), pp. 40–4.
57 It is interesting briefly to compare the above account with the use of water imagery, and elemental interplay in particular, in the work of contemporary poets. A good deal of attention has been brought to bear on this subject in the last twenty-five years: apart from the classic works of Jean Rousset and Odette de Mourgues, see for example Jean-Pierre Chauveau, 'La Mer et l'imagination des poètes au XVIIe siècle', *XVIIe Siècle*, LXXXVI–LXXXVII (1970), pp. 107–34; E. T. Dubois, 'On some aspects of baroque landscape in French poetry of the early seventeenth century', *Journal of Aesthetics and Art Criticism*, XIX (1961), pp. 253–61; Erik Michaëlsson, 'L'Eau, centre de métaphores et de métamorphoses dans la littérature française de la première moitié du XVIIe siècle', *Orbis litterarum*, XIV (1959), pp. 121–73; Alain Seznec, 'Saint-Amant, *le poète sauvé des eaux*', *Studies in Seventeenth-century French Literature presented to Morris Bishop*, Cornell, 1962, pp. 35–64. Some of these critics have found a similar sensibility at work. Saint-Amant's poetry in particular is said to be 'studded with descriptions of storms, typhoons, shipwrecks, in which water appears as nature's destructive element' and the sea is often presented as the 'instrument of divine wrath' (Seznec, pp. 41, 63). Chauveau stresses 'l'incapacité souvent manifeste à réagir spontanément, directement en face des choses sans passer par des souvenirs livresques et des figures de rhétorique' (p. 109). Perhaps the contemporary sermons help to explain this. But there are also great differences. Instead of shipwrecks, sea-storms and the *mer du monde*, poets on the whole preferred the flux of rivers, reflections in lakes and ponds, and artificial landscapes. Although, as Michaëlsson says in a notable phrase, 'On avait une nature rhétorique au lieu d'une nature sentimentale' (p. 171), it seems that preachers eschewed the decorative and pursued a more rigorously schematic rhetoric of nature than poets. The storm as a specific metaphor of political disorder, for instance, appears to be almost entirely absent from poetry.

fruitful disillusion and revelatory Nature – it would be wrong to conclude without at least sketching some of the ways in which imagery changes during this period. By selecting the flame I hope also to demonstrate the breadth and variety of uses to which a single image drawn from Nature could be put. We are fortunate too in having an almost complete compendium of possible combinations within a single work, Samuel Durant's *Trois sermons* of 1623 (C. 155). These are a continuous exploration of the text (1 Thessalonians v, 19) 'N'esteignez point l'Esprit', or rather, of the metaphor of fire implied in this text. Samuel Durant is one of the few Protestants preaching in this period before 1630 whose works are extant, and a comparison with later Protestants shows a remarkably dissimilar approach to questions of imagery. In his willingness to be led through the labyrinth of connected metaphors, he is much closer to contemporary Catholic preachers – with the important difference that he does not often stray outside the boundaries of Scriptural reference.

The exordium of the first sermon establishes the legitimacy of comparing the Spirit to fire by quoting copiously from both Testaments. But this is just the necessary starting-point, and he quickly moves on to a further stage. Since the outpouring of the Spirit is the manifestation of God's love, that love itself is a fire and expresses itself in flames. This was a source of imagery much favoured by early Catholic preachers, who evidently found it a satisfyingly concrete and immediate way of presenting a difficult idea. Antonin de Paris devotes six sermons to establishing detailed parallels between the fire in the Temple and the fire of divine love.[58] Eudemare uses it particularly well in a sermon on St Lawrence. The martyr on his gridiron is a 'sacré Phoenix, qui brusle au milieu des flammes de l'amour de Dieu', a Salamander whose bodily burning 'n'estoit que glace, à comparaison de la ferueur du sainct amour dont son coeur brusloit au dedans'.[59] In the Jesuit Suffren's sermon on the Passion, the wood of the Cross is seen as fuel to feed this fire.[60] Here we come close to the iconographic extension of this

---

58 *Tresor admirable tiré de l'Escripture saincte*, 1613 (C. 17), sermons 18–24.
59 *Tapisseries sacrées*, 1617 (C. 159), pp. 517–18. *Cf.* the passage from St François de Sales quoted above, Chapter 4, pp. 81–2.
60 *Le Victorieux et triomphant Combat de Gedeon*, 1616 (C. 290), pp. 59–62.

metaphor enshrined in the (largely Jesuit) cult of the Sacred Heart. Despite the Scriptural bases of the love/fire image, however, it is noticeably absent from later Protestant sermons. Even among Catholics its use by Molinier in a Christmas sermon (the light from the crib is like the light from a hearth) may be taken as a further sign of Molinier's conservatism of taste.[61]

A quotation from Durant illustrates the way he uses almost haphazardly the ramifications of his central metaphor. He is lamenting the decline of Huguenot fervour due to increased prosperity:

> L'ardeur de la vraye religion est presque du tout esuanouïe. Quelque beau semblant que nous facions, las en effect de suiure le flambeau de l'Esprit de Dieu, nous courons apres les feux errans de la vanité du monde, qui precipite les hommes és abysmes de perdition. (p. 8)

Within a few lines he has brought in references to the fiery cloudy pillar and the *feu follet* of the world. Although the first of these is perfectly comprehensible, the second is rather confusing in a text where all fire is being assimilated to God. This uncontrolled need to include every possible reference is not found again in the period.

Nor do later Protestants follow him in his exploration of the ambiguity of God's flame:

> Le flambeau de ceste parole par accident, au regard de la malice des hommes, mais non pas sans la Sage conduite & prouidence de Dieu, allume au monde le feu des afflictions & persecutions. Desquelles l'issue est double: Car ceux qui nous les suscitent iniustement & malicieusement, sont eux-mesmes par là conduits dans les tourmens de la gehenne du feu qui ne s'esteint point. Mais nous qui les souffrons pour nostre espreuue & pour la cause de Dieu, serons par icelle eleués à la gloire celeste. Là nostre entendement sera pleinement illuminé, & là nos volontés seront pour iamais embrasees en la dilection de nostre Dieu. (p. 28)

The closest passage to this is to be found, significantly enough, in Camus:

> Dieu est Dieu, & tout de feu. Il est de feu dans le Ciel, & de feu dans l'Enfer: mais là il est vn feu de douceur & d'Amour, icy de douleur & d'ire; là c'est vn feu luisant, & non cuisant, mais gracieux & aymable de bonté & de misericorde, icy il est feu bruslant & poignant de rigueur & de Iustice. Si qu'apres

---

61 *Sermons sur les festes des saincts*, 1648 (C. 257), vol. 1, pp. 237–66.

ceste mort nous ne pouuons euiter quelque part que ce soit les flammes eternelles.[62]

This fascination with the idea of ambiguity, with parallels, similarities, reflected here on the level of word-play ('douceur'/'douleur'; 'luisant'/'cuisant'), is a typical example of the sensibility prevalent in the early years of the reign of Louis XIII. Durant bears witness to the fact that it was not restricted to Catholics. There is in his work a love of density and allusion, a feeling for the richness of Biblical metaphors and their constant metamorphosis, which is lost precisely during our period:

Nous ne nous imaginons aucune separation entre l'Esprit de Dieu & les graces d'iceluy: non plus qu'entre le Soleil & ses rayons; ou entre le feu & la chaleur & clarté d'iceluy. (p. 18)

There is, however, one aspect of the flame as an image of the divinity and its manifestations which does persist, and indeed grows in importance. It is of course present in Durant: the flame gives light as well as heat, and this illuminates our minds as well as warming our hearts. It was touched on when he spoke of heaven as a place where 'nostre entendement sera pleinement illuminé'; elsewhere he speaks of the flame being kindled in us 'lorsqu'il nous a communiqué sa cognoissance salutaire à nous reuelée en l'Euangile' (p. 6). Durant, as we might expect, gives a further twist to this image of the true faith by using it as the basis of a controversial point:

Desia en l'Eglise Romaine & depuis plusieurs siecles ce flambeau est caché sous le boisseau d'vne langue estrangere. Il est comme du tout esteint par le desbordement des torrens de la tradition humaine, & des superstitions diaboliques. (p. 6)

A similarly aggressive use of the image (though expressed in a less concrete form) occurs only in the work of Durant's namesake and contemporary Jacques Himbert Durant.[63] As sectarian passions cooled, the metaphor was refined and attenuated:

62 *Homelies spirituelles sur le Cantique des Cantiques*, 1620 (C. 82), p. 102. Seguiran touches on this idea of the ambiguous flame in a discussion of purgatory; see his *Sermons doctes et admirables sur les Evangilles des Dimanches & Festes de l'annéé*, 1612 (C. 268), p. 973.
63 *Sermon sur ces paroles* . . . *'Prenez garde que nul ne vous butine . . .'*, 1618 (C. 153), p. 18: 'C'est vn peu de clarté parmy beaucoup de tenebres,

En vn mot toute la doctrine Chrestienne y estoit tellement couuerte d'erreurs, & offusqué de nuages, qu'il a esté impossible que ces grands hommes [sc. the Reformers] ayent fait éclorre d'vne épaisse & si profonde obscurité, vne si belle & si pure lumiere qu'est celle dont nous ioüissons maintenant, sans vne assistance tres-particuliere de la grace diuine.[64]

It nevertheless remained a metaphor, that is to say (as far as sermons are concerned) an image so closely associated with an idea that there is no need, even in this age of detailed comparisons, to establish the parallel. And while it is not restricted to unfavourable remarks on medieval religion, it is almost always contrasted with evil. Amyraut, in another sermon, lists the obstacles to a sinner's conversion as 'les tenebres de ton entendement, la peruersité de ta volonté, la violence de tes passions'.[65] Mestrezat opposes the 'ombres & figures' of Old Testament prophecy to 'la lumiere de la verité qu'on a obtenue'.[66] Daillé, alluding no doubt to 1 Corinthians xiii, 12, speaks of heaven as a place where 'en la lumiere dont nous jouyrons, nous connoistrons parfaictement toutes choses, sans qu'aucun ombrage nous cache la moindre verité'.[67] An image which was once part of a complex metaphor of God is becoming increasingly, and in fact almost exclusively, associated not with grace but with truth, the understanding, knowledge. The very treatment of it becomes more abstract as preachers begin to reject the values of concreteness and visual shock in their use of imagery. The end of the process comes with the word 'enlightenment', 'les lumières'.

The gradual restriction of this image is not limited to Protestants, although in this as in other aspects of their writing they exemplify the trend particularly well. Retz, one of the latest preachers in the period, describes the youth of St Charles Borromeo largely in terms of light:

> illusions, oracles, sentences, qu'ils suggerent à la sotte raison boursouflée de l'opinion de sa suffisance, qui discourt s'il luy semble doctement, magnifiquement des choses humaines, mondaines, charnelles, perissables, [mais] est aveugle au soleil des choses diuines, celestes, spirituelles, eternelles.'

64 Amyraut, *Sermons sur quelques sentences de l'Ecriture*, 1647, quoted from C. 16, p. 45.
65 *Sermon sur ces mots...* 'C'est Dieu...', 1640 (C. 7), p. 37.
66 *La Pasque chrestienne*, 1632 (C. 221), p. 4.
67 *Le Sacrifice des chrestiens*, 1633 (C. 110), p. 11.

> la miséricorde de Dieu fit sortir une jeune lumière qui jeta tant d'éclat dès sa naissance par les étincelles des vertus qui parurent dans ses premières années, qu'elle donna des espérances très-légitimes qu'elle dissiperoit, quand elle auroit pris plus de force, les ténèbres les plus grossières du péché et de l'ignorance.[68]

And to move out of the field of sermons for a moment, the intellectual nature of this light is made even more explicit in his celebrated portrait of Richelieu.[69]

Since we are here approaching the whole idea of the *klassische Dämpfung*, the transformation of French sensibility in the seventeenth century, a last illustration can perhaps be forgiven for straying beyond 1650. One of the few images connected with the properties of the flame not mentioned by Durant concerns the sun as a metaphor for notables. Among Catholic preachers it is frequently referred to and ingeniously explored. It was suggested in an earlier section that the king and the sun stood in a similar relationship as having the primacy of their respective levels of creation. Besse, for one, reinforces this by quoting Alexander the Great's remark on rejecting Darius's offer of a condominium, that a kingdom could have only one king just as the world has only one sun.[70] But the comparison was not restricted to kings alone; it extended to other great men – luminaries, we might call them. Both the dominant comparison and its extension are used by Boucher in his *Oraison funèbre sur le trespas de . . . Charlotte du Gué* of 1622 (C. 55). The first reference places the image firmly in the context of natural hierarchies:

> Les Anciens nous ont voulu jadis enseigner ce secret sous vne docte fable, en laquelle ils declarent que l'Honneur est tousiours glorieusement regnant prés le throsne du grand Iupiter, où il esclatte & reluit comme vn soleil: portant sur sa teste vne couronne tissuë de palmes, de lauriers, & de myrthes, enuironné de vertus, de sciences & de victoires qui le cherissent & reuerent comme leur Prince & Seigneur. (p. 6)

Here it is part of a highly allegorical exordium, but Boucher applies it later to the grieving husband, Nicolas de Verdun, and shows how easily it can be fitted into a complimentary mould:

68 *Sermon ou Panégyrique pour la fête de S. Charles Borromée*, 1646, quoted from C. 263, p. 85.
69 'Sa jeunesse jeta des étincelles de son mérite: il se distingua en Sorbonne.' *Mémoires*, ed. Allem, Paris, 1949, p. 67.
70 *Premieres conceptions theologiques sur le Caresme*, 1604 (C. 27), vol. 1, fol. 327^v.

'Nature, that universal and publick Manuscript'

> Mais tout ainsi que le Soleil durant son Eclypse n'est pas priué de lumiere en soy-mesme, car elle demeure seulement cachée à nos yeux pour vn temps: Ainsi ce grand Esprit voilé des obscuritez de la tristesse sur l'accident de cette mort, ne perdit pourtant point la lumiere de son beau iugement, & preuoyance ordinaire, qu'il fist reluire dans l'ordre merueilleux qu'il establist, & commanda d'estre obserué en la pompeuse & magnifique sepulture de cette chere Espouse.
> (p. 32)

Even the dominant comparison (king/sun) can be used to compliment lesser mortals. In Valladier's oration on Henri IV, Marie de Médicis is a

> resplendissante Lune, laquelle regardée amoureusement de ce Soleil, en la plenitude de sa vertu, est entrée en conionction de sa lumiere auecques la sienne, d'où ont esté produicts six beaux rayons, qui doiuent estre vn iour tresagreables à la France[71]

and earlier the royal family is described as

> sept planettes eclypsées en nostre hemisphere, ombragées de frayeur, voilées d'horreur, offusquées de tenebres.[72]

The fact that this sort of imagery was so prevalent early in the century partly explains, if not the choice of the *roi soleil* metaphor in later years, at least why it was so easily accepted. Nor need we leave the genre of funeral orations to trace its fortunes:

> Venez, peuples, venez maintenant; mais venez plutôt, princes et seigneurs, et vous qui jugez la terre, et vous qui ouvrez aux hommes les portes du ciel, et vous plus que tous les autres, princes et princesses, nobles rejetons de tant de rois, lumières de la France, mais aujourd'hui obscurcies et couvertes de votre douleur comme d'un nuage ...[73]

In the work of the greatest of French preachers, then, the heritage of the early 1600s is not lost. There is a process of attenuation, of increasing allusiveness; and this is made possible only by the very richness and complexity of our preachers' imagery. It is fascinating to trace the metamorphoses of *la nature rhétorique* and to examine its gradual loss of vitality. It is equally clear that later masterpieces can also be illuminated by a knowledge of this tradition.

---

71   *Harangue funebre de Henry le Grand*, 1610 (C. 297), p. 83.
72   *Ibid.*, p. 15.
73   Bossuet, *Oraison funèbre du Prince de Condé*, in *Oeuvres oratoires*, ed. Lebarq, revd Urbain and Lévesque, vol. 6, Paris, 1923, p. 457.

Postscript

An enquiry of this kind is inevitably bound to conclude not with any definitive picture but with a number of *directions de recherche*. I hope nonetheless that in the course of it some foundations have been laid upon which future research can be more firmly built. It will be remembered that in Chapter 1 three claims were made for the study of sermons. Pulpit oratory, I argued then, is a gauge of changing prose styles, a guide to the background of literary convention and sensibility in a period, and an autonomous art form. What contribution does this study make to our understanding of those three areas?

Firstly, prose style. The sermons are almost all marked by the dominance of what I have called the thesaurus method of composition. It was a method which combined reverence for the authorities of the past with a view of the world as a set of analogies to explore which was to reveal the divine pattern of life. Although it works through the literary device of the simile, it is clearly indebted to scholastic methods of argument rather than to a stylist's sensitivity to prose, and indeed in its least happy manifestations its exponents show an almost complete indifference to persuasive techniques other than the austerely intellectual. The attempt to increase the persuasive element in preaching was largely given its impetus from sources in Italian Counter-Reformation circles; and yet it had strongly divergent results. It was the effort, demonstrably based on Italian aesthetic ideals, to reduce verbosity and increase the mental stimulus of *conceptions* and *comparaisons* that led Camus to develop his extremely eccentric catenary style. On the other hand, the return to orchestrated prose originates in a new awareness of the effective power of language itself. We need not see these elements as coterminous with our period. French prose writing in the seventeenth century continues to oscillate between the rival attractions of an aphoristic tradition based on ingenuity and a rotund style which appeals to the musical rhythms of *numerus oratorius*. What does seem to belong more particularly to the sermon in this period is the mixture of these elements, the conceptist style. In its pulpit oratory, at least, early-seventeenth-century France was not so different from the rest of Europe as has often been thought. There is an important avenue here for comparative study.

The same is true of the general sensibility evinced by our preachers. A strong sense of the illusory nature of this world appears in every art form in Europe at this time, with the natural exception of music. My argument has been that this is initially a religious (and specifically a Tridentine) theme, springing from a Christian insistence on the reality of the invisible, and that the artistic commonplaces which it develops into are, in one sense, distortions of a religious view. We have also been able to see how this antithetical apprehension of life is relieved, as the period ends, of its heavily concrete overtones. The poignancy it has for an age strongly attracted by the physical appearances of things is diminished precisely by a more general acceptance of non-physical values. Molinier's invitation to the charnel-house becomes, in Bossuet, almost an apology.[1] In dealing with literary views of Nature at a time which saw the beginning of modern science we were, of course, bound to discover the same movement away from the physical and specific to the general and moral. It is the shift in the study of the world from an explanatory to an exploratory approach which ultimately kills the analogy and the prose style which enshrined it.

There has obviously to be a certain tension in an investigation which aims at surveying general trends and at the same time attempts to comment on an art form. Some of the preachers quoted here have been chosen as representative of certain themes and styles in a pure state, and are often not particularly interesting in themselves. For example, the works of Boucher or Pierre de Besse, though often extremely tedious, frequently afford the best illustration of a given point. As with any art form which has as many exponents over fifty years as we have here, there is a general consensus of ideas and forms which constitutes the background. But against

---

1 'Me sera-t-il permis aujourd'hui d'ouvrir un tombeau devant la cour, et des yeux si délicats ne seront-ils point offensés par un objet si funèbre?' Bossuet, *Sermon sur la mort*, in *Oeuvres oratoires*, ed. Lebarq, Urbain and Lévesque, Paris, 1914–26, vol. 4, p. 262.

this background certain figures stand out, and they stand out either as innovators or, more commonly, as masters of the craft. Thus St François de Sales – although he has not, for various reasons, been discussed in great detail – is clearly the major exponent of the thesaurus style.[2] Molinier, too, is not a genuine transformer of prose style, but he is, despite the constant repetition of themes in his sermons, incomparably the most interesting of the preachers who use conceptist prose. It is a style whose special virtues – brevity, ingenuity, sudden pathos, concreteness of imagery – he exemplifies to an outstanding degree, and his work clearly ought to be better known.[3] Only Du Moulin, among the Protestants who write in this style, can be compared to him. Amyraut is more difficult to place in a well-defined category; he is writing before Protestant prose acquires that classical smoothness and courtesy which characterizes, for example, Daillé's prose. But there is in his sermons – many of them unfortunately not available in major libraries – an intellectual toughness combined with a vigour of presentation which makes him perhaps the most readable of all the preachers.[4]

Some, on the other hand, deserve attention as innovators. This is particularly true of Camus, and it is an aspect of his work which has not, I think, been grasped before. His sermons, as will have been judged from the quotations I have made from them, are not the easiest of reading. Nevertheless, his concept of involving the reader dynamically in the text itself has affinities with the most modern

2   Students of the period await with interest Mlle Hélène Bordes's forthcoming study of St François's sermons.
3   The almost wholly dismissive attitude of scholars who compare French with Italian, Spanish or English 'witty' prose may be illustrated by E. R. Curtius's one-line footnote to his chapter on Mannerism in *European Literature and the Latin Middle Ages*, trans. Trask, New York, 1963, p. 301: 'The French variants (the *précieux*, etc.) are less interesting.'
4   It is surprising that his most recent interpreter judges this to be true of his thought, but not of his style: 'Yet, despite a heavy style annoyingly cluttered with appositional phrases, his writing exhibits a freedom and independence of spirit and thought which makes it refreshing reading when compared with that of his Protestant contemporaries. His sermons are only mediocre, though always attuned to the situation at hand and spiced with interesting analogies and illustrations usually taken from classical literature' (B. G. Armstrong, *Calvinism and the Amyraut Heresy*, London and Wisconsin, 1969, p. 73).

literary theories and practices, and there is evidence of a proper interest in him forming itself at last.

Unfortunately, sermons suffer from their inability to be conveniently anthologized. I am keenly aware that by discussing the trends within a genre over some fifty years I have not been able to give a sense of the span, the inner development, of a sermon as a whole entity, to examine single works on an extended wavelength. As T. S. Eliot wrote of Lancelot Andrewes, 'His sermons are too well built to be readily quotable; they stick too closely to the point to be entertaining.'[5] Obviously their contribution to the history of French prose style and the satisfaction which they, like religious poetry, can give to the modern reader have to be made known through editions or reprints of their works.

It is only then that we shall be able fully to understand the relationship in which they stand to other art forms. At various points during this study I have suggested that the most important link between sermons and poetry resides in the preachers' explanation and demonstration, week after week, of analogies between objects, thereby enabling poets to extend their repertory of metaphors and allusions without sacrificing comprehension to brevity. The link with the visual arts is much the same. As was pointed out when we examined perspectives and reflections in the sermons, they often provide the iconographical key to church decorations. A similar connexion, I suggest, ties them to the writings of later religious artists like Bossuet, although here one has to take into account substantial changes in sensibility. The relationship is a complex one, since preachers after the Fronde both react against, and are able to allude to, the tradition that precedes them. It is nevertheless clear that there is much that awaits exploration in the light of the Baroque preaching tradition.

5 *Selected Essays*, 3rd edn, London, 1966, p. 341.

Part II
Descriptive Catalogue of
printed texts

Explanatory note

The following is, with one or two exceptions, a descriptive catalogue of extant French pulpit oratory published between 1598 and 1650. The choice of these chronological limits and the principles underlying the survey are discussed in Chapter 1 of Part I. Nevertheless it is perhaps worth re-stating briefly here some of the consequences which flow from directing an enquiry solely to the question of who the preachers of this period were and what was published in their name.

There are two rather ill-defined areas where it is difficult to draw a clear line between genres. Firstly, the funeral oration. Great numbers of orations were published in the period but many, perhaps the majority, of them are civic or political rather than works of pulpit oratory. My practice has therefore been to include funeral orations only when their authors also published sermons. This gives rise to some revealing absences, such as Cospéan or Coëffeteau. Secondly, a hazy line divides the sermon from the meditation. It was a favourite practice of preachers at this time to publish sermons in the form of meditations. One of the reasons for printing a sermon at all was, of course, to furnish the devout with spiritual reading matter and thus provide a basis, or a substitute, for the discipline of meditation. Conversely, the very form of some sermons is determined by meditative techniques. I have excluded those meditations where the link with the pulpit is extremely tenuous, the acid test in these cases being almost always a purely formal one. An example of my method may be seen under Pierre Coton (Catalogue nos. 98–104). In Appendix 3 I discuss some names which readers may be surprised at not finding in the Catalogue. Similarly, I have not investigated sermons in manuscript, though modern editions of unpublished sermons by famous men (Retz, for example) have been noted. Translations have also been excluded. The absence of a list of anonymous works may appear surprising, but in fact I have discovered very few. Where an attribution was possible, works occasionally classed as anonymous have been listed under their supposed author and the reasons given. The very small remaining number of anonymous works comprises for the most part obscure single Protestant tracts.

In compiling the Catalogue the following system has been adopted: the items are numbered consecutively for easy reference, but are broken down under authors in alphabetical order; each author's works are listed chronologically. For each preacher there is a short biographical note, except in the cases of celebrated men like Richelieu or those about whose lives the usual authorities are silent; and since I have noted membership of a religious order where appropriate, it seemed useful also to indicate membership of a Protestant body (by the letter P). Often a short bibliographical note is also added. Under the individual author-headings the list is in order of the real or reconstructed date of the first edition of a work, followed immediately by the reprints or new editions, if any, which appeared up to 1650. I have permitted myself occasional excursions outside this period in order to discuss either the earliest extant edition of a work which definitely appeared during the period, or else the final volumes of a series where it seemed senseless to perform an arbitrary amputation. Where an edition has been seen in a library, it is described according to the regular practice of English and American bibliographers, i.e. with title-page, collation, and contents. This rather full description is, I think, justifiable in a catalogue which is the first to include many of these works and may be needed as a basis for distinguishing various editions. Items that have not been seen are merely given a short title and a reference to some authority for them. In the case of apparently identical copies a non-defective one of which is in the Bibliothèque Nationale, I have given the BN press-mark only, though important differences between copies (such as gross misbinding) have been noted. Modern editions are noted but not described. Appendix 1 lists some common printers' devices which it seemed unnecessary to describe each time one appeared on a title-page.

There is one major exception to the general rules I have followed. It concerns Jean-Pierre Camus, by far the most prolific and most frequently reprinted author of sermons in this period. In its original form this Catalogue applied the same method to Camus as to other preachers; such detailed labour has now been substantially rendered otiose by the excellent *Bibliographie des oeuvres de Jean-Pierre*

Camus by M. Jean Descrains.[1] M. Descrains gives a short title rather than a description, but these sermons pose in any case few bibliographical problems that might be solved by fuller description; on the other hand, he provides a very full list of the editions and their whereabouts. I have no information of substance to add to M. Descrains's list and have therefore thought it better to save considerable space here by simply listing the title and first edition of a work of Camus and the press-mark of the copy I have used, referring then to its number in Descrains and noting the total of its subsequent appearances up to 1650. Interested students are assumed to have access to M. Descrains's work. When, however, I have quoted in Part I from an edition of Camus other than the first I have noted the relevant information, including the press-mark, in this Catalogue.

Catalogues of this kind are destined to be superseded. Although I have obviously had recourse to the standard bibliographies and library catalogues (noting when necessary where I differ from them and why), I am vividly aware that a census of all the great European libraries would yield a much fuller list, especially in the case of Protestant sermons. One man can inevitably visit only a few. I shall be most grateful to those who can correct or supplement the information given here.

---

1 *Publications de la Société d'Etude du XVIIe Siècle*, I, Paris, 1971.

Abbreviations

Ars.	Bibliothèque de l'Arsenal
BHP	Bibliothèque de la Société de l'Histoire du Protestantisme français
BL	British Library
BMT	Bibliothèque Municipale de Toulouse
BMV	Bibliothèque Municipale de Versailles
BN	Bibliothèque Nationale
Bod.	Bodleian Library
ECC	Library of Emmanuel College, Cambridge
Maz.	Bibliothèque Mazarine
Mert.	Library of Merton College, Oxford
SBNU	Bibliothèque Nationale et Universitaire de Strasbourg
SG	Bibliothèque Sainte-Geneviève
ULC	Cambridge University Library

The standard authorities referred to in the Catalogue by single names (e.g. Cioranescu, Sommervogel) are listed in the select bibliography.

ABRA DE RACONIS, Charles François de
Raconis (Chartres) 1580 – Paris 1646. Studied at Paris. Preacher and Chaplain to the King. Bishop of Lavaur 1637.

1 *Riches et excellens paralleles.* Paris, 1625.
RICHES | ET EXCELLENS | PARALLELES | ENTRE DIEV | ET L'AME, LE PROTOTYPE | ET SON IMAGE. | *Preschez en vn Aduent en l'Eglise de sainct | André des Arcs l'an 1622.* | Par M. CHARLES FRANÇOIS D'ABRA | DE RACONIS, Docteur en Theologie, | Conseiller & Predicateur | ordinaire du Roy. | *Et du depuis rangez en meilleur ordre par le mesme, | pour l'vtilité du public.* | Dediez au Roy Image particuliere de la Diuinité. | [Orn.] | A PARIS, | Chez LOVYS BOVLANGER, ruë sainct | Iacques, à l'Image S. Louys. | M. DC. XXV. | *Auec Priuilege, & Approbation.* |
    8vo πA^8, $A-2X^8$

$\pi A1^r$ Title; $\pi A2^r$ Ded. au Roy [$\pi A2^r$ is numbered 3, otherwise these preliminary leaves are not paginated]; $\pi A5^r$ Sonnet signed Gerard Quatresols; $\pi A5^v$ Sonnet sur le liure; $\pi A6^r$ Autre sonnet, signed Hemart; $\pi A6^v$ Table des discours; $\pi A7^v$ Approbation dated 9 April 1625; $\pi A8^r$ Privilege for 6 years dated 10 April 1625; $A1^r$ Text, paginated 1–208/229–701; $2V6^r$ Table des matieres theologiques; $2X2^r$ Table des matieres controuersées; $2X4^v$ Table des moralitez.   [BN Rés. D 15538

2 *Oraison funebre sur le trespas de feu Mgr le Mareschal de Schomberg.* Paris, 1633.
ORAISON | FVNEBRE, | SVR LE TRESPAS | DE FEV MON-SEIGNEVR | LE MARESCHAL DE | Schomberg. | Prononcée en l'Eglise du Prieuré | de Nantheuil, le iour de son enterrement. | *Par Mre C. F. d'Abra de RACONIS,* | *Docteur en Theologie, Conseiller | & Predicateur ordinaire de | leurs Majestez.* | [Orn.] | A PARIS. | M. DC. XXXIII. |
    8vo $\tilde{a}^4$, $A-F^8$

$\tilde{a}1^r$ Title; $\tilde{a}2^r$ Ded. à Mgr le duc d'Hallwyn; $A1^r$ Text, paginated 1–92; F7 and F8 blank.   [BN Ln27 18701

Note: MS. corrections on pp. 19, 43, 47, 60. MS. notes on F7 and F8, including two signatures: Baudoyn and De raconis.

3 *Discours funebre ... du Roy Tres-Chrestien Louys le Juste.* Paris, 1643.

DISCOVRS FVNEBRE | PANEGYRIQVE | ET | HISTORIQVE, | SVR | LA VIE ET VERTVS, LA | MALADIE ET LA MORT | du Roy Tres-Chrestien | LOVYS LE IUSTE. | Prononcé le 19. et 20. Iuin, aux Seruices solennels | qui furent faits en l'Eglise des RR. PP. de | l'Oratoire du Louure. | *Par Messire* CHARLES FRANÇOIS D'ABRA | DE RACONIS, *Docteur en Theologie, Conseil-* | *ler du Roy en ses Conseils, Predicateur ordi-* | *naire de la Reyne, Euesque de l'Auaur.* | [Orn.] | *A PARIS,* | Chez NICOLAS TALON, Libraire ordinaire | de la Reyne, ruë S. Iacques, au Mortier | d'Or, pres l'Eglise de S. Benoist. | M. DC. XLIII. |

   8vo ã^8, A-0^8, P^4, Q^2

   ã1^r Title; ã2^r Ded. à la Reyne; ã7^v Privilege for 10 years dated 23 July 1643; Fautes suruenuës en l'impression; A1^r Text, pag. 1–234.
[BN X. 18890

   Note: Wants ã8 and Q2.

AMYRAUT, Moïse (P)
Bourgueil (Anjou) 1596–Saumur 1664. Professor and Pastor at the Academy of Saumur from 1626.

   There is a most useful bibliography in B. G. Armstrong: *Calvinism and the Amyraut Heresy* (London and Wisconsin, 1969) pp. 294–5, superseding those in F. Laplanche: *Orthodoxie et prédication. L'oeuvre d'Amyraut et la querelle de la grâce universelle* (Paris, 1965), in Cioranescu, and in Haag. The arabic numerals refer to the list of sermons in section 5 of the bibliography in Haag: *La France protestante*, 2nd edn, vol. 1, cols. 192–6.

4 *Sermon sur l'Apocalypse ii, 27.* Charenton, Mondiere, 1636.
8vo
(Haag 1; Armstrong).

5 *Six sermons.* Saumur, 1636.
SIX | SERMONS | DE LA NATVRE, | ESTENDVE, NE- | CESSITE', DISPENSA- | TION, ET EFFICACE | DE L'EVAN- GILE. | *Par* MOYSE AMYRAVT | *Pasteur & Professeur en Theo-* | *logie à Saumur.* | [Orn. P] | *A SAVMVR,* | Pour CLAVDE GIRARD, & | DANIEL DE LERPINIERE. | *M. DC. XXXVI.* |

   12mo ã-2ẽ^6, 2ĩ^2, A-2E^6, 2F^2

   ã1^r Title; ã2^r Preface au Lecteur; ã6^v Eschantillon de la doctrine

Amyraut, Moïse (C. 9)

de Calvin touchant la predestination; 2Ĩ2^r Textes des sermons suiuans; A1^r Text, pag. 1–338; 2F2^r Errata; Imprimé à Saumur par Jean Lesnier et Isaac Desbordes. [ULC Peterborough A. 1. 16

Note: The Bod. copy [8° A 125 Th.] has the imprint of the printers on the title-page instead of the names of Girard and Lerpinière.

6 *Trois sermons sur l'Epitre aux Ephésiens i, 16.* Charenton, 1639.
12mo
(Haag 3; Armstrong).

7 *Sermon sur ces mots . . . 'C'est Dieu . . .' [with another].*
Saumur, 1640.
SERMON | SVR CES MOTS DV | Chapitre second de l'Epistre | aux Philippiens Verset 13. | *C'est Dieu qui produit en vous auec effica-* | *ce & le vouloir & le parfaire,* | *selon son bon plaisir.* | Prononcé à Chasteleraut le iour de la | Pentecoste, lors que le Synode de | Poictou y celebroit la Cene. | *Auec vn autre prononcé à Saumur sur les* | *mesmes mots, & ceux qui les precedent.* | Par MOYSE AMYRAVT Pasteur | & Professeur en Theologie. | [Orn.] | *A SAVMVR*, | Chez ISAAC DESBORDES, | Imprimeur & Libraire, demeurant | à l'Enseigne de l'Imprimerie. | M. DC. XXXX. |
8vo A-N^4, O^2
A1^r Title; A2^r Ded. à Monsieur de S. George de Verac; A4^r Text, pag. 1–101 [the text of the second sermon begins on H2^r, p. 53]; O2^r Acheué d'imprimer le 6. iour de Septembre 1640.
[SG Rés. D 8° 11086 (6)

8 *Sermon sur 1 Corinthiens xv, 55.* Saumur, 1644.
SERMON | SVR LE VERSET | 55. du Chap. XV. de la pre- | miere Epistre de S. Paul aux | Corinthiens. | *Par M.* AMYRAVT, *Pa-* | *steur & Professeur à Saumur.* | [Orn. P] | *A SAVMVR* | Par IEAN LESNIER, Imprimeur | & Libraire, Au Livre d'Or. | M. DC. XLIV. |
12mo A-E^4
A1^r Title; A2^r Text, pag. 3–40. [BL 3900.a.45 (9)

9 *Sermon sur ces mots de l'Apocalypse i, 4 . . . 'Jean aux sept Eglises'.* Saumur, 1645.
16mo
(Haag 7; Armstrong).

10 *Sermon sur 2 Timothée i, 12.* Charenton, 1645.
SERMON | SVR LE XII. VERSET | DV CHAP. 1. DE LA 2. |
Epistre à Timothée. | *Prononcé à Charanton, par M.* | *Amyraut,
Pasteur & Professeur* | *en Theologie à Saumur, le* | *Dimanche 29.
Ianuier.* | *1465.* | [Orn.] | *Se vendent à Charenton.* | Par LOVYS
VENDOSME, | demeurant à Paris, ruë | neufue du Palais, au | Sacrifice d'Abra- | ham. | M. DC. XLV. | [1465 has been corrected in MS. to 1645.]

   12mo A-F$^{8-4}$, G^2

   A1^r Title; A2^r Text, pag. 3-76; G2^v Errata.

                                                [SBNU E. 127855

11 *Sermon sur le Psaume 14, 1.* Saumur, 1645.
   16mo
   (Haag 9; Armstrong).

12 *Deux sermons: Genèse iii, 19, 'Tu es poudre', et Jean viii, 51.*
   Saumur, 1646.
   8vo
   (Haag 10 and 11; Armstrong).

13 *Deux sermons sur 1 Jean v, 7-8.* Saumur, 1646.
DEVX | SERMONS | SVR LES VERSETS | 7. & 8. du cinquiéme chap. | de la premiere Epistre de sainct | Iean. | *Prononcés à Charenton au mois* | *d'Octobre 1645.* | *Auec vne* Action sur le Dimanche 47. | du Catechisme. | *Par* MOYSE AMYRAVT, *Pasteur* | *& Professeur en Theologie à* | *Saumur.* | [Orn.] | *A SAVMVR,* | Chez ISAAC DESBORDES, | Imprimeur & Libraire. | M. DC. XLVI. |

   8vo A-V^4

   A1^r Title; A2^r Ded. à Mme de Morins; A4^r Text, pag. 7-160.
[V3 is missigned Y3.]   [BN D^2 5496

14 *Sermon sur . . . l'Epistre aux Hebrieux x, 26.* Saumur, 1646.
SERMON | SVR CES MOTS DE | l'Epistre aux Hebrieux, | ch. 10. vers. 26. | *Si nous pechons volontairement apres* | *auoir receu la connoissance de verité,* | *il ne reste plus de sacrifice pour les* | *pechés.* | *Prononcé à la Rochelle au mois* | *d'Aoust 1644.* | *Par* MOYSE AMYRAVT *Pasteur* | *& Professeur en Theologie à Saumur.* |

[Orn.] | *A SAVMVR,* | Chez ISAAC DESBORDES, | Imprimeur & Libraire. | *M. DC. XLIV.* |
  8vo A–F⁴
  A1ʳ Title; A2ʳ Text, pag. 3–45; F4 blank.   [Maz. 36.512 (5)
  Note: Various MS. notes. Unknown to Haag, Laplanche and Armstrong.

15 *Sermons sur quelques sentences de l'Ecriture.* Saumur, I. Desbordes, 1647.
  (Armstrong).

16 *Idem.* Saumur, 1648.
SERMONS | SVR QVELQVES | SENTENCES DE | L'ECRITURE. | *Par MOYSE AMYRAVT.* | [Orn.] | *A SAVMVR,* | Chez ISAAC DESBORDES, Imprim. | & Marchand Libraire. | *M. DC. XLVIII.* |
  8vo ã⁴, A–M⁸, N⁴
  ã1ʳ Title; ã2ʳ Ded. à Henry-Charles de la Tremouille, Prince de Talmond, dated Saumur 20 November 1647; ã4ᵛ Tables des textes; A1ʳ Text, pag. 1–198.   [BHP R. 949
  Note: A second printing, according to Armstrong.

ANTONIN DE PARIS (GRAVELAIS) (Capuchin)
Nothing appears to be known of this preacher; he is noted as 'le P. Antonin' by Albert, *Dictionnaire portatif des prédicateurs,* p. 474, and Cioranescu adds nothing more. These are the only two sources which mention him; even the *Lexicon Capuccinum* is silent. His secular name is in fact found twice in the work listed below: the Latin epigram (ẽ8ʳ) calls him Renatus Antoninus Gravelais, and the French sonnet (ẽ8ᵛ) also calls him Gravelais.

Cioranescu lists two works, *Le Temple mystique,* 1613 (7647) and *Le Tresor admirable,* 1613 (7648), presumably in an attempt to reconcile Albert, who notes the former (p. 474), with the catalogue of the Bibliothèque Mazarine, which contains the latter. The title given below makes it clear that there is in fact only one work, with two interchangeable titles. Thus, despite the title-page, the running title throughout is *Le Temple mystique.*

17 *Tresor admirable tiré de l'Escripture saincte.* Paris, 1613.
TRESOR | ADMIRABLE | *TIRE' DE L'ESCRIP-* | *TVRE*

SAINCTE, | Ou est declaré come | l'Ame est le Temple Mistique de la Sa- | cree Trinité. | *Presché au temps de l'Aduant* | *Par le R. P. Anthonin* | *de Paris predicateur* | *de l'Ordre des* | *Capucins.* | *A PARIS,* | *Chez Nicolas du* | *Fosseé ruë S.ͭ Iaques* | *au vase d'or.* | *M. DC. XIII.* | *Auec priuilege du Roy.* |

[Engraved title-page, showing a Calvary with SS. Francis of Assisi and Anthony of Padua, the patrons of the Friars Minor, and SS. Antoninus of Florence and René of Angers, the author's patrons. Signed L. Gaultier sculpsit.]

8vo ã–ẽ^8, A–3Y^8, 3Z^2

ã1^r Title; ã2^r Ded. à Gabrielle de la Magdelaine, Abbesse de S. Julien d'Auxerre; ẽ2^r Aduertissement au Lecteur; ẽ4^v Concessio R. P. Generalis dated Rome 21 September 1612; Approbation des Docteurs dated 6 November 1613; ẽ5^r Privilege for 6 years dated 8 November 1613; ẽ6^r Table des sermons; ẽ8^r Latin epigram signed F. A. B.; ẽ8^v French sonnet signed Begart Guillermita; A1^r Text, pag. 1–80/91–1047; 3T8^v Table des passages de l'Escriture Saincte qui sont exposés en ce liure, pag. 1048–99.   [Maz. 24. 704

Note: MS. notes on flyleaves.

AUBERTIN, Edmé (P)
Vitry-le-François 1596 – Paris 1652. Pastor first at Chartres, then at Charenton.

The work listed under Aubertin's name in the BL *Catalogue of Printed Books* – a collection of three sermons by Aubertin, Le Faucheur, and Mestrezat – was destroyed during the second World War. Presumably it was the same work as the second entry below. The sermons by the other two preachers have also survived in different collections.

Neither of the works listed here is found in the usual authorities.

18 *Sermon de la foy des Gentils.* Charenton, 1634.
SERMON | DE LA FOY DES | Gentils en l'Euangile, | & du Seau de l'Esprit. | *Sur le Chapitre I. vers. 13. de l'Epistre* | *de S. Paul aux Ephesiens.* | Prononcé le 15, May iour de | Pentecoste à Charenton. | Par E. AVBERTIN. | [Orn.] | *Et se vendent à Charenton* | Par Iacques Lucas, dit Salliere, | demeurant à Paris ruë des | Carmes. | M. DC. XXXIIII. |

12mo A–C^{12}, D^4, E^2

A1^r Title; A2^r Text, pag. 3–84; E2^v Ce sermon a esté prononcé a Charanton le 15. May 1633.   [SG Rés. D 8° SUP 319

Note: Various MS. corrections.

19 *Sermon sur les versets 3 et 4 du Psalme 130.* Charenton, 1637.
SERMON | SVR LES VERSETS | 3. & 4. du Psalme 130. | *Fait à Charenton le 19. Nouem-* | *bre 1637. iour de ieusne.* | PAR EDME AVBERTIN | Ministre de la parole de Dieu. | Vers. 3. *Seigneur si tu prens garde* | *aux iniquitez, qui est-ce qui sub-* | *sistera?* | 4. *Mais il y a pardon par deuers toy,* | *afin que tu sois craint.* | *Et se vendent à Charenton.* | Par PIERRE AVVRAY, demeurant sur | le Quay, vis à vis le cheual de | Bronze. 1637. |

12mo A–F$^{8-4}$

A1^r Title; A2^r Text, pag. 3–71.   [SG Rés. D 8° SUP 319

Note: MS. notes *passim*.

BEAUVAIS, Charles de (P)
Nothing about this preacher in the usual sources. The BL catalogue gives some other works published in London.

20 *De la protection et sauvegarde divine.* London, 1636.
DE LA | PROTECTION, | ET | SAVVEGARDE | DIVINE. | CONTRE LES PERILS | DE LA VIE PRESENTE, | Particuliers, & | Publics. | *Par* CHARLES DE BEAVVAIS, | *Ministre de la Parole* | *de Dieu.* | A LONDRES, | Chez HVMPHREY ROBINSON, à | l'enseigne des 3. Pigeons, dans le | Cimetiere de St. Paul. | 1636. |

[The whole within an ornamented border.]

8vo A^2, B–F^8

Wants A1; A2^r Title; B1^r Text, pag. 1–31/32/31/32–75; F8 wanting.   [ECC 338. 2. 69

Note: Listed in *STC:* 1698. A microfilm copy of this work is to be found in BL Mic. A. 588 (9)

BENARD, Laurent (Benedictine)
Nevers 1573 – Paris 1620. Doctor of Theology of Paris, and Prior of the Collège de Cluny there. He joined the new community of Saint-Vannes in 1615, and was instrumental in setting up the independent Congrégation de Saint-Maur.

21 *Paraeneses chrestiennes.* Paris, 1616.
PARAENESES | CHRESTIENNES, | OV | Sermons tres-vtiles à toutes persōnes, tant | Laiques, Ecclesi- | astiques, que | Regulieres. | *Par Dom Laurent Benard | Religieux Benedictin Docteur | en Theologie et Prieur du | College de Cluny | a Paris.* | *Auec priuilege du Roy.* | *A PARIS, Chez Pierre Cheuallier ruë St Iacques a l'image St Pierre.* |

[Engraved title-page showing SS. Benedict, Maur and Hugues. Signed L. Gaultier incidit 1616.]

8vo π2, ã^8, A–3N^8

π1r Title; π2 cancelled; ã1^r Ded. à Louis de Lorraine; ã4^v Auant-Propos; ã8^r Approbation dated Paris 20 September 1616; A1^r Text, pag. 1–939; 3N6^v L'ordre des chapitres; 3N7^r Table des Paraeneses et des matieres.   [BN D 25646

BENOIST, René
Savennières 1521 – Paris 1608. He led an adventurous life closely linked with political personalities; he accompanied Mary Stuart to Scotland as her confessor, played a prominent role in the Paris of the League as Curé of Saint-Eustache (where he was nicknamed 'le pape des Halles'), and was later a friend of Henri IV, who nominated him to the See of Troyes (though this was never confirmed by Rome). His translation of the Bible was condemned for a number of years.

22 *Abrégé d'un sermon.* Paris, 1600.
ABREGE' | D'VN SERMON | PRONONCE' EN LA | PROCESSION DE L'VNIVER- | sité de Paris, faicte pour le Roy, | estant à la guerre, le 15. de Septem- | bre 1600. | *Dediê & enuoyé à la Noblesse Françoise qui* | *l'assiste fidelement.* | Par. M. R. B. Confesseur de sa Majesté, | & Doyen de la faculté de Theologie à Paris. | [Orn. IHS] | *A PARIS,* | Chez Pierre Cheuallier, au mont sainct Hilaire | à la cour d'Albret. | 1600. | *Auec Priuilege du Roy.* |

8vo A–D^4

A1^r Title; A2^2 Ded. à la Genereuse, Belliqueuse, et Heroicque Noblesse Françoise; A4^v Text. [Fols. A2, A4, B1–D4 are numbered 3, 5, 7–18.]   [BN D 25677

23 *Sermon de la disposition requise pour le lavement des pieds.* Paris, 1601.

Benoist, René (C. 24)

SERMON DE | LA DISPOSITION | REQVISE POVR LE LAVE-MENT | des pieds, pour l'adoration de la Croix | qui se fait le Vendredy sainct, & pour | gaigner le Iubilé, & pour cognoistre & | apprehender l'auctorité de nostre Sainct | Pere le Pape en la concession des Indul- | gences & pardons: | *FAICT ET PRONONCE' EN* | *la ville d'Orleans le Ieudy absolu, deuant le* | ROY, *& les Princes & Seigneurs* | *estans lors à la Cour.* | Par M. René Benoist, Doyen de la sacrée faculté de Theologie à | Paris, Confesseur du ROY, & nommé par sa Majesté, | à l'Euesché de Troyes. | [Orn.] | *A PARIS,* | Chez Pierre Cheuallier au mont. S. Hilaire, | à la cour d'Albret, | 1601. | *Auec Priuilege du Roy.* |

    8vo A-C^4

    A1^r Title; A2^r Histoire & Narration veritable, pag. 3-6; A4^r Text, pag. 7-24.   [BN D 25712

24 *Notables resolutions des presens differens de la religion.* Paris, 1608. 2 vols.

Vol. 1:
NOTABLES | RESOLVTIONS | DES PRESENS | Differens de la Religion: | *Prononcees par diuerses Predications, en plus de* | *cinquante Caresmes, preschez tant en ce* | *Royaume, que hors iceluy.* | Le tout dressé sur chacun iour de Caresme. | *Par* M. RENE' BENOIST, *Confesseur du Roy,* | *Conseiller de sa Majesté en son Conseil d'Estat & Priué* | *& son Predicateur & Aumosnier, Doyen de la* | Theologie [sic], *& Curé de S. Eustache à Paris.* | Veritas domini manet in aeternum. | A PARIS, | Par PIERRE CHEVALIER, au mont sainct | Hilaire, à la Court d'Albret. | M. DC. VIII. | AVEC PRIVILEGE DV ROY. |

    8vo ã^8, A-2X^8

    ã1^r Title; ã2^r Auant-Propos (Sommaire des themes & matieres); ã5^r Aduertissements; A1^r Text, pag. 1-704.

Vol. 2: Title as for vol. 1, except for the line division *preschez tant en ce Royau-* | *me* and the insertion of TOME SECOND after the Latin text.

    8vo a-2g^8

    a1^r Title; a2^r Text, pag. 3-477; 2g7^r Acheué d'imprimer le dernier iour de Ianuier 1608; 2g7^v Lettres patentes du Roy, for 6 years, dated 20 January 1608.   [BN D 15498

BERTAUT, Jean
Caen 1552–1611. The well-known poet. His ecclesiastical career owed a great deal to his literary talents which won him the favour of Henri III and Henri IV, under whom he became successively Abbot of Aunay (1594), first Chaplain to Marie de Médicis, and Bishop of Sées in 1606.

25 *Discours funebre sur la mort du feu Roy.* Paris, 1610.
DISCOVRS | FVNEBRE | SVR LA MORT | DV FEV ROY. | *Par Messire* I. BERTAVT *Euesque de Sees* | *premier Aumosnier de la* ROYNE. | [Orn. Royal arms] | A PARIS, | Chez la veufue ABEL L'ANGELIER, | au premier pillier de la grand' | Salle du Palais. | M. DC. X. | *Auec Priuilege du Roy.* |

8vo A–E^4

A1^r Title; A1^v Au Lecteur; A2^r Text, pag. 3–39 [pp. 33–9 mispaginated 53–9; p. 40 number wanting]; E4^r Sonnet signed Bertaut; E4^v Extraict du Privilege for 6 years dated 18 August 1610; Transport to Veuve l'Angelier. [BN Lb35 966]

26 *Sermons sur les principales festes de l'année.* Paris, 1613.
SERMONS | SVR LES | PRINCIPALES | FESTES DE L'ANNEE. | Composez par tres-Reuerend Pere en | Dieu Messire IEAN BERTAVD | Euesque de Seez, Conseiller du Roy | en son Conseil d'Estat & Priué, & pre- | mier Aumosnier de la Reyne. | *Prononcez en son Dioceze.* | Auec vn ample indice des Matieres. | EDITION PREMIERE. | [Printer's Orn.] | A PARIS, | EN LA BOVTIQVE DE NIVELLE, | Chez SEBASTIEN CRAMOISY, ruë Sainct | Iacques aux Cicognes. | M. DCXIII. | Auec Priuilege du Roy. |

8vo ã^4, A–2A^8, 2B–2C^4

ã1^r Title; ã2^r Ded. à la Reyne. signed Bertaut [the preacher's brother]; ã3^v Ta[b]le des Sermons; ã4^r Approbation dated 23 November 1612; ã4^v Extraict du Priuilege for 6 years dated 26 November 1612; A1^r Text, pag. 1–381/382/381/382–6; 2C1^r Table des principales matieres. [BN D 15503]

Note: Posthumously published by Bertaut's brother.

BESSE, Pierre de
Meymond (Corrèze) 1567 – Paris 1639. Canon of Herment 1591, Curé of Colombes 1605, Preacher to Condé, Preacher to the King 1611, Canon of Saint-Germain de l'Auxerrois 1618.

A bibliography of Pierre de Besse's works, drawn up by Auguste Bosvieux and revised by René Fage, forms the third section of E. Fage: *L'Abbé Pierre de Besse* (Tulle, 1885). Though these bibliographers relied almost entirely on private collections and occasionally based their conclusions on rather slight evidence, their work has been indispensable in building up a picture which even now remains very incomplete.

The most important internal evidence is provided by the Privilege dated 18 March 1615 which is printed in the Nicolas du Fossé 1622 edition of the *Conceptions sur les quatre fins de l'homme*. It supports its complaint against pirated editions with concrete examples (found in the list below with the note '1615 Privilege'), and supplies rather vague information as to the order in which Besse's works appeared: firstly the *Caresme*, followed by the *Quatre fins*, then 'les troisiesmes les oeuvres intitulées *Conceptions theologiques sur les dimanches, festes de toute l'année, et octave du S. Sacrement*'. These were, it states, reprinted 'six mois apres auoir esté mises en vente', by Jean de la Rivière of Cambrai. This information raises almost as many problems as it solves, since it is almost certain that the works listed together as 'les troisiesmes' were not published in that order, and that the *Festes* did not appear until 1618 (see the entry below). Of course, we are not dealing with a document aiming at scholarly accuracy; nevertheless, the apparent precision of 'six mois apres auoir esté mises en vente' remains disturbing. It is not unusual, however, for documents like Privileges and Approbations to include works which were not yet published, and even works which were never published, and so, if the Privilege really dates from 1615, the mention of the *Festes* of 1618 may well be merely further proof of the wish to put a comprehensive and effective stop to any future pirating of Besse's work.

27 *Premieres conceptions theologiques sur le Caresme.* Paris, 1604. 2 vols.

PREMIERES | CONCEPTIONS THEOLOGIQVES | *SVR LE CARESME.* | Preschees A Paris | en l'Eglise St Seuerin | l'an 1602. | *Par M. PIERRE de* | *BESSE Docteur en* | *Theologie.* | *A MONSEIGNEVR LE PRINCE.* | *Auec priuilege du Roy.* | 1604. | *A Paris* | *Chez Nicolas du* | *Fossé ruë St Iacques* | *au vase d'or.* |

[Engraved title-page showing a pope and a bishop, with the arms

of Condé. Signed L. Gaultier fecit. The engraving in this copy has been coloured.]
Vol. 1:
   8vo ã⁸, *⁴, A–2S⁸, 2T⁶
   ã1ʳ blank; ã2ʳ Title; ã3ʳ Ded. to Condé; *1ʳ Sonnet à madame la Princesse, *1ᵛ Sonnet à Monseigneur le Conte [sic]; *2ʳ L'Autheur aux Lecteurs; *3ᵛ Latin verses signed Seb. Rolliardus; *4ʳ Latin and French verses signed Simon Decubes Lymosin; *4ᵛ Quatrain signed Paulmier Crouille; A1ʳ Text of sermons up to Passion Sunday, foliated 1–334.
Vol. 2:
   8vo 3A–4C⁸, ã–ĩ⁸, õ⁶
   3A1ʳ Text of sermons from Passion Sunday to Low Sunday, foliated 1–207; 4C8ʳ Approbation dated 3 September 1603; 4C8ᵛ Extraict du Priuilege for 10 years dated 15 October 1603; ã1ʳ Table en forme de lieux communs; õ4ᵛ Acheué d'imprimer le 19. Ianuier 1604; õ5ʳ Fautes à corriger.   [BN Rés. D 25949

Note: Bosvieux and Fage (p. 104) describe this work as one volume of 1135 pages; otherwise their description tallies with the above, and this is clearly a case of two volumes being bound as one. The noting of pagination in Bosvieux and Fage is frequently erratic, and so we cannot be sure whether they had seen a foliated or a paginated copy.

28 *Idem.* Paris, 1606.
Bosvieux and Fage, p. 107. I have found no trace of this, but since it is described as having 747 pages and a smaller type, it was certainly a new edition.

29 *Idem.* Pont-à-Mousson, Melchior Bernard, 1607.
1615 Privilege. Bosvieux and Fage have presumably deduced the existence of this pirated edition from the same evidence. No one appears to have seen it.

30 *Idem.* Paris, N. du Fossé, 1611.
Bosvieux and Fage, p. 109. No evidence given. They have clearly not seen a copy.

31 *Idem.* Cambrai, Jean de la Rivière, 1618.
Bosvieux and Fage, p. 110. Entry unsupported by evidence.

32 *Idem.* Rouen, Adrien Ouyn [?], 1620.
PREMIERES | CONCEPTIONS | THEOLOGIQVES | SVR LE
CARESME. | Preschees A Paris | en l'Eglise S̊. Seuerin | l'an 1602. |
Par M. PIERRE *de* | BESSE *Docteur en* | *Theologie.* | DEDIE | A
MONSEIGNEVR | LE PRINCE. | 1620. | *A ROVEN* | *Chez Adrien
ouyn* | *dans la Court du* | *Palais.* |

[Engraved title-page showing a pope and a bishop, very clearly inspired by the engraving in no. 27. Signed Olivier Marc fecit A Rouen.]

8vo ã^8, A–3Y^8

ã1^r Title; ã2^r Ded. to Condé, ã8^r Sonnet à Madame . . .; Sonnet à Mgr le Conte [*sic*] de Belin; ã8^v Latin sonnet to Besse; French sixain signed Simon Decubes; French quatrain signed Paulmier Crouille; A1^r Text, pag. 1–1043; 3V2^v Approbation of 1603; 3V3^r Table en forme de lieux communs; 3Y8^v Acheué d'imprimer par Iacques Hollart le 14. iour d'Octobre 1623 [*sic*]. [Maz. 24.726

Note: Not listed in any of the usual sources. Unknown to Bosvieux and Fage.

33 *Idem.* Lyon, 1624.
Bosvieux and Fage, p. 110. No evidence given.

34 *Idem.* Lyon, Simon Rigaud, 1629. Bosvieux and Fage, p. 110.
No evidence given.

35 *Conceptions theologiques sur les quatre fins de l'homme.* Paris, 1606. 2 vols.

This work has presented considerable problems: the greatest initial difficulty is caused by the extraordinary fact that (apart from Albert, *Dictionnaire portatif des prédicateurs,* p. 30, and of course Bosvieux and Fage) no bibliography or catalogue, even those of the great libraries, lists this as in two volumes. This is perhaps explained and partially justified by the fact that no library possesses both volumes, and that the title-page of neither volume carries any mention of the other. Nevertheless, the internal evidence is very clear: for example, a volume on the Four Last Things which only contains sections on Heaven and Hell is unlikely to be complete in itself. The note 'Au Lecteur' begins 'Lecteur ce Lymosin a fait ce bastiment si ample, qu'il en a fallu faire deux corps de logis, ie dis en separer deux tomes' (1606 edn, vol. 2, π2^v).

Besse, Pierre de (C. 36)

Vol. 1:
CONCEPTIONS | THEOLOGIQVES | *SVR LES QVATRE* | *FINS DE L'HOMME,* | Preschéés en vn | Aduant l'an 1605. | Par | Me Pierre de Besse Doc- | teur en Theologie Aumos- | nier et Predicateur ordi- | naire de Monseigneur | le Prince de Condé. | A | Monseigneur l'Euesque | de Paris. | A Paris | Chez Nicolas du | Fossé ruë St Iacques | au vase D'or. | 1606. | Auec priuilege du Roy. |

[Engraved title-page showing SS. Peter and Paul, the title surmounted by Gondi's arms. Signed L. Gaultier sculpsit.]

8vo ã^8, ẽ^6, A–Z^8, 2a–2x^8, 2y^2

ã1^r Title; ã2^r Quatrain à Mgr l'Euesque de Paris; ã2^v Engraving of Henri de Gondy; ã3^r Ded. to the Bishop; ẽ1^v Sonnet to Pierre de Gondy; ẽ2^r Sonnet to Philippe-Emmanuel de Gondy; ẽ2^v Sonnet to Henry de Gondy; ẽ3^r Sonnet to Jean de Gondy; ẽ3^v Au Lecteur; ẽ5^v Privilege of 1606; A1^r Text, pag. 1–680; 2V5^r Table; 2Y2^v Acheué d'imprimé pour la premiere fois le 25. Aoust, 1606. [P. 188 carries an engraving of a death-bed scene, a burial, and the Last Day.]

[BMV Pératé c.4

Vol. 2: Title as for Vol. 1.

8vo π^4, A–3D^8, 3E^6

π1r Title; π2^r Au Lecteur; π2^v Quatrain signed Paulmier; π 3^r two Sonnets signed I. le Verrier Curé de Hebitrenon en Constantine; π3^v Engraving of Heaven and Hell; wants π^4; A1^r Text, pag. 1–776; 3C5^r Privilege for 10 years dated 21 July 1606 [mentions 'le tout en deux volumes']; 3C7^r Approbation dated 12 July 1606; 3C7^v Table des Matieres contenues en la seconde partie de l'Aduent.

[BN D 25939

Note: The BL copy [846.4.13] has 3E3 and 3E4 bound in after A2. The Ars. copy [8° T 6252] has very fine coloured and gilded engravings.

36 *Idem*. Douai, J. Bogard, 1607.
1615 Privilege. I assume that Bosvieux and Fage, p. 116, base their entry on the same evidence, since they offer none. I have found no copies.

37 *Idem*. Paris, N. du Fossé, 1609. 2 vols.
Vol. 1: Title engraved as in no. 35, except for the changed date. Contents as in no. 35, vol. 1, except that there is no Acheué d'imprimer. [ECC 330.7.117

Vol. 2: Title engraved showing a pope and a decapitated queen.
Contents as in no. 35, vol. 2. [BMV Pératé c.5

Note: A reprint or re-issue of the 1606 edition with a newly engraved title-page.

38 *Idem.* Paris, 1622.
CONCEPTIONS | THEOLOGIQVES | *SVR LES QVATRE* | *FINS DE L'HOMME,* | Preschéés en vn | Aduant. | *Par M.ᶜ Pierre de Besse* | *Docteur en Theologie* | *Ausmosn.ʳ et Pred.ʳ ordin.ᵉ* | *du Roy et de Monsei* | *gneur le Prince.* | A PARIS, | *Chez Nicolas du Fossé* | *ruë S.ᵗ Iacques au vase d'or.* | *Auec priuilege du Roy.* | M. DC. XXII. |

[Engraved title-page. SS. Peter and Paul are this time seated beneath the episcopal arms. Signed L. Gaultier sculpsit.]

8vo ã⁸, ẽ⁴, A–3P⁸

ã1ʳ Title; ã2ʳ Quatrain à Mgr le Cardinal de Reths; ã2ᵛ Engraving of Henri de Gondy; Ded. to Cardinal Bishop; ẽ1ʳ Sonnet to Pierre Card. de Gondy; ẽ2ʳ Sonnet to Philippe Emmanuel de Gondy; ẽ2ᵛ Sonnet to Henry de Gondy; ẽ3ʳ Sonnets to Book and Author; ẽ3ᵛ Approbation; ẽ4ʳ Quatrain to Besse; ẽ4ᵛ Engraving of Death, Burial, and the Last Day [as on p. 188 of no. 35, vol. 1]; A1ʳ Text, pag. 1–940; 3N6ᵛ Privilege; 3N8ᵛ Transport dated 12 April 1618; Ces conceptions theologiques ont esté acheuées d'imprimer pour la premiere fois de cette nouuelle correction le 7. iour de May. 1622; 301ʳ Table des matieres. [BN D 25940

Note: Clearly a new edition. Unknown to Bosvieux and Fage, and the usual authorities. It achieves its single-volume brevity by omitting the sermons for the feasts which fall in Advent.

39 *Conceptions theologiques sur tous les dimanches de l'année.* Paris, 1609. 2 vols.
This edition does not appear to be extant; Bosvieux and Fage have not seen a copy, nor does one exist in any of the libraries checked in this survey. I have presumed 1609 to be the date largely on the evidence of the 1619 Cambrai Jean de la Rivière edition (see below) which contains an Approbation of Paris dated 5 April 1609. The Paris approbation is normally a safe indication of the date of the first privileged edition. Further, the title of Cambrai 1619, which is clearly based on a Paris first edition, makes no mention of Besse's position as Preacher to the King, to which he was appointed in 1611.

Cioranescu (11941) quite unaccountably lists this work as Paris, 1604.

40 *Idem.* Cambrai, Jean de la Rivière, 1613.
See evidence below.

41 *Idem.* Cambrai, Jean de la Rivière, 1619. 2 vols.
I have been unable to find vol. 1.
Vol. 2:
CONCEPTIONS | THEOLOGIQVES | SVR TOVS LES | DIMANCHES DE | L'ANNEE, | Preschees en diuers | lieux | *Par M. PIERRE DE BESSE* | *Docteur en Theologie, Au-* | *mosnier & Predicateur ordinaire de Mr. le Prince de* | *Condé.* | Tome Second. | A | CAMBRAY, | Chez IEAN DE LA RIVIERE | M. DC. XIX. |
[Engraved title-page. The title panel is surmounted by two angels bearing the letters IHS, and supported by six panels showing Moses, David, and the four evangelists. Unsigned.]
8vo ã^8, A–2Z^8
ã1^r Title; ã2^r Ded. à M. de Lomenie; ã8^v Sonnet to Besse; A1^r Text, pag. 1–474/5/8/479–718; 2Y6^v Approbation of Paris 5 April 1609; 2Y7^r Table en forme de lieux communs; 2Z8^v Approbation of Cambrai dated 31 July 1613.   [BN D 25941

42 *Idem.* Douai, Pierre & Martin Bogard, 1632. 2 vols.
Bosvieux and Fage, p. 121.

43 *Conceptions theologiques sur l'octave du Saint-Sacrement.*
    Paris, Nicolas du Fossé, 1614.
Bosvieux and Fage, p. 131; Cioranescu 11947.

44 *Idem.* Pont-à-Mousson, Melchior Bernard, 1614.
Bosvieux and Fage, p. 135.
I have seen no copies of these editions, which I suppose to be in private hands. A description of the first edition may be found in Bosvieux and Fage. However, the loss is not irremediable, since according to René Fage ('Notice supplémentaire', p. 160) all the sermons contained here were reprinted in the 1618 *Festes.*

45 *Conceptions theologiques sur toutes les festes des saincts.* Paris, 1618. 3 vols.

Besse, Pierre de (C. 46)

CONCEPTIONS | THEOLOGIQVES | *SVR TOVTES LES* |
FESTES DES SAINCTS | & autres solemnelles | de l'Annéé. |
Preschéés en diuers lieux | Par M.ᵉ *Pierre de Besse* | *Docteur en Theolo-* | *gie et Predicateur* | *Ordinaire du Roy.* | TOME I. | A
PARIS, | *Chez Nicolas du* | *Fossé ruë Sainct* | *Iacques au vase* |
D'or. | 1618. | *Auec priuilege du Roy.* |

[Engraved title-page. The title within a border of nine representations of saints. Signed L. Gaultier incidit.]
Vol. 1:

8vo ã–õ⁸, ū⁴, A–3Y⁸

ã1ʳ Title; ã2ʳ blank; ã2ᵛ Arms of Nicolas le Jay; ã3ʳ Ded. to Nicolas le Jay dated Paris 4 April 1618; ẽ6ᵛ Preface de l'Autheur; õ6ᵛ Aduis au Lecteur; ū1ᵛ Approbation dated 1 April 1618; ū2ʳ Table des Sermons; ū2ᵛ Greek verses; ū3ʳ Latin verses signed Stephanus Fouquet; ū3ᵛ Sonnet to P. de B.; ū4ʳ Voeu de l'autheur; ū4ᵛ Engraving of Besse [aetat. 50. 1618; signed L. Gaultier.]; A1ʳ Text, pag. 1–1070 [pagination very confused throughout]; 3V6ʳ Privilege; 3V8ᵛ Transport dated 12 April 1618; Acheué d'imprimer pour la premiere fois le vingtiesme iour d'Auril 1618; 3X1ʳ Table des matieres; 3Y8 blank.   [ECC 326.6.49

Vol. 2:

8vo π², ã⁴, A–3F⁸, 3G⁴

π1ʳ Title; π2 cancelled; ã1ʳ Aduis au Lecteur; ã4ʳ Approbation; ã4ᵛ Table; A1ʳ Text, pag. 1–655/666–820; 3E6ʳ Privilege; 3E8ᵛ Transport etc; 3F1ʳ Table.   [ECC 326.6. 50

Vol. 3:

8vo π², ã⁴, A–3G⁸, 3H⁴

π1ʳ Title; π2 cancelled; ã1ʳ Aduis au Lecteur; ã4ʳ Approbation; ã4ᵛ Table; A1ʳ Text, pag. 1–826; 3F7ʳ Privilege; 3G1ʳ Transport etc; 3G1ᵛ Table; 3H4 blank.   [ECC 326.6.51

Note: Cioranescu (11952) gives the Rouen 1628 as the only edition.

46 *Idem.* Rouen, 1628. 3 vols.
Vol. 1:
CONCEPTIONS | THEOLOGIQVS | SVR TOVTES LES |
FESTES DES SAINCTS, | & autres solemnelles | de l'Année. |
Preschées en diuers lieux par M. PIERRE | DE BESSE *Docteur en* | *Theologie, &* | *Predicateur ordinaire* | *du Roy.* | TOME PREMIER. |

Besse, Pierre de (C. 47)

[Orn. IHS] | A ROVEN, | Chez RICHARD L'ALLEMANT, prés le Col- | lege des Peres Iesuites. | M. DC. XXVIII. |
    8vo ã–ĩ⁸, A–3H⁸
    ã1ʳ Title; ã2ʳ Ded. to Le Jay; ẽ2ʳ Preface; ĩ4ᵛ Aduis au Lecteur; ĩ7ʳ Approbation of Paris 1618; ĩ7ᵛ Sonnet; ĩ8ʳ Latin verses signed Fouquet; ĩ8ᵛ Table des sermons contenus en ce premier tome; A1ʳ Text, pag. 1–834; 3G2ʳ Table des matieres.   [BN D 25942
    Note: I have been unable to find copies of vols. 2 and 3.

47 *Secondes et nouvelles conceptions theologiques sur tous les jours du Caresme.* Paris, 1629. 2 vols.
Vol. 1:
SECONDES | ET NOVVELLES | CONCEPTIONS | THEOLO- GIQVES, | SVR TOVS LES IOVRS | du Caresme Preschees à | Paris. | Par M. PIERRE DE BESSE | Docteur en Theologie | Predicateur Ordinaire | du Roy et de Monsei- | gneur le Prince. | TOME PPEMIER [*sic*]. | A PARIS, | *Chez Claude Sonnius &* | *Pierre Baillet, ruë s. Iac-* | *ques à l'Escu de Basle, & à la Nauire d'Or. 1629.* | *Auec Priuilege du Roy et du duc de Lorraine.* |
    [Engraved title-page. The title is supported by figures of SS. Germain and Vincent, the whole surmounted by a Coronation of the Virgin. Unsigned.] False Title: SECOND | ET | NOVVEAV | CARESME | DE M. BESSE. | Tome premier. |
    8vo ã–ĩ⁸, A–3Z⁸
    ã1ʳ False title; ã2ʳ Engraved title; ã3ʳ Ded. à MM. les Doyens, Chanoines, & Chapitre de ... Saint-Germain de l'Auxerrois, dated 14 August 1628; ẽ3ᵛ Quatrain to Saint-Germain de l'Auxerrois; ẽ4ʳ Preface; ĩ4ʳ Approbation dated 20 February 1628; ĩ4ᵛ Extraict du Priuilege to Sonnius for 9 years, dated 13 March 1628; ĩ5ʳ Extraict des Registres du Parlement dated 30 August 1628; ĩ5ᵛ Acheué d'imprimer pour la premiere fois le 15. Septembre 1628; ĩ6ʳ Privilege of the Duke of Lorraine, to Sonnius for 8 years, dated Nancy 24 June 1628; ĩ8ᵛ Engraving of Besse [Aetat. 60. Signed C. de Pas delineauit et fecit.]; A1ʳ Text, pag. 1–1044; 3V3ʳ Table des choses plus rares ... contenuës en ce premier Tome.
                                                    [Ars. 8° T 6253
    Note: I have been unable to discover vol. 2. This work is unknown to Bosvieux and Fage, and to Cioranescu.

BLANCHOT, Pierre (Minim)
Paris 1589 – Beauvais 1637. Minim in 1617.

48 *Le Vray Accomplissement des desirs de l'homme.* Paris, 1635.
LE VRAY | ACCOMPLISSEMENT | DES DESIRS DE L'HOMME | EN LA VIE PRESENTE | Presché durant l'Aduent | en l'Eglise de Sainct | Mederic. | Par P. F. PIERRE BLANCHOT | Religieux Minime. | Parisien. | Auec Priuilege du Roy. | *A PARIS,* | *Chez Sebastien Cramoisy,* | *Imprimeur ordinaire du* | *Roy rue S.ᵗ Iacques aux* | *Cicognes.* | *MDCXXXV.* |

    8vo ā⁸, A–2Y⁸, 2Z⁴

    ā1ʳ Engraved title-page [unsigned; device of Cramoisy in lower right-hand panel]; ā2ʳ second title; ā3ʳ Ded. to the Church of St Mederic dated 7 March 1634; ā6ʳ Approbation des Docteurs dated 1 September 1634; ā6ᵛ Approbation des Theologiens dated 14 March 1634; ā7ʳ Extraict du Priuilege dated 7 March 1634; ā7ᵛ Table des desirs accomplis; A1ʳ Text, pag. 1–701; 2X7ᵛ Table des Autheurs; 2Y1ʳ Table des Matieres; 2Z3ᵛ Stances, signed F. P. DV-VAL, Minime; 2Z4ʳ Fautes suruenuës en l'impression.

                                          [BMV Fénelon c. 458

Note: Not mentioned by any authorities.

49 *Sermons pour les festes principales de l'année et octave du S. Sacrement.* Paris, 1645.
SERMONS | POVR LES FESTES PRIN- | CIPALES DE L'ANNEE, | ET | OCTAVE DV S. SACREMENT. | Composez & prononcez en diuers lieux par feu | le R. P. PIERRE BLANCHOT, Parisien, | Religieux de l'Ordre des Minimes. | Reueus & mis en lumiere par le R. P. F. MICHEL | DE LA NOÜE, Parisien, Religieux du mesme | Ordre. | *Auec deux tables, l'vne des Sermons & de leurs des-* | *seins, l'autre des matieres principales.* | [Engraving of device: Fleur de lis with the motto 'Spes mea Deus'] | A PARIS. | Chez Charles Rouillard, ruë S. Iacques | à la Fleur de Lis. | M. DC. XLV. | *Auec priuilege du Roy, & Approbation.* |

    8vo ã–ẽ⁸, A–2V⁸, 2X⁴

    ã1ʳ Title; ã2ʳ Ded. to Fr. de la Noüe, dated 1645; ã7ʳ Licence des Superieurs, dated 25 April 1645; ã7ᵛ Approbation dated 18 May 1645; ã8ʳ Tesmoignage des Theologiens de l'ordre of 20 April 1645; ã8ᵛ Extraict du priuilege; Acheué d'imprimer, dated 1 June 1645; ẽ1ʳ Aduis au Lecteur; ẽ1ᵛ Tables des Sermons; A1ʳ Text, pag. 1–667 [very much mispagination]; 2T5ʳ Table des Matieres; 2X3ʳ Erreurs d'impression; 2X4 blank. [BMV Fonds A. in-8°. 0.355.h

  Note: Wants gatherings sig. X and Y. Cioranescu (12371) gives only the (less defective) edition of Rouen, J. Besongne, 1656. It is to be found at BN D 26157.

BOSQUIER, Philippe (*Recollet*)
Mons (Hainault) 1562 – Avesnes (Hainault) 1636.

50 *Harangue funebre sur la mort de Messire Charles de Croy, duc d'Arschot, faite et prononcée par Philippe Bosquier, au service celebré par les officiers de sa Terre et Pairie d'Avesnes.* Douai, 1612. Title-page wanting.
  8vo A–F⁸, G²
  Wants A1 Title; A2ʳ Ded. à MM. les Officiers Ducaulx de la terre, pairie et seigneurie d'Avesnes, pag. 3–4; A3ʳ Text, pag. 5–100; G2ᵛ Permission of Censor, dated Douai 27 August 1612; Verse to the Croy family, signed F. P. B. M. [BN Ln27 5197

51 *Sermons sur toute la parabole du prodigue evangelique.* Paris, 1612. 4 vols.
Vol. 1:
SERMONS | SVR TOVTE | LA PARABOLE | DV PRODIGVE | EVANGELIQVE | *Preschez en diuers lieux &* | *saisons de l'annee.* | Diuisez en IIII. Tomes | AV ROY. | Par R. P. F. Philippe | Bosquier obseruantin | de l'ordre de S. Fran' | COIS [sic], en la Prouince | de Flandre. | *Auec priuilege du Roy.* | TOME II. | *A PARIS,* | *Chez Oliuier de,* | *Varennes, ruë Sainct* | *Iacques. A' la Victoire,* | M. D. C. XII. |
  [Clearly this should read TOME I.]
  [Engraved. The title panel is surrounded by six panels showing the progress of the Prodigal, and two panels bearing the arms of the king and of Paris. Signed Iaspar Isac fecit 1612.]
    8vo ã–ĩ⁸, A–2X⁸, 2Y²
  ã1ʳ Title; ã2ʳ Ded. Au Roy; ã5ʳ Au Lecteur; ẽ8ʳ Auctor ad Lectorem; ĩ1ʳ Acrostic; Le mesme à l'autheur; ĩ2ʳ D. Laurentii Baii Melinensis ... Carmen; ĩ2ᵛ Sonnet à l'Autheur; Latin verses signed I. Sonnius; ĩ3ʳ Ad auctorem, signed Franciscus Boueault Atrebas; In vetus anagramma auctoris; In nouum; ĩ3ᵛ In homilias signed Philippe

Mayero Atrebatio; ĩ4ʳ Apographum Licentiae Praelati, dated Brussels 23 June 1607; ĩ4ᵛ Extraict du Priuilege, to O. de Varennes & Adrien de Launay, for 6 years, dated 9 October 1611; ĩ5ʳ Acheué d'imprimer le 28. de Decembre 1611; ĩ5ᵛ Table des arguments et sommaires des sermons; A1ʳ Text, pag. 1–688; 2X1ʳ Table des matieres. [Ars. 8° T 6257¹]

Vol. 2:
SERMONS SVR | LA PARABOLE DV | PRODIGVE EVANGE-LIQVE. | *Traictans plusieurs singulieres remarques, doctes | Questions, & resolutions. | Soubs la figure duquel | est representé le miserable estat auquel l'homme se | precipite par le peché: & est enseigné le vrai che- | min de son salut. | Preschés en diuers lieux & saisons | diuerses de l'annee. | TOME II. | Par R. P. F. Philippe Bosquier, Obseruantin de l'Ordre | de S. François, en la Prouince de Flandres.* | [Orn.] | A PRAIS [*sic*], | Chez OLIVIER DE VARENNES, ruë Sainct | Jacques à la Victoire. | M. DC. XII. | *Auec priuilege du Roy.* |

8vo π², a–2c⁸, 2d⁴, 2ã⁴

π1ʳ Title cancellans; a1ʳ Text, pag. 1–404; 2c3ʳ Table des matieres; 2ã1ᵛ Apographum . . .; 2ã2ʳ Table des sommaires et arguments; 2ã4ʳ Privilege; 2ã4ᵛ Acheué d'imprimer [as for vol. 1].

[Ars. 8° T 6257²]

Vol. 3: Title as for vol. 2
8vo π², 2A–3K⁸, 3ã⁴

π1ʳ Title; π1ᵛ Apographum; π2ʳ Privilege; π2ᵛ Acheué d'imprimer . . .; 2A1ʳ Text, pag. 1–508; 3I7ʳ Table des matieres; 3ã1ʳ Table des arguments [wants 3K8]. [Ars. 8° T 6257³]

Vol. 4: Title as for vol. 1
8vo π², 4ã⁴, a–3t⁸

π1ʳ Title cancellans; 4ã1ʳ Table des arguments; 4ã3ᵛ Approbation; 4ã4ʳ Privilege; 4ã4ᵛ Acheué d'imprimer; a1ʳ Text, pag. 1–998; 3r4ʳ Table des matieres. [Ars. 8° T 6257⁴]

Note: The copy in the BN [Rés. D 15502] wants vols. 2 and 3. The BN also has a copy [D 26604, four volumes bound as three] which is identical to the work described above, except that it bears throughout the imprint of Pierre Chevalier. This is clearly a case of a shared edition.

BOUCHER, Jean (Franciscan)
Le Mans 1560 – 1631. Professed 1578. Spent a number of years in Poitiers before being elected Warden of the Le Mans convent in 1613. Well known for his book on the Holy Land, *Le Bouquet sacré*.

A 'Notice sur Jean Boucher', containing biographical and bibliographical information, by Antoine de Serent, is to be found in *La France franciscaine*, III(1914), pp. 215-55.

52 *Oraison funebre de ... Emery de Barbezieres.* Poitiers, 1609.
ORAISON | FVNEBRE | DE HAVT ET PVISSANT | SEIGNEVR MESSIRE EMERY DE | BARBEZIERES CHEVALIER DES DEVX | ordres du Roy, Conseiller en ses Conseils | d'Estat & Priué, grand Mareschal des | logis du corps & armées de sa Ma- | jesté, Comte de Ciuray, & Sei- | gneur de la Roche Chemeraut. | *Declamée à Marigné le 9. Iuin. par le R. P.* | *Boucher, Religieux de l'ordre S. François.* | [Orn. A swan with the motto 'Ut in cute albus intus'] | A POICTIERS, | Chez IVLIAN THOREAV, Imprimeur | de l'Vniuersité. 1609. |
  8vo A-D^4
  A1^r Title; A2^r Ded. à Mme Claude de l'aubepinne Contesse de Ciuray; A4^r Text [unpaginated, except for no. 1 on A4^r]; D3^v Oraison. [BN Ln27 24425
  Note: The BN Catalogue lists this as a 12mo, and gives the collation as a-d.

53 *Les Magnificences divines.* Paris, 1620.
LES MAGNIFICENCES DIVINES | *chantées par La Vierge S. sur les Montagnes de Iudéé Et* | *preschées dans l'Eglise des PP. Cordelliers de Paris par* | *le P. Boucher religieux du dit Ordre* | *Dediées à Monseigneur l'Illustrissime Cardinal de Rets.* | A. PARIS | *Par Antoine Estiene,* | *Imprimeur ordinaire du* | *Roy, ruë St Iacques* | [pres? word obliterated by library stamp] St *Yues.* 1620. | *Auec Priuilege du Roy.* |
  [Engraved. Shows Virgin and Child in glory surrounded by allegorical figures seated on clouds. Signed Iaspar Isac fecit.]
  8vo ã^8, ẽ^4, A-2E^8, 2F^6
  ã1^r Title; ã2^r Voeu et priere à la Mere de Dieu, pag. 3-10; ã6^r Ded. au Cardinal de Retz, pag. 11-20, dated 9 September 1620; ẽ2^r Au Lecteur; ẽ3^v Approbation dated 15 September 1620; ẽ3^v Approbation du Gardien, dated 16 September 1620; A1^r Text, pag.

1–447; 2F1^r Table des matieres; 2F5^r Extraict du priuilege, to
Estienne and Denis Moreau, for 10 years, dated 20 September 1620.
[BN D 26735

Note: Sig. D misbound between sigs. B and C; sig. P misbound
between sigs. M and N.

54 *L'Epitome des merveilles de Dieu presché durant l'octave du S.
Sacrement dans l'eglise des PP. Cordeliers de Paris en l'an 1619.*
Paris, D. Moreau, 1619.

Noted by Albert, p. 349, and Cioranescu (1·5069). Serent, p. 252,
gives a brief description of it, referring to a copy in the Bibliothèque
Sainte-Geneviève. Not only is no copy listed in the SG Catalogue,
but the press-mark Serent gives is not of the modern SG type at all.
I have found no copy elsewhere.

55 *Oraison funebre sur le trespas de . . . Charlotte du Gué*. Paris,
1622.

ORAISON | FVNEBRE | SVR LE TRESPAS | DE MADAME M. |
CHARLOTTE DV GVE', | en son viuant Espouse de Monseigneur
M. | Messire NICOLAS DE VERDVN, Cheualier, | Conseiller du
Roy en ses Conseils d'Estat | & Priué, premier President au Parlement | de Paris, & Chancelier de MONSEIGNEVR | M. Frere
Vnique de sa MAIESTE'. | [Orn.] | A PARIS, | Chez DENYS
MOREAV, ruë sainct | Iacques, à la Salemandre. | M. DC. XXII. |

4to A–D^4, E^2

A1^r Title; A2^r Led. à Messire Nicolas de Verdun, pag. 3–4; A3^r
Text, pag. 5–34 [wants E2].   [BN Ln27 20203

56 *Idem*. Paris, 1622.

Title virtually identical to the above: the ornament is different.

8vo A–C^8, D^6

A1^r Title; A2^r Ded., pag. 3–6; A4^r Text, pag. 7–60.
[BN Ln27 20203A

Note: It was not uncommon, of course, for a work to be printed
in two editions. The quarto is presumably the preferable, as the
edition destined for presentation.

Serent, p. 250, is unaware of the quarto edition, noting only the
octavo in the BN and an identical copy in the Mazarine [Maz.
32.851] which he wrongly gives as a 12mo (p. 328).

57 *Sermons ou Thresors de la pieté chrestienne.* Paris, 1623.
This edition is not listed in the usual sources, nor does it appear to be extant. Nevertheless, all the evidence in Paris 1627 (see next entry) points to its existence. Serent, p. 251, comes to the same conclusion.

58 *Idem.* Paris, 1627.
SERMONS OV | THRESORS | DE LA PIETE' | CHRESTIENNE, | *Cachez dans les Euangiles* | *des Dimanches de* | *l'Année.* | *Nouuelle Edition* | *Dediés à Monsigneur* | *Monsig. le Prince* | *Par le P. Boucher* | *Predicateur de lordre* | *des PP. Cordeliers.* | A PARIS. | *Chez Louys Boullenger* | *rue S.ᵗ Iacques alimage* [sic] | *Sᵗ Louys.* | *Auec Priuilege du Roy. 1627.* |

[Engraved. The title is on a background of fleur-de-lis between salomonic columns surmounted by two angels bearing the arms of Condé. Unsigned.]

8vo ã⁸, A–3K⁸

ã1ʳ Title; ã2ʳ Ded. to Condé dated Paris 14 January 1623; ã4ʳ Aduertissement au Lecteur; ã4ʳ Table des sermons; ã7ʳ Permission des Supérieurs, dated 10 January 1623; ã7ᵛ Approbation dated 6 October 1622; ã8ʳ Privilege, for 6 years, dated Lyon 12 December 1622; ã8ᵛ Transport to Boulanger dated 10 January 1623; A1ʳ Text, pag. 1–885; 3K3ᵛ Table des matieres.   [BN D 26737

59 *Idem.* Rouen, 1629.
SERMONS | OV THRESORS DE LA | PIETE' CHRESTIENNE. | *Cachez dans les Euangiles des* | *Dimanches de l'année.* | *Dediés à Monseigneur Monseigneur* | *le* PRINCE. | *Par le P. Boucher Predicateur de* | *l'ordre des PP. Cordeliers.* | DERNIERE EDITION. | [Orn. Two angels bearing the arms of Condé] | *A ROVEN,* | Chez MANASSEZ DE PREAVLX, | deuant le Portail des Libraires. | M. DC. XXIX. |

8vo ã⁸, A–3K⁸

ã1ʳ Title; ã2ʳ Ded.; ã5ʳ Aduertissement au Lecteur; ã5ᵛ Table des sermons; ã8ʳ Permission of 1623; ã8ᵛ Approbation of 1622; Acheué d'imprimer le second iour de Mars, mil six cens vingt-neuf; A1ʳ Text, pag. 1–885; 3K1ᵛ Table des matieres.   [BN D 26738

60 *Sermons pour tous les jours du Caresme.* Paris, Rouillard or Taupinart, 1631.
See evidence below.

61 *Idem.* Paris, 1635.
SERMONS | POVR TOVS LES | IOVRS DE CARESME. | PAR LE | R. P. BOVCHER, | DE L'ORDRE S. FRANÇOIS, | Predicateur de la Reyne. | *Mis en lumiere, par le commandement des Superieurs de son Ordre.* | [Taupinart's device: an astrolabe] | A PARIS, | Chez ADRIEN TAVPINART, ruë S. | Iacques, à la Sphere. | M. DC. XXXV. | *Auec Approbation, & Priuilege du Roy.* |
 8vo ã–ẽ⁸, A–3C⁸

ã1ʳ Title; ã2ʳ Ded. to Daniel Baudry, signed F. L. G.; ã8ʳ Au Lecteur; ẽ4ʳ Approbation dated 20 July 1631; ẽ4ᵛ Permission des Supérieurs dated 20 July 1631; ẽ5ʳ Privilege, to Adrien Taupinart and Charles Roüillard for 6 years, dated Monceaux 1 August 1631; ẽ6ᵛ Table des sermons; A1ʳ Text, pag. 1–752; 3B1ʳ Table des matieres; 3C8 blank. [BN D 26739

Note: Posthumously published by Louis Gautier.

BOURGOING, François (Oratorian)
Paris 1585 – Paris 1662. Superior of the Oratory 1641–61. Ingold, *Essai de bibliographie oratorienne*, p. 32, mentions the following work:

62 *Homelies chrestiennes sur les Evangiles des dimanches et principales festes de l'année.* Paris, 1642.

Of the subsequent editions mentioned by Ingold, only the following appears to be extant:

63 *Idem.* Paris, 1665.
HOMELIES | CHRESTIENNES, | SVR LES EVANGILES | DES DIMANCHES | ET | DES FESTES PRINCIPALES | DE L'ANNE'E. | AVEC CINQ AVTRES HOMELIES | sur la Doctrine Chrestienne. | *Par le* R. P. FRANÇOIS BOVRGOING, *Prestre* | *& Superieur General de la Congregation de* | *l'Oratoire de* IESVS-CHRIST N. *Seigneur.* | [Orn. The lion of Venice] | A PARIS, | Chez FREDERIC LEONARD, ruë | S. Iacques, à l'Escu de Venise. | M. DC. LXV. | *Auec Approbation & Priuilege.* |
 8vo ã⁸, ẽ⁴, A–3C⁸

ã1ʳ Title; ã2ʳ Preface; ã5ᵛ Approbation for the Homelies Chrestiennes dated 27 May 1650; Approbation for the Cinq Homelies da d 9 August 1639; ã6ʳ Extraict du Priuilege for 10 years dated

24 February 1665; ã6ᵛ Table des Homelies; ē3ᵛ Table des Homelies sur les vertus de la Sainte Vierge; ē4ᵛ Table des Homelies sur la doctrine chrestienne; A1ʳ Text of the Homelies sur les Euangiles des Dimanches, pag. 1–191/192/191/192–623; 2R1ᵛ Text of the Homelies pour les Festes de la Vierge, pag. 624–734; 3A1ʳ Title for the Homelies sur la doctrine chrestienne; 3A2ʳ Preface, pag. 737–8; 3A3ʳ Text, pag. 739–82.   [BN D 15301

Note: Wants 2Y5 and 2Y6. Jacquinet, *Des prédicateurs du XVIIᵉ siècle avant Bossuet*, p. 135, states that none of Bourgoing's French sermons are extant.

BURLAT, Hugues
Nothing known about this preacher except what appears on the title-page. Author of some Latin works, the earliest of which is dated 1571. He is not mentioned in either of the Cioranescu bibliographies.

64 *Deux sermons de la resurrection du Lazare.* Paris, 1603.
DEVX SERMONS | DE LA RESVRREC- | TION DV LAZARE. | Par lesquels est verifiée l'Interces- | sion des Saincts, la Confession | auriculaire, & le Purgatoire. | *A tres-reuerend Pere en Dieu Mes- | sire* RENAVD DE BEAVNE, | *Archeuesque de Sens, Primat des | Gaules & de Germanie, Grand | Aumosnier de France.* | Par M HVGVES BVRLAT, Docteur | en Theologie, Chanoine Theologal | & Penitencier de l'Eglise | d'Orleans. | [Orn.] | Par IEAN RICHER, ruë S. Iean de Latran | à l'Arbre verdoyant. | 1603. |

8vo ã⁸, A–L⁸, M⁴

ã1ʳ Title; ã2ʳ Ded. to Renaut de Beaune, dated 15 March 1603; ã5ᵛ Ten dedicatory poems in Latin and French; A1ʳ Text, foliated 1–90; M3ʳ Attestation des docteurs, dated 15 March 1603; M4 blank.   [BN D 15500

CAMUS, Jean-Pierre
Paris 1584 – Paris 1652. Bishop of Belley in 1609. In 1640 he resigned his see, and spent the rest of his life working at the Hôtel des Incurables in Paris. Best known for his friendship with François de Sales, and for his spiritual novels.

For the method followed in this section, see my Explanatory

note (above, pp. 188–9). M. Jean Descrains's *Bibliographie des oeuvres de Jean-Pierre Camus* (1971) supersedes the bibliographies of Depéry (in his edition of the *Esprit du bien-heureux François de Sales*, Paris, 1840, vol. 1, pp. cxv–cxli), V. Gastaldi (*Jean-Pierre Camus. Romanziere barocco e vescovo di Francia*, Catania, 1964), and A. Garreau (*Jean-Pierre Camus Parisien, Evêque de Belley*, Paris, 1968).

65 *Panegyrique de la Mere de Dieu.* Paris, Chappelet, 1608.
   Descrains no. 001
   Reprints, etc. 2   [BN D 27698

66 *Homelie des trois simonies, ecclesiastique, militaire et judicielle.*
   Paris, Chappelet, 1615.
   Descrains no. 013
   Reprints, etc. 2   [BN Le^{17} 9

67 *Homelie des trois fleaux des trois Estats de France.* Paris, Chappelet, 1615.
   Descrains no. 014   [BN D 15298(1)

68 *Homelie des desordres des trois ordres de cette Monarchie.*
   Paris, Chappelet, 1615.
   Descrains no. 015
   Reprints, etc. 1   [BN Le^{17} 27

All three of these harangues before the States-General are reprinted in:
69 *Collection intégrale et universelle des orateurs sacrés*, ed. Migne, vol. 1, cols. 11–88.

70 *Homélies des Etats généraux*, ed. J. Descrains, Geneva and Paris, 1970.

71 *Premieres homelies quadragesimales.* Paris, Chappelet, 1615.
   Descrains no. 016
   Reprints, etc. 7   [BN D 15515(1)

72 *Premieres homelies dominicales.* Paris, Chappelet, 1617.
   Descrains no. 017
   Reprints, etc. 8

Edition quoted in Part I:
73 *Idem.* Paris, Chappelet, 1619.
   Descrains no. 017-02   [BN 27707

74 *Premieres homelies festives.* Paris, Chappelet, 1617.
   Descrains no. 018
   Reprints, etc. 10   [BMV Fonds A. in-8°, 0.37.e

Edition quoted in Part I:
75 *Idem.* Paris, Chappelet, 1619.
   Descrains no. 018-02   [BN D 27708

76 *Homelies sur la Passion.* Paris, Chappelet, 1617.
   Descrains no. 019
   Reprints, etc. 4

Edition quoted in Part I:
77 *Idem.* Paris, Chappelet, 1623.
   Descrains No. 019-02   [BN D 27676

78 *Premieres homelies eucharistiques.* Paris, Chappelet, 1618.
   Descrains no. 022
   Reprints, etc. 2   [BN D 15516

79 *Metanee, ou de la penitence.* Paris, Chappelet, 1619.
   Descrains no. 024
   Reprints, etc. 1   [BN D 81680

80 *Premieres homelies diverses.* Paris, Chappelet, 1619.
   Descrains no. 025
   Reprints, etc. 2   [BN D 27705

81 *Premieres homelies mariales.* Paris, Chappelet, 1619.
   Descrains no. 026
   Reprints, etc. 2   [BN D 27710

82 *Homelies spirituelles sur le Cantique des Cantiques.* Paris, Chappelet, 1620.
   Descrains no. 027   [BN D 15519

83 *Metaneacarpie, ou des fruicts de la penitence.* Paris, Chappelet, 1620.
   Descrains no. 028
   Reprints, etc. 2   [BN D 27691]

84 *Meslange d'homelies.* Paris, Chappelet, 1622.
   Descrains no. 034   [BN D 15520]

85 *Homelies panegyriques de S. Ignace de Loyola.* Lyons, J. Gaudion, 1623.
   Descrains no. 037   [BN D 15522]

86 *Homelies panegyriques de sainct Charles Borromée.* Paris, Chappelet, 1623.
   Descrains no. 040   [BN D 15521]

87 *Harangue funebre ... de ... Josias ... de ... Ransau.* Paris, G. Meturas, 1650.
   Descrains no. 256   [BN Ln27 16984]
For Camus's *Prônes* and *Instructions* see Appendix 2.

CAUSSIN, Nicolas (Jesuit)
Troyes 1583 – Paris 1651. Entered the Society in 1607, taught rhetoric, and became famous as a preacher. Louis XIII chose him as his spiritual director against the wishes of both the Jesuits and Richelieu; he was quickly disgraced, and exiled first to Rennes, then to Quimper. He was celebrated for his religious dramas.

88 *Les Devoirs funebres rendus à l'heureuse memoire de Mme ... de Beauvillier.* Paris, 1634.
LES | DEVOIRS | FVNEBRES | rendus à l'heureuse memoire | de MADAME | CATHERINE HENRIETTE | MARIE DE BEAV-VILLIER, | dite de saincte Gertrude, | Coadiutrice de Madame l'Abbesse | de Mont-martre. | *Par le* R. P. NICOLAS CAVSSIN, | *de la Compagnie de* IESVS. | [Orn.] | A PARIS, | Chez ADRIEN TAVPINART, ruë | S. Iacques, à la Sphere. | M. DC. XXXIIII. | *Auec Permission.* |
   8vo π^2, A–C^8, D^6

π1ʳ Title cancellans; A1ʳ Text, pag. 1–59; D6ᵛ Permission du R. P. Provincial for 3 years, dated 7 October 1634.

[BN Ln27 1375

89 *Le Buisson ardent.* Paris, 1647.
LE | BVISSON | ARDENT. | FIGVRE DE L'INCARNATION, | Contenant vingt-quatre Discours sur les | Mysteres de l'Aduent. | *Par le R. Pere* NICOLAS CAVSSIN *de la* | *Compagnie de* IESVS. | [Orn. Hand bearing ears of wheat, from a cloud, with motto 'Fertilior cultu'] | A PARIS, | Chez IEAN DE BRAY, ruë sainct Iacques, | aux Espics meurs. | M. DC. XLVII. | *Auec Priuilege & Approbation.* |

8vo ã⁸, ẽ⁴, A–2V⁸, 2X⁴

ã1ʳ Title; ã2ʳ Ded. to Mazarin; ã5ʳ Au Lecteur; ã8ʳ Table des discours; ẽ2ᵛ Extraict du priuilege dated 16 October 1647, for 10 years; ẽ3ʳ Acheué d'imprimer pour la premiere fois le vingt-cinq Nouembre 1647; ẽ3ᵛ Permission du R. P. Provincial, dated 28 April 1647; ẽ4ʳ Approbation dated 13 November 1647; A1ʳ Text; 2V1ʳ Table des matieres; 2X4ᵛ Fautes suruenuës en l'impression.

[BN D 29418

90 *Idem.* Paris, 1648.
A reprint of no. 89. Title and contents identical.

91 Migne, *Orateurs sacrés*, vol. 1, cols. 761–868, reprints the first seventeen sermons; he has, unusually, printed straight from the text, with old spelling; only certain abbreviations are expanded.

CHARRON, Pierre

92 *Discours chrestiens.* Paris, 1604. 3 parts.
DISCOVRS | CHRESTIENS | DE | *LA DIVINITE* | *CREATION RE-* | *DEMPTION ET* | octaues du | Sainct Sa- | crement. | PAR | Mᵉ *PIERRE CHARRON* | *Parisien Docteur Theolo-* | *gal Chanoine en l'E-* | *glise de Condon.* | *Auec Priuilege du Roy.* | *A Paris.* | *Chez Pierre Bertault* | *Libraire Iuré au mont Sᵗ Hilaire a l'estoille* | *d'or couronnée.* | 1604. |

[Engraved. The title is surrounded by panels showing the subjects discussed. Signed L. Gaultier fecit.]

8vo π^2, ā^4, ē^2, A-R^8, A-2M^8, 2N^2

$\pi 1^r$ Title cancellans; ā1^r Ded. à Mgr Messire Claude Dormy Euesque de Boulogne; ā4^r Table des discours; ē2^v Privilege for 10 years dated 27 March 1604; A1^r Text of first part, pag. 1-268; R7 and R8 blanks;

A1^r Text of second part, pag. 1-187; M7^r Text of third part, pag. 1-356; 2M1^r Table des remarques principales; 2N2^v Ce Liure a esté acheué d'imprimer le 2. Auril M. DCIII. Par FLEVRY BOVRRIQVANT. | [BL 850.d.8

Note: Posthumously published by Gabriel Michel de Rochemaillet: see Ded. I have included this work because, although the discourses are much shorter and more theoretical than most sermons, the 'division' is absolutely in sermon form.

CHARRUAU, Nicolas (Franciscan)
B? Died 1655. Warden of the Rennes convent c. 1639. Bibliography and notes in Bernard Kirsch: 'Nicolas Charruau', *La France Franciscaine*, III (1914), pp. 255-7.

93 *Harangue funebre . . . de feu M. . . . du Bourblanc*. Nantes, 1639.
HARANGVE FVNEBRE | FAICTE AVX OBSEQVES | RENDVS A LA MEMOIRE DE FEV | Monsieur le President, | du Bourblanc, | Dans l'Eglise des Religieux reformés | de S. François de Rennes le 18. Avril | 1639. en presence du Parlement | assistant en corps. | *PAR FRERE NICOLAS CHARRVAV,* | Docteur en Theologie de la faculté de Paris, & Gardien | du mesme Couvent. | A NANTES | Par GVILLAVME MONNIER, | Imprimeur & Libraire. | M. DC. XXXIX. |

4to A-B^4, C^2 [the first gathering is unsigned]
A1^r Title; A1^v Au Lecteur, pag. 2; A2^r Text, pag. 3-14.
               [BN Ln 27 6363

94 *La Jerusalem celeste*. Paris, Simon le Febvre, 1641.
Listed by Cioranescu (18851). Kirsch, p. 257, describes a copy he has seen in a private collection. See also the evidence of documents in Paris 1650 below.

95 *Idem*. Paris, L. Boullanger, 1648. 'Derniere edition'.
Noted by Louis Jacob, *Bibliographia parisina*, III, p. 11.

96 *Idem.* Paris, 1650.
LA | IERVSALEM | CELESTE, | *OV* | SERMONS POVR TOVS LES | iours de l'Aduent, sur la prise de | possession du Paradis, & les | moyens d'y paruenir. | *PAR LE R. P. F. NICOLAS CHARRVAV,* | *Docteur en Theologie de la Faculté de Paris,* | *Religieux de l'Ordre des R. P. Cordeliers.* | AVEC VNE TABLE D'INSTRVCTION | pour sçauoir detacher chaque Sermon de | son suiet, afin de s'en seruir à d'autres occa- | sions, n'y en ayant aucun qui ne soit appliqué | à trois ou quatre suiets differens, tant du | Caresme, que des Dimanches & Festes | de l'Année. DERNIERE EDITION. | [Orn.] | A PARIS, | Chez LOVIS BOVLLANGER, ruë sainct Iacques, | à l'Image S. Louis, deuant S. Yues. | M. DC. L. | *Auec Approbation, & Priuilege.* |

8vo ā–ē^8, A–2L^8

ā1^r Title; ā2^r Ded. à la Comtesse de Soissons; ā5^r Au Lecteur; ā7^r Permission du Provincial, dated Tours July 1640; ā7^v Approbation dated 3 October 1640; ā8^r Privilege to Charruau for 5 years, dated 27 November 1640; Acheué d'imprimer le huictiesme Ianuier 1641; ē1^r Table; A1^r Text, pag. 1–525; 2K7^v Table des matieres, pag. 526–41. [BN D 29752]

Note: This copy wants 2L8, which was presumably a blank.

COSTEBADIE, Jean (or COSTE-ABADIE, Jean de) (P)
Minister first at Lalinde, then at Clairac from 1635 to 1661.

97 *Deux sermons.* Charenton, 1642.
DEVX SERMONS | DE IEAN | COSTEBADIE, | Ministre de la parole | de Dieu en l'Eglise | de Clairac. | [Orn.] | *Se vendent à Charanton,* | Par LOVIS VENDOSME, demeurant | à Paris ruë de la Pelleterie, | à l'enseigne S. Nicolas. | *M. DC. XLII.* |

12mo A–F$^{8-4}$

A1^r Title; A2^r Ded. à Monsieur Rivet, docteur en theologie à Leiden; A3^r [missigned A2] Text of first sermon, pag. 5–34; C6^r Text of second sermon, pag. 35–70; F4 blank.
[SBNU E 127855]

Note: Unknown to Cioranescu.

COTON, Pierre (Jesuit)
Néronde (Loire) 1564 – Paris 1626. Entered the Society in 1583.

Preacher and Confessor to Henri IV; Provincial of the Society in France.

98 *Sermons sur les principales et plus difficiles matieres de la foy.*
Paris, 1617.
SERMONS | SVR LES PRIN- | CIPALES ET PLVS | DIFFICILES MATIERES | de la foy | Faicts par le R. Pere | Pierre Coton de la cō- | pagnie de Iesus. Confes- | seur et Predicateur | ordinaire du Roy. Redu- | icts par luy mesme en | forme de meditation. | Dediés à la Royne. | Auec priuilege du Roy. | A PARIS | Chez Sebastien Huré | Ruë Sainct Iacques au | coeur-bon. | 1617. |

[Engraved. The title panel supported by figures of a bishop and a woman saint, and surmounted by a Christ in majesty with angels. Signed Mich: faute. fecit.]

8vo πA^8, π^2, A–3L^8

$\pi A1^r$ Title; $\pi A2^r$ Ded. à la Royne; $\pi A6^v$ Aux Lecteurs; $\pi A8^v$ Approbation dated 3 October 1616; $\pi 1^r$ Repertoire des sermons; $\pi 2^r$ Extraict du priuilege to Coton dated 5 October 1616; $\pi 2^v$ Transport to Huré for 10 years dated 4 October 1616; A1^r Text, pag. 1–547/558–922. [BN D 15531

99 *Idem.* Pont-à-Mousson, Melchior Bernard and Charles Marchant, 1617.
Sommervogel, p. 1554. I have not found a copy.

100 *Idem.* Arras, Guillaume de la Riviere, 1617.
Sommervogel, p. 1554. I have not found a copy.

101 *Idem.* Paris, 1624.
Title: As for Paris 1617 except dated 1624.

8vo π^2, πA^8, A–2V^8, χA^8

$\pi A1$ blank; $\pi 1^r$ Title cancellans; $\pi A2^r$ Ded.; $\pi A5^r$ Aux Lecteurs; $\pi A6^v$ Approbation of 1616; $\pi A7^r$ Privilege of 1616; $\pi A7^v$ Transport of 1616; $\pi A8^r$ Repertoire; A1^r Text, pag. 1–688; $\chi A1^r$ Table des matieres. [ULC E.6.1.

102 *Idem.* Rouen, 1626.
SERMONS | SVR LES | PRINCIPALES | ET PLVS DIFFICILES | MATIERES DE LA FOY. | Faicts par le R. P. P. COTTON, de la com- | pagnie de IESVS, Confesseur & Pre- | dicateur du ROY. |

REDVITS PAR LVY-MESME EN | *forme de Meditations.* |
DEDIE' A LA ROYNE. | [Orn. Hand holding out roses from a
thorn bush; motto: 'Ex dolore gaudium'] | A ROVEN, | Chez
Iacques Besongne, dans la Court | du Palais, joignant la grand'
porte. | M. DC. XXVI. |

 8vo πA^8, A–2V^8, χA^8

 $\pi A1^r$ Title; $\pi A2^r$ Ded.; $\pi A5^r$ Aux Lecteurs; $\pi A6^v$ Approbation of Paris 1616; $\pi A7^r$ Repertoire; $\pi A8$ blank; A1^r Text, pag. 1–688; $\chi A1^r$ Table des matieres.   [BN D 31211

 Note: This edition follows Paris 1624 closely; they both reduce the size of Paris 1617 by using a much smaller type.

103 *Idem.* Rouen, 1629.
Title, Collation and Contents as Rouen 1626, of which it is a reprint.   [ECC 330.7.128

104 Migne, *Orateurs sacrés*, vol. 1, cols. 363–700, reprints the
 1617 Paris text.
For a clarification of the 'reduction' to meditation form, Coton's *Epistre au Lecteur* (O.S. vol. 1, cols. 563–5) is important. He emphasizes the difficulty of publishing sermons without disappointing those who originally heard them, and without breaking rules that are necessary in writing but not in speaking. He appears to solve this problem by a superficial change in the name of the work, and he actually indicates precisely how we may reconstruct the sermon most easily: 'Les poincts contiennent l'exorde et la narration; les Profits la confirmation et amplification; le Colloque la conclusion, qu'ils appellent vulgairement la Peroration.' Obviously there are no profound changes.

105 *Oraison funebre sur le trespas de feu M. de Villeroy.* Lyons,
 1618.
ORAISON | FVNEBRE SVR | LE TRESPAS DE | FEV
MONSIEVR | de Villeroy. | *Faitte & recitee à Lyon le second iour* | *de la presente année* 1618. | Par le Pere Pierre Coton, de la Comp- | agnie de IESVS, Predicateur | ordinaire du Roy. | [Orn.] | *A LYON,* | PAR CLAVDE LARJOT. | M. DCXVIII. | *Auec permission.* |

 8vo A–H^4

Croï, Jean de (C. 107)

A1^r Title; A2^r Ded. au Roy; A3^r Text, pag. 5-61; H3^r Permission to Larjot dated 20 January 1618.

[BN Rés. Z. Fontanieu 299 (12)

Note: This copy wants H4. It is mounted on quarto sheets and bound in a collection.

106 *Idem.* Paris, 1618.
ORAISON | FVNEBRE | SVR LE TRESPAS DE | MONSIEVR DE VILLEROY, | FAITE ET RECITEE A | Lyon, le second iour de la presente | année 1618. | *Par le Pere* PIERRE COTON, *de la Com-* | *pagnie de* IESVS, *Predicateur ordi-* | *naire du Roy.* | [Orn. IHS] | A PARIS, | Chez SEBASTIEN HVRE', ruë sainct | Iacques, au Coeur-bon. | M. DC. XVIII. | *Auec permission.* |
  8vo A-E^4
A1^r Title; A2^r Ded., pag. 3-4; A3^r Text, pag. 5-40.

[BN Ln27 20520

CROÏ, Jean de (P)
Uzès? - Uzès 1659. Pastor at Béziers. Son of François de Croï, a celebrated Protestant theologian.

107 *Le Dernier Jugement.* Paris, 1645.
LE DERNIER | IVGEMENT. | ou | SERMON | SVR LA VISION | DE SAINT IEAN APOCALYPSE. | Chap. XX.V.11.12.13.14.& 15. | Prononcé à Charenton, le 15. iour de l'an | 1645. en la presence du Synode National | qui y estoit conuoqué, par permission | du Roy. | *Par I. de* CROY. | [Orn. P] | Se vend à Charenton Par SAMVEL | PETIT, demeurant à Paris, | dans la Cour du Palais | à la Bible d'or. | M. DC. XLV. |
  12mo A-F$^{8-4}$, G^6
A1^r Title; A2^r Text, pag. 3-82; G6 blank.

[BN D^2 4250 *bis*

DAILLÉ, Jean (P)
Châtellerault 1594 - Paris 1670. A close friend of Duplessis-Mornay. After two years spent in Italy as a young man, he became minister at Saumur and later, in 1626, at Charenton. Moderator of the Synod of Loudun.

The picture of Daillé's works which can be built up from extant editions in the libraries consulted is still a very fragmentary one. Despite considerable doubts I have included all the works listed by Haag (*La France protestante*, 2nd edn, vol. 5, cols. 28–36), and Roman numerals refer to that list.

108 *Sermon sur le Pseaume 90.* Charenton, 1632.
SERMON | SVR | LE PSEAVME XC. | vers. 12. 13. 14. 15. 16. & 17. | *Fait à Charenton le Ieudy* | *premier iour de l'an 1632.* | Par IEAN DAILLE' | Ministre du sainct Euangile | en l'Eglise Reformee | de Paris. | [Orn.] | *Et se vendent à Charenton,* | Par Melchior Mondiere, demeurant à | Paris, ruë neufue du Palais, aux | deux Viperes. | M. DC. XXXII. |
    12mo A–D$^{8-4}$, E^4, F^2
    A1^r Title; A2^r Text, pag. 3–60.   [Bod. 8° R 117. Th.
    Note: Unknown to Haag.

109 *Sermon de la vocation des fideles à la foy et au salut.*
    Charenton, Pierre des Hayes, 1633.
    12mo
    Haag I.

110 *Le Sacrifice des chrestiens.* Charenton, 1633.
LE | SACRIFICE | DES | CHRESTIENS. | SERMON FAIT A CHARENTON | le 2. de l'an 1633. jour de Cene, | sur le 12. chap. de l'Epistre | aux Rom. vers. 1. | *Par* IEAN DAILLE', *Ministre du* | *Sainct Euangile en l'Eglise* | *Reformée de Paris.* | [Orn.] | Se vendent à Charenton, | Par MELCHIOR MONDIERE, demeurant | à Paris dans la court du Palais, | aux deux viperes. | M. DC. XXXIII. |
    12mo A–B^{12}, C^{10}
    A1^r Title; A2^r Text, pag. 3–58/69–77; C10^v Fautes suruenuës en l'impression.   [BHP R. 16.065
    Note: Unknown to Haag.

111 *Christ mort et ressuscité pour nous.* Charenton, 1633.
CHRIST MORT | ET RESSVSCITE' | POVR NOVS. | Rom. 4 v. 25. | SERMON FAICT A | Charenton le iour de Pasques | de la presente année 1633. | *Par* IEAN DAILLE' *Ministre du sainct* | *Euangile en l'Eglise Reformée de Paris.* | [Orn.] | *Et se vendent à*

Charenton. | Par IACQVES LVCAS, dit Salier, | demeurant à Paris, ruë | des Carmes. | M. DC. XXXIII. |
    12mo A–F$^{8-4}$, G^2
    A1^r Title; A2^r Text, pag. 3–76.   [SG Rés. D 8° SUP 319
    Note: Haag (IV) gives the date of this as 1639.

112 *Sermon sur la charité chrestienne.* Charenton, Mondiere, 1633.
    12mo
    Haag V.

113 *Sermon sur 1. Pierre i, 12.* Charenton, Mondiere, 1636.
    12mo
    Haag IX.

114 *Sermon sur 1. Pierre i, 22–4.* Charenton, Vendosme, 1636.
    12mo
    Haag X.

115 *Sermon pour le jeusne celebré à Charenton le Jeudy 21 Aoust 1636.* Charenton, 1636.
SERMON | POVR LE IEVSNE | CELEBRE' A CHARENTON, | le Ieudy 21. Aoust 1636. | *Sur le 12. Chap. de S. Luc. Vers. 32.* | Par IEAN DAILLE', Ministre de | la Parole de Dieu. | [Printer's Orn.] | *Se vendent à Charenton,* | Par MELCHIOR MONDIERE, de- | meurant à Paris dans la cour du Palais, | ioignant le bastiment neuf du Tre- | sor, aux deux Viperes. | M. DC. XXXVI. |
    12mo A–D$^{8-4}$, E^2
    A1^r Title; A2^r Text, pag. 3–51.   [ECC 9.5.93[7]
    Note: Unknown to Haag or other authorities.

116 *Idem.* Geneva, 1637.
In *Sermons faits au jour du Jusne celebré à Charenton pour la prosperité des armes du Roy, le Jeudy 21 Aoust 1636.* Geneva, Jean de la Planche, 1637, pp. 154–97.   [BHP 8° 20.309

117 *Idem.* Charenton, Mondiere, 1638.
    12mo
    Haag XIII.

118 *Deux sermons sur 1 Colossiens.* Charenton, Mondiere, 1643.
12mo
Haag XVI.

119 *Quatre sermons sur divers textes.* Charenton, 1644.
QVATRE | SERMONS | SVR DIVERS TEXTES, | PRONONCES | A CHARENTON, | *Par* IEAN DAILLE', *Ministre* | *du S. Euangile.* | [Orn. P] | *Et se vendent à Charenton,* | Par IACQVES AVVRAY l'aisné, demeu- | rant à Paris sur le Pont neuf, au Prince | d'Orange. | M. DC. XLIV. |

12mo ā^6, A–F^{12}, G^6

ā1^r Title; ā2^r Ded. à Madame Madame de la Jurie, pag. 3–7, dated Paris 31 December 1643; ā4^v Errata; A2^r Text, pag. 3–156.

[BN D^2 6986

Note: Wants A1.

120 *Exposition de la divine Epître de S. Paul aux Filippiens en XXIX sermons.* Charenton, 1644–7. 2 vols.
Haag (XVIII) gives this as in two volumes 1644; since I have found only a first volume of 1644, and only a second volume dated 1647, I incline to believe that the two volumes were issued in different years. See the evidence of the dedications.
Vol. 1:
EXPOSITION | DES | DEUX PREMIERS | CHAPITRES DE L'EPITRE | DE SAINCT PAVL | aux Filippiens, | *EN SEIZE SERMONS,* | *prononcés à Charenton,* | Par IEAN DAILLE' Ministre | du Sainct Euangile. | [Printer's Orn.] | *Se vendent à Charenton* | Par MELCHIOR MONDIERE, demeurant à | Paris, en la Court du Palais, aux 2. Viperes. | M. DC. XLIIII. |

8vo ā^6, A–2S^8, 2T^4

ā1^r Title; ā2^r Ded. à Anne de Mornay, Duchesse & Maréchale de la Forse, dated Paris 19 November 1643, pag. 3–9; A1^r Text, pag. 1–663; 2T4^v Errata. [BHP 22.262

Note: Wants ā6. MS. notes on flyleaves and throughout.
Vol. 2:
EXPOSITION | DES | TROIS ET QVA- | TRIESME CHAPITRES | DE L'EPISTRE DE S. PAVL | aux Philippiens, | *EN TREIZE SERMONS,* | *prononcez à Charanton* | Par IEAN DAILLE'. | [Printer's Orn.] | *Se vendent à Charenton.* | Par MELCHIOR MONDIERE, demeurant | à Paris à la grande montée du Palais, | deuant le May, aux deux Viperes. | M. DC. XLVII. |

Daillé, Jean (C. 122)

8vo π⁴, A–2L⁸, 2M²

π1ʳ Title; π2ʳ Ded. à Mme de Dangeau, dated Paris 14 April 1647; A1ʳ Text, pag. 1–267/270–301/304–550; 2M2ᵛ Errata.

[BN D² 4043

Note: Wants π4. The last two leaves are mere fragments in this copy. A later edition of this work, both volumes, was published in Geneva in 1659.

121 *Sermon sur 1 Corinthiens xi, 31–2*. Charenton, 1645.
SERMON | SVR LES VERSETS | TRENTE ET VN, ET TRENTE | deuxiesme, de l'onziesme | Chapitre de la premiere Epi- | stre de sainct Paul aux Corin- | thiens. | *Prononcé à Charenton le 4. de May,* | *iour de ieusne.* | PAR IEAN DAILLE'. | [Orn.] | *Se vend à Charenton,* | Par La Vefue L. PERIER, | ET | Par NICOLAS PERIER, demeu- | rans à Paris ruë Neufue du Palais, | au Roy de Suede. | M. DC. XLV. |

12mo A–E⁸⁻⁴

A1ʳ Title; A2ʳ Text, pag. 1–62.

[BN D² 6988

Note: This copy wants E8. Unknown to Haag.

122 *Sermons sur l'Epître aux Colossiens*. Charenton, 1648. 3 vols.
Vol. 1:
SERMONS | DE IEAN DAILLE' | Sur l'Epître de l'Apôtre Saint Paul | aux Colossiens. | PREMIERE PARTIE, | *Qui contient l'exposition du premier cha-* | *pitre, en quinze Sermons.* | [Orn.] | Se vendent à Charenton, | Par LOVYS VENDOSME, demeurant | à Paris en la Gallerie des Oyseaux, | à la Caille, & au Sacrifice | d'Abraham. | M. DC. XLVIII. |

8vo ã⁸, A–2M⁸

ã1ʳ Title; ã3ʳ Ded. à M. de Candal, Seigneur de Fontenaille, dated Paris 1 April 1648; ã8ʳ Errata; A1ʳ Text, pag. 1–557.

[BN D² 4044 (1) [Uncatalogued]

Vol. 2:
'Qui contient l'exposition du Chapitre second, en seize Sermons'.

8vo ã⁸, A–2L⁸, 2M⁴

ã1 blank; ã2ʳ Title; ã3ʳ Ded. à M. Bigot, Seigneur de Lahonville, dated Paris 1 April 1648; ã7ʳ Errata; A1ʳ Text, pag. 1–552.

[BHP 7587

Daillé, Jean (C. 123)

Vol. 3:
'Qui contient l'exposition des deux derniers chapitres, en dix-huict sermons'.

8vo ã^4, A–2S^8

ã1^r Title; ã2^r Ded. à M. de Rambouillet; A1^r Text, pag. 1–653; 2S7^v Errata. [BN D^2 4044 (3)]

123 *Sermon sur le Psaume 74, 16 et 17, prononcé à Charenton le jour de l'an.* Charenton, Vendosme, 1648.
8vo
Haag XX. This work is listed in the BHP catalogue, but the copy in that library is missing.

124 *Deux sermons . . . prononcéz à Charenton, les deux Dimanches, 5. & 12. de Septembre 1647.* Charenton, 1647 [1649?].
DEVX | SERMONS | DE | IEAN DAILLE'. | *Prononcez à Charenton, les deux Diman-* | *ches, 5. & 12. de Septembre 1647.* | *iours de Cene;* | L'vn sur I Cor. 10. 16. | L'autre sur 2. Tim. 2.8. | [Orn. P] | *Se vendent à Charenton,* | Par LOVYS VENDOSME, demeurant à Paris, | sur le Quay de Gévre, à la Caille. | M. DC. XLIX. |

8vo Λ I^4, K^2

A1^r Title; A2^r Text, pag. 3–75; K2^v Errata.
[BHP 6297 (9)]
Note: MS. correction of the date on the title-page to 1647; this tallies with the other date in the title. Unknown to Haag.

125 *Sermon sur Jean i, 39.* Charenton, 1649.
SERMON | SVR LE VERSET | XXIX. DV PREMIER | Chapitre de l'Evangile selon Saint | Jean, | *Prononcé à Charanton par JEAN* | *DAILLE' Ministre du Saint* | *Evangile.* | [Orn.] | *Et se vend à Charenton.* | Par LOVIS VENDOSME, Marchand | Libraire à Paris, demeurant sur le Quay | de Gesvre, à l'Enseigne de la Caille. | M. DC. XLIX. |

8vo A–F^4

A1^r Title; A2^r Text, pag. 3–45; F3^r, pag. 45, Errata; F4 blank.
[BN D^2 4280 (6)]
Note: MS. notes on title-page: 'le iour de la feste S. Iean Baptiste 24 Iuin 1648'. 'Don de l'autheur ce 25. Iuin 1649'. The two faults given in the errata have been corrected in MS.

DRELINCOURT, Charles (P)
Sedan 1595 – Paris 1669. Minister at Charenton 1620. Roman numerals refer to the list in Haag, 2nd edn, vol. 5, cols. 488–95.

126 *Sermon pour le jeusne . . . le Jeudy 21. Aoust 1636.* Charenton, 1636.
SERMON | POVR LE IEVSNE | CELEBRE' A CHARENTON | le Ieudy 21. Aoust 1636. | Sur le Pseaume 60. | ψ. 13. & 14. | Auec la Priere faite à la fin | de l'action. | Par CHARLES DRELINCOVRT, | Ministre de la Parole de Dieu. | [Orn.] | *Se vendent à Charenton,* | Par SAMVEL PETIT, demeurant à | Paris dans la Court du Palais, place du | Change, à la Bible d'or. | M. DC. XXXVI. |
    12mo A–K$^{8-4}$
    A1^r Title; A2^r Text, pag. 1–106; I6^r Prayer, pag. 107–19.
                                                      [SG Rés. D 8° SUP 319
    Note: Unknown to Haag.

127 *Idem.* Quevilly, 1636.
SERMON | POVR LE | IVSNE | CELEBRE' A CHARENTON | pour la prosperité des armes du Roy, | le Ieudy 21. Aoust 1636. | Sur le Pseaume 60 ψ. 13. & 14. | Auec la Priere faite à la fin | de l'Action. | Par | CHARLES DRELINCOVRT, Ministre de la Parole de Dieu. | [Orn.] | *Se vendent à Queuilly,* | Par CLAVDE LE VILLAIN, Et | IACQVES CAILLOÜE. | M. DC. XXXVI |.
    12mo A–F^6
    A1^r Title; A2^r Text, pag. 3–66; F4^r Priere faite apres l'Action, pag. 67–72.   [BHP R. 16.065

128 *Idem.* Geneva, 1637.
In *Sermons faits au jour de jusne, etc.* Geneva, Jean de la Planche, 1637, pp. 60–153.

129 *La Vanité du monde, sermon sur Hebreux xiii, 14.* Charenton, 1639.
    12mo
    Haag XII. Reprinted in *Recueil de sermons sur divers passages de l'Escriture saincte*, Geneva, Tournes, 1658–64, vol. 1, pp. 335–98.
                                                      [BHP 8° 14.927

130 *De la foy des esleus, et de l'incredulité des reprouvez.*
    Charenton, S. Petit, 1639.

12mo
Haag XIII. Reprinted in *Recueil, etc.* (as above) vol. 1, pp. 401-60.

131 *Sermon sur Esaïe lxiv, 6-9.* Charenton, 1645.
SERMON | SVR LE CHAP. | 64. du Prophete Esaye | vers. 6.7.8. & 9. fait à | Charenton le 4. de May | 1645, pour la sanctifica- | tion du Ieusne. | Auec l'Acte du Synode | National. | *Par* | CHARLES DRELINCOVRT | Ministre de Iesus-Christ. | [Orn.] | *Se vend à Charenton* | Par LOVIS VANDOSME de- | meurant à Paris, ruë neuve du | Palais, au Sacrifice | d'Abraham. | M. DC. XLV. |
12mo ã^4, A-P$^{8-4}$
ã1^r Title; ã2^r Extraict des Actes du Synode National; A1 wanting; A2^r Text, pag. [beginning A2^v] 4-179; P8 wanting.
[BN D^2 7212

Note: Unknown to Haag.

132 *Sermon sur la paix.* Charenton, Vendosme, 1649.
8vo
Haag XXV.

DU BEC, Philippes
1524-1605. Successively Bishop of Vannes and of Nantes, and Archbishop of Rheims.

133 *Sermon de la Samaritaine.* Paris, 1600.
SERMON | DE LA SAMARITAINE | OV | DE NOSTRE VOCA- | TION | à la Grace, à quoy ce S. Iubilé | nous appelle. | Faict par Messire PHILIPPES DV BEC, Arche- | uesque Duc de Rheims, premier Pair de Fran- | ce, Legat nay du S. Siege, Conseiller du Roy en | son Conseil d'Estat, & Commandeur de l'ordre | du S. Esprit. | [Orn. Figure of peace, with motto: 'Pax certa melior quam separata victoria'] | A PARIS, | Chez LEGER DELAS, rue S. Iacques, | au Soleil d'or. | M. DC. |
8vo ã^4, A-D^4, E^2
ã1^r Title; ã2^r Ded; A1^r Text, pag. 1-35.
[BN Rés. D 15495 (1)

Note: ã4 has been torn out of this copy.

134 *Sermon de la paix.* Paris, 1600.
SERMON DE LA PAIX | SVR LA PAIX | DE FRANCE, SVYVIE | de l'année de Paix | du S. Iubilé. | Faict par Messire PHILIPPES DV BEC, Arche- | uesque & Duc de Rheims, Legat nay du S. Sie- | ge, Conseiller du Roy en son Conseil d'Estat, & | Commandeur de l'ordre du sainct Esprit: à son | entrée, en mesme temps, audit Rheims. | [Orn. as for no. 133] | A PARIS, | Chez LEGER DELAS, rue S. Iacques | au Soleil d'or. | M. DC. |
   8vo ã6, A–E^4

ã1^r Title; ã2^r Ded. to Clement VIII; ã5^r Hebrew poem signed Vignal Professor Regius; ã5^v Greek epigram; ã6^r Latin verse signed C. P. P.; ã6^v Presage à la France, signed C. P. P.; A1^r Text, pag. 1–38; E4 blank.   [BN Rés. D 15495 (2)]

DU MOULIN, Pierre (the elder) (P)
Buhy (Normandy) 1568 – Sedan 1658. Studied at Sedan and in England. Professor of Philosophy at Leiden at the age of 24. Pastor at Charenton in 1599. Summoned to England by James I to attempt (unsuccessfully) the reunion of Protestantism. Forbidden by Louis XIII to attend the Synod of Dordrecht, and eventually exiled from Charenton to Sedan where he spent his last years. Well known as a prolific and powerful controversialist.

   Roman numerals refer to the bibliography in Haag, 2nd edn, vol. 5, cols. 815–20. There are occasional bibliographical references in Lucien Rimbault: *Pierre du Moulin, 1568–1658, un pasteur classique à l'âge classique* (Paris, 1966). He discusses (p. 34) two very early works, *Théophile, ou traité de l'amour de Dieu* (La Rochelle, 1609) and *Héraclite, ou de la vie humaine* (1609), which he says are 'une suite de sermons composés sur un thème commun'. Later (p. 48), he remarks that 'ces méditations sont de toute évidence, des sermons, mais des sermons d'un genre spécial, formant un tout organisé'. In view of my remarks in the Explanatory note I have excluded them.

135 *Sermon sur Daniel ix, 1–9.* Sedan, 1623.
   Haag XL.

136 *Sermon de la priere en temps d'affliction.* Geneva, 1624.
SERMON DE LA PRIE- | RE EN TEMPS D'AF- | fliction. Pseaume

50. ɣ. 15. |

Printed in *Du combat chrestien*, Geneva, P. Aubert, 1624, pp. 128-57. [BHP O. 22.27

Note: According to Rimbault, p. 100, this was published at Geneva by P. Chouet in 1622. I have found no edition of that year.

137 *Sermons sur quelques textes.* Geneva, 1625.
SERMONS | SVR QVELQVES | TEXTES DE L'ES- | criture Saincte. | *PAR* | PIERRE DV MOVLIN, | *Ministre de la Parole de Dieu, & Professeur* | *en Theologie en l'Academie de Sedan.* | L'Indice desquels se void à la fin desdits | Sermons. | [Orn. Storm-tossed ship at sea] | *A GENEVE,* | Pour PIERRE AVBERT. | M. DC. XXV. |

8vo A-O⁸

A1ʳ Title; A2ʳ Text, pag. 1-224; O8ᵛ Indice des VII. Sermons.
[BHP 13. 847

138 *Idem.* Geneva, 1636.
SERMONS | *SVR* | QVELQVES TEXTES | de l'escriture Saincte. | *PAR* | PIERRE DV MOVLIN, | *Ministre de la Parole de Dieu, & Professeur en* | *Theologie en l'Academie de Sedan.* | L'INDICE des-quels se void à la fin desdits SERMONS. | [Orn. Sheep frolicking, shepherd sleeping, wolf approaching] | *A GENEVE,* | Chez PIERRE AVBERT, Imprimeur | de la Republique & Academie. | M. DC. XXXVI | *Auec permission & priuilege.* |

8vo A-O⁸

A1ʳ Title; A2ʳ Text, pag. 3-224; O8ᵛ Indice des VII. Sermons.
[BL 3901. a. 51 (2)

Dix décades de sermons. 1637-53.
The fragmentary state of the extant editions makes the dating of the series, and consequently the decision as to which is the best text, extremely difficult. It seems, however, likely that the 1637 Sedan edition of the first *décade*, the 1639 Hubert Raoult Sedan edition of the *Troisième décade*, and the 1649 François Chayer edition of the *Huitième décade* are first editions. The dedications are dated the same year as the edition in the case of the latter two, and in the November of the previous year in the case of the 1637 edition, and we know that Du Moulin was living at Sedan at the time.

It appears to follow from this that the only method of dating the remaining *décades* is from the dedications. This is the complete list:

1. 10 November 1636
2. Undated
3. 29 July 1639
4. 10 September 1640
5. 17 February 1642
6. 1 January 1647
7. 24 September 1647
8. 19 October 1649
9. 6 June 1652
10. 18 July 1653

We may therefore tentatively give the dates of the work as 1637–53. This presents a rather different picture from Haag's somewhat cursory notice (col. 820) '*Dix décades de sermons,* Genève 1641–1654'. In particular, many must have received their final form much earlier than one might suppose from Haag.

This is the theoretical set of dates. The extant works present the difficulty that the two complete collections were printed in Geneva, and are clearly not first editions. One way of determining the care of the Geneva printers for the integrity of the text is to examine the fate of the 'fautes à corriger' listed in the 1639 Sedan edition of the *Troisième décade*; these faults are not only typographical, but involve the expansion of elliptical or obscure expressions and allusions, and seem to have an authoritative source. They have all been carefully inserted into the text of Geneva 1642–3. Other faults may, of course, have crept in; but on a rapid examination the text does not seem to be corrupt.

What is the relationship between the two Geneva collections? They come from the same family printing house; the pagination is identical. But on closer examination it appears that the 1653–5 edition of the first five *décades* is a new edition: there are considerable differences in spelling and abbreviation.

The following are the extant texts I have been able to discover, and on which the above arguments are based:

139 *Decade de sermons.* Sedan, 1637.
DECADE | DE | SERMONS. | *Par PIERRE DV MOVLIN* | *Ministre de la parole de Dieu.* | [Orn. A coat of arms] | A SEDAN, | Par IEAN IANON. | *Et se vendent à Charenton,* | Par NICOLAS BOVRDIN, & LOVIS PERIER, | demeurans à Paris, ruë Neufue du | Palais, au Roy de Suede. | M. DC. XXXVII. |

8vo ã⁴, A-2B⁸, 2C²

ã1ʳ Title; ã2ʳ Ded. à M. de Maupeou, dated Sedan 10 November 1636; ã4ʳ Table des sermons; A1ʳ Text, pag. 1-402; 2C2 blank.

[Mert. 74.b.1

Note: Bound up with Du Moulin's *Jugement sur le livre du sieur de la Milletiere*.

140 *Deuxiesme decade de sermons*. Quevilly, ?1638.
DEVXIESME | DECADE | DE SERMONS. | *Par* PIERRE DV MOVLIN, | *Ministre de la Parole de Dieu*. | [Hole in page: probably the device cut out] | *A Queuilly*. | Chez CENTVRION LVCAS, tanan [. . . | sa boutique dans la Court du P [. . . | du costé des Greffe [. . . | M. DC. XXX [. . . | [The title-page has been badly cut and torn, so that the date remains uncompleted.]

8vo, ã⁴, A-2A⁸, 2B⁴

ã1ʳ Title; ã2ʳ Ded. à Mademoiselle Le Roy, undated; ã4ʳ Table des textes des dix sermons; A1ʳ Text, pag. 1-163/154-364; 2B4 blank. [SBNU E 169307

Note: Logically, the date should fall between that of the first *décade* (1637) and the third (1639). There is, however, an air of mystery about this work, the only *décade* with an undated dedication. a-

141 *Troisiesme decade de sermons*. Sedan, 1639.
TROISIESME | DECADE | DE SERMONS, | *Par PIERRE DV MOVLIN*. | *Ministre de la Parole de Dieu à Sedan*, | *& Professeur en Theologie*. | Par | approbation du Conseil des Moderateurs. | [Orn. P] | A SEDAN, | Par Hubert Raoult. | M. DC. XXXIX. |

8vo ã⁶, A-Y⁸, Z²

ã1ʳ Title; ã2ʳ Ded. à Mme la duchesse de la Trimouille, pag. 3-7; ã5ʳ Table; ã6 blank; A1ʳ Text, pag. 1-354; Z2ʳ Fautes à corriger.

[BN D² 7277 (3)

142 *Cinquième decade de sermons*. Charenton, 1642.
CINQVIEME | DECADE | DE | SERMONS. | *PAR* | *PIERRE DV MOVLIN*, | *Ministre de la parole de Dieu, &* | *Professeur en Theologie à Sedan* | [Orn. A coat of arms] | *Se vendent à Charenton*, | Par N. BOVRDIN & L. PERIER, | demeurans à Paris, ruë Neufve du | Palais, au Roy de Suede. | M. DC. XLII. |

8vo ã⁴, A-O⁸, P⁴

ã1ʳ Title; ã2ʳ Ded. à Mademoiselle Rivet ma soeur, dated Sedan

17 February 1642; ã4ʳ Table des textes des dix sermons; A1ʳ Text, pag. 1-228; P3 and P4 blank. [SBNU E 179776

143 *Premiere-cinquiesme decades de sermons.* Geneva, 1642-3.
5 parts.
PREMIERE | DECADE | DE | SERMONS. | Par | *PIERRE DV MOVLIN,* | Ministre de la Parole de Dieu à Sedan, | & Professeur en Theologie. | [Orn. Sower sowing seed] *A GENEVE,* | Pour Iaques Chouët. | M. DC. XLIII. |
Part I: 8vo ã⁴, A-Q⁸, R⁴, S⁴
   ã1ʳ Title; ã2ʳ Ded.; ã4ʳ Table; A1ʳ Text, pag. 1-272.
Part II: 8vo ¶⁴, A-P⁸, Q⁴, R⁴
   ¶1ʳ Title; ¶2ʳ Ded.; ¶4ʳ Table; A1ʳ Text, pag. 1-252; R3 and R4 blank.
Part III: 8vo ¶⁴, A-P⁸, Q⁴
   ¶1ʳ Title; ¶2ʳ Ded.; ¶4ʳ Table; A1ʳ Text, pag. 1-248.
Part IV: 8vo ¶⁴, A-Q⁸, R⁴
   ¶1ʳ Title; ¶2ʳ Ded.; ¶4ʳ Table; A1ʳ Text, pag. 1-263 [p. 263 mispaginated 163]; R4 blank.
Part V: 8vo ã⁴, A-O⁸, P⁴
   ã1ʳ Title; ã2ʳ Ded.; ã4ʳ Table; A1ʳ Text, pag. 1-228; P3 and P4 blank. [BN D² 7276

144 *Huictieme decade de sermons.* Sedan, 1649.
HVICTIEME | DECADE | DE SERMONS. | PAR PIERRE DV MOVLIN, | Ministre de la Parole de Dieu | à Sedan, & Professeur | en Theologie. | [Orn. P] | A SEDAN, | Par FRANÇOIS CHAYER, deuant | la Maison de Ville. | M. DC. XLIX. |
   8vo ã-ẽ⁸, A-V⁸, X⁴
   ã1ʳ Title; ã2ʳ Ded. à mes fils; ẽ7ᵛ Table; A1ʳ Text, pag. 1-327.
[BN D² 7272

145 *Premiere-dixiesme decades de sermons.* Geneva, Chouet, 1653.
2 vols. 10 parts. Parts I-V as for no. 143.
Part VI; 8vo ¶⁶, A-O⁸, P²
   ¶1ʳ Title; ¶2ʳ Ded.; ¶6ʳ Table; A1ʳ Text, pag. 1-225; P2 blank.
Part VII: 8vo ¶⁴, A-M⁸, N⁴, O⁴
   ¶1ʳ Title; ¶2ʳ Ded.; ¶4ʳ Table; A1ʳ Text, pag. 1-207.
Part VIII: 8vo ã-ẽ⁸, A-P⁸
   ã1ʳ Title; ã2ʳ Ded; ẽ8ʳ Table; A1ʳ Text, pag. 1-237; P8 blank.

Du Moulin, Pierre (C. 146)

Part IX: 8vo ¶⁶, A–M⁸, N²

¶1ʳ Title; ¶2ʳ Ded.; ¶4ʳ Table; ¶6 blank; A1ʳ Text, pag. 1–196.
Part X: 8vo *⁴, A–P⁸, Q⁴
*1ʳ Title; *2ʳ Ded.; *4ʳ Table; A1ʳ Text, pag. 1–245; Q4 blank
[? – wanting in this copy]. [BN D² 18097

146 *Trois sermons faits en presence des Peres Capucins.* Paris, 1641.
TROIS SERMONS | FAITS EN PRESENCE | DES PERES CAPVCINS, | qui les ont honorez de leur | presence. | *PAR PIERRE DV MOVLIN* | *Ministre de la Parole de Dieu.* | [Orn.] | Se vendent à Charenton. | Par SAMVEL PETIT, demeurant à Paris, dans la | Cour du Palais, à la Bible d'Or. | M. CD. XXXXI [*sic*] |

8vo †², A–L⁴

†1ʳ Title; †2ʳ Preface; A1ʳ Text, pag. 1–88. [BN D² 7287

147 *Idem.* Geneva, 1641.
TROIS | SERMONS | FAITS EN PRESENCE | DES PERES CAPVCINS, | qui les ont honorez de | leur presence. | PAR | *PIERRE DV MOVLIN* | *Ministre de la Parole de Dieu.* | Auec approbation du Conseil des Moderateurs. | [Orn.] | *A GENEVE,* | Pour Iaques Chouët. | M. DC. XLI. |

8vo a–e⁸, f⁴

a1ʳ Title; a2ʳ Preface, pag. 3–4; a3ʳ Text, pag. 5–88.

[BL 3901. b. 43

Note: Bound up with other anti-Capuchin works by Du Moulin.

148 *Sermon de l'image de Dieu en l'homme.* Charenton, 1647.
SERMON | *DE* | L'IMAGE | DE DIEV EN | l'homme: | Sur le I. chap. de Genese ⅄. 26. | *Faisons l'homme à nostre image,* | *selon nostre semblance, &c.* | Fait par PIERRE DV MOVLIN, | Professeur en Theologie, & | Pasteur en l'Academie & | Eglise de Sedan, | *En la LXXVI. année de son aage.* | [Orn.] | *Se vend à Charenton,* | Par LOVIS VENDOSME, demeu- | rant à Paris ruë neufue du Palais, | au Sacrifice d'Abraham. | M. DC. XLVII. |

12mo *A*⁸, *B*⁴, *C*⁴, *D*² [The signatures are italicized, a very unusual practice.]

A1ʳ Title; A1ᵛ L'Imprimeur aux Lecteurs; A2ʳ Text, pag. 3–35.

[SG Rés. D 8° SUP 319

Note: Unknown to Haag.

149 *De la mort du fidele, et de sa resurrection.* Sedan, 1649.
DE LA | MORT DV | FIDELE, ET DE | SA RESVRRECTION. |
Sermon sur le Pseaume 16. ℣. 9. | *Ma gloire s'est esgayée, aussi ma chair* | *habitera en asseurance.* | Par PIERRE DV MOVLIN, Ministre | de la Parole de Dieu à Sedan, & | Professeur en Theologie. | [Orn. P] | A SEDAN, | Par FRANÇOIS CHAYER, deuant | la Maison de Ville. | M. DC. XLIX. |
    8vo A–B^8
    A1^r Title; A2^r Text, pag. 3–32.   [SG Q 8° 74 Rés. Inv. 953
    Note: Unknown to Haag.

DU PERRON, Jacques Davy, Cardinal

150 *Les diverses oeuvres de l'Illustrissime Cardinal du Perron, Archevesque de Sens, etc.*, 1st edn, Paris, A. Estienne, 1622. This collection, which ran into a number of editions, contains several oratorical works which are either purely political, or else too early to be included in this Catalogue. Those which conform to our criteria are the *Sermon fait en l'Eglise de Nostre Dame, le jour de la Pentecoste* (pp. 681–93), the *Sermon faict à Sens le iour de la Toussainct* (pp. 694–704) and the *Commencement du premier sermon faict à sainct Mederic* (pp. 709–13: this is merely an *Avant-Propos*, and ends with the customary Ave Maria). The first two of these are reprinted in:

151 Migne, *Orateurs sacrés*, vol. 88, cols. 213 and 226.

DURANT, Jacques Himbert (or HIMBERT DURANT, Jacques) (P)
Pastor at one of the towns called La Ferté. Nothing more known about him. Haag does not contain an entry.

152 *Sermon sur ces paroles, 'Nostre ayde au nom de Dieu'.* La Rochelle, 1616.
SERMON SVR | CES PAROLES, | *Nostre ayde au nom de Dieu qui* | *a fait le ciel & la terre.* Psal. 124.8 | PRONONCE' EN DEVX | ACTIONS EN L'EGLISE RE- | formée d'Orleans le premier Dimanche | d'Octobre 1615. | *Par I. H. D. M. de la parole de Dieu.* | [Orn.] | A LA ROCHELLE, | Pour IAQVES LVCAS marchand | libraire à Paris. | M. DC. XVI. |

8vo A–H⁴, I²

A1ʳ Title; A2ʳ Ded. à Vertueuse et Chrestienne Damoiselle Mlle Palot, pag. 3–6; A4ʳ Text, pag. 7–66; I2 blank.

[BN D² 4037 (2)]

Note: The ECC copy [338.2.69] is identical except that it does not carry an imprint.

153 *Sermon sur ces paroles* ... *'Prenez garde que nul ne vous butine...'.* N.p., 1618.
SERMON | SVR CES PAROLES | COLOSS. 2.8.9.10. | *Prenez garde que nul ne vous butine* | *par la Philosophie & vaine de-* | *ception, selon la tradition des* | *hommes, selon les rudimens du* | *monde, et non point selon Christ.* | etc. | Par I. H. D. | [Orn.] | M. DC. XVIII. |

8vo A–H⁴

A1ʳ Text; A2ʳ Ded. à M. le baron de Montathere, & à MM. de Magdaillon ses freres, pag. 3–6; A4ʳ Text, pag. 7–62; H4 blank.

[BN D² 4037 (3)]

DURANT, Samuel (P)

Geneva *c*. 1580 – Paris 1626. Chaplain to the Landgrave of Hesse, Minister at Charenton. Moderator of the Synod of Charenton 1623. Noted for his anti-Arminianism.

154 *Six sermons sur quelques textes.* Sedan, 1623.
SIX | SERMONS | SVR | QVELQVES TEXTES | DE L'ESCRITVRE SAINTE, | qui sont marqués apres | la preface. | *PAR* | SAMVEL DVRANT, Ministre | de la parole de DIEV. | [Orn.] | A SEDAN. | Par IEAN IANON. | *M. DC. XXIII.* | Et se vendent à Charenton par Nicolas | Bourdin. |

12mo ã⁴, A–P¹², q², Q–S¹², T⁶

ã1ʳ Title; ã2ʳ Ded. à Mlle Durant ma mere; ã3ʳ Table of texts; ã4 blank; A1ʳ Text, pag. 1–335/blank/345–407/388/389–410/367/392–427.

[BL 4452. a. 15

Note: Unknown to Haag.

155 *Trois sermons sur ces mots* ... *'N'esteignez point l'Esprit'.* Sedan, 1623.
TROIS | SERMONS | SVR CES MOTS | DE S. PAVL EN LA |

premiere aux Thessaloni- | ciens [sic] chapitre 5. vers. 9. | *N'esteignez point l'Esprit.* | Par SAMVEL DVRANT, Ministre | de la Parole de Dieu en l'Eglise | de Paris. | [Orn.] | A SEDAN, | Par IEAN IANNON Imprimeur | de l'Academie. | M. DC. XXIII. |

12mo A–K⁶, L⁴

A1ʳ Title-page; A2ʳ Ded. à Mme la duchesse de Bouillon, pag. 3–4; A3ʳ Text, pag. 5–126. Wants L4. [BN D² 4250 (4)]

156 *L'Histoire de la tentation de nostre Seigneur.* Geneva, 1627.
L'HISTOIRE | *DE LA* | TENTATION | *DE* | NOSTRE SEIGNEVR | IESVS CHRIST. | *Exposée en* XVIII. SERMONS, *en l'E-* | *glise Reformée de Paris.* | Par SAMVEL DVRANT MINISTRE | de la Parole de Dieu. | [Orn.] | *A GENEVE,* | Chez PIERRE AVBERT | Imprimeur ordinaire de la Republique | & Academie. | M. DC. XXVII. | *Auec Priuilege.* |

8vo ¶⁴, 2¶², A–2R⁸, 2S⁴, 2T²

¶1ʳ Title; ¶2ʳ Ded. à Anne de Rohan, signed Spanheim, dated 20 February 1627, pag. 3–12; A1ʳ Textes des sermons, pp. 1–2 unpag.; A2ᵛ Text, pag. 4–651. [BN D² 7331]

157 *Sept sermons.* Geneva, 1627.
SEPT | SERMONS | *SVR* | L'ESCHELLE DE IACOB. | L'AGNEAV PASCHAL. | LA REMISSION DES PECHE'S. | LA PERSEVERANCE. | *Faits en l'Eglise Reformee* | *de Paris.* | Par SAMVEL DVRANT | Ministre de la Parole | de Dieu. | [Orn.] | *A GENEVE,* | POVR IACQVES CHOVET. | M. DCXXVII. |

8vo *⁸, B–V⁸

*1ʳ Title, *2ʳ Ded. à M. Arnauld, Conseiller & Secretaire du Roy, signed Spanheim, dated 4 June 1627; *7ᵛ Fautes à corriger; *8 blank; B1ʳ Text, pag. 1–299; V7 and V8 blank.

[SBNU E 157781]

Note: The BN copy [D² 7333] wants all but a fragment of the title-page, and also V8.

158 *Seize sermons sur Esaïe liii.* Geneva, 1628.
SEIZE | SERMONS | SVR LE LIII. CHA- | PITRE DV PRO- | phete Esaie | *Faits en l'Eglise Reformee* | *de Paris.* | Par SAMVEL DVRANT | Ministre de la parole | de Dieu. | *Auec vn* INDICE *des doctrines* | *plus importantes.* | [Orn. A crown] | *A GENEVE,* | Pour Pierre Chouët | M. DC. XXVIII. |

8vo ¶⁸, A–2R⁸, 2S⁶

¶1ʳ Title; ¶2ʳ Ded. à M. Durant, signed Spanheim, dated 18 January 1628; ¶7 and ¶8 blank; A1ʳ Text, pag. 1–640; 2S1ʳ Indice; 2S6 blank. [BL 3615. aa. 39

Note: The BN possesses a copy [D² 7332] with the imprint of Estienne Gamonet which wants ¶7 and ¶8. The Maz. copy [26.347] also carries the Gamonet imprint and wants all the preliminary leaves, and A1. Nos. 156–8 were posthumously published by Friedrich Spanheim.

EUDEMARE, François de
Rouen? – Rouen 1635. Canon of Rouen. Author of a widely read history of William the Conqueror (1629), some other religious works, and a sonnet to Henri IV on his entry to the city in 1596.

159 *Tapisseries sacrées*. Paris, 1617.
TAPISSERIES | SACREES. | *A l'honneur de l'eglise de Dieu* | *sur Chacun Jour des princi-* | *pales festes de Nostre Seigneur* | *De la tressaincte Vierge et* | *Autres Sainctz Celebrez* | *par l'Eglise Diuisées en* | *Deux Liures: et Dediées* | *A la Sacree Vierge,* | *Mere de Dieu.* | *Par* | F. D'EVDEMARE | *Prebstre et chanoine* | *en l'Eglise cathedral* [sic] | *A Rouen.* | *Auec Priuilege Du Roy* | A. PARIS. | *Chez Sauinian Pigoreau li-* | *braire demt au Mont S.ᵗ hy-* | *laire a l'Image S.ᵗ Claude* | *pres le puis certain* | 1617. |

[Engraved. The title panel is supported by SS. Gabriel and Michael, and surmounted by symbols of the Trinity, the Virgin and Child, and S. Peter. The imprint is supported by SS. Luke and Augustine. Signed Jaspar Isaac fecit.]

8vo ã⁸, ẽ⁸, ĩ⁴, *–2*⁸, A–3M⁸

ã1ʳ Title; ã2ʳ Ded. to the Virgin; ã8ʳ Ded. to François de Harlay, Abp. of Rouen; ẽ6ʳ Preface au Lecteur; ĩ2ᵛ Stances aux lecteurs, signed Pierre de Coudray; ĩ3ʳ Approbation dated 19 October 1617; Approbation of Rouen Theologal dated Rouen 20 July 1617; ĩ3ᵛ Fautes suruenuës en l'impression; ĩ4ʳ Extraict du priuilege for 6 years dated 19 October 1617; ĩ4ᵛ Chappitres des tapisseries contenuës en ce premier liure; *1ʳ Table des choses remarquables leuës aux deux liures des Tapisseries; A1ʳ Text of Book 1, pag. 1–451; 2F3ʳ Title for Book 2, pag. 453; 2F3ᵛ Chapitres des tapisseries contenues en ce second liure, pag. 454; 2F4ʳ Text of Book 2, pag. 455–874; 316ʳ Passages expliquez ou alleguez de l'Escriture saincte. [BN Rés. D 15533]

There are a number of engravings bound in as follows, facing the following pages:
32: St Stephen [L. Messag. ex.]; 54: St John the Evangelist [L. Messager excud.]; 98: Circumcision [I. Messager excudit] [L. Gaultier sculpsit]; 122: Adoration of the Magi; 190: St Matthew; 334: St James the Less; 484: St Peter [Ian Messager excud.]; 516: St Lawrence [I. Messag. exc.]; 574: St Augustine [I. Messager ex.]; 726: St Luke [L. Messager excudit]; 782: Paradise; 816: St Martin; 847: Immaculate Conception.

160 *L'Evangile en son trosne.* Rouen, 1631.
L'EVANGILE | EN SON TROSNE. | *SERMONS* | Sur la Parole de Dieu, contre le | Calvinisme. | *Par* FR. D'EVDEMARE, | *Prestre, & Chanoine en l'Eglise* | *Cathedrale nostre Dame* | *de Roüen.* | ET VN AVTRE OPSCVLE DV | mesme Autheur, sur la Priere du Canon | de la Messe, contre P. du Moulin, | Caluiniste. | [Orn.] | *A ROVEN,* | Chez Michel l'Allemant, tenant sa Bouti- | que au Portail des Libraires. | M. DC. XXXI. | *AVEC APPROBATION.* |

8vo ã⁴, ẽ⁴, ĩ⁴, A–F⁴, G–2P⁸, 2Q⁴

ã1ʳ Title; ã2ʳ Aux lecteurs catholiques; ĩ1ʳ Catalogue, representant sommairement ce qui est declaré aux Sermons; ĩ4ᵛ Approbation of Rouen Gardien dated 11 October 1631; Errata; A1ʳ Text, pag. 1–373/376–569. [BN D 33948]

Note: The work against Du Moulin mentioned in the title has a different collation and pagination.

It seems unlikely that this should be the first edition, but there is nowhere an indication of an earlier, privileged edition.

EUSTACHE, David (P)
Dauphiné 1595 – Montpellier 1672. Pastor in various southern towns, finally settling in Montpellier. President of the Provincial Synod of 1654.

161 *Sermon sur ... Matthieu xxvi, 26: 'Ceci est mon corps'.*
Geneva, 1648.

SERMON | Sur les paroles du Cha- | pitre xxvj. de S. Matth. | verset xxvj. | *Ceci est mon corps.* | PRONONCE' A MONTPELLIER, | par DAVID EVSTACHE, Ministre | du Saint Euangile. | [Orn. Hart drinking from stream] | *A GENEVE,* | Par PHILIPPE GAMONET. | M. DC. XLVIII. |

    8vo π^2, A–E^8, F^4

    $\pi 1^r$ Title cancellans; A1^r Ded. à M. d'Hillaire, dated Montpellier 14 January 1648, pag. 1–6; A5^r Au Lecteur, pag. 7–9; A7^r Text, pag. 11–38.   [BHP 23.086 R.

162 *Idem.* Charenton, 1649.
SERMON | SVR LES PAROLES | DV CHAP. XXVI. DE | S. Matth. vers. 26. | *Cecy est mon Corps.* | PRONONCE' A MONTPELLIER | par DAVID EVSTACHE, Ministre | du Sainct Euangile. | *Reueu & corrigé de nouueau par l'Autheur.* | [Orn.] | *Iouxte la copie imprimée à Geneve.* | Et se vend à Charenton par LOVYS | VENDOSME, demeurant à Paris | en la Gallerie des Oyseaux, | à la Caille. | M. DC. XLIX. |

    8vo A–K^4

    A1^r Title; A2^r Ded. to Hillaire, pag. 3–6; A4^r Au Lecteur, pag. 7–8; B1^r Text, pag. 9–79.   [BHP 23.086 R.

    Note: Unknown to Haag.

163 *Idem.* Orange, 1649.
SERMON | SVR LES PAROLES DV | Chapitre XXVI. de Sainct Matthieu | verset xxvj. *Cecy est mon corps.* | AVEC | La RESPONSE au Liure que le Sieur Richard | Mercier Iesuite a publié sur l'Eucharistie, où | il examine particulierement ledit Sermon. | ENSEMBLE | *Vne Conference auec le mesme, sur le* | *mesme sujet.* | Par DAVID EVSTACHE Ministre du Sainct | Euangile à MONTPELIER. | [Orn.] | *A ORANGE,* | Chez EDOVARD RABAN, Impri- | meur & Libraire de son Altesse, de la | Ville & Vniversité. | M. DC. XLIX. |

    8vo *–2*^{8}, A–2C^8, 2D^6, χ^2

    *1^r Title; *2^r Ded. à M. de Rambouillet; *2*3^r Preface; 2*6^r Table; 2*8 blank; A1^r Text of sermon, pag. 1–79/90–101; F7^r Response, pag. 103–438; $\chi 1^r$ Fautes à corriger.   [BN D^2 7559

    Note: This copy wants 2C. In the *fautes à corriger*, the author notes that the page reference system found in the *Response* 'se rapporte aux pages de la premiere Edition dudit Sermon, & non aux pages de celle-cy qui est la troisiesme'.

164 *Idem.* Charenton, 1650.
SERMON | SVR LES PAROLES | DV CHAP. XXVI. DE | S. Matth. vers. 26. | *Cecy est mon Corps.* | PRONONCE' A MONTPELLIER | par DAVID EVSTACHE, Ministre | du Sainct Euangile. | *Reueu & corrigé de nouueau par l'Autheur.* | [Orn.] | *Iouxte la copie imprimée à Genéve.* | Et se vend à Charenton par LOVYS | VENDOSME, demeurant à Paris en | la ruë de la Harpe, proche le Pont | S. Michel, au Sacrifice d'Abraham. | M. DC. L. |

8vo A–L^4

A1^r Title-page; A2^r Ded. to Hillaire, pag. 3–6; A4^r Au Lecteur, pag. 7–8; B1^r Text, pag. 9–88.   [BN D^2 5065

165 *Sermon sur la Passion.* Charenton, 1650.
SERMON | SVR LA PASSION | DE | IESVS-CHRIST | *Prononcé à Montpellier par* DAVID | EVSTACHE *Ministre du S. Euangile.* | [Orn. P] | *Se vend à Charenton,* | Par LOVYS VENDOSME, demeurant à | Paris sur le Quay de Gévre à la Caille. | M. DC. L. |

8vo A–E^4, F^4 [F missigned C]

A1^r Title; A2^r Text, pag. 3–43; F3 and F4 blank.

[BN D^2 5065

FERROUILH (or **FARROUILH**), Etienne (Franciscan)
No details of his life in any of the sources.

166 *Homelies adventuelles sur la salut angelique.* Paris, 1618.
Les | HOMELIES | ADVENTVELLES | *sur la* [sic] *salut Angelique* | *Ensemble les Dimanches* | *et festes de laduent* | *Par* R. P. F. E. | *Ferrouilh* | *Predicateur Or^{din}* | *Du* ROY | *du Conuent de* | *Bourdeaux* | DEDIE AV ROY | *A PARIS* | 1618. | *Chez Iean* | *Petit Pas Rue* | *St Iacques A lescu* | *de Venise pres les* | *Mathurins* | *Auec priuilege du* | ROY. |

[Engraved. Shows the Annunciation, the king, and a figure wearing a dalmatic and holding a palm whom I take to be St Stephen. Signature illegible]

8vo ã^8, A–2R^8, 2S^4

ã1^r Title; ã2^r Ded. au Roy; ã4^v Voeu de l'Autheur à la Vierge; ã5^v Latin epigram and ode signed God. de Lormeau, Vindoc.; ã6^v Au lecteur; ã8^r Approbation dated Paris 9 July 1618; ã8^v Approbation du Gardien dated 9 July 1618; A1^r Text, pag. 1–622; 2Q8^r

Table des matieres; 2S2ᵛ Privilege for 10 years dated 14 July 1618; 2S4 blank. [BN Rés. D 15299

FRANÇOIS de SALES, Saint
Only one oratorical work was published in St François's lifetime:

167 *Oraison funebre sur le trespas . . . du Duc de Mercoeur*. Paris, 1602.
ORAISON | FVNEBRE SVR | LE TRESPAS DE TRES- | hault & tres-Illustre Prince PHILLIPPE | EMANVEL de Lorraine Duc de Mer- | coeur et de Pentheure, Pair de France, | Prince du S. Empire & de Martigues, &c. | Lieutenant general de l'Empereur en ses | armées d'Hongrie. | *Faicte & prononcée en la grande Eglise de Nostre-* | *Dame de Paris le 27. Auril 1602. par* | Messire FRANCOIS DE SALES | *Coad. & esleu Euesque de Geneue.* | [Orn.] | A PARIS, | Chez Rolin THIERRY, & Eustache | FOVCAVLT, ruë S. Iaques, | à la Coquille. | 1602. AVEC PERMISSION. |
  8vo A–H⁴
  A1ʳ Title; A2ʳ Text, pag. 3–61; H3ᵛ Ded. à Mlle Françoise de Lorraine, fille vnique . . ., pag. 62–4. [BN 8° Ln27 14012

There are considerable problems surrounding the text of his sermons: the authentic texts, fragments, and recorded sermons, as well as a discussion of the textual difficulties, are to be found in:

168 *Edition complète des oeuvres*, Annecy, 1892–1935, vols. 7–10. This naturally supersedes the finding-list appended to Sauvage: *S. François de Sales prédicateur*, Paris, 1874, pp. 271–4.

GOYON, Simon de (P)
Minister at Bordeaux.

169 *La Cognoissance incomprehensible de la dilection de Christ*. Charenton, 1645.
LA | COGNOISSANCE | INCOMPREHENSIBLE | DE LA DILECTION | de CHRIST. | OV | SERMON | SVR CES PAROLES | de S. Paul, écriuant aux Ephe- | siens, chap. 3. v. 19. Et que vous | puissiez cognoître la dilection | de CHRIST, laquelle surpasse | toute cognoissance. | *Prononcé à Charenton le 26. Ianuier* | 1645. *Pour la*

cloture du Synode na- | tional, qui y estoit conuoqué, par | permission du Roy. | Par SIMON de GOYON, M. D. S. E. | à Bordeaux. | Se vend à Charenton, | Par LOVIS VENDOSME, demeurant | à Paris, ruë neufve du Palais, au Sa- | crifice d'Abraham. M. DC. XLV. |
   12mo A–F$^{8-4}$
   A1^r Title; A2^r Text, pag. 3–72.   [SBNU E 127855
   Note: Various MS. notes.

170 *La Conversion de Ninive.* Geneva, 1647.
LA | CONVERSION | DE NINIVE, | *OV* | SERMON PRONONCE' | à Begle le quatriesme iour | de May 1645. | *Pour la celebration du Ieusne indict par* | *le Synode Nationnal* [sic] *tenu à Cha-* | *renton l'an 1644.* | Par SIMON DE GOYON Ministre de la | Parole de Dieu, à Bourdeaux. | [Orn. A snail] | *A GENEVE,* | Pour Iaques Chouët. | *M. DC. XLVII.* |
   12mo A–B^{12}, C^6
   A1^r Title; A2^r Text, pag. 3–60.   [BN D^2 4250 (6)

GUERSON, François
Nothing known except that he was a preacher to the king. Cioranescu has overlooked him. The other works in the BN appear to be mainly political and polemical; one of them is a pamphlet in favour of the Jesuits, but as he is called 'le Sieur Guerson' in other titles, the hypothesis that he was a Jesuit is not very plausible. Certainly, Sommervogel has nothing.

171 *Sermons, ou Analogies divines.* Paris, 1620.
SERMONS | OV | ANALOGIES | DIVINES DV | VERBE, FILS DE DIEV, | ET DE IOSEPH, FILS DE | Iacob mocqué & vendu | par ses Freres. | Preschés en l'Aduent de l'an 1619. en l'Eglise S. Iean | en Greue. | *Par F. GVERSON Docteur en Theologie, Con-* | *seiller & Predicateur ordinaire du Roy.* | *Dedié* à LOYS LE IVSTE Roy de France & | de Nauarre. | Auec vn Panegyre de S. Augustin. | [Orn.] | A PARIS, | Chez SIMON LE FEBVRE ruë S. Iacques, à l'Image Sainct | François, deuant les Iesuites. | M. DC. XX. | *Auec priuilege du Roy & Approbation.* |
   8vo ã^8, A–Z^8
   ã1^r Title; ã2^r Ded. au Roy; ã4^r Table des matieres; ã7^r Printer's

Note; ã7ᵛ Extraict du priuilege for 6 years dated 3 April 1620; ã8ʳ Approbation, undated; A1ʳ Text, pag. 1–111/102/133–388.

[BN Rés. D 15536

The printer's note to the reader (ã7ʳ) is worth quoting:

Tres-cher Lecteur, ie te presente Ioseph mocqué & vendu par ses freres, s'il t'est agreable ie te promets Ioseph adoré par ses freres; tu excusera en celuy-cy quelques fautes suruenues en l'impression que l'Autheur n'a peu voir & examiner; car il prechoit le Caresme à Sainct Paul. Si ce premier essay t'agrée, il te promet vne octaue du Sainct Sacrement, des commentaires sur l'Apocalypse, & autres oeuvres qu'il a en main.

None of this substantial collection is extant, and it may well not have been published.

HERAULT, Louis (P)
Sedan c. 1604 – London? Studied at Sedan. Minister at Alençon, and later at the Walloon Church in London. Returned to France during the English Civil War, but at the Restoration was made a Canon of Canterbury. This event brought forth a postscript to the present work, *Le Pacifique royal en joye*, Amsterdam, 1665.

172 *Le Pacifique royal en deuil.* Saumur, 1649.
LE | PACIFIQVE | ROYAL | EN DVEIL [sic] | COMPRIS EN DOVZE | Sermons sur quelques tex- | tes de l'Escriture. | *Par* | *LOVIS HERAVLT,* | *Ministre du sainct Euangile.* | [Orn.] | *A SAVMVR,* | Par IEAN LESNIER, Imprimeur | & Libraire, au Liure d'Or. | *M. DC. XLIX.* |

   8vo ¶⁸, 2¶⁴, 3¶², A–2B⁸, χ²

   ¶1ʳ Title; ¶2ʳ Ded. to Charles II of England; A1ʳ Text, pag. 1–272/287–410; χ1ʳ Fautes à corriger.   [BN D² 4048

173 *Idem.* Saumur, 1650.
A reprint of 172. Although this copy wants the *fautes à corriger*, the text is uncorrected.   [BN D² 8282

HERSENT, Charles
Paris? – Brittany 1660. Joined the Oratory in 1615, but left in 1625 because of difficulties over preferment. Chancellor of Metz in 1627. He rejoined the Oratory, but was later excluded by Condren

because of his fierce anti-monastic invectives. He was known to his contemporaries as a violent, tempestuous man, strongly opposed to monks and Jesuits. For his suspected Jansenist sympathies he was excommunicated at Rome in 1650.

174 *Eloge funebre de ... Mme ... la Duchesse de la Valette.* Paris, 1627.
ELOGE | FVNEBRE | DE TRES-HAVTE ET TRES- | PVISSANTE PRINCESSE MADAME | GABRIELE DE BOVRBON | Duchesse de la Valette. | *Compris en trois Discours prononcez dans* | *l'Eglise Cathedrale de S. Estienne de Metz.* | Par R. P. CHARLES HERSENT | Theologien & Predicateur. | *Timenti Dominum bene erit in extremis, & in die defunctionis* | *suae benedicetur.* | Ecclesiast. 1. | [Orn.] | A PARIS, | Chez THOMAS BLAISE, ruë sainct | Iacques au Mercure Arresté. | M. DC. XXVII. |
Part I: 8vo ã^8, A–C^8, D^2
 ã1^r Title; ã2^r Ded. à la Reyne, pag. 3–11; ã6^v Preface [ã7^v pag. 14; wants ã8]; A1^r Text, pag. 1–50.
Part II: 8vo †^{4}, a–c^8
 †1^r Title; †2^r Ded. à Mgr l'Euesque de Metz; a1^r [missigned D] Text, pag. 1–48.
Note: The preliminary leaves have been misbound between sigs. a and b.
Part III: 8vo **^{4}, ã^8, ẽ^8, õ^8, ũ^4
 **1^r Title; **2^r Ded. à Mgr le duc de la Valette; ã1^r Text, pag. 1–53; ũ4 blank.   [BN 8° Ln27 11765

175 *Le Sacré Monument dedié à la memoire de ... Louis le Juste.* Paris, 1643.
LE SACRE' | MONVMENT | DEDIE' A LA MEMOIRE | DV TRES-PVISSANT, ET TRES- | Inuincible Monarque | LOVIS LE IVSTE, | Compris en trois Discours. | *Premier discours prononcé le 29. May dans l'Eglise* | *S. Germain de l'Auxerrois.* | DEDIE' A LA REINE, | Par CHARLES HERSENT Predicateur, Chan- | cellier de l'Eglise de Metz. | *Non possumus quae vidimus & audiuimus, non loqui.* Act. 4. | A PARIS, | Chez NOEL CHARLES, ruë S. Iacques, aux | trois Couronnes, deuant les Mathurins. | M. DC. XLIII. | *Auec Priuilege du Roy.* |
Part I: 8vo ã^4, ẽ^4, A–D^8
 ã1^r Title; ã2^r Ded. à la Reine; ẽ1^r Aduis au lecteur; A1^r Text, pag. 1–64.

Hersent, Charles (C. 176)

Part II: 8vo ē⁴, ī², A–D⁸, E⁴

ē1ʳ Title; ē2ʳ Ded. to Mazarin; A1ʳ Text, pag. 1–69; E3ᵛ Privilege to Hersent for 10 years dated 20 July 1643; E4ᵛ Transport to Noel Charles.

Note: Wants ī2.

Part III: 8vo õ⁴, ũ², A–D⁸

õ1ʳ Title; õ2ʳ Ded. à Mgr l'Illustrissime & Reuerendissime Euesque de Beauuais, Duc & Pair de France, & Ministre d'Estat; A1ʳ Text, pag. 1–63.

Note: Wants ũ2. [BN Lb36 3388]

176 *Le Scandale de Jesus-Christ dans le monde.* N.p. 1644.
LE SCANDALE | DE IESVS CHRIST | DANS LE MONDE. | Presché par le sieur Hersent dans l'Eglise de sainct Ger- | uais le second Dimanche des Aduens, en la presence | de Monseigneur le Coadjuteur de Paris. | *Et presenté à Monseigneur le Duc d'Orleans.* | Nos stulti propter Christum. I Cor. 4. | M. DC. XLIV. |

4to π⁴, A–D⁴ [of which D1 is the title leaf]

D1ʳ Title; π1ʳ Ded. to duc d'Orleans; π3ʳ L'auditeur au lecteur; A1ʳ Text, pag. 1–29. [BN D 8090]

Note: D1 has been folded round the other gatherings to make a title; in this copy π3 and π4 have been misbound between sigs. C and D. The circumstances of this pamphlet are explained in the note 'Au lecteur' as well as in the Dedication. Retz had apparently been so angered by the sermon that he had forbidden Hersent to preach, and placed a general ban on discussion of Grace and frequent Communion in the pulpit. This probably explains the absence of an imprint.

177 *L'Empire de Dieu dans les saincts.* Rome, Mascardi, 1650.
See evidence below.

178 *Idem.* 1651.
L'EMPIRE DE DIEV | DANS LES SAINCTS, | Ou bien | L'ELOGE DE SAINCT LOVIS | ROY DE FRANCE. | Prononcé à Rome le iour de sa Feste: Et dedié au Pape | auec la permission & agréement de sa Saincteté. | *Par le sieur Hersent Predicateur ordinaire du Roy, & Chancelier* | *de l'Eglise Cathedrale de Mets.* | Veu, approuué, & permis de publier auec l'Epistre, par le | R. P. Candide Maistre du Sacré Palais. | *Et depuis à l'insceu de sa Saincteté tres-iniustement*

persecuté par | *certains Religieux Politiques, ennemis declarés de la Grace* | *de Iesus-Christ en faueur du Pelagianisme.* | Iouxte la coppie imprimée à Rome l'An 1650. par | Mascardy: Auec la permission des Superieurs. | M. DC. LI. |

 4to A–D^4, E^2

 A1^r Title-page; A2^r Italian ded., pag. 3–6; A4^r French ded.; [B1^r is pag. 9]; B1^v Text, pag. 10–35.   [BN 4° Lb18 86

 Note: Unknown to Cioranescu.

Clearly another controversial sermon, hence no imprint.

HUMBLOT, François (Minim)
Verdun? – Tours 1612. Preacher to the Queen and Provincial of Touraine. An account of Humblot's life and death is to be found in A. Chavineau: *Les Derniers Souspirs d'une âme religieuse* (Paris, 1613), but it contains no information which would be useful here.

179 *Discours funebres . . . de feu . . . le Duc de Montpensier, et*
   de . . . Pere Ange de Joyeuse. Lyon, 1608.
DISCOVRS | FVNEBRES | ET PANEGYRICS: | Faicts en memoire de feu M^{gneur} | le Duc de Montpensier, | *Et de feu tresreuerend Pere Ange de Joyeuse,* | *Prouincial de la Prouince de France,* | *de l'Ordre des Capucins.* | Par F. Fr. HVMBLOT, Minime. | [Orn.] | *A LYON,* | Par Claude Morillon, Imprimeur de Madame | la Duchesse de Montpensier, 1608. | *Auec permission des Superieurs.* |

 12mo †^{8}, A–S^{12}, T^4

 †1^r Title; †2^r Ded. à Mme de Montpensier, dated 30 October 1608; †4^v Epistre à MM. de la Cour de Parlement de Dombes; †5^v L'Argument des deux discours; †8^r General permission to Humblot to publish, by the General of the Order, dated Rome October 1607; †8^v Provincial's permission, dated November 1608; A1^r Text of Montpensier discours, pag. 1–156; H1^r Title-page of 2nd disc.; H2^r Ded. to Cardinal de Joyeuse; H4^r Text of disc.; pag. 163–423; T2^v, pag. 424, Attestation of Censor, dated 24 November 1608; T3^r, pag. 425, Approbation, dated 24 November 1608; T3^v, pag. 426, Permission to Morillon to print, dated 24 November 1608, for 3 years; T34^r Fautes suruenuës à l'impression.

            [BN 8° Ln27 14725

The following works were published posthumously by Pierre Chevalier. The only work hitherto known to have survived was the *Conceptions . . . sur Jeremie* of 1618, although it would have been

possible to deduce the hypothetical existence of the others from
the General Privilege of 1615, which gives a list:

Nostre bien aymé PIERRE CHEVALIER, Imprimeur & Libraire Iuré en nostre
Vniuersité de Paris, nous a fait dire & remonstrer qu'il a recouuert Les
Sermons sur tous les Dimanches & Festes de l'année, le Sacrifice d'Isaac, auec
toutes les circonstances d'iceluy rapporté au Sacrifice de la nouuelle Loy, pres-
chez durant l'Octaue du Sainct Sacrement: Entrée de l'homme en l'estat
d'innocence, son seiour desastreux en l'estat du peché, & son noble retour en
l'estat de grace, representé durant l'Aduent: Le tout presché en diuers lieux,
par feu R. P. F. François Humblot, Religieux Minime de la Congregation de
sainct François de Paule, Prouincial du mesme Ordre en la
Prouince de Touraine. Lesquels Sermons il desireroit imprimer, ou faire
imprimer . . .

Second editions of the other works are in the Cambridge University
Library. The date of their first editions is not at all certain; the
Sacrifice d'Isaac is in a second edition by 1617, and though it contains no revealing Approbation, it must therefore be of 1615 or
1616. The *Festes de l'année* contains an Approbation of January
1617, which we may therefore take to be the year of the first
edition. The very defective second volume of the *Dimanches* contains no evidence. However, Albert's *Dictionnaire des prédicateurs*
(p. 310) notes a work by Humblot called *Conceptions sur tous les
Evangiles*, 2 vols. in 8°, Paris, Chevalier, 1618; this is a plausible
alternative title for the *Dimanches*, and though Albert may have
been noting a later edition, there is no contrary evidence for believ-
ing that the first edition came any earlier. It is therefore possible to
establish a tentative list:

180 *Le Sacrifice d'Isaac.* Paris, 1615 or 1616.

181 *Idem.* Paris, 1617.
LE | SACRIFICE | D'ISAAC, | *Auec toutes les circonstances
d'iceluy, rapportees* | *au Sacrifice de la nouuelle Loy.* | Presché
durant l'Octaue du sainct Sacrement, par vn | des plus renommez
personnages, & l'vne des | grandes memoires de nostre temps. |
Seconde edition, reueue & corrigee. | [Orn. IHS with sun in crown
of thorns] | A PARIS, | Chez PIERRE CHEVALIER, ruë S.
Iacques | à l'image sainct Pierre prés les Mathurins. | M. DC. XVII. |
Auec priuilege du Roy, & Approbation. |
   8vo π^2, A–T^8, V^6

Humblot, François (C. 185)

π1ʳ Title; π2ʳ Extraict du priuilege [of 1615]; A1ʳ Text, pag. 1-288; T3ᵛ Table des matieres. [ULC E.6.2²

Note: Wants gathering sig. E, pp. 65-80.

182 *Conceptions admirables sur toutes les festes de l'année.* Paris, 1617.

183 *Idem.* Paris, 1619.
CONCEPTIONS | ADMIRABLES SVR | TOVTES LES FESTES | de l'Année. | *Preschées en diuers lieux, par vn des plus re-* | *nommez personnages, & l'vne des grandes* | *memoires de nostre temps.* | Seconde edition, reueuë, corrigee, & augmentee | de plusieurs Sermons qui ont esté obmis | à la premiere edition. | [Orn. IHS with sun in crown of thorns] | A PARIS, | Chez PIERRE CHEVALIER, ruë sainct | Iacques, à l'Enseigne de sainct Pierre, | pres les Mathurins. | M. DC. XIX. | *Auec Priuilege du Roy: Et Approbation.* |

8vo ã⁸, *², A-3E⁸, 3F⁴

ã1ʳ Title; ã2ʳ Ded. à Messire Jean Jacques de Mesme, Seigneur de Roissy, signed C. M.; ã6ʳ Aduertissement au Lecteur; ã7ʳ Privilege of 1615; ã8ᵛ Approbation dated Paris, 17 January 1617; *1ʳ Table des Sermons; A1ʳ Text, pag. 1-112/117-292/283-634/633-760; 3C1ʳ Table des matieres. [ULC E.6.3

184 *Conceptions admirables sur tous les dimanches de l'année.* Paris, ?1618. 2 vols.

185 *Idem.* Paris, ?
We have vol. 2 in a very defective copy. I reconstruct the collation of this volume as follows:

8vo A-2H⁸, 2I², a-l⁸

Wants A-K (pp. 1-160); Begins with text, L1ʳ, pag. 161-470; 2G4ʳ Table des matieres contenuës en ce second tome; a1ʳ Sermons qui ont esté adioustez en cette seconde edition des Dimanches du P. Humblot, pag. 1-171; l7 and l8 blank. [ULC E.6.2¹.

Note: Apart from the remark in the *Table des matieres*, one can be certain that this is vol. 2 inasmuch as the text begins with the sermon for the sixth Sunday after Pentecost; one could never reach that in 161 pages.

186 *Conceptions admirables sur les lamentations de Ieremie.* Paris [1618].

CONCEPTIONS | ADMIRABLES SVR | les lamentations de Ieremie, | Contenant l'entrée de | l'Homme en l'estat d'in- | nocence, son seiour des- | astreux en l'estat du peché, | et son noble retour en l'estat | de la grace, le tout repre- | senté durant l'Aduent. | Par l'vn des plus Celebres per- | sonnages et des plus grandes | memoires de nostre temps. | A PARIS, | Chez Pierre Cheuallier | ruë St Iacques à l'image S.^{t} | Pierre, pres les Mathurins | Auec priuilege du Roy | et Approbation. |

[Engraved: shows various subjects of the lamentations. Unsigned.]

8vo ã^4, A–3A^8, 3B^4 [3B missigned 2B]

ã1^r Title; ã2^r Ded. to Henry de Mesmes, signed C. M.; ã4^r Au Lecteur; ã4^v Approbation dated 30 July 1618; A1^r Text, pag. 1–695; 2X5^r Table des matieres les plus belles; 2B2^v Privilege of 1615.

[BN D 38208

LA FITE, Jean de (P)
Minister at Pau.

187 *Sermon sur Colossiens i, 13.* Orthez, 1631.
4to
Cioranescu 38376

188 *Deux sermons faits en deux synodes de Béarn.* Orthez, 1631.
4to
Cioranescu 38377

189 *Sermon sur Jean i, 51.* Charenton, 1645.
SERMON | SVR CES PAROLES | DE IESVS-CHRIST. | IEAN. 1. 51. | En verité, en verité ie vous dis, desormais | vous verrez le Ciel ouuert, & les Anges | de Dieu, montans & descendans | sur le Fils de l'Homme. | *Prononcé à Charenton, le 1. de l'An 1645. iour* | *de Cene, & premier Dimanche de la tenuë* | *du Synode National.* | Par IEAN LA FITE, F. M. D. S. E. | en l'Eglise de Pau, deputé de la Pro- | uince de Bearn. | [Printer's Orn.] | *Se vendent à Charenton.* | Par MELCHIOR MONDIERE, de- | meurant à Paris, en la court du Palais | aux deux Viperes. | M. DC. XLV. |
12mo A–H$^{8-4}$

A1ʳ Title; A2ʳ Text, pag. [3]–96. [SBNU E 127855]

Note: This sermon is listed in Haag (1st edn, vol. 6, p. 208) with a footnote: 'A l'exception de ce sermon, nous ne sachions pas qu'il ait rien publié.'

LANGLE, Jean Maximilien de Baux, Seigneur de (P)
Evreux 1590 – Rouen 1674. Pastor at Rouen for 52 years.

190 *Sermon sur S. Luc xiii, 1–3*. Quevilly, 1636.
SERMON | FAIT A QUEVILLY, | le 28. Aoust 1636. en vn iour | de Iusne, celebré en toute la | prouince de Normandie par | nos Eglises, pour la prosperité | des armes du Roy. | *Sur les vers. 1. 2. & 3. du 13. Chap. de* | *l'Euangile selon S. Luc.* | Par IEAN MAXI-MILIEN DE | L'ANGLE Ministre de la | Parole de Dieu, à Roüen. | [Orn.] | *Se vendent à Queuilly,* | Par ROBERT VALENTIN, Et | CENTVRION LVCAS, | dans la Court du Palais. | M. DC. XXXVI. |
12mo A–I⁶
A1ʳ Title; A2ʳ Text, pag. 3–105; wants I⁶. [SBNU E 127396]

191 *Idem*. Geneva, 1637.
In *Sermons faits au jour de Jusne, &c.* Geneva, Jean de la Planche, 1637. [BHP 20.309. 8°

192 *Sermon sur Apocalypse ii, 4–5*. Charenton, 1645.
SERMON | SVR LES PAROLES | DV SECOND CHAPITRE | de l'Apocalypse v. 4.5. pronon- | cé à Charenton, le huitiéme | iour de l'an 1645. En la presen- | ce du Synode national qui y | estoit conuoqué par permis- | sion du Roy. | *Par I. M. de L'Angle.* | [Orn.] | *Se vend à Charenton.* | Par N. BOVRDIN, & la vefve | L. PERIER, demeurant à Paris | ruë Neufve du Palais, au Roy | de Suede. | M. DC. XLV. |
12mo A–H⁸⁻⁴
A1ʳ Title; A2ʳ [missigned ãii] Ded. à l'Eglise que Dieu a commise à mon soin, qui fait sa demeure à Rouen; A3ʳ Text, pag. 5–95.
[BN 8° Ld176 128

Note: Unknown to Haag. The SBNU copy [E 127855] has the imprint of Louis Vendosme.

LE FAUCHEUR, Michel (P)
Geneva *c.* 1585 – Paris 1657. Began his ministry at Annonay, and was soon much in demand for his oratorical talents. Pastor at Montpellier 1625; was sent on a peace mission to Nîmes, but fell into Richelieu's disfavour and was forbidden to preach for a while. Pastor at Charenton, 1634–57. Roman numerals refer to the list in Haag, 1st edn, vol. 6, pp. 495–6.

193 *Sermon sur le Psaume 42, 4 et 5.* 1613.
12mo

Haag I. In view of the very slight information given, and the similarity to the sermon of 1641 with the same title, this entry is very doubtful indeed.

194 *Huict sermons sur divers textes.* Sedan, 1625.
The two works which make up this item are often listed (in Haag, for instance, or the BL Catalogue) as if they were additional to it. In reality, the title-page is merely a cover for two separate groups of four sermons each, as described below. The second edition may be responsible for this confusion.

1. SERMONS | FAITS EN | L'EGLISE DE | MONTPELLIER, | sur | La perseuerance en la Reli- | gion. | Le iugement de Dieu de- | noncé à Felix. | Le dormir de S. Estienne. | Le rauissement d'Elie. | *Par* MICHEL LE FAVCHEVR, | *Ministre de la parolle de Dieu* | *en ladite Eglise.* | [Orn.] | A SEDAN. | Et se vendent à Charenton, par Nicolas | Bourdin, & Samuel Petit. | M. DC. XXV. |

12mo π^4, A–H^{12}

$\pi 1^r$ General title [Huict Sermons]; $\pi 2^r$ Title [as above]; $\pi 3^r$ Ded. à Mlle de Roham [*sic*]; A1^r Text, pag. 1–190; H12^r Fautes suruenuës à l'impression.

Note: Gathering sig. F printed in much smaller type.

2. QVATRE | SERMONS | FAITS EN | DIVERS TEMPS, | & sur diuerses occasions, | en l'Eglise de Montpel- | lier. | *Par* MICHEL LE FAVCHEVR, | *Ministre de la parolle de Dieu* | *en ladite Eglise.* | [Orn.] | A SEDAN | Et se vendent à Charenton, par Ni- | colas Bourdin, & Samuel Petit. | M. DC. XXV. |

12mo π^2, A–I^{12}

$\pi 1^r$ Title; $\pi 2^r$ Ded. à Monsieur Arnaud; A1^r Text, pag. 1–213; wants I^{12}. [BL 846.k.20

195 *Idem.* Sedan, 1626.
HVICT | SERMONS | FAITS EN L'EGLISE | DE MONTPELLIER, | Sur, | *La perseuerance en la Religion.* | *Le iugement de Dieu denoncé à Felix.* | *Le dormir de S. Estienne.* | *Le rauissement d'Elie.* | *La Priere pour la paix de Ierusalem.* | *La vocation de Timothee au S. ministere.* | *La desolation de l'Eglise, & retour de* | *grace enuers icelle.* | *Les Chastimens enuoyez sur l'Eglise pour* | *r'allumer son zele à repentance.* | Par MICHEL LE FAVCHEVR, Ministre | de la parolle de Dieu en | ladite Eglise. | [Orn.] | *A SEDAN.* | Et se vendent à Charenton, par Nicolas | Bourdin, & Samuel Petit. | M. DC. XXVI. |

 12mo A–2K$^{8-4}$, 2L^2

 A1^r Title; A2^r Ded. à Mademoiselle de Roham [*sic*]; A3^r Text, pag. 5–403.   [SBNU E 159216

196 *Sermon sur . . . Jean iii, 14 et 15* [with another]. Charenton, 1632.
SERMON | SVR CES PAROLES | DE L'EVANGILE SELON | S. Iean, Chap. 3. vers. 14. & 15. | *Or comme Moyse esleua le Serpent au desert:* | *ainsi faut-il que le Fils de l'homme soit* | *esleué.* | *Afin que quiconque croit en luy ne perisse* | *point, mais qu'il ait vie eternelle.* | Prononcé en l'Eglise de Charenton | le 14. Septembre, 1631. | *Par* MICHEL LE FAVCHEVR, | *Ministre de la Parole de Dieu, en l'Eglise* | *Reformée de Montpellier.* | [Orn.] | *Et se vendent à Charenton,* | Par N. BOVRDIN, & L. PERIER, de- | meurans à Paris, ruë Neufue du | Palais, au Roy de Suede. | M. DC. XXXII. |

 12mo A^{12} B^8 C^4 D^4 E^2 F^8 G^4 H^8 I^4 K^4

 A1^r Title; A2^r Text of sermon, pag. 3–60; F1^r Text of another sermon, on Psalm 102, vv. 14 and 15, pag. 61–115.
               [BHP 10.548

 Note: Unknown to Haag.

197 *Trois sermons.* Charenton, 1632.
TROIS | SERMONS, | Dont le premier est de la vie | spirituelle. | Le second, du preseruatif & | remede contre le peché. | Le troisiesme, de la certitude | du salut. | *Prononcez à Charenton cette* | *année 1632.* | Par MICHEL LE FAVCHEVR, | Ministre de la Parole de Dieu en | l'Eglise Reformée de | Montpellier. | [Orn.] | *Et se vendent à Charenton.* | Par IEAN MARTIN & LOVYS | VENDOSME,

demeurans à Paris sur | le Pont S. Michel à l'Anchre double, | & dans la court du Palais à la | ville de Venise. 1632. |

    12mo A–I^{12}, K^6

    A1^r Title-page; A2^r Text, pag. 3–225; K6 blank.

                                                                             [BHP 10.548

    Note: Unknown to Haag.

198 *Sermon des souffrances des fideles.* Charenton, 1632.
SERMON | DES SOVFFRANCES | DES FIDELES | & de leur gloire. | PAR | *MICHEL LE FAVCHEVR* | *Ministre de la Parole de Dieu* | *en l'Eglise Reformée de* | *Montpellier.* | [Orn.] | *Se vendent à Charenton,* | PAR PIERRE AVVRAY, demeurant | à Paris en l'Isle du Palais à | la fleur de Lys. | M. DC. XXXII. |

    12mo A–C$^{8-4}$, D^2

    A1^r Title-page; A2^r Text, pag. 3–43.   [BHP 10.548

    Note: Unknown to Haag.

199 *Sermon sur Jean vi, 56.* Charenton, 1632.
SERMON | SVR CES MOTS | DE L'EVANGILE SELON | S. Iean Chapitre 6. vers. 56. | *Celuy qui mange ma chair & qui boit mon* | *sang demeure en moy, & moy en luy.* | Prononcé en l'Eglise de Charenton | le iour de Pasques, 1632. | *Par* MICHEL LE FAVCHEVR, | *Ministre de la Parole de Dieu, en l'Eglise* | *Reformée de Montpellier.* | [Orn.] | *Et se vendent à Charenton et à Paris.* | Chez IEAN MARTIN, sur le Pont S. | Michel, à l'Anchre double. | LOVYS VENDOSME, dans la | Court du Palais. | PIERRE AVVRAY, en l'Isle du | Palais, à la fleur de Lys. | [All bracketed together] M. DC. XXXII. |

    12mo A–C^{12}

    A1^r Title; A2^r Text, pag. 3–69. Wants C12. [SG D 8° Rés. 11.174

    Note: Of the two identical copies in the BHP, one carries the imprint of Jean Martin only [BHP R. 16.065], the other that of Pierre Auvray only [BHP 10.548]. None of these is known to Haag.

200 *Sermon faict pour le Jeusne celebré le 19. Novembre 1637.*
    Charenton, 1638.
SERMON | FAICT POVR LE | Ieusne celebré le 19. | Nouembre 1637. | Sur les Lamentations de | Ieremie chapitre 5. | verset 21. | Par MICHEL LE FAVCHEVR | Ministre de la Parole | de Dieu. | [Orn.] | *Se vendent à Charenton* | Par Louis de Vendosme demeu-

Le Faucheur, Michel (C. 205)

rant | à Paris, en la Court du Palais, | à la ville de Venize. | M. DC. XXXVIII. |
 12mo A-E$^{8-4}$
 A1^r Title; A2^r Text, pag. 3-61.   [SBNU E 156928

201 *Sermon sur les paroles du Psaume 42, 1-3.* 1640.
Haag VI.

202 *Sermon sur le Pseaume 42, 4, 5 & suivans.* Charenton, 1641.
SERMON | SVR | LE PSEAVME | XLII. Versets 4. 5 & suiuans | jusques à la fin du Chapitre. | Par MICHEL LE FAVCHEVR, Mi- | nistre du Sainct Euangile. | [Orn. P] | *Se vendent à Charanton* | Par SAMVEL PETIT, demeurant à | Paris, dans la Cour du Palais à la | Bible d'Or. | M. DC. XLI. |
 8vo A-C^8, D^4
 A1^r Title; A2^r Text, pag. 1-54. Wants D4. [BHP 8154
 Note: In a somewhat fragmentary state.

203 *Sermons sur Ephesiens iv.* 1641.
Haag VII.

204 *Idem.* Charenton, 1642.
SERMONS | SVR LE QVATRIESME | Chapitre de l'Epistre de S. | Paul aux Ephesiens. | Par MICHEL LE FAVCHEVR, | *Ministre du Sainct Euangile.* | [Orn. P] | *Se vendent à Charenton,* | Par SAMVEL PETIT, demeurant à Paris, | dans la Cour du Palais, à la Bible d'Or. | M. DC. XLII. |
 8vo A-2P^8, 2Q^4
 A1^r Title; A2 blank; A3^r Text, pag. 1-612.
            [SBNU E 159217
 Note: The BHP copy [1253] appears to be missing from that library.

205 *Sermon prononcé le jour du Jeusne . . . 4. May 1645.*
 Charenton, 1645.
SERMON | PRONONCE' | LE IOVR DV IEVSNE, | celebré à Charenton le | Ieudy 4. May 1645. | Sur le 66. Chap. d'Esaie v.2. | *Par* MICHEL *le* FAVCHEVR | *Ministre de la Parole de Dieu.* | [Orn. P] | Ce [*sic*] vend à Charenton par SAMVEL PETIT | demeurant à Paris, dans la Cour | du Palais à la Bible d'Or. | M. DC. XLV. |

12mo A–F$^{8-4}$, G^4
A1^r Title; A2^r Text, pag. 3–79.   [BN D^2 8884
Note: Unknown to Haag.

LE GAULT, Ignace (*Recollet*)
B? – Paris 1652. *Recollet* in 1601. Warden of the Paris convent.

206 *Homelies sur les dimanches et festes de l'année.* Paris, 1629–31. 2 vols.

Cioranescu (41764); Albert (p. 366). The latter notes the work as Paris, D. Moreau, 1628. I have found only vol. 2:
HOMELIES | SVR LES | DIMANCHES | ET FESTES DE L'ANNEE. | *Composees par le* R. P. IGNACE DE LA GAVLT, *Gardien* | *des Peres Recolects de Mets.* | TOME SECOND. | [Printer's Orn.] | A PARIS, | chez DENYS MOREAV, ruë S. Iacques, à la | Salemandre d'Argent. | M. DC. XXXI. | *Auec Priuilege du Roy, & Approbation des Docteurs.* |
    8vo ã^8, A–2Q^8, 2R^4
    ã1^r Title; ã2^r Ded. to Hercule de Rohan, dated Metz 30 May 1625; ã5^v Licence du R. P. Prouincial, dated Metz 27 June 1625; Approbation des Docteurs, dated Paris 31 May 1625; ã6^v Privilege for 9 years, dated Compiègne 6 June 1624; ã7^v Table des Sermons; A1^r Text, pag. 1–602 [Sermons for 1st Sunday in Lent to Trinity]; 2P6^r Table des Matieres; 2R4 blank.
                        [BMV Fonds A. in-8°. 0. 31. E

207 *Sainctes exhortations sur tous les Evangiles du Caresme.* Paris, 1633.
SAINCTES | EXHORTATIONS | SVR TOVS | LES EVANGILES | DV CARESME. | Auec vn Sermon de Sainct Ioseph, & de | l'Annonciation de la VIERGE. | *Composées par le R. P.* IGNACE LE GAVLT, | *Gardien des PP. Recollets de Paris.* | Ensemble vne Table, contenant deux ou trois Sermons | sur châque iour, tirez de ses Homelies Dominicales. | [Printer's Orn.] | A PARIS, | Chez Denys Moreau, ruë S. Iacques, à la Salemandre. | M. DC. XXXIII. | *Auec Priuilege, & Approbation.* |
    8vo ã^8, ẽ^4, A–4C^8, 4D^4
    ã1^r Title; ã2^r Ded. à Mgr Georges de la Porte, dated Paris 2 March 1633; ã5^v Aduis au Lecteur; ã7^v Table; ẽ3^r Approbation du

Prouincial dated 20 November 1632; ẽ3ᵛ Approbation des
Theologiens, dated 20 February 1633; ẽ4ʳ Privilege for 10 years,
dated 3 March 1633; A1ʳ Text, pag. 1–1111; 4A4ᵛ Table des
matieres; 4D3ʳ Fautes suruenuës . . .; 4D4 blank.
[BN D 41227
Sbaraglia (Supplement to Wadding, vol. 2, no. 1012) notes 'Conciones de Adventu et Quadragesima tomis pluribus in-8 gallicè'. I have found no other mention of an Advent series.

LOR, Antoine de (Carmelite)
B? – Toulouse 1631. Doctor of Theology, Toulouse, in 1602;
Prior of the Carmel 1622; elected Provincial of the Basque province 1628.

208 *Sermons salutaires sur tous les jours de l'Advent.* Toulouse, 1623.
SERMONS | SALVTAIRES | SVR TOVS LES IOVRS | de l'Aduent,
pour conduire les Ames | pecheresses au chemin du Ciel, | *COM-POSEZ ET PRESCHEZ* | *par le* R. P. ANTOINE DE LOR *Docteur* | *en saincte Theologie, & Prieur du grand* | *Conuent de la Vierge Marie du* | *Mont Carmel en Tholose.* | [Orn. Shepherd with sheep] | *A TOLOSE,* | Chez PIERRE BOSC Marchand Libraire. | M. DC. XXIII. | Auec Priuilege. |
   8vo ã⁸, A–2Q⁸, 2R⁴
   ã1ʳ Title; ã2ʳ Ded. à Messire Marc de Calviere; ã5ʳ Aduertissement au Lecteur; ã7ᵛ Licentia R. P. Magistri Generalis, for all Lor's works, dated Rome 10 July 1621; ã7ᵛ Approbation, dated Toulouse 1 February 1623; ã8ʳ Permission du Vicaire General dated 13 February 1623; ã8ᵛ Extraict du priuilege dated 18 February 1623; A1ʳ Text, pag. 1–588; 207ʳ Fautes plus remarquables qui se sont glissées en l'impression; 207ᵛ Table generale des matieres.
[Ars 8° T 6262¹⁻²
   Note: Though the text is continuous, this copy is bound in two volumes, the second beginning on p. 383. This explains the entry of two volumes in Nyon's La Valliere catalogue (no. 993).
The *Biblioteca carmelitana* (p. 175, no. 238) notes 'scripsit 1) Sermones Adventuales, tom. 1 in-8, 2) Sermones Quadragesimales, tom. 1 in-8, 3) Sermones de Sanctis, tom. 1 in-8. Tres hi tomi editi fuerunt Tolosae, anno 1623, apud Petrum Bosc'. Although only the

one work listed above appears to be extant, evidence for the others is found in the Approbation, Permission, and Privilege, all of which are for 'les Sermons pour tous les jours de l'Aduent & Caresme'.

The General's Licence of 1621 goes much further: it is for 'Centum octuaginta Sermones compositos et habitos à dicto Patre in multis regni Galliae civitatibus, singulis diebus Adventus, & Quadragesimae, necnon omnibus Dominicis & Festis totius anni, cum aliquibus aliis pro defunctis'. This is of course a complete series, and may well be based on Lor's hopes rather than his manuscripts.

MACÉ, Jean (in religion, LEON DE SAINT-JEAN) (Carmelite) Rennes 1600 – Paris 1671. Carmelite in 1617. Much of his life was spent in the world of political as well as religious authority; he attended Richelieu at his death.

209 *La Couronne des saints.* Paris, 1637.
Cioranescu (42668). See the evidence listed below. This is noted by the *Bibliotheca Carmelitana* (col. 240) as Paris, P. J. Cottereau, 1637; however, as the 1642 edition is also noted as published by Cottereau this should not worry us too greatly.

210 *Idem.* Paris, 1642.
LA | CORONNE | DES SAINTS, | COMPOSEE DE DIVERS | SERMONS PANEGYRIQVES. | EDITION NOVVELLE. | *Reueuë, corrigée & augmentée par le R. P. F.* | LEON, *R. Carme Reformé.* | A TRES-SAGE, TRES-VERTVEVX | ET TRES-ILLVSTRE SEIGNEVR, | MESSIRE | MATTHIEV MOLE', | PREMIER PRESIDENT | AV PARLEMENT DE PARIS. | [Orn.] | A PARIS, | Chez CHARLES ROÜILLARD, ruë S. Iacques, | à la Fleur de Lys Coronnée. | M. DC. XLII. | *Auec Priuil. du Roy, & Approbation des Doct.* |

8vo ã⁶, A–2L⁸, 2M²

ã1ʳ Title; ã2ʳ Ded.; ã3ᵛ Vn mot au Lecteur; ã4ʳ Printer's note; ã5ʳ Approbation dated 25 November 1637; Extraict du priuilege, to Pierre Billaine for 7 years dated 1 December 1637; 'Les heritiers du deffunt Pierre Billaine . . . ont transporté leur droit . . . à Charles Roüillard'; ã6ʳ Les fleurons dont est composée la Coronne des Saincts; A1ʳ Text, pag. 1–532; 2L3ʳ Table des matieres.

[BN D 41380]

211 *Le Pontife innocent, ou sermon du Bienheureux François de Sales.* Paris, 1637.
Cioranescu 42672; *Bibliotheca Carmelitana* col. 240.

212 *Panegyrique de S. Louis.* Rome, 1648.
SAINT LOVYS, | LE S.^{NT} DES ROYS, | & | LE ROY DES SAINTS. | Sermon Panegyrique, | Presché à Rome, dans l'Eglise de Saint | Louys de la Nation Françoise. | *Le xxv. d'Aoust. de l'an M. DC. XLVIII.* | PAR LE R. P. LEON DE SAINT IAN, | Exprouincial des Carmes Reformes de | la Prouince de Touraine, Visiteur | general du mesme Ordre en Fran- | ce, & Predicateur ordinaire | de sa Majesté tres | Chrestienne. | *Mis en lumiere par M. Ian Marquier, Prestre de Bretagne,* | *& Curè de Saint Yues de Rome.* | A Rome, par Bernardin Tani. 1648. | *Auecque permission des Superieurs.* |
 4to π^2, $2\pi^2$, A–C^4

 $\pi 1^r$ Title; $2\pi 1^r$ Ded. au Roy, signed Ian Marquier, dated Rome 15 September 1648; $2\pi 2^v$ Two imprimaturs, both undated; A1^r Text, pag. 1–26.   [BN 4° L46 190 (1)]

 Note: $\pi 2$ has been wrapped around so as to form the final leaf of the text, and is signed D.

213 *La Tres-eloquente Harangue funebre du Pere Joseph.* Paris, 1649 [1639?]
LA | TRES-ELOQVENTE | HARANGVE | FVNEBRE | QVI FVT PRONONCEE PAR | LE P. LEON CARME, A L'ENTERREMENT | DV PERE IOSEPH | CAPVCIN, | Fort entendu & employé aux affaires d'Estat aupres du | Cardinal de Richelieu. | *Sacramentum Regis abscondere bonum est opera autem Dei* | *reuelare & confiteri honorificum est.* Tob. 12. | [Orn.] | A PARIS | Chez NICOLAS BESSIN, Imprimeur & Libraire, au Palais, | en l'allée S. Michel. | M. DC. XLIX. |
 4to A–D^2, χ^1

 A1^r Title; A2^r Text, pag. 3–17.   [BN 4° Ln27 25495]

 Note: χ is a loose leaf pasted on to D2. Joseph de Paris, the 'éminence grise', died in 1638, of course, and this raises the problem of the date. Since the oration is entirely normal, and refers to Joseph as recently dead, we can, I think, assume that the date on the title-page is a mistake.

MACHON, Louis
Nothing seems to be known of this preacher except that at the time of the publication of the following works he was Archdeacon of Port and Canon of Toul (see the Dedication and Privilege). Cioranescu notes that he was Curé of Tourne after 1672.

214 *Discours ou sermon apologetique, en faveur des femmes.* Paris, 1641.
DISCOVRS | OV | SERMON | APOLOGETIQVE, | EN FAVEVR | DES FEMMES. | *QVESTION NOVVELLE,* | *curieuse, & non jamais* | *soustenuë.* | [Orn.] | A PARIS, | Chez T. BLAISE, ruë Sainct Iacques, | prés Sainct Yues. | M. DC. XLI | *Auec Priuilege du Roy, & Approbation.* |

8vo ã^6, A-G^8, H^2

ã1^r Title; ã2^r Ded. à la Marquise de Coislin; ã6^r Extraict du Priuilege to Machon for two sermons, dated Paris 29 April 1641; Transport to Blaise; Acheué d'imprimer, le 15. iour de May, 1641; A1^r Text, pag. 1–115. [BN R 24043

Note: Despite its unconventional theme, this work is in normal sermon form.

215 *Sermon pour le jour de l'Assomption.* Paris, 1641.
SERMON | POVR LE IOVR DE | l'Assomption Nostre Dame, au | retour de la Procession gene- | rale, establie par le Roy LOVIS | XIII. surnommé LE IVSTE, | en l'an 1638. | [Orn.] | A PARIS, | Chez T. BLAISE, ruë Sainct Iacques, | prés Sainct Yues. | M. DC. XLI. | *Auec Priuilege du Roy, & Approbation.* |

8vo ã^6, A-D^8

ã1^r Title; ã2^r Ded. to Richelieu; ã6^r Privilege, Transport and Achevé as for no. 214; A1^r Text, pag. 1–62; D8 blank.
[BN R 24044

MESTREZAT, Jean (P)
Geneva 1592 – Paris 1657. Studied brilliantly at Saumur. Minister at Charenton; President of the Synod of Charenton 1631. Well known as a controversialist; even Retz had reason to fear him. Roman numerals refer to the list in Haag, 1st edn, p. 400. Most of the works listed here are unknown to Haag, and I have not noted this in each case. It merely underlines, as did the list for Le Faucheur, the dangers of reliance on this authority.

216 *Trois sermons sur Ephesiens ii, 5–10.* Sedan, 1625.
DV | FRVICT | QVI NOVS REVIENT | DE LA COMMVNION | à Iesus-Christ. | Et de la maniere de nostre | iustification. | OV | TROIS SERMONS SVR | *l'Epistre de S. Paul aux Ephes. ch. 2.* | ℣. 5.6.7.8.9.10. | Par IEAN MESTREZAT, Ministre | de la Parole de Dieu, en l'Eglise | reformée de Paris. | [Orn.] | *A SEDAN,* | Par Iean Ianon, & se vendent a Charenton | par SAMVEL PETIT, demeurant | à Paris, ruë S. Iacques au cheual | rouge, pres S. Seuerin. | M. DC. XXV. |

12mo ¶⁴, A–S⁸⁻⁴, T²

¶1ʳ Title; ¶2ʳ Ded. à M. Bigot, Sieur de la Honville [undated]; A1ʳ Text, pag. 1–219. [Bod. 8° R 117 Th.

Note: This is not listed in any of the authorities.

217 *Sermon faict en un jour de Noël.* Sedan, 1625.
MEDITATION | *SVR* | L'INCARNATION | DE I. CHRIST NOSTRE SEIGNEVR, | *ET SVR* | Le legitime honneur de la Bien- | heureuse VIERGE. | ou | *SERMON FAICT EN VN* | *iour de Noël sur S. Luc chap. 1.* | vers. 39.40.41.42.43. | Par Iean Mestrezat, Ministre de la Parole de | Dieu, en l'Eglise Reformée de Paris. | [Orn.] | *A SEDAN,* | Et se vendent à Charenton par SAMVEL | PETIT, demeurant a Paris, rue S. Iac- | ques au Cheual rouge, pres S. Seuerin. | M. DC. XXV. |

12mo A–F⁸⁻⁴

A1ʳ Title; A2ʳ Text, pagination beginning A2ᵛ, 4–72.

[Bod. 8° R 117 Th.

218 *Idem.* Sedan, 1625.
Reprinted at the end of Du Moulin's *Traicté de la cognoissance de Dieu*, Sedan, 1625, pp. 273–388. [BL 1482.a.35

219 *Idem.* Charenton, 1631.
MEDITATION | *SVR* | L'INCARNATION | DE IESVS CHRIST | NOSTRE SEIGNEVR. | *ET SVR* | La legitime honneur de la Bien- | heureuse VIERGE. | Ou | *SERMON FAICT EN VN* | *jour de Noël sur Sainct Luc chap. 1.* | vers. 39. 40. 41. 42. 43. | Par IEAN MESTREZAT, Ministre de | la Parole de Dieu, en l'Eglise Reformée | de Paris. | Seconde Edition reueuë & corrigée. | [Orn.] | *Iouxte la copie Imprimée à SEDAN.* | Et se vendent à Charenton, par MELCHIOR | MONDIERE, demeurant à Paris, en | l'Isle du Palais, aux deux Viperes. | M. DC. XXXI. |

12mo A–D$^{8-4}$, E^4
A1^r Title; A2^r Text, pag. 3–54.   [SG Rés. D 8° SUP 319
Note: This copy wants E4.

220 *Sermons sur divers textes.* Sedan, 1625.
Haag III.

221 *La Pasque chrestienne.* Charenton, 1632.
LA | PASQVE | CHRESTIENNE. | *Par IEAN MESTREZAT* |
Pasteur de l'Eglise Reformée | *de Paris.* | [Orn.] | *Se vendent à*
Charenton | Par PIERRE AVVRAY, demeurant à | Paris en l'Isle
du Palais à | la fleur de Lys. | M. DC. XXXII. |
12mo A–E$^{8-4}$, F^2
A1^r Title; A2^r Text, pag. 3–59.   [SG Rés. D 8° SUP 319
Note: The copy BHP R.16.065 carries the imprint of Mondiere;
the copy Bod. 8° R 117 Th. carries the imprint of Samuel Petit.
The SG copy has MS. notes *passim* by a reader signed 'Boisselet'
(p. 59).

222 *Exhortation à repentance.* Paris, 1632.
EXHORTATION | A | REPENTANCE, | SVR ESAIE CHAPITRE |
LVII. VERSET XV. | *Par IEAN MESTREZAT Pasteur* | *de l'Eglise*
reformée de Paris. | [Orn.] | *Se vendent à Charenton* | Par N.
BOVRDIN, & L. PERIER | demeurans à Paris, ruë neufve du |
Palais, au Roy de Suede. | M. DC. XXXII. |
12mo A–D$^{8-4}$, E^2
A1^r Title; A2^r Text, pag. 3–51.   [Bod. 8° R 117 Th.

223 *La Pentecoste chrestienne.* Charenton, 1633.
LA | PENTECOSTE CHRESTIENNE, | ou | SERMON FAIT EN
VN IOVR | de Pentecoste sur Act. | ch. 2. vers. 16. 17. 18. | *Par*
IEAN MESTREZAT, *Pasteur* | *de l'Eglise Reformée de Paris.* |
[Orn.] | Se vendent à Charenton, | Par MELCHIOR MONDIERE,
demeu- | rant à Paris, dans la court du Palais, | place du Change, aux
deux Viperes. | M. DC. XXXIII. |
12mo A–F$^{8-4}$, G^2
A1^r Title; A2^r Text, pag. 3–74.   [BHP R. 16.065
Note: Wants G2.

224 *Idem.* Quevilly, 1633.
LA | PENTECOSTE | CHRESTIENNE, | OV | SERMON FAIT LE

Mestrezat, Jean (C. 229)

IOVR DE | la Pentecoste sur Act. | ch. 2. vers. 16. 17. 18. | *Par* IEAN MESTREZAT, | *Pasteur de l'Eglise Refor-* | *mée de Paris.* | [Orn.] | Se vendent à Queuilly, | Par CLAVDE LE VILLAIN. | M. DC. XXXIII. |
   12mo A–D⁶
   A1ʳ Title; A2ʳ Text, pag. 3–48.   [SG Rés. D 8° SUP 319
   Note: MS. notes on pp. 34 and 42.

225 *Sermon de la venue de Jesus-Christ.* Charenton, 1634.
SERMON | DE LA | VENVE | DE IESVS-CHRIST | AV MONDE. | Faict à Charenton le jour de | Noël 1633. Sur Hebrieux | Chap. 10. ℣. 5.6.7. | *Par* IEAN MESTREZAT. | [Orn.] | *Se vendent à Charenton,* | Par PIERRE DES-HAYES. | M. DC. XXXIIII. |
   12mo A–F⁸⁻⁴
   A1ʳ Title; A2ʳ Text, pag. 3–71.   [BHP R.16.065

226 *Sermon faict au jour de Jeusne celebré . . . le 21. Aoust 1636.* Charenton, 1636.
SERMON | FAICT AV IOVR | DV IEVSNE CELEBRE' | à Charenton le 21. Aoust 1636. | *Par* IEAN MESTREZAT | [Orn. P] | Et se vend à Charenton | Par NICOLAS BOVRDIN, & LOVÏS | PERIER, demeurans à Paris, à la | ruë Neufue du Palais, au | Roy de Suede. | M. DC. XXXVI. |
   12mo A–F⁸⁻⁴
   A1ʳ Title; A2ʳ Text, pag. 3–72.   [SG Rés. D 8° SUP 319

227 *Idem.* Quevilly, 1636.
SERMON | FAICT AV IOVR | DV IVSNE CELEBRE' | à Charenton le 21. Aoust 1636. | *Par* IEAN MESTREZAT | [Orn. P] | Et se vend à Queuilly, | Par CLAVDE LE VILLAIN, ET | IACQVES CAILLOVE. | M. DC. XXXVI. |
   12mo A–H⁴⁻²
   A1ʳ Title; A2ʳ Text, pag. 3–47.   [SBNU E 127396

228 *Idem.* Geneva, 1637.
In the collection publ. Jean de la Planche.   [BHP 8° 20.309]

229 *Sermon faict au jour de Jeusne celebré à Charenton . . . le 19. Nouemb. 1637.* Charenton, 1637.
SERMON | FAICT AV IOVR | DV IEUSNE CELEBRE' | à

Charenton le 19. Nouemb. 1637. | *Sur Apocal. Chap. 3. Vers. 1. 2. 3. 4. & 5.* | Par IEAN MESTREZAT | [Orn. P] | *Se vend à Charenton,* | Par NICOLAS BOVRDIN, & LOVÏS PERIER | demeurans à Paris, à la | ruë Neufue du Palais, au | Roy de Suede. | M. DC. XXXVII. |

 12mo A–G$^{8-4}$, H^2

A1^r Title; A1^v Scriptural text; A2^r Text, pag. 3–91.

[SG Rés. D 8° SUP 319

230 *Sermons sur la justification.* Geneva, 1639.
 12mo
 Haag XI.

231 *Sermons sur les deux premiers chapitres de l'Epistre aux Hebreux.* Charenton, 1639.
SERMONS | SVR LES | DEVX PREMIERS | CHAPITRES DE L'EPISTRE | aux Hebreux. | Par IEAN MESTREZAT *Ministre du* | *Sainct Euangile.* | [Printer's Orn.] | *Se vendent à Charenton* | Par MELCHIOR MONDIERE, demeu- | rant à Paris en la cour du Palais, | aux deux Viperes. | M. DC. XXXIX. |

 8vo π^2, A–3A^8, 3B^4

π1^r Title; π2^r Ded. à la Mareschalle de Chastillon, dated Paris 24 November 1638; A1^r Text, pag. 1–760.   [BL 3266.a.8

Note: The series continued out of our period. Two further volumes containing an exposition of Hebrews III–X appeared at Geneva (S. Chouet) in 1653, with a dedication dated Paris, 4 June 1652.

232 *De la sacrificature de Jesus-Christ.* Charenton, 1640.
DE LA | SACRIFICATVRE | DE IESVS CHRIST | nostre Seigneur. | OV, | SERMONS | SVR LES CHAPITRES | septiéme, huictiéme, neufuiéme, & | partie du dixiéme de l'Epistre aux | Hebreux, prononcés à Charenton. | *Par IEAN MESTREZAT,* | *Ministre du Sainct Euangile.* | [Orn.] *Se vendent à Charenton,* | Par PIERRE DES-HAYES, | Imprimeur & | Marchand Libraire, demeurant à Paris | ruë de la Harpe, à la Rose Rouge. | M. DC. XL. |

 8vo π^2, A–3B^8, 3C^2

π1^r Title cancellans; π1^v Fautes suruenuës en l'impression; A1^r Text, pag. 1–781.   [BN D^2 4039

233 *Sermon du combat de la chair et de l'esprit.* 1642.
12mo
Haag XIII.

234 *De la vertu de la foy.* Charenton, 1644.
DE LA | VERTV DE LA FOY, | OV | SERMONS SVR LE | CHAPITRE ONZIESME | de l'Epistre aux Hebreux, | *Prononcés à Charenton,* | *Par IEAN MESTREZAT.* | [Orn. P] | *Se vendent à Charenton,* | Par NICOLAS BOVRDIN, & la Vefue L. PERIER, | demeurans à Paris, ruë Neufve du Palais, | au Roy de Suede. M. DC. XLIV. |
8vo π^2, A–3E^8
$\pi 1^r$ Title cancellans; A1^r Text, pag. 1–814; 3E7^v Fautes . . .
[BN D^2 4040
Note: BN D^2 18261 is an identical copy carrying the imprint of Louis Vendosme, with MS. corrections on pp. 468 and 509.

235 *Idem.* Charenton, 1645.
Description as for no. 224, of which it is a simple reprint.
[BHP R. 3724

236 *Sermon sur le Pseaume 130, 1–4.* Charenton, 1645.
SERMON, | SVR LE PSEAVME | CXXX. VERS. 1.2.3. & 4. | *Prononcé à Charenton au iour* | *du Ieusne 4. May 1645.* | *Par Iean Mestrezat.* | [Orn. P] | Se vend à Charenton, Par SAMVEL | PETIT, demeurant à Paris, | dans | la Cour du Palais | à la Bible d'Or. | M. DC. XLV. |
12mo A–G$^{8-4}$, H^2 [These last two leaves are in fact unsigned.]
A1^r Title; A2^r [missigned A] Text, pag. 3–89; H2 blank.
[BN D^2 9376

237 *Sermon sur ces mots 'La Parole a esté faicte chair.'* Charenton, 1645.
SERMON | SVR CES MOTS | La Parole a esté faicte chair, | &c. Iean chap. 1. vers. 14. | *Prononcé à Charenton le iour de Noël* | 1644. *à l'ouuerture du Synode* | *National conuoqué par permission du Roy.* | *Par* IEAN MESTREZAT Ministre du | Sainct Euangile. | [Printer's Orn.] | *Se vend à Charenton,* | Par MELCHIOR MONDIERE, de- | meurant à Paris en la Court du | Palais, aux deux Viperes. | M. DC. XLV. |

12mo A-H$^{8-4}$
A1^r Title; A2^r Text, pag. 3-96. [SG Rés. D 8° SUP 319

238 *Trois sermons sur la venue et naissance de Jesus-Christ.* Geneva, 1649.
TROIS | SERMONS | *SVR LA* | VENVE ET NAISSANCE | DE IESVS CHRIST | au monde. | Le I. sur Malachie, chap. IV ℣. 2. | le II. sur Esaie, chap. VII. ℣. 14. | *Prononcés à Charenton le 20. & 25.* | *Decembre 1648.* | Le III. sur S. Luc, ch. 1, ℣. 39. 40. 41, 42. 43. | Par | IEAN MESTREZAT. | [Orn. Sower sowing seed] | *A GENEVE,* | Imprimé pour Pierre Chouët. | *M. DC. XLIX.* |
8vo ¶^{4}, A-H^8, I-K^4
¶1^r Title; ¶2^r Ded. to author's brother, dated Paris 22 March 1649; A1^r Text, pag. 1-444. [F8 is unpaginated and blank.]
[BHP 937

MOLINIER, Etienne
Toulouse? – Toulouse 1647. First a lawyer, later ordained. Took doctorates in civil law, canon law, and theology. Celebrated as a preacher in Provence and Paris, as well as in his home province. The myth that he preached at Louis XIII's coronation has been disproved more than once, but continues to be propagated.
A bibliography is to be found in J. Contrasty: 'Le Prêtre toulousain Etienne de Molinier, précurseur des orateurs du siècle de Louis XIV', *Revue historique de Toulouse,* XXXVI (1949), pp. 6-8, to which the Roman numerals refer.

239 *Panegyrique du Roy S. Louys.* Paris, 1618.
PANEGYRIQVE | Du Roy S. Louys, | *SVR LE SVBIECT DE* | *la celebration de sa feste, ordonnée* | *par nostre S. Pere, à la requeste du* | *Roy tres-Chrestien Louys XIII. à* | *present regnant.* | Auec vne oraison en vers au Roy sainct | LOVYS pour la prosperité du Roy. | Par E. MOLINIER *Tholozain, Prestre,* | *& Docteur és Droicts.* | Dedié à sa Majesté. | [Orn.] | A PARIS, | Par René Giffart, demeurant contre la | porte sainct Iacques. | M. DC. XVIII. |
8vo π^2, A-E^4
π1^r Title cancellans; A1^r Ded., pag. 1-2; wants A2, pag. 3-4; A3^r Text of Panegyric, pag. 5-37; E3^r Oraison en vers, pag. 37-40.
[BN 8° Lb18 81

Note: Reprinted in *Mystere de la Croix.*

240 *Discours funebre sur la mort de Mgr du Vair.* Paris, n.d. [1621].
DISCOVRS | FVNEBRE SVR | LA MORT DE MON- | seigneur du VAIR, Euesque de | Lysieux, & Garde des Sceaux de | France. | PAR. E. MOLINIER | *Tholozain, Prestre & Docteur.* | DEDIE' A MONSEIGNEVR | l'Euesque de Riés. | *In requie mortui requiescere fac memoriam eius.* | Ecclesiastique Chapitre 38. | [Orn.] | A PARIS, | Chez GVILLAVME LOYSON, au Palais en la | Gallerie des Prisonniers, prés la Chancellerie. | *Auec Permission.* |
  8vo ã^4, A–F^4
  ã1^r Title; ã2^r Ded.; A1^r Text, pag. 1–46; F4 blank.
  [BN 8° Ln27 6974
Note: Reprinted in *Mystere de la Croix*. Not noted by Contrasty. No date: Guillaume du Vair died in 1621. This date is confirmed in the 1628 reprint.

241 *Le Mystere de la Croix, et de la Redemption du monde.* Toulouse, 1628.
LE MYSTERE | DE LA CROIX, | ET DE | LA REDEMPTION | DV MONDE, | Expliqué en dix Sermons preschez dans la Chapelle | des Penitens Noirs de Tolose. | *Par* E. MOLINIER *Tolos. Prestre & Docteur.* | Auec quelques autres oeuures du mesme Autheur. | *Le tout dedié à Monseigneur le Reuerendissime* | *Archeuesque de Tolose.* | Dominus regnavit à ligno. | [Orn. A cross with crown of thorns] | *A TOLOSE,* | Par RAYMOND COLOMIEZ, Imprimeur | ordinaire du Roy, & de l'Vniuersité. | M. DC. XXVIII. |
  8vo ã–ẽ^8, A–3B^8, 3C^2
[I give a fuller list of contents than normal, since this is of considerable importance for later added material. Contrasty does not discuss later editions of the *Mystere*.]
  ã1^r Title; ã2^r Ded. to Charles de Mont-Chal; ã5^r L'Autheur au Lecteur; ẽ7^v Table des oeuures; ẽ8^v Attestation des docteurs dated Toulouse 21 September 1627; Approbation of Vicar General dated Toulouse 22 September 1627; A1^r Text of 8 sermons for the Octave of the Invention 1615, pag. 1–238; P8^r Sermon for Invention 1610, pag. 239–61; R3^v Serm. for Feast of Exaltation 1623, pag. 262–93; T3^v Panegyrique du Roy S. Louys, pag. 294–334; X8^r Panegyrique de S. Fr. Xavier, pag. 335–75 [reprinted in 1648 *Festes des Saincts*]; 2A4^v Oraison funèbre de M. Pons de Bardion, pag. 376–400; 2C1^r O. F. Noble d'Hebrail, pag. 401–34; 2E2^r O. F. Du Vair, pag. 435–

82; 2H2^r Abregé de la Passion, pag. 483–510; 2L4^r Serm. de la Nativité de la Vierge, pag. 511–37 [reprinted in 1648 *Festes*]; 2L5^v Serm. de l'Assomption, pag. 538–76 [reprinted in 1648 *Festes*]; 2O1^r Serm. de S. Jean l'Evangeliste, pag. 577–619 [reprinted in 1648 *Festes*]; 2Q6^v Serm. de l'Image de nostre Dame de Pitié tenant Jesus-Christ dans ses bras, pag. 620–42; 2S2^r Discours sur l'institution des Penitens Noirs, pag. 643–770; 3C2^r Fautes suruenuës en l'Impression; 3C2^v Extraict abregé du priuilege, for 6 years, dated La Rochelle 23 October 1627; Acheué d'imprimer le 3. Decembre 1627.

[BMT 273/A

242 *Idem.* Toulouse, 1635.
Title as for no. 241, except SECONDE EDITION | Reueuë, corrigée, & augmentée de sept diuers Sermons | de nouueau adioustez. | The imprint is of Arnaud Colomiez, the date 1635.

8vo ã–ẽ^8, A–3K^8

ã1^r Title; ã2^r Ded.; ã5^r Au Lecteur; A1^r Text, pag. 1–688 [the same items as in 1628, though in different order]; p. 689: 'Pieces adioustez en cette seconde edition: S. des Indulgences, S. pour l'anniversaire de l'institution de l'ordre de la redemption des captifs, O. F. de Noble Hebrail Fils, Exhortation aux parents du sieur defunct, Deux sermons de S. Nicolas' [of which the first is reprinted in the 1648 *Festes*]; 3K5^r Table; 3K6^v Attestation of 1627; Approbation of 1627; 3K7^r Extraict du priuilege, for the 2nd edn, for 9 years, dated 27 March 1635; Acheué d'imprimer le 28. iour de Iuin 1635. [BN D 44928

243 *Idem.* Toulouse, 1643.
Title as for no. 241. TROISIESME EDITION | etc. . . . Date 1643.
8vo ã–ẽ^8, A–2L^8, 2M^4

ã1^r Title; ã2^r Ded.; ã5^r Au Lecteur; A1^r Text, pag. 1–551.

[BN D 44929

This edition does not contain the following works found in 1628: 1616 Feast of the Invention sermon; Pan. de S. Louys; Pan. de S. François Xavier; Sermons of the Nativity of our Lady, the Assumption, and St John. The only work from the 1635 *Pieces adioustez* to be reprinted here is the Sermon des Indulgences. It contains the following new work, p. 380: a reprint of the Oraison funèbre du R. P. Gabriel Ranquet, published in 1642.

244 Migne, *Orateurs sacrés*, vol. 1, cols. 869–989, reprints the Preface and the eight sermons for the Octave of the Invention. It appears at first sight that he printed off a 1635 text, for it is this he mentions, col. 869; he has altered the spelling and punctuation, and his text contains a number of new errors. However, many of his departures from 1635 in fact derive from 1643, which leads one to suspect that he used that text without acknowledging it. In any case, the Migne text is unreliable.

245 *Sermons pour tous les dimanches de l'année.* Toulouse, 1631. 2 vols. I have only been able to find vol. 1.
SERMONS | POVR TOVS | LES DIMANCHES | DE L'ANNEE. | Diuisez en deux Volumes. | *Composez & Preschez par Estienne Molinier,* | *Docteur, & Recteur de Sauuens* | *au Diocese de Tolose.* | Dediez à Monseigneur l'Illustrissime & Reue- | rendissime Archeuesque de Tolose. | *TOME PREMIER.* | [Printer's Orn.] | A TOLOSE, | Par RAIM. COLOMIEZ Imprimeur ordinaire | du Roy & de l'Vniuersité. | 1631. | *Auec approbation & Priuilege du Roy.* |
  8vo ã^8, ẽ^4, A–3G^8, 3H^2

  ã1^r Title; ã2^r Ded.; ẽ1^v Approbation dated 3 March 1631; Permission dated 3 March 1631; ẽ2^r L'Imprimeur au Lecteur; ẽ2^v Table des matieres; ẽ3^v Fautes plus remarquables; ẽ4^v Extraict du priuilege for 6 years dated 19 April 1631; Acheué d'imprimer le 16. Iuin 1631; A1^r Text, pag. 1–752/757–855.   [BN D 44934

  Note: Contrasty (VI) describes briefly his own two-volume copy. This BN copy lacks the engraved title-page Contrasty describes (but see next entry).

246 *Idem.* Toulouse, 1635. 2 vols.
Vol. 1: Title as for no. 245, except SECONDE EDITION. | Reueuë, corrigée, & augmentée par l'Autheur.
  8vo π^2, ã^8, A–2G^8, χ^2

  ã1^r Title; π1^r Engraved title piece [see note below]; ã2^r Ded.; ã8^v Approbation & Permission of 1631; A1^r Text, pag. 1–848; χ1^r L'Imprimeur au Lecteur, of 1631; χ1^v Table des matieres; χ2^r Privilege of 1631.   [BMT 273/A

  Note: Vol. 1 of the BN copy [BN D 44935] wants the two leaves χ. This is of some importance, since the note 'Au Lecteur' apologizes for faults in the 1631 text which the author has not been present to revise; and its absence could lead us to trust 1635 more than it deserves. Both the BN and the BMT copies contain the engraved title which Contrasty describes for his 1631 edition. However, it bears the date M. DC. XXXV.

The BMT copy wants vol. 2.

Vol. 2:

8vo ã², A–3C⁸

ã1ʳ Title; ã2ʳ Table des matieres; A1ʳ Text, pag. 1–765; 3B7ᵛ Oratio habita in Synodo . . . [This copy wants all of 3C; but see 1639 edn in next entry.]   [BN D 44935

247 *Idem.* Toulouse, 1639. 2 vols.
Title as before, except CINQVIESME EDITION, | reueuë, &c. . . .
Vol. 1: 8vo ã⁸, π², A–3G⁸

ã1ʳ Title; ã2ʳ Ded.; ã8ʳ Approbation; ã8ᵛ Permission; π1ʳ L'Imprimeur au Lecteur, of 1631; π1ᵛ Table; A1ʳ Text, pag. 1–848.
Vol. 2: 8vo π², A–3M⁸, 3N⁶

π1ʳ Title; π2ʳ Table; A1ʳ Text, pag. 1–765; 3B7ᵛ Oratio habita Tolosae in Synodo . . . 1631; 3D1ʳ Title for *Sermons divers adioustez*; 3D2ʳ Text of new sermons, pag. 787–938; 3N6ʳ Approbation des sermons adioustez, dated 25 May 1639; 3N6ᵛ Extraict du Priuilege for the Sermons adioustez, undated.   [BN D 44936

Note: Not mentioned by Contrasty. I have found no trace of third or fourth editions. Clearly this edition is most important, not only for the material here added for the first time, but also for the Latin oration which is defective in 1635. Contrasty gives two (presumably unprivileged) editions, Rouen 1643 and Rouen 1653. Contrary to his usual practice, he makes no reference to extant copies and has clearly not seen them.

248 *Le Banquet sacré de l'Eucharistie.* Toulouse, 1635.
LE | BANQVET | SACRE' | DE L'EVCHARISTIE, | Pour l'Octaue du S. Sacrement. | *Par* Mᵉ. ESTIENNE MOLINIER, | *Prestre & Docteur.* | Venite ad me omnes, & ego reficiam vos. | *Matth.* II. | [Printer's Orn.] | A TOLOSE, | Par A. COLOMIEZ, Imprimeur ordinaire | du Roy, & de l'Vniuersité. 1635. | *Auec Priuilege, & Approbation.* |

8vo ã⁸, A–V⁸, X⁴

ã1ʳ Title; ã2ʳ Ded. to Séguier, signed Colomiez; ã5ʳ L'autheur au lecteur; ã7ᵛ Approbation dated 26 April 1635; ã8ʳ Permission dated 27 April 1635; A1ʳ Text, pag. 1–325; X3ᵛ Privilege for 9 years

dated 27 March 1635; X4ʳ Acheué d'imprimer le 16. May 1635.
[BN D 44921]

249 *Idem.* Toulouse, 1640.
Title and Contents as for no. 248, except that the title carries the notice SECONDE EDITION. Despite its closeness to 1635, this really is a corrected edition. [BN D 44922]

250 *Idem.* Toulouse, 1647.
Title as for no. 248, except TROISIESME EDITION.

8vo ã⁴, ẽ², A–V⁸, X²

ã1ʳ Title; ã1ᵛ Extraict du Priuilege, for 10 years, dated 1640; ã2ʳ Ded.; ã4ʳ L'autheur au lecteur; ẽ2ᵛ Approbation and Permission of 1635; A1ʳ Text, pag. 1–324. [BN D 44923]

Note: The date of the Privilege is most interesting. There was no new Privilege in the 1640 edition.

251 *Les Douze Fondemens de la Cité de Dieu.* Toulouse, 1635.
LES DOVZE | FONDEMENS | DE LA CITE' | DE DIEV, | OV LES DOVZE ARTICLES DV | Symbole des Apostres, expliqués par les douze pierres | precieuses de l'Apocalypse, en XXI Discours, | par forme de Catecheses accomodées | au temps de l'Aduent. | *Dediés à Monseigneur de* MESMES, *President* | *au Parlement de Paris.* | Par ESTIENNE MOLINIER Tolosain. | *Credidi propter quod locutus sum.* Psal. 115. | [Printer's Orn.] | A TOLOSE, Par ARN. COLOMIEZ, Imprimeur | ordinaire du Roy, & de l'Vniuersité. 1635. | *Auec Priuilege, & Approbation.* |

8vo ã⁸, π², ẽ⁴, A–3P⁸, 3Q⁶

ã1ʳ Title; ã2ʳ Ded. dated 12 November 1635; ẽ2ʳ Table des douze pierres precieuses rapportées aux douze articles du Symbole; ẽ2ᵛ Aduis au lecteur; ẽ3ᵛ Approbation de Mon. le Coad. de Montauban dated 1 November 1635; Approbation des docteurs dated 20 February 1635; ẽ4ʳ Permission de l'Archeuesque dated 23 February 1635; ẽ4ᵛ Extraict du Priuilege for 9 years dated 27 March 1635; Acheué d'imprimer le 12. Nouembre 1635; π1ʳ French sonnet to Mesmes signed G.; π1ᵛ French sonnet signed Baynaguet nepueu de l'Autheur; π2ʳ Autre sonnet par le mesme; π2ᵛ Autre sur le mesme suiet; French quatrain to Molinier signed A. D.; A1ʳ Text, pag. 1–908; 3L8 blank; 3M1ʳ Indice des matieres; 3Q5ᵛ Fautes plus notables. [BN D 44925]

Note: The BMT copy [273/A] has the leaves π inserted between sigs. ā and ē. My own copy wants the leaves π. That they were inserted afterwards is made clear by the fact that the BMT copy has ā2 blotted on the verso of ā1.

252 *Idem*. Toulouse, 1642.
Title as for no. 241, except that no dedication is mentioned. It is SECONDE EDITION, and is dated 1642.

8vo ā⁸, ē⁴, A–3P⁸, 3Q⁴

ā1ʳ Title; ā2ʳ Ded. [despite the title-page]; ē2ʳ Table des douze pierres; ē2ᵛ Aduis au Lecteur; ē3ᵛ and ē4: Approbation etc. as for 1635; A1ʳ Text, pag. 1–910; 3M1ʳ Indice des matieres.

[BMT 273/A

Note: The faults listed in 1635 have been corrected.

253 *Sermons pour toutes les feries, et dimanches du Caresme.*
Toulouse, 1641. 2 vols.
Vol. 1:
SERMONS | POVR TOVTES | LES FERIES, | ET | DIMANCHES | DV CARESME, | Composés & preschés par E. MOLINIER, | Prestre, Tolosain. | *Diuisés en deux Volumes.* | Dediés à Monseigneur l'Illustrissime, & Reuerendissime | Euesque de Commenge. | TOME PREMIER. | *Declaratio sermonum tuorum illuminat.* Psalm. 118. | [Orn.] | A TOLOSE, | Par ARNAVD COLOMIEZ, Imprimeur ordinaire | du Roy, & de l'Vniuersité. 1641. | *AVEC PRIVILEGE.* |

[Preceded by an engraved title piece showing Christ and Satan on either side of the Tree. Unsigned]

Vol. 1: 8vo π², ¶⁸, ā², A–3K⁸, 3L⁴

π1ʳ Engraved title cancellans; ¶1ʳ Title; ¶2ʳ Ded.; ¶8ʳ French sonnet signed Dupho; Latin epigram signed Dupho; ¶8ᵛ Attestation dated 1 October 1641; Approbation dated 7 October 1641; ā1ʳ Extraict du priuilege for 9 years dated 27 March 1635; Acheué d'imprimer pour la premiere fois le 24. d'Octobre, 1641.; ā1ᵛ Table; A1ʳ Text, pag. 1–903.

Vol. 2: 8vo ē², A–3Q⁸, 3R⁴

ā1ʳ Title; ē2ʳ Table; A1ʳ Text, pag. 1–1000. [BN D 44938

254 *Idem*. Toulouse, 1645. 2 vols.
I have only been able to find vol. 1: Title as for 1641.

8vo †⁸, ā², A–3K⁸, 3L⁴

Contents as for no. 253, vol. 1. [BMT 273/A

255 *Idem.* Lyon, 1650. 2 vols.
SERMONS | SVR TOVTES | LES FERIES, | ET DIMANCHES | DV CARESME, | Composez & preschez par E. MOLINIER, | Prestre, Tolosain. | *Diuisez en deux Volumes.* | Dediez à Monseigneur l'Illustrissime, & Reuerendissime | Euesque de Commenge. | TOME PREMIER. | *Declaratio sermonum tuorum illuminat.* Psalm. 118. | [Orn. IHS with motto 'Laudabile nomen domini'] | *A LYON,* | Chez PIERRE BAILLY, ruë Marciere. | *M. DC. L.* |
Vol. 1: 8vo †⁸, ã², A–3K⁸, 3L⁴
†1ʳ Title; †2ʳ Ded.; †8ʳ Dupho's verses; †8ᵛ Attestation of 1641; ã1ʳ Approbation of 1641; ã1ᵛ Table; A1ʳ Text, pag. 1–903.
Vol. 2: 8vo ē², A–3Q⁸, 3R⁴
ē1ʳ Title [Identical in all other respects to the title of vol. 1, it bears the imprint of Nicolas Gay.]; ē2ʳ Ded.; A1ʳ Text, pag. 1–1000.
[BN D 44939

256 *Oraison funebre sur la mort du R. P. Gabriel Ranquet.*
Toulouse, 1643.
ORAISON | FVNEBRE | SVR LA MORT | DV R. P. GABRIEL RANQVET, | DE L'ORDRE S. DOMINIQVE, | Inquisiteur de la Foy | à Tolose. | *Prononcée dans l'Eglise du Conuent du | mesme Ordre en Tolose, le 30. De | cembre 1642.* | Par Mᵉ ESTIENNE MOLINIER, | Prestre & Docteur. | [Orn.] | A TOLOSE, | Par ARNAVD COLOMIEZ, Imprimeur ordinaire | du Roy, & de l'Vniuersité. | 1643. |
8vo A–C⁸, D²
A1ʳ Title; A2ʳ Text, pag. 3–52.   [BN 8° Ln27 16981
Note: Reprinted in the 1643 *Mystere.*

257 *Sermons sur les festes des saincts.* Toulouse, 1648. 3 vols.
SERMONS | SVR | LES FESTES | DES SAINCTS. | COMPOSEZ ET PRESCHEZ | Par E. MOLINIER, Prestre Tolosain, | & diuisez en trois Tomes. | TOME I. | *Corpora Sanctorum in pace sepulta sunt,* | *& Viuent nomina eorum in aeternum.* | [Printer's Orn.] | A TOLOSE, | Par ARNAVD COLOMIEZ, Imprimeur ordinaire | du Roy, & de l'Vniuersité. 1648. | *Auec priuilege du Roy.* |
Vol. 1: 8vo ã⁸, A–3N⁸, 3O⁴
ã1ʳ False title; ã2ʳ Title; ã3ʳ Ded. to Claude d'Advisard, signed J. A. Baynaguet, neveu de l'autheur; ã6ᵛ Extraict du priuilege for 7 years dated 18 May 1648; ã7ʳ Acheué d'imprimer le 30. Iuin 1648;

ā7ᵛ Permission dated 15 June 1648; ā8ʳ Table des Sermons contenus en ce premier Tome; A1ʳ Text, pag. 1-951.
Vol. 2: 8vo π², A-2V⁸, 2X⁶
   π1ʳ Title; π2ʳ Table des sermons . . .; A1ʳ Text, pag. 1-700.
Vol. 3: 8vo π², A-2N⁸, 2O⁴
   π1ʳ Title; π2ʳ Table des sermons . . .; A1ʳ Text, pag. 1-582.
[Maz. 24.742-4

Note: Posthumously published by Baynaguet. Contrasty (XV) notes the first edition of this work as 1652, Douai, Marc Wion. Possibly he is following Albert (*Dictionnaire*, p. 181), who gives the same information. They have both been followed by Cioranescu. A Douai first edition is of course highly improbable in itself, and the more so when the copy which Contrasty refers to in the BN is in fact the 1652 Toulouse reprint (see below). It should have been clear from Toulouse 1652 that 1648 was the date of the first edition, although this is the first time that the first edition has been noted in any list of Molinier's writings.

258 *Idem*. Toulouse, 1652.
Title and Contents as for no. 257. A reprint of Toulouse 1648.
[BN D 44937

259 Migne, *O.S.*, vol. 1, cols. 989-1228, reprints the following panegyrics from this work: Ambroise, Luce, Sylvestre, Sebastien, Jean Chrysostome, Blaise, Gregoire, Pantaleon, Philippe & Jacques, Barnabé, les 40 martyres. He cites as his only source an edition of Douai 1652: a further example of Migne's unreliability.

PRIMROSE (or **PRIMEROSE**), Gilbert (P)
A Scotsman, and none other than the seventeenth-century Bishop of Ely. He ministered in several French churches, notably Bordeaux, and remained in France until banished by Louis XIII in 1623. He then became successively pastor of the French Church in London, Chaplain to the King, Canon of Windsor, and Bishop of Ely.

260 *La Trompette de Sion*. Bergerac, 1610.
LA | TROMPETTE | DE SION: | *OV EXHORTATION* | *A Repentance & à Iusne.* | *Par* GILBERT PRIMROSE *Ministre* | *de la parole de Dieu en l'Eglise* | *de* BORDEAVX. | ESAIE 58. | I. Crie à plein

gosier, ne t'espargne point, esleue ta voix com- | me vne TROM-
PETTE, & declare à mon peuple leur forfait, | & à la maison de
Iacob leurs pechez. | HIER. AD NEPOTIANVM. | *Lachrymae
auditorum, laudes tuae sint.* | [Orn. Motto 'sic omni tempore
verno'] | *A BERGERAC,* | Par GILBERT VERNOY. | M. DC. X. |
  8vo (.)^8, (.)(.)^8, (.)(.)(.)^4, A–2N^8, 3A–3P^8
  (.)1^r Title; (.)2^r Ded. to Anne de la Chaussade; 3(.)4^v Au lecteur;
A1^r Text of part I, pag. 1–572; 2N8 blank; 3A1^r Text of part II,
pag. 1–237; 3P7^v Carmen, signed D. Home: Distichon signed I. P. F.;
3P8^r Sonnet signed Gautier. [Bod. 8° P 107 Th.

Note: Wants 2K8, which is the cancelled butt of 2K1; the text,
however, is continuous: the catch-word 'en' on 2K7^v is correct for
2L1^r; the pagination is continuous. MS. note on front flyleaf: 'Don
de l'autheur, moy estant a Oxfort au mois de Juillet 1611'. The BN
copy [D^2 10262] is defective: it wants the whole of sig. 2A,
pp. 369–84. This defect is not noted in the BN Catalogue.

261 *Six sermons de la reconciliation de l'homme avec Dieu.* Sedan,
  1624.
SIX | SERMONS | DE LA | RECONCILIATION | DE L'HOMME
AVEC DIEV. | *PRESCHEZ* | *Par* GILBERT PRIMEROSE, |
Ministre du Sainct Euangile. | [Orn.] | A SEDAN. | M. DC. XXIV. |
  8vo ã^4, A–Y^4
  ã1^r Title; ã2^r Ded. to George Villiers, Duke of Buckingham; A1^r
Text, pag. 1–172; Y3^r Sommaire des sermons; Y4 blank.
[BN D^2 10261

  The *Panegyrique à trés-grand et trés-puissant prince Charles,
prince de Galles*, Paris, P. Auvray, 1624, is not a work of pulpit
oratory.

RETZ, Jean-Paul-François de Gondi, Cardinal de
Only one of Retz's sermons was published in his lifetime:

262 *Sermon de S. Louis.* Paris, 1649.
SERMON | DE S. LOVIS | ROY DE FRANCE, | FAIT ET PRO-
NONCE' DEVANT | le Roy & la Reyne Regente sa Mere. | *PAR
MONSEIGNEVR L'ILLVSTRISSIME* | *& Reuerendissime I. F.
Paul de Gondy Archeuesque de* | *Corinthe, & Coadjuteur de Paris:* |
A PARIS DANS L'EGLISE DE S. LOVIS | des PP. Iesuites, au iour

& Feste dudit saint | Louis, l'an 1648. | A PARIS, | M. DC. XLIX. |
4to A–C²
A1ʳ Title; A2ʳ Text, pag. 1–12 [mispag. 22].

[BN 4° Lb37 341

There are three copies of a work of this name in the BN: they are listed in the BN Catalogue as three separate editions, although 341B is in fact identical to the edition described above. 341A, however, contains an engraving of the Coadjutor [signed N. Moncornet excudit cum Privilegio Regis.], and has a definitely corrected text. The question is whether this is a second edition, or whether the not insubstantial differences are press-corrections.

The editor of the *Grands Ecrivains* edition (vol. 9) states that there are no differences between the three BN copies he has collated, and notes that he has established variants from a further edition of his own. If the text he gives is compared to any of the above, it is clear that there has been a considerable amount of silent correction.

263 *Oeuvres de Retz.* Paris, 1887, vol. 9, ed. R. Chantelauze (*Grands Ecrivains* series). Contains the following unpublished works:

'Sermon ou Panegyrique pour la fête de S. Charles Borromée, 1646'; 'Sermon pour le mercredi des cendres'; 'Sermon sur l'hypocrisie'; and two sermon plans found in the Cardinal's pocket when he was arrested in December 1652.

RICHELIEU, Armand-Jean du Plessis, Cardinal de
For the *Instruction du Chrestien*, Poitiers, 1621 (and very many subsequent editions) see Appendix 2.

None of Richelieu's sermons which were actually delivered was published in his lifetime. A.-M.-P. Ingold edited a MS. copy of an early sermon:

264 *Un Sermon inédit de Richelieu (Noël 1608).* Luçon, 1889.

SAUVAGE, Jean (P)
Nothing seems to be known of his life other than that he ministered at Lavandac and later at Bergerac, and was charged at Paris in 1644 with publicly dishonouring the Virgin Mary.

Sauvage, Jean (C. 267)

265 *La Voye veritable de la vie.* Charenton, 1645.
LA VOYE VERITABLE | DE LA VIE, | ou | SERMON | SVR CES PAROLES | DE IESVS CHRIST. | *Ie suis la Voye, la Verité, & la Vie.* | *Iean 14. Verset 6.* | Prononcé à Charanton le dixhuict | Decembre 1644. | *Par* IEAN SAVVAGE *Ministre* | *du Sainct Euangile à Bergerac.* | [Orn.] | *Se vend à Charenton.* | Par la Veuue LOVIS PERIER. | ET | NICOLAS PERIER à Paris ruë neufue | du Palais, au Roy de Suede. | M. DC. XLV. |
    12mo A–I$^{8-4}$, K^2
    A1^r Title; A2^r Ded. à M. Sauuage mon pere, dated Bergerac 25 April 1645, pag. blank/4–7; A5^r Text, pag. 9–108.

[BN D^2 4250 (5)

266 *Idem.* Quevilly, 1645.
LA VOYE VERITABLE | DE LA VIE, | SERMON | SVR CES PAROLES | de IESVS CHRIST, | *Ie suis la Voye, la Verité, & la Vie.* | Iean 14. vers. 6. | Prononcé à Charenton le dix-huict | Decembre 1644. | *Par* IEAN SAVVAGE *Ministre du* | *sainct Euangile à Bergerac.* | [Orn.] | *Se vend à Queuilly,* | Chez IEAN BERTHELIN. | M. DC. XLV. |
    12mo A–F$^{8-4}$, G^4
    A1^r Title; A2^r Ded.; A4^r Text, pag. 1–74.

[SG Rés. D 8° SUP 319

Note: Not listed in Cioranescu.

267 *Sermon sur 1 Corinthiens i, 30.* Charenton, 1646.
12mo
Noted in Haag, 1st edn, vol. 9, p. 193.

SEGUIRAN, Gaspar de (Jesuit)
Aix 1569 – Paris 1644. Entered the Society 1584. Taught belles lettres, rhetoric, philosophy and theology before devoting himself to preaching. He was sent, without much success, to La Rochelle by Henri IV. Confessor and preacher to Louis XIII 1626–30. Rector of the professed house at Paris. The works listed in this catalogue are attributed to Seguiran by the BN and others largely on the strength of contemporary MS. notes found in them; it is unlikely, for example, that Coëffeteau, whose ex libris in MS. is found in one of them, should be unaware of their proper author. It would

be interesting to know whether the anonymity indicates that the author has not been consulted on the printing of his works, or whether it is the result of a proper religious modesty. The tone of the following note 'Au Lecteur' is not entirely ingenuous:

> Ceste pieuse intention nous a faict prendre vne resolution de le mettre soubs la presse, afin qu'vn chacun soit participant de ses fruicts, bien qu'à nostre regret il faille qu'il soit veu sans nom, & sans Autheur, nous estant incogneu, d'autant que fortuitement (heureusement toutesfois pour l'vtilité publicque) ceste coppie nous a esté apportée par vn certain Religieux, (meu d'vne saincte intention de profiter à tous) & mise par iceluy entre nos mains, sans nous auoir donné aucune instruction ny de l'Autheur, ny de son nom, toute delabree sans tiltre, & sans reclame.

At the same time one may wonder why the specifically Jesuit device IHS is so prominent on the title-pages of all these works.

268 *Sermons doctes et admirables sur les Evangilles des Dimanches & Festes de l'anneé.* Paris, 1612.
SERMONS | DOCTES ET AD- | MIRABLES SVR LES | Euangilles des Diman- | ches & Festes de l'année: | & octaues du S^t. Sacramēt | *Diuisé en huict Paraboles tirees* | *de la Saincte escripture,* | *Preschez en diuers lieux par vn* | *Docte et celebre person-* | *nage de nostre temps.* | A PARIS, | *Chez Nicolas du Fossé ruë* | S^t. *Iacques au vase d'or,* | ET | *Pierre Cheuallier au mont* | S^t. *Hilaire a la court d'albret* | Auec priuilege du Roy. |
[Engraved. Shows two Fathers, and the title surmounted by angels adoring IHS. Signed L. Gaultier sculpsit 1612.]
8vo ã^6, A–3S^8, 3T^2, 3V–3X^8, 3Y^4
ã1^r Title; ã2^r Aux lecteurs; ã4^r Latin verse signed I. D. M.; ã4^v Privilege to Chevalier for 10 years dated 16 May 1611; ã6^v Approbation dated 26 May 1611; A1^r Text, pag. 1–1030; 3V1^r Table des matieres. [BN D 52267]
Note: Unknown to Sommervogel and to Cioranescu.

269 *Idem.* Paris, 1617/18.
Noted by Sommervogel and Cioranescu; I have not found a copy.

270 *Idem.* Paris, 1622.
SERMONS | DOCTES ET | ADMIRABLES SVR | les Euangiles des Dimanches, & Fe- | stes de l'annee: & Octaue du sainct | Sacrement. | DIVISE'ES EN HVICT | *Paraboles tirees de la S. Escriture.* | PRES-

Seguiran, Gaspar de (C. 276)

CHEZ EN DIVERS LIEVX | par vn Docte & celebre personnage | de nostre temps. | [Orn. IHS] | A PARIS, | Chez NICOLAS DE LA VIGNE, | Imprimeur ruë Clopin à l'Escu de France, | pres le petit Nauarre. | M. DC. XXII. |
    8vo ã^4, A-3S^8, 3V^8, 3X^4 [3V is missigned V]
    ã1^r Title; ã2^r Au Lecteur; ã4^r Latin verse; ã4^v Approbation of 1611; A1^r Text, pag. 1-370/353-70 [the text is continuous]; 3S3^r Table.   [BN D 52268]

271 *Idem.* Lyon, 1622.
This edition is nowhere listed, but the Approbation of Lyon 1622 printed in Rouen 1630 is evidence for it.

272 *Idem.* Rouen, Louis Loudet, 1629.
Sommervogel and Cioranescu.

273 *Idem.* Rouen, 1630.
SERMONS | DOCTES ET | ADMIRABLES | SVR LES EVAN- GILES | des Dimanches & festes de l'année, | & octaue du S. Sacrement. | *DIVISE'E EN HVICT PARABOLES* | *tirées de la saincte Escriture.* | Preschez en diuers lieux par vn docte & | celebre Personnage de nostre temps. | [Engraving of Jesus and Mary] | *A ROVEN,* | Chez IEAN BOVLEY, ruë aux Iuifs, | entre les deux portes du Palais. | M. DC. XXX. | *AVEC APPROBATION DES DOCTEVRS.* |
    8vo ã^4, A-4F^8
    ã1^r Title; ã2^r Au Lecteur; ã3^v Latin verse; ã4^r Approbation of 1611; two Attestations, dated Lyons, 18 and 30 January 1622; A1^r Text, pag. 1-1154; 4D2^r Table des matieres.   [BN D 52269]

274 *Idem.* Rouen, 1634.
Title as for no. 273, except it has engraving of two saints, and carries the imprint of Daniel Loudet.
Contents as for no. 273.   [BN D 52270]
    Note: This is a further edition based on Rouen 1630. The type is different.

275 *Idem.* Paris, Pierre Chevallier, 1643. 2 vols.
Sommervogel; I have found no other trace of such an edition.

276 *Sermons sur la parabole de l'enfant prodigue.* Paris, 1612.
SERMONS | SVR LA PARA- | BOLE DE L'ẼFANT | PRODIGVE, |

ou sont representées les | felicitez de l'homme en | son innocence, les mal- | heurs & miseres qui l'ont | suiuy apres son peché, et | les graces et faueurs q'uil [sic] | reçoit en sa Iustification, | Auec le premier Dimanche | de l'Aduent festes de la | Circoncision et des Roys, | Preschez par vn docte et | celebre personnage de | nostre temps. | A PARIS, | Chez Nicolas du Fossé | ruë St Iacques au vase d'or. | ET | Pierre Cheuallier au mont | St Hilaire a la cour d'albret. 1612. | Auec priuilege du Roy. |

[Engraved: seven panels showing the progress of the Prodigal. Signed L. Gaultier sculp.]

8vo ā⁸, A–3K⁸

ā1^r Title; ā2^r Aduertissement au lecteur; ā4^r Sommaires des sermons; ā7^v Extraict du priuilege to Chevalier for 10 years dated 16 May 1611; ā8^v Approbation dated 27 May 1611; A1^r Text, pag. 1–368/371–855; 3H3^v Table des matieres.   [BN D 52279

Note: Unknown to Sommervogel and Cioranescu.

277 *Sermons doctes et admirables sur tous les jours de Caresme.*
   Paris, 1613.
SERMONS | DOCTES ET | ADMIRABLES | *SVR TOVS LES* | iours de Cares- | me & feriees [sic] | de Pasques. | PRESCHEZ A PARIS | *PAR* | *Vn celebre personnage* | *de nostre temps.* | A PARIS, | Ruë S. Iacques | *Chez Nicolas du Fossé* | *au vase d'or* | *Et Pierre Cheuallier* | *a l'image S. Pierre* | M. DC. XIII. | *Auec priuilege du Roy.* |

[Engraved. Shows two Fathers, and the title surmounted by angels adoring IHS. Signed L. Gaultier incidit.]

8vo ā⁴, A–3M⁸

ā1^r Title; ā2^r Aduertissement au lecteur; ā4^r Approbation dated 24 July 1613; A1^r Text, pag. 1–880/877–90; 3K7^v Privilege to Chevalier for 6 years dated 14 August 1614; 3L1^r [missigned A] Table des matieres.   [BN D 52271

SPANHEIM, Friedrich (P)
Amberg (Palatinate) 1600 – Leiden 1649. Studied at Heidelberg, Geneva, Paris, and in England. Professor of Philosophy at Geneva in 1627, and of Theology 1631. Professor of Theology at Leiden 1642. Enjoyed a reputation for great learning and immense intolerance.

278 *Le Throne de grace.* 1644.
See evidence below.

279 *Idem.* Leiden, 1649.
LE THRONE | DE GRACE. | *Ou Sermon* | Sur les paroles Hebr. 4.
16. | *Allons donc avec asseurance au* | *throne de grace.* | *Fait en*
l'Eglise Reformée de Paris, | *assemblée à Charenton le 7. Septembre* |
de l'An 1642. Iour du Cene [sic]. | PAR | FRIDERIC SPANHEIM, |
Docteur & Professeur en Theologie en | *l'Vniversité, & Pasteur en*
l'Eglise | *Francoyse de Leiden.* | Deuxiesme edition, nouvellement
corrigée. | [Orn.] | *Imprimé à* LEIDEN, | Chez *Iean du Pré,* |
demeurant pres de l'Eglise | Walonne, au livre à Escrire, 1649. |
    12mo *^{6}, A–G^{12}, H^6
    *1^r Title; *2^r Ded. to Duc de la Force, dated Leiden 25 June
1644; *6^v L'Imprimeur au Lecteur; A1^r Text, pag. 1–179.
                                                             [BN D^2 4049 (1)]

280 *Le Throne de jugement.* Leiden, 1646.
See evidence below.

281 *Idem.* Leiden, 1650.
LE THRONE | *DE* | IUGEMENT. | *Ou Sermon* | Sur le dernier
Jugement, representé Apoc. XIV, 14. 15. 16. | *Fait devant la*
ROYNE *de* BO- | HEME *à* Riswijck *en la Maison* | *de* S. A.
D'ORANGE | *le 24. Sept. 1645.* | Par | F. SPANHEIM. | Deuxiesme
Edition, nouvellement corrigée. | [Orn.] | *Imprimé à LEIDEN,* |
Chez *Iean du Pré,* demeurant pres de l'Eglise | Walonne, au livre à
Escrire, 1650. |
    12mo A–H^{12}
    A1^r Title; A2^r Ded. à la Serenissime Princesse Elizabeth, dated
25 October 1646; A5^r Text, pag. 1–184.   [BN D^2 4049 (2)]

282 *Le Throne de gloire.* Leiden, 1649.
LE THRONE | DE GLOIRE, | *Où [sic] Sermon* | Sur la Vision du
Throne | de DIEV, representée | en Esa. VI. 1. 2. 3. 4. | *Fait* | En
l'Eglise Françoyse de la | Haye le 15. Ianv. 1643. | PAR | F.
SPANHEIM. | [Orn.] | A LEYDEN, | Chez *Guillaume Christian.*
1649. |
    12mo (? ¿ ?)^6, A–E^{12}, F–G^6
    sig. 1^r Title; sig. 2^r Ded. à Guillaume Frederic, Comte de Nassau,

dated 3 February 1649; sig. 6ʳ Fautes à corriger; A1ʳ Text, pag.
1–144. [BN D² 4049 (3)]

283 All three works were reprinted in an edition published by E. Maupeau, Geneva, 1649.

SUAREZ DE SAINTE-MARIE, Jacques (Franciscan)
Lisbon 1552 – Paris 1614. Bishop of Sées in 1611. Known in Paris as 'le Père portugais'.

284 *Sermons pour les octaves du S. Sacrement.* Paris, 1605.
SERMONS | POVR LES OCTA- | *VES DV S.ᵗ SACRE-* | *MENT DE L'AVTEL.* | Contenantz huict causes | pour lesquelles nr̃e Sei- | gneur nous a laissé sa chair | et son sang reallement [*sic*] et | substantiellement en ce tres | auguste Sacrement. | *DEDIE' | A LA ROYNE MARGVERITE.* | *Preschez à Paris par le R. P. F.* | *Iacques Suares de S.ᵗᵉ Marie obser-* | *uantin Portugais Docteur en* | *Theologie et Predicateur or-* | *dinaire du Roy, et par luy* | *reueus et mis en lumiere.* | 1605. | *A PARIS,* | *Chez Nicolas du Fossé* | *ruë Sainct Iacques* | *au vase d'or.* | *AVEC PRIVILEGE DV ROY.* |
[Engraved. Panels showing the Last Supper and the prophets who foretold its institution]
8vo ã⁸, A–2C⁸
ã1ʳ Title; ã2ʳ Ded.; ã4ᵛ Au lecteur catholique; ã6ʳ Privilege, to Suarez for 10 years, dated 29 July 1605; Transport to Du Fossé undated; ã8ᵛ Approbation dated 12 August 1605; A1ʳ Text, foliated 1–193; 2Bʳ Oraison, foliated 193–4; 2B2ᵛ Les Marguerites recueillies par tout ce liure [i.e. index]; 2C7ʳ Acheué d'Imprimé le vingtiesme Septembre, 1605, De l'Imprimerie de PIERRE CHEVALIER au mont S. Hilaire. [BN D 52756]

285 *Trésor quadragésimal.* Paris, N. du Fossé, ? 1607 or 1608.
8vo
Noted by Dagens: *Bibliographie de la littérature de la spiritualité*, for the year 1607. There is supporting evidence, though the dates conflict. Wadding, p. 106, notes a '*Thesaurum Quadragesimalem*, pluribus divinorum eloquiorum ac sanctorum Patrum sententiis plenum, primo lingua Gallica editum, deinde ab ipso authore Latine publicatum. Prodiit apud eundem Cardonem anno 1610.' Weigert:

Graveurs du XVIIe siècle, vol. 4, p. 472, notes that Gaultier executed a frontispiece for Suarez de Sainte-Marie's *Trésor quadragésimal*, Paris, N. du Fossé, 1608.

Cioranescu does not list such a work, but does include a translation of a Spanish Lenten series: *Considerations admirables sur tous les Evangiles et feries du Caresme*, Paris, 1605 (63658).

286 *Vingt discours sur le XIIe chapitre de l'Apocalypse de S. Jean.* Paris, 1608.
8vo

Cioranescu 63656. Weigert: *Graveurs du XVIIe siècle*, vol. 4, pp. 467 and 472, notes that Gaultier executed the frontispiece for N. du Fossé.

287 *Sermon funebre, fait aux obseques de Henry IIII.* Paris, 1610. SERMON FVNEBRE, | FAIT AVX OBSEQVES | DE HENRY IIII. ROY DE | France & de Nauarre, le 22. | de Iuin 1610. dans l'Eglise de | S. Iacques de la Boucherie. | *Par Fr.* IACQVES SVARES | *Obseruantin Portugays, Docteur* | *en Theologie, Predicateur ordi-* | *naire & Conseiller de sa* | *Maiesté.* | [Orn. IHS in crown of thorns] | A PARIS, | Chez NICOLAS DV FOSSE' ruë | S. Iacques au Vase d'Or. | clc. lcc.x | *Auec Priuilege du Roy.* |
    8vo ã², A–H⁴, I²

ã1^r Title; ã2^r Ded. à la Royne; A1^r Avant-Propos, pag. 1–4; A3^r Text, pag. 5–67; I2^v Privilege, to Suarez for 6 years, dated 9 July 1610; Transport dated 9 July 1610.   [BN 8° Lb35 1002

288 Reprinted in G. du Peyrat's *Les oraisons funebres . . . sur le trespas de Henry le Grand*, Paris, 1611, pp. 109–45.
[BN 8° Lb35 980

SUFFREN (or SOUFFRAND, or SOUFFRANT), Jean (Jesuit) Salon 1571 – Flushing 1641. Entered the Society in 1586. Confessor to Louis XIII and Marie de Médicis; he followed the Queen Mother into exile.

289 *Le Victorieux et triomphant Combat de Gedeon.* Bordeaux, 1616.
See evidence below. Noted by Sommervogel.

290 *Idem.* Bordeaux, 1616.
LE | VICTORIEVX | ET TRIOMPHANT | COMBAT DE GEDEON. | *Presché à Paris, au iour de la Pas- | sion du Fils de Dieu, en l'an 1612. | en l'Eglise de S. Seuerin.* | En presence de la Serenissime | Royne Marguerite. | *Par le R. P. Souffrand, Predicateur | celebre de la compagnie de Iesus.* | *Reueue & corrigée outre la precedente impression.* | [Orn.] | Imprimé à Bordeaux, pendant | le sejour de leurs Majestez. | M. DC. XVI. | *Auec Approbation.* |

12mo π^6, A–M^{12}

$\pi 1^r$ Title; $\pi 2^r$ Aux lecteurs chrestiens; $\pi 3^v$ Diuision de cét oeuure; $\pi 4^v$ Approbation dated Bordeaux 3 November 1615; A1^r Text, pag. 1–288. [BN D 52533

291 *Idem.* Paris, 1616.
LE | VICTORIEVX | ET TRIOMPHANT | COMBAT DE GEDEON. | *Representé à Paris, au iour de la Pas- | sion du fils de Dieu, en l'an 1612. | en l'Eglise de S. Seuerin.* | En presence de la Serenissime ROYNE | MARGVERITE. | [Orn. IHS] | A PARIS, | Derniere Edition, corrigée des fautes | passees à celle de Bordeaux. | M. DC. XVI. |

12mo πA^8, A^8, B–P$^{8-4}$, Q^6

πA1^r Title; πA2^r Aux lecteurs chrestiens; πA3^v Diuision de cét oeuure; A1^r Text, pag. 1–195 [mispaginated 165]; Q6^v Approbation of Bordeaux 1615. [BN D 15512

292 *Idem.* Paris, 1626.
LE | VICTORIEVX | ET TRIOMPHANT | COMBAT DE GEDEON. | *Representé à Paris, le iour de la Pas- | sion du Fils de Dieu, en l'Eglise | de sainct Seuerin.* | Par le R. P. Souffrand, Predicateur ce- | lebre de la Compagnie de IESVS. | [Orn.] | A PARIS, | Chez Charles Hulpeau, au bout du pont | sainct Michel, en allant aux | Augustins. | M. DC. XXVI. |

12mo A–Q$^{8-4}$, R^4, S^2

A1^r Title; A2^r Aux lecteurs chrestiens; A4^r Diuision . . .; A5^r Text, pag. 9–202; S2^r Approbation of Bordeaux 1615.
[Ars. 8° T 6363

293 *Sermons rares et pleins de doctrine . . . sur les 52 dimanches de l'année.* Paris, Pierre Chevalier, 1622, 2 vols.
8vo

Sommervogel, and Cioranescu 63682. According to Sommervogel this is an anonymous work.

294 *Testament du Patriarche Jacob.* Paris, 1623.
TESTAMENT | DV PATRIARCHE | IACOB: | OV | *LES PRO-PHETIES DE* | *Maledictions & Benedictions prononcees* | *par Iacob au lict de la mort sur ses douze* | *enfans.* GENES. XLIX. | OV EST DESCRITE L'OECO- | nomie generale du Royaume Spirituel que | le Verbe Eternel est venu establir par son | Incarnation: fondé sur les deux colomnes de crainte & d'amour. | *PRESCHE'A PARIS DVRANT* | *l'Aduent en l'Eglise de S. Mederic en l'an 1620.* | [Orn.] | A PARIS, | Chez PIERRE CHEVALIER, ruë sainct | Iacques à l'Image S. Pierre, prés les Mathurins. | M. DC. XXIII. | *Auec Priuilege & Approbation des Docteurs.* |

8vo π⁶, A–3I⁸, 3K⁴

π1 blank; π2ʳ Title; π3ʳ Au lecteur; π4ʳ Table des sermons; π6ʳ Approbation dated 22 October 1622; π6ᵛ Extraict du Priuilege for 10 years dated 12 September 1622; Acheué d'imprimer pour la premiere fois le 28. Octobre. 1622; A1ʳ Text, pag. 1–400/399/400–862; 3I1ʳ Table des matieres.   [BN D 53081

Note: Attributed to Suffren by Sommervogel on good evidence. The *Epistre au lecteur* is not signed C. M. as Sommervogel states, but it does contain the words he quotes.

La Reduction de la Rochelle, avec l'entrée victorieuse du Roy, et le sermon du P. Souffrant de la Compagnie de Jesus, Niort, Jean Bureau, 1628 [Maz. 27.287], contains not a sermon but a very brief account of the preacher's themes as a part of the general narrative. So, contrary to Sommervogel and Cioranescu, this should not be listed as a sermon, nor even as a work by this author.

TROUSSET, Alexis (Franciscan)
Dates unknown. A doctor of Paris, he belonged to the convent at Tours.

295 *Conceptions evangeliques sur toutes les Beatitudes.* Paris, 1619.
CONCEPTIONS | *euangeliques sur toutes* | *les Beatitudes preschées à* BLOIS. | *Par le* R. P. ALEXIS TROVSSET *Bachelier* | *en Theologie Religieux de S.ᵗ François du Con-* | *uent des Cordeliers de*

Tours. Ou sont conte- | nuës plusieurs belles sentences tirees de la | Saincte Escripture et Anciens docteurs | de l'Eglise. | AV ROY. | A PARIS. | Chez la Vefue Iacques du Clou, et | Denis Moreau rue S.ᵗ Iacques a | la Salamendre. i6i9 [sic] | Auec priuilege du Roy. |

[Engraved. Shows Christ preaching the Sermon on the Mount amidst numerous allegorical symbols which are fully explained in the 'Epistre au Lecteur']

8vo πA–πB⁸, A–2M⁸, 2N²

πA1ʳ Title; πA2ʳ Ded.; πB2ʳ Greek verse to the king signed F. T. du Mas; Latin verses Ad Lilia, signed by the same; πB2ᵛ Au Lecteur; πB5ʳ Sonnet to Trousset signed Frere G. Galhaut; πB5ᵛ Latin verses signed F. I. Dubie; πB6ʳ French verses by the same; πB6ᵛ Sixain au liure signed F. I. Desroches; Quatrain to the author signed I. Bourdois; πB7ʳ Sonnet to the author signed F. P. Boyer; πB7ᵛ Approbation dated 9 July 1619; πB8ʳ Permission; πB8ᵛ Extraict du priuilege for 10 years dated Tours 17 July 1619; A1ʳ Text, pag. 1–544/541/542; 2M2ʳ Table des matieres.   [BN Rés. D 15534

296 *Le Gage precieux de la vie eternelle, presché à Blois.* Paris, 1620.

Cioranescu 95055; Wadding, p. 10a: 'Sermones de Eucharistia quos inscripsit 'Le Gage precieux'.

Sbaraglia, Supplement to Wadding, vol. 3, p. 48, notes a *Panégyrique de Sainte Claire*, but gives no solid information.

VALLADIER, André

Saint-Paul-de-Chalençon (Loire) 1565 – Metz 1638. He entered the Society of Jesus in 1586, taught rhetoric and the humanities, and then gave himself to preaching; he left the Society in 1607. He then became Chaplain and Preacher to the King, and Vicar General of Metz. Eventually he joined the Benedictines and was appointed Abbot of Saint-Arnoul-de-Metz. He appears to have had no small difficulty in taking possession of his abbey, and his life thereafter seems to have consisted principally of struggles with the local authorities.

297 *Harangue funebre de Henry le Grand.* Paris, 1610.

HARANGVE | FVNEBRE | DE HENRY LE | GRAND QVA-TRIESME DE | ce nom, tres-inuincible & incomparable | ROY, de

Valladier, André (C. 300)

France et de Nauarre, | d'eternelle memoire. | *PAR Mre ANDRE' VALLADIER,* | *Docteur en Theologie, Protonotaire Apostolique, Conseiller* | *Aumosnier, & predicateur ordinaire du Roy, & Vicaire* | *General de Monseigneur l'Illustrissime Cardinal de Giury* | *en l'Euesché de Mets.* | Prononcee en la grande Eglise Cathedrale de Mets, le 21. | Iour de Iuin durant l'office funebre, & depuis. | DEDIEE A LA ROYNE. | *Dixi quia Dii estis, & filii excelsi omnes.* | Psalm. 81. | [Printer's Orn.] | A PARIS, | EN LA BOVTIQVE DE NIVELLE. | Chez SEBASTION CRAMOISY, ruë sainct | Iacques aux cicognes. | M. DC. X. | *AVEC PRIVILEGE DV ROY.* |

8vo A–Q⁴, R²

A1ʳ Title; A2ʳ Ded.; B2ʳ Text, pag. 1–119; R1ᵛ Privilege for 6 years dated 12 July 1610. [BN 8° Lb35 1004]

Note: Corrections in MS.

298 *Idem.* Paris, 1610.
Title as for 1st edn, except: *Seconde Edition reueuë, & corrigée par l'Autheur.*

8vo A–F⁸, G⁴

A1ʳ Title; A2ʳ Ded. pag. 3–8; A5ʳ L'Autheur au Lecteur, pag. 9–10; A6ʳ Text, pag. 11–98; G2ʳ In omnia authoris opera Carmen, pag. 99; G2ᵛ Sonnet à l'honneur de l'autheur, pag. 100; G3ʳ Privilege, of 1610; G4 blank. [BN 8° Lb35 1004A

299 Reprinted in Du Peyrat, *Recueil*..., pp. 265–360.

300 *Parenese royale.* Paris, 1611.
PARENESE | ROYALE: | SVR LES CEREMONIES | du Sacre du Tres-chrestien | LOVYS XIII. Roy de | France & de Nauarre. | *Pour le lendemain du Sacre, iour de S. Luc, &* | *de la ceremonie des Cheualiers du S. Esprit,* | *faicte en l'Eglise Cathedralle de nostre Dame* | *de Rheims.* | Par ANDRE' VALLADIER, Docteur en | Theologie, Protonotaire Apostolique, Con- | seiller, Aumosnier, Predicateur ordinaire du | Roy, Vicaire general de Monseigneur l'Illu- | strissime Cardinal de Giury, en l'Euesché de | Metz. | AV ROY. | [Orn.] | A PARIS, | Chez PIERRE CHEVALIER au mont | S. Hilaire, à la Court d'Albret. | M. DC. XI. | *Auec Priuilege de sa Maiesté.* |

8vo π², ã⁸, A–G⁸

π1ʳ Title cancellans; ã1ʳ Ded.; L'Autheur au lecteur; Sonnet

signed F. Champ-flour; Privilege for 6 years dated 23 March 1611;
[A1ʳ] Text, pag. 1-112.   [BN Lb36 114

Note: This copy wants sig. A.

301 *Epitaphe panegyrique, ou le Pontife chrestien.* Paris, 1612.
EPITAPHE | PANEGYRIQVE, | OV | LE PONTIFE CHRESTIEN. | Sur la vie, les moeurs, & la mort de | l'Illustriss. ANNE D'ESCARS, dict | Cardinal de Giury, Euesque de | Metz, & Prince du S. Empire, de- | cedé le XIX. Auril 1612. | *Prononcé en l'Eglise Cathedrale de Metz, le* | *28. Auril iour de son Office funebre.* | Par M. ANDRE' VALLADIER, Docteur en | Theologie | Conseiller, Aulmosnier, & Predi- | cateur ordinaire du Roy, Chanoine en ladicte | Eglise, Theologal, & Vicaire general en l'Eues- | ché de Metz. | A PARIS, | Chez PIERRE CHEVALIER, au mont | S. Hilaire, à la Court d'Albret. | M. DC. XII. | *Auec priuilege du Roy.* |

4to ã⁴, A-T⁴, V²

ã1ʳ Title; ã2ʳ Ded. to S. Charles Borromeo; ã3ᵛ Tumulus; A1ʳ Sonnet on the work; A1ᵛ Tumulus; Acrostichon seculare; A2ʳ Text, pag. 3-154; V² Privilege [see note below].   [BN 8° Ln27 7168

Note: A royal privilege dated 31 July 1612 gave Valladier the right to have 'tous & chacuns ses sermons' printed by any printer 'pour le terme qu'il accordera'. Henceforward I shall refer to this as 'General Privilege'.

302 *Les Divines Paralleles de la saincte Eucharistie.* Paris, 1613.
LES | DIVINES | PARALLELES | *DE LA SAINCTE EVCHARISTIE,* | Sermons pour l'octaue | du Sainct Sacrement | presches a Paris a Sᵗ | Medric l'an 1612. | *PAR* | *ANDRE VALLADIER* | *Abbé de Sainct Arnoul de* | *Metz Ordre de Sᵗ Benoist,* | *Docteur en Theologie, pre-* | *dicateur ordinaire du Roy.* | A PARIS, | Chez Pierre Cheuallier ruë S. Iacques à | l'image Sᵗ Pierre pres les Mathurins | *Auec priuilege du Roy.* |

[Engraved. The title panel rests on figures of the Gorgon and the New Law, and is surmounted by the Trinity with the Host. Signed L. Gaultier incidit. 1613.]

8vo π², ã⁸, A-2H⁸, 2L², χ²

π1ʳ Title cancellans; ã1ʳ Ded. à Monseigneur de Sillery; ã6ʳ General Privilege; ã7ʳ Acheué d'imprimer le 1. d'Octobre, 1613; ã7ᵛ Transport for 10 years dated 15 April 1613; ã8ʳ Approbation dated 15 April 1613; ã8ᵛ Verse of Ps. 110; A1ʳ Text, pag. 1-473; 2G5ᵛ

Table des Matieres; χ2ʳ Fautes suruenuës.
[BN 8° Z Le Senne 11686
Note: The other BN copy [D 53948] wants χ2.

303 Idem. Paris, 1617.
Title as for no. 302, except for the change of date.
  8vo ã⁸, A-2M⁸
  ã1ʳ Title; ã2ʳ Ded.; ã6ʳ General Privilege; ã7ʳ Acheué d'imprimer le dix-huictiesme Mars 1616; ã7ᵛ Transport of 1613; ã8ʳ Approbation of 1613; A1ʳ Text, pag. 1-473; 2G5ᵛ Text of a sermon for SS. Peter and Paul, pag. 474-532; 2L3ʳ Table des matieres.
[BN D 53950
  Note: The mistakes listed in 1613 have been corrected.

304 La Saincte Philosophie de l'ame. Paris, 1614.
LA SAINCTE | PHILOSOPHIE | DE L'AME, | Sermons pour l'Aduant | preschez a Paris A Sᵗ | Medric l'an 1612. | Par ANDRE VALLADIER | ABBE DE Sᵗ ARNOVL de | Metz Ordre de Sᵗ Benoist, | predicateur ordinʳᵉ du Roy. | A PARIS, | Chez Pierre Cheuallier ruë Sᵗ | Iacques a l'image Sᵗ Pierre | pres les Mathurins. | Auec priuilege du Roy. | 1614. |
  [Engraved. Title panel supported and surmounted by allegorical figures of Spirit, Soul, and Mind. Signed L. Gaultier incidit.]
  8vo π², ã⁸, A-4C⁸
  π1ʳ Title cancellans; ã1ʳ Ded. à la Royne Regente; ã5ᵛ Table des sermons; ã7ʳ General Privilege; ã8ᵛ Transport dated 15 April 1613; Approbation dated 15 April 1613; A1ʳ Text, pag. 1-1108; 4A3ʳ Table des matieres.   [BN D 15504
  Note: Cioranescu (65387) gives the date as 1613.

305 Idem. Lyons, 1625.
LA SAINCTE | PHILOSOPHIE | DE L'AME. | Sermons pour l'Aduent preschez à Paris | à Sainct Medric, l'an 1612. | Par ANDRE' VALLADIER | Abbé de Sainct Arnoul de Mets, Ordre | de Sainct Benoist, Predicateur | ordinaire du Roy. | [Engraved Orn. A knight with sword and book on winged horseback, and the motto 'Ocyus ut totum doctrinam portet in orbem'] | A LYON, | Chez MICHEL CHEVALIER | en ruë Merciere. | M. DCXXV. | Auec approbation des Docteurs. |
  8vo ã⁴, A-2X⁸, 2Z⁸, 3A⁴

ã1ʳ Title; ã2ʳ Ded.; ã4ʳ Table des sermons; ã4ᵛ Approbation of Paris 1613; A1ʳ Text, pag. 1–695; 2X5ʳ Table des matieres; 3A4 blank. [Maz. 48.920

Note: There is no sig. Y; the text is continuous; sig. 2Z1 is also signed Yy. This edition is not listed in the usual authorities. The BN catalogue notes another edition: 16° D 1718 — 'Ex. incomplet, sans page de titre, d'une édition différente de celles qui sont cataloguées ci-dessus. Comprend les p. 543–1100 et la table.'

306 *Metaneologie sacrée.* Paris, 1616. 2 vols.
METANEOLOGIE | *SACREE,* | SERMONS | Sur toutes [sic] les Euangi- | les du Caresme | *Preschés à Paris à Sᵗ Iacques* | *de la Boucherie, l'An 1609.* | *AV ROY.* | *PAR ANDRE VALLADIER* | *Docteur en Theologie, Abbé de* | *Sᵗ Arnoul de Metz, Ordre de* | *Sᵗ Benoist Conseiller Au-* | *mosnier et predicateur* | *ordinaire du Roy.* | *A PARIS, Chez Pierre Cheuallier ruë Sᵗ Iacques a l'image Sᵗ Pierre* | *Auec priuilege du Roy.* |
[Engraved. Panels depict allegorical figures of prayer, fasting and alms-giving, and their opposite sins; the whole surmounted by the Temptation in the wilderness. Signed L. Gaultier incidit.]
Vol. 1: 8vo π², ã⁸, ē⁴, A–3N⁸

π1ʳ Title cancellans; ã1ʳ Ded.; ē2ʳ Table des sermons; ē4ᵛ Approbation dated 26 September 1616; A1ʳ Text, pag. 1–944.
Vol. 2: 8vo π², 3O–5I⁸, 5K⁶

π1ʳ Title; π2ʳ General Privilege; 2V Transport for 10 years; Acheué d'imprimer pour la premiere fois le 22. Octobre 1616; 3O1ʳ Text, pag. 945–1572; 5G3ʳ Table des matieres.
[BN Rés. D 15506

Note: The copy in the Mazarine [Maz. 24.725] is bound as one volume.

307 *Idem.* Rouen, 1628. 2 vols.
METANEOLOGIE | SACRE'E. | SERMONS | SVR TOVTES [sic] LES | EVANGILES DV | Caresme. | *Preschez à Paris à S. Iacques de la Boucherie.* | AV ROY. | Par ANDRE' VALLADIER, Docteur en | Theologie, Abbé de S. Arnoul de Metz, ordre de | S. Benoist, Conseiller, Aumosnier & Pre- | dicateur ordinaire du Roy. | [Engraving of Jesus and Mary] | *A ROVEN,* | Chez LOVYS LOVDET, ruë aux | Iuifs pres le Palais. | M. DC. XXVIII. | *Auec Approbation.* |
Vol. 1: 8vo π², ã⁸, ē⁴, A–3N⁸

π1ʳ Title cancellans; ã1ʳ Ded.; ã2ʳ Table; ẽ4ᵛ Approbation of Paris 1616; A1ʳ Text, pag. 1-944.
Vol. 2: 8vo π², 30–5I⁸, 5K⁶
π1ʳ Title; 301ʳ Text, pag. 945-1572; 5G3ʳ Table des matieres; 5K6ᵛ Acheué d'Imprimer. Chez DAVID GEVFFROY, le 7. de Iuillet. 1628. [BN D 53951

308 *Le Mariage divin et spirituel.* Paris, 1623.
LE | MARIAGE DIVIN | ET SPIRITVEL | *ENTRE DIEV ET* | *L'HOMME,* | *EN LA SAINCTE EVCHARISTIE.* | Octaue Seconde. | *DES DIVINES PARALLELES* | *PAR* | *F. ANDRE' VALLADIER,* | *Docteur en Theologie, Conseille* [sic] | *aulmonier et predicateur ordi-* | *naire du Roy, Abbé de Sᵗ Arnoul* | *de Metz ordre de Sᵗ Benoist* | *A PARIS,* | *Chez Pierre Cheuallier ruë S. Iacques à* | *l'image Sᵗ Pierre pres les Mathurins.* | *Auec priuilege du Roy.* |
[Engraved as for 302. Signed L. Gaultier incidit 1623.]
8vo π², ã–õ⁸, ā–ĩ⁸, χ², A–2I⁸, 2K⁴
π1ʳ Title; π2ʳ blank; π2ᵛ Engraving of a coat of arms; ã1ʳ Ded. to Duc de la Valette, dated Paris 13 July 1623; õ6 blank; õ7ʳ Table des sermons; õ8 blank; ā1ʳ Ded. à Mme la duchesse de la Valette; χ1ʳ General Privilege; χ2ʳ Transport for 10 years dated 31 July 1623; Acheué d'Imprimer le dernier Iuillet 1623; χ2ᵛ Approbation dated 15 May 1623; A1ʳ Text, pag. 1-272/271/272-365/362/3/4/5-490; 2Iʳ Table des matieres. [BN D 15507
Note: Sig. 2A2 is badly torn in this copy.

309 *Les Stromes sacrés de la poenitence.* Paris, 1623. 2 vols.
LES | STROMES SACRES | *DE LA POENITENCE,* | *ET VIE DES SAINCTS.* | Sermons, | Pour toutes les festes | des Saincts. | *Par Mᵉ. Andre Valladier Docteur en* | *Theologie, Conſ! Aulmosnier et pred!* | *ord! du Roy, Abbè de Sainct Arnoul.* | *A MONSIEVR FRERE DV ROY* | *A PARIS,* | *Chez Pierre Cheuallier ruë Sᵗ Iacques* | *à l'image Sainct Pierre.* | *Auec priuilege du Roy.* |
[Engraved. The title is supported by scenes from the life of Christ, and surmounted by the Coronation of the Virgin. It carries the arms of Gaston d'Orléans and of Valladier. Signed L. Gaultier incidit.]
Vol. 1: 8vo π², ã–ẽ⁸, A–3C⁸, 3D⁴
π1ʳ Title cancellans; ã1ʳ Ded.; ẽ6ʳ Au lecteur; ẽ8ʳ Table des sermons; A1ʳ Text, pag. 1-770; 3C2ʳ Table des matieres; 3D4 blank.

Note: Probably because of the incorrect substitution of corrected leaves, the following faults occur: for 02 202, for 07 207, for 2E3 E3, and for 2E6 E6. These substituted leaves are slightly different from those which occur in their proper place. Between pp. 402 and 417 the sigs. are: 2C1, 2B2, 2B1, 2C2-2C7, 2B8, 2B7, 2C8, 2D1. Vol. 2: 8vo ã⁸, A-2Z⁸, 3A²

ã1ʳ Title; ã2ʳ Table des sermons; ã3ʳ General Privilege; ã4ʳ Transport for 10 years; Acheué d'imprimer le dernier Iuillet 1623; ã4ᵛ Approbation dated 22 February 1623; A1ʳ Text, pag. 1–742.
[BN Rés. D 15509

Note: Cioranescu (65402) notes an edition of Paris, 1627. I have been unable to find any other evidence for its existence.

310 *Les Triumphes et solennités de Jesus-Christ.* Paris, 1623.
LES TRIVMPHES | *ET SOLENNITES DE* | IESVS CHRIST. | Sermons, | Pour toutes les festes de | Nostre Seigneur, | *Par M. André Valladier Docteur en | Theologie, Conf.ʳ Aumosnier et pred.ʳ | ord.ᵉ du Roy, Abbé de S.ᵗ Arnoul.* | *AV ROY.* | A PARIS, | *Chez Pierre Cheuallier ruë S.ᵗ Iacques | à l'image Sainct Pierre.* | *Auec priuilege du Roy.* |

[Engraved as for no. 309. MS. note: 1623.]
8vo π², ã-2ã⁸, 2ẽ², A-3D⁸, 3E⁴, 3F⁸, 3G⁴

π1ʳ Title cancellans; ã1ʳ Ded.; 2ẽ1ʳ Table des sermons; 2ẽ2ᵛ Approbation dated 22 February 1623; A1ʳ Text, pag. 1–805; 3E3ᵛ General Privilege; 3E4ᵛ Transport for 10 years; 3F1ʳ Table des matieres; 3G4 blank. [BN Rés. D 15511

311 *Paralleles et celebritez partheniennes.* Paris, 1626.
PARALLELES, ET | CELEBRITEZ | PARTHENIENNES | *POVR TOVTES | LES FESTES DE | LA GLORIEVSE | MERE DE DIEV | Sermons. | Preschez a Paris a S. | Estienne des Grecs durant | l'octaue de son Assumptiõ | Par ANDRE VALADIER | Docteur en Theologie | Conseiller Aulmosnier, et | Predicateur ordinaire du | Roy. ABBE DE SAINCT | ARNOVL.* | *A la Royne mere* | A PARIS | *Ches Pierre* | *Cheualier* | *rue* | S.ᵗ *Iacques* | *à limage Saint* | *Pierre.* | M. DC. XXVI. | *Auec Priuilege du Roy, & Approbation.* |

[Engraved. The title is surrounded by panels showing scenes from the life of the Virgin. Signed G. David f.]
8vo π², ã-ũ⁸, 2ã⁴, A-2V⁸, 2Y⁴

π1ʳ Title cancellans; ã1ʳ Ded.; õ3ᵛ Epistre aux confreres de N.

Dame de Bonne Deliurance; 2ã2ᵛ Approbation; 2ã3ʳ General Privilege; 2ã3ᵛ Transport; 2ã4ʳ Table des sermons; A1ʳ Text, pag. 1–528/ 549–668; 2S5ʳ Table des matieres; 2Y4 blank.

[BN Rés. D 15514

Note: There is no gathering signed X; the text is continuous. 2T2 and 2T4 are missigned 2V2 and 2V4. The other BN copy [D 15513] is highly defective.

Jacquinet, *Des prédicateurs du XVIIᵉ siècle avant Bossuet*, p. 63, note 1, mentions an oration over 'le fameux ligueur Montgaillard'. Montgaillard died in 1628. I have found no further evidence for such a work, and Jacquinet supplies no concrete information.

VOYER D'ARGENSON, Claude de
Dates unknown. Chaplain to the King, Abbé de Chartres-lès-Cognac.

312 *L'Enneade sacrée*. Paris, 1622.
Cioranescu 7781.

313 *Idem*. Paris, 1628.
This must be a new edition of the first work, not a new work. See the evidence below with which to oppose Cioranescu's.
   SERMONS | SVR | QVELQVES PRINCIPALES | FESTES ET DIMANCHES | de L'Année. | DANS LE DERNIER DESQVELS, QVI EST | DES ANGES, A ESTE' INTRODVIT VN TRAICTE' DE | neuf Vertus, rapportées auec neuf Ordres Celestes, | & des vices opposez à icelles. | *AVEC VN AVANT-PROPOS, QVI COMPREND* | *TOVT CE QVI CONCERNE, TANT L'ORIGINE ET LES* | *Parties de la Predication que l'Office du Predicateur.* | DEDIE' A MONSEIGNEVR L'ABBE DE S. DENYS, | PAR CLAVDE DE VOYER D'ARGENSON, PRESTRE, | Conseiller & Aumosnier du Roy, Preuost de Sainct Laurent de | Parthenay, Dignité de l'Eglise Cathedrale de Luçon. | *NOVVELLE EDITION, REVEVË ET CORRIGEE.* | [Orn.] | A PARIS, | Chez LOVYS BOVLANGER, ruë sainct Iacques, à l'Image S. Louys, | prés Sainct Yues. | M. DC. XXVIII. | *Auec Priuilege & Approbation.* |
   [Followed by an engraved frontispiece, the title panel of *L'Enneade sacrée* of 1622. It consists of an inner ring of panels showing the Muses, and an outer ring of the Christian mysteries, the whole surmounted by the parallel figures of Apollo and Christ – 'Verus Apollo ecclesiasticus'. Signed C D f.]

Voyer d'Argenson, Claude de (C. 313)

Folio ã⁸, A–2D⁶

ã1ʳ Title; [ã2 wanting]; ã3ʳ Engraved frontispiece; ã4ʳ Ded. to Henry of Lorraine, dated Paris 7 September 1622; ã7ᵛ Au lecteur catholique; ã8ʳ Engraving of Henry de Lorraine and Godefroy de Bouillon with a verse comparing them; ã8ᵛ Approbation dated 18 September 1622; Extraict du priuilege dated 19 October 1622; Acheué d'imprimer le 26 Octobre.; A1ʳ Text of Avant-Propos, pag. 1–47; E1ʳ Text of sermons, pag. 49–317; 3D3ᵛ Table des matieres; 3D6ᵛ Fautes suruenuës en l'impression.   [Ars. fol. T 1599

Note: ã2 has been excised and its butt glued to ã3, the engraving, but the leaves are signed so as to disguise this: thus ã4 is signed ãiij and ã5 is signed ãiiij. MS. comment on the front fly-leaf (presumably by a later seventeenth-century reader): 'Ces Sermons doivent me paroistre bons puisque l'Auteur etoit mon Grand Oncle. d'ailleurs l'Allegorie des neuf Muses est Singuliere.'

Appendix 1:
Some printers' devices

For the sake of brevity I have not given a description of a current device each time it appears on a title-page. The following are the commonest devices.

References are to L.-C. Silvestre, *Marques typographiques*, Paris, 1867.

Orn. P: A winged figure holding a book (sometimes open at the words 'Religion chrestienne') standing over a skeleton.
Silvestre, no. 894, gives this as the device of Jérôme Haultier of La Rochelle. It is used in different sizes and with several variations by most printers of Protestant works.

Claude Chappelet: A unicorn holding a shield with the initials I. K. Listed in Silvestre, no. 53, as the device of Jacques Kerver, Printer at Paris 1535-83.

Arnaud and Raymond Colomiez: An aureole containing a Christ in majesty, surrounded by the words 'Timor domini initium sapientiae'.

Sebastien Cramoisy: Two storks in a garland of flowers. Listed in Silvestre, no. 201, as the device of Sébastien Nivelle, Printer at Paris 1550-1603.

Jean de la Rivière: An ornamented oval showing a river with the words 'Madent a flumine valles'. Silvestre, no. 889, gives this for Guillaume de la Rivière, Printer at Arras 1591-1637.

Nicolas du Fossé: Two pitchers of water with the motto 'Petit à petit'. The pitchers occasionally appear inconspicuously on his engraved title-pages. Silvestre, no. 1200.

Melchior Mondière: Two entwined vipers with the words 'Quod tibi fieri non vis alteri ne feceris'.

Denis Moreau: A crowned salamander amidst flames, encircled by the words 'Timentibus Deum nil deest'.

Jean Osmont: An ornamented oval showing rocks and palm trees, with the words 'Deus beat. quos vult'.

Adrien Taupinart: An astrolabe.

Appendix 2:
A note on *prônes* and similar material

The two chief representatives of this genre are Richelieu, whose *Instruction du Chrestien* appeared in 1621 and went through an immense number of editions during the period, and Camus, whose *Prônes* and *Instructions* appeared in 1649–50.

These are essentially handbooks for country parishes, and provide short talks, or frameworks for short talks, which relieve country priests from the task of preparing a suitable sermon themselves. They were also written to prevent rural congregations from being subjected to sermons taken wholesale from published collections intended for use in cultured Paris (though this has wrongly been seen as a reaction against 'rhetoric' in general). They are not examples of sermons in the normal sense, although a *history* of the pulpit at this time would have to take them into account.

Appendix 3:
Some surprising exclusions

The following names are often encountered in past works on early-seventeenth-century pulpit oratory. Some had a considerable reputation in their own time. I give a brief explanation of their absence in my main list.

ABBADIE, Pierre, Minister at Pau (P)
Cioranescu (6487–90) lists four works which I have been unable to find. The *Gesamtkatalog der Preussischen Bibliotheken*, vol. 1 (1931), notes that three of these were in the Preussische Staatsbibliothek (nos. 1656–8), but this is not necessarily a guarantee that they are still extant.

BENING, François (Jesuit)
Widely famed for his *Bouclier d'honneur*, which is a funeral oration on Crillon and was frequently reprinted, but there appear to be no sermons.

BERULLE, Pierre (Oratorian)
Although Cardinal Bérulle's influence on the ecclesiastical atmosphere, and therefore on preaching, was immense, he left no printed sermons. He seems to have suffered from great timidity in the pulpit.

BIROAT, Jacques (Jesuit for a time)
Preacher to the king. Works published out of our period. Migne reprints an *Avent* of 1660.

BOULANGER, André (Augustinian)
Known as 'le petit-père André', and perhaps the most frequently cited example of burlesque preaching from the seventeenth century down to our own day. All this is unfortunately based on contemporary gossip, since the only text which survives (and to which reference is never made) is an *Oraison funèbre sur la mort de ... Marie de Lorraine*, Paris, 1627.

CASTILLON, André (Jesuit)
Only one work, a funeral oration over the Cardinal de la Rochefoucauld, is in our period.

COEFFETEAU, Nicolas (Dominican)
I have only been able to discover one work, the funeral oration for Henri IV, of 1610. This went through several editions, and is presumably the basis for the numerous remarks found in the standard works.

CONDREN, Charles de (Superior of the Oratory)
Migne, *Orateurs sacrés*, vol. 88, cols. 563–655, reprints his *Discours*, but their very titles, as well as their form, belie the hypothesis that they are sermons: *Essai sur les équivoques*, for example.

COSPÉAN, Philippe de
Despite his prominence in past studies, and conjectures as to his influence on Bossuet, I have only been able to find one work, the funeral oration on Henri IV.

DU BOIS (or OLIVIER), Jean (Celestine)
Preacher to Henri IV, and a vehement opponent of the Jesuits, whom he accused of implication in the king's assassination. This may account for the celebrity of his one extant oratorical work, the *Pourtraict de Henry le Grand*.

EUDES, Saint Jean
André Pioger, *Un Orateur de l'école française*, pp. 3–4, remarks:

> Enfin, si nous n'avons pas le texte intégral de ses sermons, les auteurs sont unanimes pour affirmer que beaucoup de chapitres de ses Traités nous présentent tantôt un premier crayon de ses oeuvres oratoires, tantôt un écho direct de sa parole, et même une transcription littérale.

This might also be said of very many other works of devotion and is, in my opinion, no case for considering the texts we have of his as examples of extant pulpit oratory.

FENOUILLET, Pierre de
We have a number of funeral orations, and speeches of a civic or political nature.

GODEAU, Antoine
The frequenter of literary salons who was nominated to the see of Grasse with a celebrated pun. He was an Academician, and is associated with contemporary movements for linguistic control and regularization. Several orations and sermons were published out of our period (see Migne, vol. 1, cols. 89–362).

GONTERY (or GONTIER), Jean (Jesuit)
Found in most accounts of early-seventeenth-century preaching. Apart from a funeral oration, his only work is *La Vraye Procedure pour terminer le different en matiere de religion. Extraict des*

sermons faicts à Caen, Paris, Macé, 1606. This is purely a work of controversy, and nothing remains of the sermon form in which the arguments may first have been proposed.

LEJEUNE, Jean (Oratorian)
The indefatigable missioner and famous preacher to the peasantry. None of his works was published in our period, though it is certain that a large number must have been preached before 1650. Although he is credited with a large part in the 'reform' of the pulpit, it is clear that taste moved slowly, for his works were not published in a collected edition until 1669–71. The Abbé Renoux discusses the impossible difficulty of dating his sermons in the introduction to his *Le P. Lejeune, sa vie, son oeuvre, ses sermons*, Paris, 1875.

LINGENDES, Claude de (Jesuit)
One of the most famous and influential preachers of the mid-century. He wrote, however, in Latin, though we may suppose that he preached in French, and modern editions (e.g. Migne, vol. 2, cols. 9–561) are translations which take into account the notes of copyists present at the sermons.

LINGENDES, Jean de
Brother of the above, and a court celebrity. He appears to have confined himself to the fashionable funeral oration.

METEZEAU (or MITEZEAU), Paul (Oratorian)
No oratorical works extant. There are some treatises though.

NOUET, Jacques (Jesuit)
He had a successful preaching career, according to Sommervogel, and Labbe, *Bibliotheca anti-Janseniana*, p. 23, calls him 'concionator insignis' – but I have only been able to discover one funeral oration.

OGIER, François
A celebrated preacher and writer of the school of Balzac. Apart from an oration over Louis XIII, his published sermons – the *Actions publiques* – are of 1652.

SENAULT, Jean-François (Superior of the Oratory)
Entered the Oratory in 1618, and dedicated himself to preaching for forty years. He was also a great teacher: Mascaron was one of his pupils. None of his early sermons was published. In fact, his only published work is a collection – very widely read in its time – of *Panégyriques des saints* of 1655, and some funeral orations.

SINGLIN, Antoine
Strongly influenced first by Vincent de Paul, then by Saint-Cyran;

Appendix 3

he was a very popular preacher at Port-Royal, and was eventually forbidden to preach because of his Jansenist leanings. All his works were published well out of the period. The Bibliothèque de l'Arsenal has a copy of his *Instructions chrestiennes*, 6 vols., dated Avignon 1644 [Ars. 8° T 6265], which may lead to confusion. It is quite clear, however, from the internal evidence that the date on the title-page should in fact read 1744.

SIRMOND, Antoine (Jesuit)
Not to be confused with his more famous uncle, the learned Jacques Sirmond. A popular preacher who has been much studied despite the fact that there seem to be no extant sermons. There are, however, two works on preaching theory.

VINCENT de PAUL, Saint
The most painful exclusion. Migne, vol. 88, cols. 383–554, prints his *Conférences, discours, exhortations et fragments divers*. The conferences however are memoirs of the Sisters, records of instruction given by the saint during conversation and official instruction. They have been retouched many times. Most were written down out of our period, and were naturally published only much later: see J. Leonard, *The Conferences of St Vincent de Paul*, London, 1938–40, vol. 1, Introduction.

It is worth noting Jacquinet's reaction to an edition of Vincent de Paul's 'sermons':

Tout récemment, en 1858, ont paru deux volumes de *Sermons de saint Vincent de Paul, de ses coopérateurs et successeurs immédiats pour les missions des campagnes*, recueillis par l'abbé Jeanmaire. Cette publication ne contient en réalité que des sermons des premiers Pères des Missions, revus et remaniés en 1712, par ordre du supérieur J. Bonnet, pour servir de modèles aux membres de la société.

(*Des Prédicateurs du XVIIe siècle*, p. 130, note 1)

Select bibliography

Note: In order to reduce this book-list to manageable proportions, Section 2 lists only the editions used, and Section 4 contains only works referred to in Part I or Part II. The sermons and funeral orations themselves are of course listed in the Catalogue.

1. Sources of bibliographical information

Bourgeois, E., and André, L. *Les Sources de l'histoire de France*, vol. 6, *Histoire religieuse*, Paris, 1932.

British Museum General Catalogue of Printed Books, 263 vols., London, 1965-6.

Bure, G. de *Catalogue des livres de la bibliothèque de feu M. le duc de La Vallière, Première partie*, 3 vols. and a supplement, Paris, 1783.

Caplan, H., and King, H. 'Latin tractates on preaching: a book-list', *Harvard Theological Review*, XLII (1949), pp. 185-206.

'Italian treatises on preaching; a book-list', *Speech Monographs*, XVI (1949), pp. 243-52.

'French tractates on preaching; a book-list', *Quarterly Journal of Speech*, XXXVI (1950), pp. 296-325.

'Spanish tractates on preaching: a book-list', *Speech Monographs*, XVII (1950), pp. 161-70.

Catalogue général des livres imprimés de la Bibliothèque Nationale, Paris, 1897-1976.

Chambers, D. 'A catalogue of the library of Bishop Lancelot Andrewes', *Transactions of the Cambridge Bibliographical Society*, V (1970), pp. 99-121.

Cioranescu, A. *Bibliographie de la littérature française du seizième siècle*, Paris, 1959.

Bibliographie de la littérature française du dix-septième siècle, 3 vols., Paris, 1965-67.

Claudin, A. *Bibliographie des éditions originales d'auteurs français*

composant la bibliothèque de feu M. A. Rochebilière, Paris, 1882.
Catalogue des livres rares et anciens en tous genres composant la bibliothèque de feu M. A. Rochebilière, Paris, 1884.
Côme de Villiers. *Bibliotheca Carmelitana*, Orléans, 1752.
Dagens, J. *Bibliographie chronologique de la littérature de spiritualité et de ses sources (1501–1610)*, Paris, 1952.
Descrains, J. *Bibliographie des oeuvres de Jean-Pierre Camus*, Paris, 1971.
Edelman, N. *A Critical Bibliography of French Literature*, vol. 3, *The Seventeenth Century*, Syracuse, 1961.
François, Dom J. *Bibliothèque générale des écrivains de l'ordre de Saint Benoît*, 4 vols., Bouillon, 1777–8.
Gesamtkatalog der Preussischen Bibliotheken, vols. 1–12, Berlin, 1931–8.
Goujet, Abbé C. *Bibliothèque françoise*, vols. 1 and 2, Paris, 1740.
Grente, G., et al. *Dictionnaire des lettres françaises*, vol. 4, *XVIIe siècle*, Paris, 1954.
Haag, E. and E. *La France protestante*, 10 vols., Paris, 1846. Second edn, 6 vols. (*Aba-Gas* only), Paris, 1877–88.
Hoefer, J.-C. *Nouvelle biographie générale*, 46 vols., Paris, 1862–6.
Hurter, H. *Nomenclator literarius theologiae catholicae*, 3rd edn, vol. 3 (1564–1663), Innsbruck, 1907.
Ingold, A.-M.-P. *Essai de bibliographie oratorienne*, Paris, 1880–2.
Joannes à Sancto Antonio. *Bibliotheca universa franciscana*, 3 vols., Madrid, 1732–3.
Labbe, P. *Bibliotheca anti-janseniana*, Paris, 1654.
La Croix du Maine, G. de *Les Bibliothèques françaises*, ed. Rigoley de Juvigny, 6 vols., Paris, 1772–3.
Lanson, G. *Manuel bibliographique de la littérature française moderne*, revd edn, Paris, 1921.
Le Petit, J. *Bibliographie des principales éditions originales d'écrivains français du XVe au XVIIIe siècle*, Paris, 1888.
Lexicon Capuccinum: promptuarium historico-bibliographicum Ordinis Fratrum Minorum Capuccinorum (1525–1950), Rome, 1951.
Liste des prédicateurs qui doivent prescher en cette ville et fauxbourgs de Paris l'Avent de la présente année 1633, Paris, 1633.
Louis Jacob de Saint-Charles. *Bibliographia parisina*, 5 vols., Paris, 1645–51.

Select bibliography 307

 Bibliographia gallica universalis, 4 vols., Paris, 1646–54.
Migne, J.-P. *Collection intégrale et universelle des orateurs sacrés*, 99 vols., Paris, 1844–66.
Nyon, J. L. *Catalogue des livres de la bibliothèque de feu M. le duc de La Vallière, Seconde partie*, 6 vols., Paris, 1784.
Peignot, G. *Dictionnaire critique, littéraire et bibliographique des principaux livres condamnés au feu, supprimés ou censurés*, 2 vols., Paris, 1806.
Picot, E. et al. *Catalogue des livres composant la bibliothèque de feu M. le baron James de Rothschild*, Paris, 1884 in progress.
Quetif, J. and Echard, J. *Scriptores Ordinis Praedicatorum recensiti*, 2 vols., Paris, 1719–21.
Sallier, C. *Catalogue des livres imprimez de la bibliothèque du Roy*, 6 vols., Paris, 1739–53.
Silvestre, L. *Marques typographiques*, 2 vols., Paris, 1867.
Sommervogel, C. *Bibliothèque de la Compagnie de Jésus*, revd edn, 10 vols., Brussels and Paris, 1890–1909.
Sorel, C. *La Bibliothèque françoise*, Paris, 1664.
Tchemerzine, A. *Bibliographie d'éditions originales et rares d'auteurs français des XVe, XVIe, XVIIe et XVIIIe siècles*, 10 vols., Paris, 1927–33.
Vacant, A., et al., *Dictionnaire de théologie catholique*, 15 vols., Paris, 1923–50.
Villaume, X. *Tables générales de la collection intégrale et universelle des orateurs sacrés*, Paris, 1892.
Wadding, L., and Sbaraglia, F., *Scriptores Ordinis Minorum. Editio novissima*, 4 vols., Rome, 1906–36.
Watt, R. *Bibliotheca Britannica; or a General Index to British and foreign Literature*, 4 vols., Edinburgh, 1824.
Weigert, R. A. *Graveurs du XVIIe siècle*, Paris, 1939 in progress.

2. Primary texts other than pulpit oratory
Acquaviva, C. *Epistola . . . de formandis, ac bene instituendis nostris concionatoribus* (14 August 1599), in *Epistolae praepositorum generalium*, Rome, 1615, pp. 297–300.
 Epistola . . . monita complectens, formandis concionatoribus accomoda (28 May 1613), in *Epistolae praepositorum generalium*, Rome, 1615, pp. 373–96.
Alciati, A. *Omnia emblemata, cum commentariis . . . per Claud. Minoem*, Paris, 1618.

Aristotle. *The Art of Rhetoric*, trans. Freese, London, 1926.
Augustine, St. *De doctrina christiana libri IV*, ed. H. J. Vogels, Bonn, 1930 (*Florilegium Patristicum XXIV*).
Balinghem, A. de *Scriptura sacra in locos communes... ad concionum usum digesta*, Douai, 1621.
Bertaut, J. *Oeuvres poétiques*, ed. A. Chenevière, Paris, 1891.
Binet, E. *Essay des merveilles de la nature et des plus nobles artifices. Piece tresnecessaire à tous ceux qui font profession d'éloquence*, Rouen, 1621.
Borja, St Francis de *De ratione concionandi libellus*, in Binsfield, P., *Enchiridion theologiae pastoralis*, Trier, 1609, pp. 686-715.
Borromeo, St Charles *Pastorum concionatorumque instructiones*, in *Acta ecclesiae Mediolanensis*, Milan, 1583, fols. 212-21.
Botero, G. *De praedicatore verbi Dei libri V*, Paris, 1585.
Calvin, J. *Institution de la religion chrestienne* (1560), ed. J.-D. Benoît, 5 vols., Paris, 1957-63.
Caussin, N. *De eloquentia sacra et humana libri XVI*, Paris, 1643.
Cicero, *De oratore*, trans. Sutton and Rackham, with *De partitione oratoria*, trans. Rackham, 2 vols., London (Loeb), 1959-60.
Council of Trent. *Diariorum, actorum, epistularum, tractatum nova collectio*, ed. Societas Goerresiana, vol. 5, Freiburg im Breisgau, 1911.
Dadré, J. *Loci communes similium et dissimilium*, Cologne, 1603.
Docreta Societatis Iesu, 7 vols., Avignon, 1827-38.
Diez, P. *Summa praedicantium*, 2 vols. in 1, Lyons, 1596.
Du Vair, G. *Les Oeuvres... comprises en cinq parties*, Paris, 1619.
Estella, D. de *Modo de predicar y Modus concionandi*, ed. P. Sagüés Azcona, 2 vols., Madrid, 1951.
Gody, S. *Ad eloquentiam christianam via*, Paris, 1648.
Granada, L. de *La Réthorique de l'Eglise ou l'eloquence des prédicateurs*, trans. Nicolas Binet, 2 vols., Paris, 1698.
Sylva locorum communium, Lyons, 1586.
Hyperius, A. *De formandis concionibus sacris, seu de interpretatione Scripturarum populari libri II*, Basle, 1573.
Joannes à Sancto Geminiano. *Summa de exemplis*, ed. Gravatius, Venice, 1576.
Keckermann, B. *Rhetoricae ecclesiasticae, sive artis formandi et habendi conciones sacras libri II*, 3rd edn, Hanau, 1606.
La Mothe Le Vayer, F. de *Oeuvres*, 2nd edn, vol. 1, Paris, 1656.

Laval, A. de *Des Prédicateurs qui affectent de bien dire*, in trans. of *Homélies de S. Jean Chrysostome*, Paris, 1621.
Mansi, G. D., et al., *Sacrorum conciliorum nova et amplissima collectio*, 56 vols., Rome, 1759-1927.
Marulić, Marko. *Dictorum factorumque memorabilium libri VI*, Paris, 1586.
Mazarini, G. *Practique pour bien prescher*, trans. J. Baudoin, Paris, 1618.
Migne, J. P. (ed.) *Patrologiae cursus completus. Series latina*, 221 vols., Paris, 1844-55. (Referred to in the text as Migne, *P.L.*)
Patrologiae cursus completus. Series Graeco-latina, 161 vols. in 166, Paris, 1857-66. (Referred to as Migne, *P.G.*)
Panigarola, F. *L'Art de prescher et bien faire un sermon*, trans. G. Chappuis, Paris, 1604.
Modo di comporre una predica . . . per quelli che cominciano, in *Dell'eloquenza ecclesiastica opere diverse*, Venice, 1643, pp. 564-604.
Rapin, R. *Les Réflexions sur l'éloquence, la poétique, l'histoire et la philosophie*, in *Oeuvres diverses*, 3 vols., Amsterdam, 1693-5, vol. 2.
Ratio, atque Institutio studiorum Societatis Iesu, Rome, 1616.
Reggio, C. *Orator christianus*, Rome, 1612.
Sales, St François de *Epistre à Frémiot*, in *Oeuvres complètes*, vol. 12, Annecy, 1902, pp. 299-325.
Sherry, R. *A Treatise of Schemes and Tropes*, ed. H. W. Hildebrandt, Ann Arbor and London, 1958.
Soarez, C. *De arte rhetorica libri III ex Aristotele, Cicerone, ac Quintiliano praecipue deprompti*, Paris, 1573.
Talon, Omer. *Rhetorica e Petri Rami . . . praelectionibus observata*, Paris, 1577.
Trujillo, T. de *Thesaurus concionatorum*, vol. 2, Paris, 1585.
Valiero, A. *De rhetorica ecclesiastica libri III*, Verona, 1583.
La Rhétorique du prédicateur, trans. Dinouart, in Migne (ed.), *Nouvelle encyclopédie théologique*, vol. 6, cols. 955-1128.
Vossius, G. *Commentariorum rhetoricorum, sive Oratoriarum institutionum libri VI*, Leiden, 1643.

3. Studies of French preachers and preaching 1598-1650

Albert, A. *Dictionnaire portatif des prédicateurs françois*, Lyons, 1757.

Armstrong, B. G. *Calvinism and the Amyraut Heresy*, London and Wisconsin, 1969.
Bayley, P. J. 'Les Sermons de Jean-Pierre Camus et l'esthétique borroméenne' in *Critique et création littéraires en France au XVIIe siècle*, ed. M. Fumaroli, Paris, 1977, pp. 93–8.
Boucher, E. *L'Eloquence de la chaire, histoire littéraire de la prédication*, Lille, 1894.
Bremond, H. *Histoire littéraire du sentiment religieux en France*, 11 vols., Paris, 1916–36.
Cabanac, P. *Un Prédicateur protestant au XVIIe siècle: Michel Le Faucheur*, Montauban, 1901.
Calvet, J. *La Littérature religieuse de François de Sales à Fénelon*, Paris, 1956.
Chavineau, A. *Les Derniers Souspirs d'une ame religieuse, tirez sur l'heureuse et pieuse mort du Révérend Père François Humblot*, Paris, 1613.
Contrasty, J. 'Le Prêtre toulousain Etienne de Molinier, précurseur des orateurs du siècle de Louis XIV', *Revue historique de Toulouse*, XXXVI (1949), pp. 1–109.
Dagens, J. *Bérulle et les origines de la restauration catholique (1575–1611)*, n.p., 1952.
'L'Ecrivain et l'orateur chrétien suivant Jean-Pierre Camus', *Studi Francesi*, VI (1958), pp. 379–94.
Damien, A. 'Etude sur l'éloquence de la chaire en France au commencement du XVIIe siècle', *Mémoires et procès-verbaux de la Société Agricole et Scientifique de la Haute-Loire*, IV (1883–5), pp. 199–223.
André Valladier: La Saincte Philosophie de l'âme, Paris-Auteuil, 1890.
Depéry, L. 'Notice sur la vie et les écrits de M. Camus', in his edition of J.-P. Camus, *L'Esprit du bien-heureux François de Sales*, 3 vols., Paris, 1840, vol. 1, pp. xxi–cxli.
Descrains, J. 'La Rhétorique dans les homélies de Jean-Pierre Camus aux Etats Généraux de 1614', *XVIIe Siècle*, LXXX–LXXXI (1968), pp. 61–78.
Du Bled, V. 'Les Prédicateurs avant Bossuet', in *La Société française*, Paris, 1901, vol. 2, 2e série.
Duval, L. 'Un Sermon de J.-P. Camus, Evêque de Belley', *Revue normande et percheronne*, II (1893), pp. 278–85.

Fage, E., et al., *L'Abbé Pierre de Besse, prédicateur du roi Louis XIII*, Tulle, 1885.
Feret, P. *Le Cardinal du Perron, orateur, controversiste, écrivain. Etude historique et critique*, Paris, 1877. 2nd edn, Paris, 1879.
  Portraits du vieux temps, Paris, 1891 (pp. 239-314 are on Besse).
Garreau, A. *Jean-Pierre Camus Parisien, Evêque de Belley*, Paris, 1968.
Gastaldi, V. *Jean-Pierre Camus, Romanziere barocco e vescovo di Francia*, Catania, 1964.
Gisbert, B. 'Histoire critique de la chaire française', *Revue Bourdaloue*, I (1902), pp. 365-426.
Hennequin, J. 'La Rhétorique dans les oraisons funèbres prononcées à la mort du roi Henri IV', *XVIIe Siècle*, LXXX-LXXXI (1968), pp. 45-60.
Hocking, G. D. *A Study of the 'Trageodiae sacrae' of Father Caussin (1583-1651)*, Baltimore, 1943.
Jacquinet, P. *Des Prédicateurs du XVIIe siècle avant Bossuet*, Paris, 1863. 2nd edn, Paris, 1885.
Jobit, P. 'Saint François de Sales et les influences espagnoles', *Les Lettres romanes*, III (1949), pp. 83-104.
Julien-Eymard d'Angers (C. Chesneau) *Du stoïcisme chrétien à l'humanisme chrétien: les 'Diversitez' de Jean-Pierre Camus*, Meaux, 1952.
Kehrli, P. 'Rhétorique et poésie. Le *De eloquentia sacra et humana* (1618) du P. Nicolas Caussin', *Travaux de linguistique et de littérature*, Strasbourg, XIV, 2 (1976), pp. 21-50.
Kies, A. 'Montaigne et saint François de Sales sont-ils baroques?', *Les Lettres romanes*, XII (1958), pp. 235-50.
Kirsch, B. 'Nicolas Charruau', *La France franciscaine*, III (1914), pp. 255-7.
Laplanche, F. *Orthodoxie et prédication. L'Oeuvre d'Amyraut et la querelle de la grâce universelle*, Paris, 1965.
Lemaire, H. *Les Images chez Saint François de Sales*, Paris, 1962.
Leonard, J. Introduction to his edition of *The Conferences of St Vincent de Paul*, 4 vols., London, 1938-40.
Lézat, A. *De la prédication sous Henri IV*, Paris, 1871. Reprinted, Paris, 1903.
Massip, J. *Un vieux Prédicateur huguenot. Essai sur les sermons de Pierre du Moulin*, Montauban, 1888.
Mor, A. *San Francesco di Sales scrittore*, Rome, 1960.

Pioger, A. *Un Orateur de l'école française, Saint Jean Eudes (1601–1680)*, Paris, 1940.
Renoux (also found as Reroux), G. *Le P. Lejeune, sa vie, son oeuvre, ses sermons*, Paris, 1875.
Rimbault, L. *Pierre du Moulin, 1568–1658, un pasteur classique à l'âge classique*, Paris, 1966.
Rochemonteix, C. de *Nicolas Caussin, confesseur de Louis XIII et le cardinal Richelieu*, Paris, 1911.
Rolland, L. C. 'François de Sales et Jeremy Taylor', *Revue de littérature comparée*, XLII (1968), pp. 557–62.
Saigey, C. E. *Moïse Amyraut. Sa vie et ses écrits*, Strasbourg, 1849.
Sauvage, H. *Saint François de Sales, prédicateur*, Paris, 1874.
Serent, A. de 'Notice sur Jean Boucher', *La France franciscaine*, III (1914), pp. 215–55.
Vincent, F. *Le Travail du style chez saint François de Sales*, Paris, 1923.
Vinet, A. *Histoire de la prédication parmi les réformés en France au XVIIe siècle*, Paris, 1860.

4. Other works referred to

Adam, A. 'Le Sentiment de la nature au XVIIe siècle en France dans la littérature et dans les arts', *Cahiers de l'Association Internationale des Etudes Françaises*, VI (1954), pp. 1–15.
Auerbach, F. *Mimesis*, trans. Trask, New York, 1957.
   Literary Language and its Public in late Latin Antiquity and in the Middle Ages, trans. Manheim, London, 1965.
Bally, C. *Traité de stylistique française*, 3rd edn, 2 vols., Geneva and Paris, 1951.
Barnard, H. C. *The French Tradition in Education*, Cambridge, 1922.
   The Port-Royalists on Education, Cambridge, 1918.
Belin, F. *Histoire de l'ancienne Université de Provence*, vol. 1, Paris, 1896.
Blench, J. W. *Preaching in England in the late Fifteenth and Sixteenth Centuries*, Oxford, 1964.
Broutin, P. *La Réforme pastorale en France au XVIIe siècle*, 2 vols., Paris, 1956.
Brun-Durand, J. 'Règlements de l'Académie protestante de Die (1604–1663)', *Bulletin historique et philologique* (1890), pp. 305–24.
Brunot, F. *Histoire de la langue française des origines à 1900*,

vol. 3, *La Formation de la langue classique (1600-1660)*, Paris, 1909.
Buisson, F. (ed.) *Répertoire des ouvrages pédagogiques du XVIe siècle*, Paris, 1886.
Cantel, R. *Les Sermons de Vieira, étude du style*, Paris, 1959.
Cave, T. C. *Devotional Poetry in France c. 1570-1613*, Cambridge, 1969.
Charmot, F. *La Pédagogie des Jésuites*, Paris, 1943.
Chauveau, J.-P. 'La Mer et l'imagination des poètes au XVIIe siècle', *XVIIe Siècle*, LXXXVI-LXXXVII (1970), pp. 107-34.
Croll, M. W. *Style, Rhetoric, and Rhythm*, ed. J. Max Patrick *et al.*, Princeton, 1966.
Curtius, E. R. *European Literature and the Latin Middle Ages*, trans. Trask, New York, 1963.
Dainville, F. de *Les Jésuites et l'éducation de la société française*, vol. 2, *La Naissance de l'humanisme moderne*, Paris, 1940.
  'L'Evolution de l'enseignement de la rhétorique au XVIIe siècle', *XVIIe Siècle*, LXXX-LXXXI (1968), pp. 19-43.
Dejob, C. *De l'influence du Concile de Trente sur la littérature et les beaux-arts chez les peuples catholiques*, Paris, 1884.
Delumeau, J. *Le Catholicisme entre Luther et Voltaire*, Paris, 1971.
Dubois, E. T. 'On some aspects of Baroque landscape in French poetry of the early seventeenth century', *Journal of Aesthetics and Art Criticism*, XIX (1961), pp. 253-61.
Edelman, N. *Attitudes of Seventeenth-century France toward the Middle Ages*, Morningside Heights, N.Y., 1946.
Eliot, T. S. 'Lancelot Andrewes', *Selected Essays,* 3rd edn, London, 1966, pp. 341-53.
Flachaire, C. *La Dévotion à la Vierge dans la littérature catholique au commencement du XVIIe siècle*, ed. A. Rebelliau, Paris, 1916.
Fumaroli, M. (ed.) 'Aspects de l'humanisme jésuite au début du XVIIe siècle', *Revue des Sciences Humaines*, CLVIII (1975), pp. 245-93.
France, P. *Racine's Rhetoric*, Oxford, 1965.
  Rhetoric and Truth in France, Oxford, 1972.
Gardner, H. *The Business of Criticism*, Oxford, 1959.
Genette, G. *Figures I*, Paris, 1966.
Gilson, E. 'Michel Menot et la technique du sermon médiéval', *Revue d'histoire franciscaine*, II (1925), pp. 301-50.

Goldin, J. 'Jeux de l'esprit et de la parole, d'une rhétorique à un art de la pointe', in *Critique et création littéraires en France au XVIIe siècle*, ed. Fumaroli, Paris, 1977, pp. 129-37.

Graves, F. P. *Peter Ramus and the Educational Reformation of the Sixteenth Century*, New York, 1912.

Guillaumie, G. *J.-L. Guez de Balzac et la prose française*, Paris, 1927.

Guiraud, P. *La Stylistique*, 5th edn, Paris, 1967.

Higman, F. M. *The Style of John Calvin in his French Polemical Treatises*, Oxford, 1967.

Holmès, C. E. *L'Eloquence judiciaire de 1620 à 1660*, Paris, 1967.

Hopper, V. F. *Medieval Number Symbolism*, New York, 1938.

Huizinga, J. *The Waning of the Middle Ages*, Eng. trans., Harmondsworth, 1955.

Kenyon, J. P. (ed.) *The Stuart Constitution*, Cambridge, 1966.

Labitte, C. *De la démocratie chez les prédicateurs de la Ligue*, 2nd edn, Paris, 1865.

Lanson, G. *L'Art de la prose*, Paris, n.d. [1908].

Lantoine, H. *Histoire de l'enseignement secondaire en France au XVIIe et au début du XVIIIe siècle*; vol. 2 of his *Oeuvres*, Paris, 1919.

Leake, R. E. 'The relationship of two Ramist rhetorics: Omer Talon's *Rhetorica* and Antoine Fouquelin's *Rhetorique françoise*', *Bibliothèque d'humanisme et Renaissance*, XXX (1968), pp. 85-108.

Mandrou, R. *Magistrats et sorciers en France au XVIIe siècle*, Paris, 1968.

Martz, L. *The Poetry of Meditation*, revd edn, New Haven and London, 1962.

Massebieau, L. *Schola aquitanica. Programme d'études du Collège de Guyenne*, Paris, 1886.

Maurel, M. 'Fastes mortuaires et déploration. Essai sur la signification du baroque funèbre dans la poésie française', *XVIIe Siècle*, LXXXII (1969), pp. 37-54.

Mazzeo, J. A. *Renaissance and Seventeenth-century Studies*, New York and London, 1964.

Michaëlsson, E., 'L'Eau centre de métaphores et de métamorphoses dans la littérature française de la première moitié du XVIIe siècle', *Orbis litterarum*, XIV (1959), pp. 121-73.

Mitchell, W. F. *English Pulpit Oratory from Andrewes to Tillotson. A Study of its Literary Aspects.* London, 1932.

Mourgues, O. de *Metaphysical, Baroque and Précieux Poetry*, Oxford, 1953.
Nicolas, M. *Histoire de l'ancienne Académie protestante de Montauban (1598–1659)*, Montauban, 1885.
Ong, W. J. *Ramus and Talon Inventory*, Cambridge, Mass., 1958.
  Ramus. Method and the Decay of Dialogue, Cambridge, Mass., 1958.
Ortali, R. *Un Poète de la mort: Jean-Baptiste Chassignet*, Geneva, 1968.
Owst, G. R. *Preaching and Pulpit in Medieval England*, Cambridge, 1933.
Poupé, E. 'Livres de classe en usage au Collège de Toulon en 1624–1625', *Bulletin philologique et historique* (1932–3), pp. 133–41.
Reymond, P. *L'Eau, sa vie, et sa signification dans l'Ancien Testament*, Leiden, 1958.
Richardson, C. *English Preachers and Preaching 1640–1670. A Secular Study*, London, 1928.
Rousset, J. *La Littérature de l'âge baroque en France. Circé et le Paon*, Paris, 1954.
  Anthologie de la poésie baroque française, 2nd edn, 2 vols., Paris, 1968.
Ruthven, K. K. *The Conceit*, London, 1969.
Saulnier, V.-L. 'L'Oraison funèbre au XVIe siècle', *Bibliothèque d'humanisme et Renaissance*, X (1948), pp. 124–57.
Sayce, R. A. *The Essays of Montaigne, a Critical Exploration*, London, 1972.
Schimberg, A. *L'Education morale dans les collèges de la Compagnie de Jésus en France*, Paris, 1913.
Seznec, A. 'Saint-Amant, le poète sauvé des eaux', in *Studies in Seventeenth-century French Literature presented to Morris Bishop*, ed. Demorest, Cornell, 1962.
Sharratt, P. 'Peter Ramus and the Reform of the University: The Divorce of Philosophy and Eloquence', in *French Renaissance Studies*, ed. P. Sharratt, Edinburgh, 1976.
Snyders, G. *La Pédagogie en France au XVIIe et XVIIIe siècles*, Paris, 1965.
Sonnino, L. A. *A Handbook to Sixteenth-century Rhetoric*, London, 1968.
Thomas, K. *Religion and the Decline of Magic*, London, 1971.

Topliss, P. *The Rhetoric of Pascal*, Leicester, 1966.
Truchet, J. 'La Division en points dans les sermons de Bossuet', *Revue d'histoire littéraire de la France*, LII (1952), pp. 316–29.
  'Prédication classique et séparation des genres', *L'Information littéraire*, VII (1955), pp. 127–33.
  La Prédication de Bossuet, étude des thèmes, 2 vols., Paris, 1960.
  'Pour un inventaire des problèmes posés par l'étude de la rhétorique au XVIIe siècle', *XVIIe Siècle*, LXXX–LXXXI (1968), pp. 6–17.
Tuve, R. *Elizabethan and Metaphysical Imagery*, Chicago, 1947.
Varga, A. Kibédi *Rhétorique et littérature*, Paris, 1970.
Vickers, B. W. *Francis Bacon and Renaissance Prose*, Cambridge, 1968.
  Classical Rhetoric in English Poetry, London, 1970.
Wartburg, W. von *Evolution et structure de la langue française*, 3rd edn, Berne, 1946.
Webber, J. *Contrary Music. The Prose Style of John Donne*, Madison, 1963.
Welter, J. T. *L'Exemplum dans la littérature religieuse et didactique du moyen âge*, Paris and Toulouse, 1927.
Willaert, L. *La Restauration catholique 1563–1648*, Paris, 1960 (vol. 18 of Fliche and Martin, *Histoire de l'Eglise*).
Williamson, G. *The Senecan Amble. A Study in Prose Style from Bacon to Collier*, London, 1951.
Woodward, W. H. *Studies in Education during the Age of the Renaissance, 1400–1600*, Cambridge, 1906.
Yates, F. *The Art of Memory*, London, 1966.

Index to Part I

Abra de Raconis, Charles François de, 94, 98, 109, 116–17, 150, 163
Acquaviva, Claudio, 57–8, 59
actio, 23, 24, 28, 47, 49, 63, 66
Adam, A., 150n.
Advent courses of sermons, 13, 14–15, 166n.
Albert, Antoine, 80, 93
Alciati, Andreas, 84, 89
allegory, 54–5, 74, 107, 108
amplificatio, 25, 63, 66, 112, 126–7, 132
Amyraut, Moïse, 98–9, 108, 110, 111, 117, 120, 140, 150–2, 164–5, 173, 177, 182
analogy, 77, 80–5, 90, 91, 94, 153–60, 180–1, 183; *see also* simile *and* exempla
Andrewes, Lancelot, 4, 183
Antonin de Paris, 79, 86, 174
application, 104, 109, 110, 116, 117
Argenson, *see* Voyer d'Argenson
Aristotle, 19, 21, 23, 31, 32, 37, 81
Armstrong, B. G., 182n.
Arnauld, Antoine, 21, 68
art:
  as metaphor of rhetoric, 51, 60, 63, 87–8, 92
  as symbol of illusion, 139–40
Artemidorus of Daldis, 96n.
artes praedicandi, 8, 13, 38–71, 72, 78
  classification of, 40
Aubertin, Edmé, 110
Auerbach, E., 42n.
Augustine, St, 15, 40–3, 46, 49, 50, 51n., 62, 111
Aulus Gellius, 59, 68

Austen, Jane, 3, 91
avant-propos of sermons, 54, 74, 75, 76, 95, 101, 103, 107, 109, 112, 114

Balinghem, Antoine de, 68, 70
Bally, C., 13
Barnard, H. C., 20, 21n.
baroque, 14, 89, 123, 128, 135n., 183
Baudoin, J., 59n.
Beauvais, Charles de, 109, 170n.
Belin, F., 19n.
Benoist, René, 76, 77, 103
Bernard, St, 100, 108
Bertaut, Jean, 73–6, 90, 100, 138, 139, 144, 170
Bertaut, Pierre, 73
Bérulle, Pierre de, 10, 83
Besse, Pierre de, 79, 83, 90, 100, 115, 145, 160n., 178, 181
Bible, *see* Scripture
Binet, Etienne, 70, 112, 155
Blench, J. W., 106n.
Boileau-Despréaux, Nicolas, 10
Bordes, H., 182n.
Bosquier, Philippe, 136n.
Bossuet, Jacques-Bénigne, 4, 102, 105, 179, 181, 183
Botero, Giovanni, 49–51, 52, 88
Boucher, E., 7, 8n.
Boucher, Jean, 79, 80, 82, 103–4, 105n., 127–8, 136n., 141, 157, 161, 178–9, 181
Bourdaloue, Louis, 15
Bourgoing, François, 170, 171
Bremond, H., 12n., 53
Brisson, Barnabé, 34

Index to Part I

Broutin, P., 12n., 38n., 46n.
Browne, Sir Thomas, 149
Brun-Durand, J., 20n.
Brunot, F., 35
Burlat, Hugues, 76, 160-1, 162, 165

Calvin, Jean, 150, 151
Calvinism, 73; *see also* Protestants
Camus, Jean-Pierre, 15, 72, 75,
    85-91, 92, 96n., 97, 98, 100,
    103, 104, 114, 115n., 122-3,
    130, 138, 144n., 145, 146-7,
    152, 154, 158-9, 165, 166-7,
    169-70, 172n., 175-6, 180,
    182-3
Cantel, R., 6n.
Caplan, H., 39n.
captatio benevolentiae, 74, 118
catenary prose, 72, 85-91, 92, 93,
    96, 98, 104, 112, 180
Caussin, Nicolas, 93-5, 97, 98, 100,
    104, 105n., 130, 133n., 161-2
    De eloquentia sacra et humana,
    22, 32-3, 66-7, 93n.
Cave, T. C., 111, 123n.
Chappuis, Gabriel, 52n.
Charles Borromeo, St, 40, 44, 45n.,
    46-7, 48, 49, 51, 63, 88, 91
Charmot, F., 21n.
Chauveau, J.-P., 173n.
Church councils:
  French, 40, 43-5, 67, 68, 133
  Milanese, 44
  see also Trent, Council of
Cicero, 19, 20, 21, 22, 23, 24, 25,
    26, 31, 37, 39, 51, 54, 68, 98
Ciceronian style, 29, 31, 80n., 93
Claude, Jean, 110
coeli enarrant gloriam Dei topos,
    65, 135, 150-3, 155
commonplace-books, 26, 42, 53, 54,
    56, 58, 59, 65, 67, 70, 78, 91;
    see also thesauri *and exempla*
conceits and conceptist prose, 36,
    52-3, 72, 79, 83-4, 88, 91-7,
    112, 115, 116, 132, 142, 155,
    181-2; *see also* wit

Contrasty, J., 11n.
controversy, as subject of preaching,
    99, 109, 110, 111, 114n., 119,
    128-9, 142, 158-9, 176
copia, 27, 60, 75, 120
Coton, Pierre, 16n., 136n.
Counter-Reformation, 88, 180; *and
    see* Trent, Council of
Cressolles, Louis de, 23, 24n.
Croï, Jean de, 98, 166
Croll, M. W., 5, 35, 89
Curtius, E. R., 182n.

Dadré, Jean, 70
Dagens, J., 12n.
Daillé, Jean, 95, 98, 111, **117-21**,
    122, 128, 130, **138**, 160, 168n.,
    177, 182
Dainville, F. de, 21
Dejob, C., 46n.
Delumeau, J., 12n., 38n.
Demosthenes, 20
Descrains, J., 85, 91n.
Diez, Felipe, 59, 65, 70
digests, *see* thesauri
dispositio, 24, 25, 26-7, 29, 32, 49,
    52, 57, 60, 62, 87, 104
division into points, 55, 60, 61-2,
    65, **101-11**, 119
doctes merveilles, 79, 82, 155; *and
    see* conceits
Donne, John, 3, 6n., 80n.
dream *topos*, **129-30**, 136
Drelincourt, Charles, **124-5**, 129,
    134n.
Du Bec, Philippes, 75, 90, 171
Du Bellay, Joachim, 89
Du Bled, V., 8n.
Dubois, E. T., 173n.
Du Moulin, Pierre, 8, 15, 82, 106-7,
    109-10, 129, 131-2, 137, 140,
    142n., 146, 147, 154, 162-3,
    164, 170, 182
Du Perron, Jacques Davy, 73
Durant, Jacques Himbert, 13, 176-7
Durant, Samuel, 13, 154, **174-6**
Du Vair, Guillaume, 26, **33-5**

Eachard, John, 149-50
elements, the four, 135, 160-2, 165-73
Eliot, T. S., 4, 183
elocutio, 24, 27-8, 29, 30, 31, 32, 47, 49, 57, 60, 62, 63, 87, 88, 92
emblems, 75-6, 84, 85, 89, 94, 124
encyclopaedias, 70, 78; *and see* thesauri
Erasmus, Desiderius, 27, 62
Escars, Anne de, 100, 108
Estella, Diego de, 39n., 53, 54-6, 60, 62, 65, 66, 70, 102, 106n.
etymology, 22, 41, 62, 110
Eudemare, François de, 147, 174
Eustache, David, 128-9
exempla, 26, 34, 46, 47, 55, 57, 59, 65, 68, 70, 77-8, 80, 85, 119, 127; *see also* commonplace books *and* thesauri
exordium, 26, 47, 55, 60, 90, 101, 105, 109, 110, 112-13, 118-19, 178

fables, condemnation of, 44, 65, 67, 68, 92
Fage, E., 11n.
Flachaire, C., 83n.
flames, imagery of, 173-9
Fouquelin, Antoine, 29n.
France, P., 17n., 18n.
Francis Borgia, St, 57
François de Sales, St, 5, 11, 16n., 63-6, 70, 81-2, 155, 174n., 182
Frémiot, André, 63, 105
Frondes, 9, 127, 183
Fumaroli, M., 23n.
funeral oration:
  as example of epideictic oratory, 26, 48
  as separate genre, 15, 105
  themes of, 133, 134, 136, 161, 163, 179
  themes of, decreed by Councils, 45, 68, 133

Gardner, H., 106n.

Genette, G., 17n.
Gerson, Jean, 5, 100, 104
Gilson, E., 7, 101
Gody, Simplicien, 68
Goldin, J., 94n.
Góngora, Luis de, 96
Gracián, Baltasar, 94n.
Granada, Luis de, 48, 53-4, 59, 62, 70
Graves, F. P., 29n.
Guez de Balzac, Jean-Louis, 5
Guicciardini, 89
Guillaumie, G., 5
Guiraud, P., 14n.

Haag, E. and E., 19
Hennequin, J., ix
Henri III, 73
Henri IV, 4, 73, 79n., 100, 107, 144, 169, 179
Heraclitus, 131
Hersent, Charles, 105, 134n., 164n.
Higman, F. M., 14, 77n.
Hildebrandt, H. W., 29n.
hinds calving *topos*, 160n.
Holmès, C., 36n.
homily:
  as distinct from sermon, 14, 43, 49
  Camus's use of the term, 90-1
  on the Gospel of the day (*sermo evangelicus*), 49, 52, 54-6, 61, 62, 65, 102-3, 104
Hopper, V. F., 106n.
Horace, 37
Huizinga, J., 4
humanism, devout, 88, 89
Humblot, François, 78n., 136n.
Hyperius, Andreas, 55, 61-2

Ignatius Loyola, St, 91, 141n.
inventio, 24, 25-6, 29, 32, 46-7, 52, 60, 87, 90, 148
inventio textualis, *see* homily
Isocrates, 20
Italian influences on preaching, 40, 45-53, 69n., 87-8, 92, 180

Index to Part I

Jacquinet, P., 8, 10-12, 66n.
Jansenism, 12
  educational ideas of, 18, 21
Jesuits, 38, 83, 84, 175
  educational system of, 18, 19, 21, 22-3, 24n., 32
  theories of preaching, 40, 56-60
jewelled prose, 112-15, 143
Joannes a Sancto Geminiano, 56, 70n.
John Chrysostom, St, 46, 66, 69n., 88n.
John Eudes, St, 11
jokes, condemnation of, 44, 47, 59

Keckermann, Bartolomaeus, 62-3, 102
Kehrli, P., 32n.
Kibédi Varga, A., 17n., 18n.
King, H., 39n.

Labitte, C., 4n., 52n.
La Bruyère, Jean de, 39, 69, 101
La Mothe Le Vayer, François de, 35-6
Langle, Jean-Maximilien de, 168-9
Lanson, G., 5
Lantoine, H., 20n.
La Tour, Georges de, 135-6
Laval, Antoine de, 69
Leake, R., 29n.
Le Faucheur, Michel, 110, 139n., 156, 160, 171
Lemaire, H., 5, 155
Lemaire de Belges, Jean, 89
length of sermons one hour, 16
Lenten courses of sermons, 13, 14-15, 91
  material for, 59
Leo, St, 100
Lézat, A., 8, 11
Lipsius, Justus, 32
Lor, Antoine de, 78n., 79, 132, 140, 146, 166n., 172n.
Louis XIII, 99, 176
Ludham, John, 61n.
lycanthropy, 79n., 146

Macé, Jean, 97, 105n., 114, 127, 163
macrocosm/microcosm, 135, 151, 162
Maillard, Olivier, 5
make-up, feminine, as anti-rhetorical *topos*, 47, 50, 51, 67, 92-3
Malherbe, François de, 10
Mandrou, R., 146n.
mannerism, 14
Mansi, G. D., 43n.
manuals of rhetoric, 13, 17-37, 97
Marie de Médicis, 107, 170, 179
Martz, L., 111n.
Marulić, Marko, 70n.
Massebieau, L., 19
Maurel, M., 135n.
Mazarini, Giulio, 58, 59-60, 65, 66, 70, 87
Mazzeo, J. A., 83, 155n.
meditation, 57, 70, **111**, 115, 116n., **133-8**
Melanchthon, Philip, 20
memoria, 24, 28-9, 49, 62, 106
Menot, Michel, 7n.
mer du monde topos, 170-3
Mestrezat, Jean, 110, 162, 177
metaphor, as distinct from simile, 76, 85, 98, **127**, 171, 177, 183
Michaëlsson, E., 173n.
Mignault, Claude, 89
Migne, J. P., 9n., 48n.
miracles, 143-5
mirror *topos*, 140-2
Mitchell, W. Fraser, 7
Molinier, Etienne, 11, 72, 83, 91-7, 98, 105, 112-13, 115-16, 123, **126-7**, 131, **133-7**, 142n., 143, 146, 147-8, 153, 156-7, 159, 160n., 169n., 175, 181, 182
Montaigne, Michel de, 5, 73, 75n., 78
Montesquieu, Charles de Secondat de, 165
Monteverdi, Claudio, 4
Mor, A., 5

Index to Part I

Morel, Abbé, 68n.
mots bas, 27, 32, 57, 69
Mourgues, O. de, 173n.
mythology, pagan, 147–8

Nantes, Edict of, 4, 9
neo-platonism, 34, 151–2, 162–3
Nicolas, M., 21n., 22n.
number systems, 106
numerus oratorius (oratio numerosa), 28, 30, 32, 36, 41, 51, 113, 120, 180–1

Ong, W. J., 23n., 29n., 30n.
oratio numerosa, see *numerus oratorius*
Oratorian education, 18, 21
orchestrated prose, 72, 97–100, 116, 120, 125, 180
Ortali, R., 122
Owst, G. R., 6n.

Panigarola, Francesco, 52–3, 54, 60, 65, 66, 70, 88, 102
paronomasia, *see* word-play
partitio, 102, 104; *and see* division into points
Pascal, Blaise, 5, 17
Paul, St, as model of preacher, 41, 42, 51, 65, 91, 118–19, 150
peacock *topos*, 128
pearls/tears *topos*, 96, 113, 142, 159
peroration, 27, 28, 77, 108, 109, 110, 112, 113, 116, 117, 120
personification, 74, 75
Petrarch, 59, 68
Pioger, A., 11
plain prose, 72, 76–7, 80
Pliny, 70, 112, 155
poetic prose, 73–6, 90
Poupé, E., 21n.
Pozzo, Padre, 141n.
préciosité, 100
Primrose, Gilbert, 103
prône, 91
pronuntiatio, 23, 28, 29, 30, 32, 47, 63

propositio, *see* division into points
Protestants:
  central importance of preaching among, 15, 61
  education of, 18, 19, 20–1, 22
  few works surviving from early years, 13, 174
  influence of Ramism upon, 31, 97–8
  special emphases of, 82, 97–8, 128, 131–2, 137–8, 147, 150, 159–60, 182
  structure of sermons among, 102–3, 106, 109–11, 117–21
  theories of preaching, 61–3, 102

Quintilian, 19, 21, 23, 31, 33, 37, 39, 54, 68

Racine, Jean, 17, 130
rainbow *topos*, 128, 142
Ramism, 19–20, 25, 29–31, 97–8
Rapin, René, 69
Ratio studiorum, 19, 21, 22
Raymond, P., 167n.
Reggio, Carlo, 58–9
religious orders, rarity of preachers from, 13
Répertoire des ouvrages pédagogiques du XVIe siècle, 20
Retz, Cardinal de, 99–100, 114, 172, 177–8
Richards, I. A., 82
Richardson, C., 20n.
Richelieu, Cardinal, 108–9, 172, 178
Rimbault, L., 8
river of time *topos*, 131–3
rose/thorns *topos*, 159–60
Rousset, J., 83, 173n.
Ruthven, K. K., 155n.

Sagüés Azcona, P., 39n., 54n., 61n.
Saint-Amant, Marc-Antoine de Gérard, de, 173n.
Saint-Cyran, Abbé de, 10
Saulnier, V.-L., 45, 48n.
Sauvage, H., 10, 64n.

Sayce, R. A., 75n.
Scaliger, J. C., 32
Schimberg, A., 57n.
science, 149–50, 154–8
Scripture, interpretation of, 40–1, 49, 54–5, 61, 65, 82, 99, 102–3, 106–8, 176
sea-storm *topos*, 167–73
secular preachers, predominance of, 13
Seguiran, Gaspar de, 78, 82, 83, 84, 96n., 107, 113, 115, 124, 139, 141–2, 143, 155–6, 160n., 176n.
seminaries, insignificance of, 18, 38
Senecan style, 80n.
sermo evangelicus, see homily
Seznec, A., 173n.
Sharratt, P., 29n.
Sherry, Richard, 29n.
shipwreck *topos*, 167–70
simile, as distinct from metaphor, 76, 142–3, 171, 180
Simpson, E., 3
Snyders, G., 22n.
Soarez, Cypriano, 20, 21, 23–9, 30, 31, 34, 36
Sommervogel, C., 24n.
Sonnino, L. A., 18
Spanish influences on preaching, 40, 53–6, 69n.
Spiegler, F. J., 141n.
spirituality, French School of, 12
stage, see theatre
Stella, Didacus, see Estella
Stuart Constitution, The, 102
style:
  Ciceronian, 29, 31, 80n., 93
  periodic, 28, 36, 37, 69
  style coupé, 35
Suarez de Sainte-Marie, Jacques, 16n., 107
Suffren, Jean, 84, 109n., 115n., 174
sun-spots, 156
Swift, Jonathan, 71

Talon, Omer (Audomarus Talaeus), 20, 21, 29–31, 97; *and see* Ramism
Tesauro, Emmanuele, 94n.
theatre *topos*, 129–30, 133, 134
thesauri, 29, 56, 58, 59, 65, 70, 86
  prose style based on, 37, 60, 67, 70–1, 72, 77–85, 88, 92, 93, 96, 97, 98, 112, 113, 114, 115, 116, 156–7, 180–2
  see also exempla and common-place-books
Thomas, K., 146n.
Topliss, P., 17n.
transcription of sermons, 15–16
transubstantiation, 73, 142, 144–5
Trent, Council of, 38, 39, 40, 43–5, 51, 60, 63, 67, 128, 181; *see also* Church councils
trompe-l'oeil, 138–42
Truchet, J., 14n., 68n., 80n., 101, 102, 105
Trujillo, Tomás de, 59, 70
Tuve, R., 30

university education, 20, 32
utile dulci, 128

Valiero, Agostino, 45n., 47–9, 51 2, 59, 62
Valladier, André, 79–80, 100, 107–8, 113, 114, 115, 134n., 142, 145, 146, 147, 167–8, 169, 179
Vickers, B. W., 6, 14, 17n., 30, 102n.
Vieira, António, 6n.
Villavicencio, Lorenzo de, 61
Vincent de Paul, St, 10, 12
Vinet, A., 8
Vossius, Gerardus, 20, 22, 31–2
Voyer d'Argenson, Claude de, 16, 67–8, 86, 106, 114–15, 125–6, 144n., 168

Wartburg, W. von, 5n.
Webber, J., 6n., 80n.
Welter, J. T., 78n.
Willaert, L., 12n.
Williamson, G., 6

wit and witty prose, 36, 72, 82, 94, 123; *see also* conceits
witchcraft, 79, **146**
Woodward, W. H., 20n.
word-pairs, 75, 77

word-play, 28, 30, 49, 76, 94, 97, 98, 99, 111, 114, 126, 176

Yates, F., 106